WORK/FAMILY CONFLICTS

WORK/FAMILY CONFLICTS

Private Lives—Public Responses

BRADLEY K. GOOGINS

 *Auburn House*
New York · Westport, CT · London

Library of Congress Cataloging-in-Publication Data

Googins, Bradley K.
   Work/family conflicts : private lives—public responses / Bradley
K. Googins.
     p. cm.
   Includes bibliographical references.
   ISBN 0-86569-003-0. — ISBN 0-86569-011-1 (pbk.)
   1. Work and family—United States. I. Title.
HD4904.25.G66   1991
306.3'6'0973—dc20   90-36656

British Library Cataloguing in Publication Data is available.

Library of Congress Catalog Card Number: 90–36656
ISBN: 0-86569-003-0
    0-86569-011-1 (pbk.)

First published in 1991

Auburn House, 88 Post Road West, Westport, CT 06881
An imprint of Greenwood Publishing Group, Inc.

Printed in the United States of America

∞

The paper used in this book complies with the
Permanent Paper Standard issued by the National
Information Standards Organization (Z39.48–1984).

10 9 8 7 6 5 4 3 2 1

Copyright Acknowledgments

The author and publisher gratefully acknowledge the following sources for granting permission to
use copyrighted material:

Excerpted from *The Nation's Families: 1960–1990*, George Masnick and Mary Jo Bane (Auburn
House Publishing Co., Dover, MA, an imprint of Greenwood Publishing Group, Inc., Westport,
CT, 1980), pp. 2–3, 10–11, 40. Copyright © 1980 by the Joint Center for Urban Studies of MIT
and Harvard University.

Reprinted with permission of The Free Press, a Division of Macmillan, Inc., from *Domestic Revolutions: A Social History of American Family Life* by Steven Mintz and Susan Kellogg. Copyright © 1988 by The Free Press.

CONTENTS

PREFACE

As America moves into the 1990s it faces some of the most difficult challenges of this century. Not only are geopolitical forces revolutionizing the world but our immediate society is also in the midst of fundamental change on almost every front. Although change is an inevitable part of every era, some of the changes that have taken place during the past several decades were accompanied by dramatic cultural shifts, the types that are as rare and as radical as the natural phenomenon of an earthquake or a volcanic explosion. Recent social earthquakes have caused changes in the behaviors and functioning of the two most basic institutions in society—the family and the workplace. What makes these changes dramatic and different from the naturally occurring changes of seasons and time are their pervasiveness throughout the social fabric of our country and their consequences for our nation's culture and its social policies. America is just beginning to feel some of the aftershocks that are reverberating throughout its society. Because most of us are in the midst of this cultural shift, we are perhaps too close to the scene to gain an accurate perspective. We may not have fully appreciated the effect these changes have had on our lives.

Consider a few random events recently reported in the national press tucked away in human interest columns. All of these seemingly isolated situations are indicators of work/family situations in today's America. To social archaeologists of the future, each of these events is a tiny bit of skeletal evidence of a social phenomenon now taking place before our eyes.

- Wayne Gretsky, perhaps the greatest hockey player ever to play the game, announced that he was moving from Calgary to Los Angeles for the sake of his wife's career. His decision touched off a national outcry throughout Canada. This story illustrates how some of the basic, unwritten rules that have traditionally guided behaviors at home and at work have suddenly been reconceived. His decision to adjust his career and life for the sake of his wife's work broke longstanding cultural norms whereby the career of the husband was preeminent and the wife subjugated her life to that of her husband.

- A survey conducted by the Whirlpool Corporation determined that more than 50 percent of the calls to its consumer information hot line for appliance servicing were made by children home alone after school. While our nation bemoans problems such as teenage drug abuse, pregnancy, and poor academic progress among our youth, there are an increasing number of households in which children fend for themselves after school until their parents return from work.

- Today most Americans spend more time caring for their parents than they do caring for their children. More elders are living longer at a time when fewer women are at home to provide the needed care that was traditionally given by full-time homemakers. There are fewer family resources to care for the increasing number of elders who need assistance. The tables have turned on today's adults.

- For the first time in recorded history more cats are kept as pets than are dogs. This reflects yet another subtle change that might be portrayed as an ironic twist of fate in American lifestyles. There are fewer households in which an adult is at home full time, and families are choosing pets that are more self-sufficient during the workday.

All of these seemingly unrelated events offer evidence of the changing worlds of work and family and their conflicts. The conflicts, in turn, reflect the inability of society to readily adjust and accommodate to these changes.

At one point not too long ago it appeared that work and home life were two separate entities. In fact, the dichotomy was more real than imagined. The reality facing today's families makes it all but impossible to continue to ignore the interactions and interconnections between the two domains in our lives that Freud conceptualized as work and love. And yet, in many ways, the economic, social, political, and cultural systems in our society continue to function as if the interdependence between love and work did not exist. As a consequence, we have not developed adequate social and institutional supports that might address some of the work/family conflicts.

It is the premise of this book that there are a number of inherent conflicts surrounding the complexity of work/family issues—conflicts felt within the family, within the corporation, and within society at large. These conflicts are felt most immediately by those individuals and families who by necessity have struggled to find a work/life balance. This has become aggravated by the absence of support in either the corporate or governmental arena. Although recent responses by a number of corporations to employees with dependent care responsibilities is encouraging, the overall picture is not an optimistic one. Awareness of the increasing levels of stress among employees attempting to balance work and home demands remains low for both corporate and public policy makers. The lack of fit between organizational structure and culture and the new generation of employees with major family and life roles and responsibilities outside the workplace has not been widely recognized or responded to in any significant fashion. The boundaries between public and private roles continue to be vague, undifferentiated, and largely not discussed within the larger socioeconomic environment.

My own awareness of the realm of work/family conflicts began with quite narrow parameters that focused on single parents. Having been grounded in the "employee assistance" field for many years, I was introduced to an employee assistance program in a Connecticut insurance company whose largest single group of clients, unlike others in which alcoholics predominated, were single parents. Wanting to explore this further, I spent the next year at a *Fortune* 500 company in the fashion of an anthropologist trying to understand how single parents functioned in this work environment. This excursion, which took me from the top of the company to the bottom, became an exciting and genuine learning process in the complexity and extent of work/family issues. My perspective was broadened during a meeting when a labor representative blurted out, "Why do you just talk about single parents? Most of us are married with kids, and we have the same problems you have been talking about. And besides, if you just talk about single parents, you are going to miss all the men."

The next phase in my educational odyssey came when I began to understand that the symbolic corporate door would begin to shut when these issues were raised. One supervisor commented, "Family—what has that got to do with work? That is totally separate and belongs outside of here." Workplaces have been able to ignore the work/family issue for so long that it is difficult for them to appreciate its relevance to bottom-line concerns. Corporations and workplaces, like most individuals and institutions, primarily act in terms of vested self-interest. It thus becomes necessary to expand the understanding of work/family conflicts and their impact on the corporation in ways that corporate interests are tied to effective responses.

As the 1990s bring even greater focus on work/family issues it is becoming clearer that what began over concerns with child care, supermom, and the attempt by families to have it all is beginning to uncover more basic societal conflicts, conflicts that touch the very cultural values and norms that underlie life in the United States. Any attempt to keep the work/family problem bottled up within the family can no longer succeed. The growing, yet reluctant revolution is forcing corporations and governmental bodies to come to grips with their roles and responsibilities. Simplistic programs and services are no substitute for the more fundamental changes that are necessary to find effective solutions.

The conflicts that continue to defy easy solutions and keep work/family issues at the head of the agenda bump up against a wide array of fundamental social, economic, and cultural realities that only further complicate the problem. Make no mistake about it—this issue and these conflicts will not easily or readily disappear as passing fads. American productivity and competitiveness with Japan and Europe, which have strategies and supports that address balancing work and family issues, depend on a better set of solutions. The American family is under considerable strain as the result of cultural and social policies that leave it in a quasi-schizophrenic existence, acknowledging the impossibility of maintaining traditional family roles in light of the demands of the workplace. And finally, the corporation itself is faced with genuine organizational and cultural change, if it hopes to get at the root of the work/family conflicts within its boundaries. These are the challenges of the decade and beyond. They require a new honesty in acknowledging the complexity of the issues and the ownership of these issues beyond the family. These same issues cry out for aggressive and articulate leadership and advocacy within the public and private sectors. In the final analysis, work/family conflicts require creative solutions, new partnerships, and a courage to confront dysfunctional structures, attitudes, and social arrangements, if we hope to achieve healthy and productive families and workplaces.

ORGANIZATION OF THE BOOK

This book focuses on the roles played by society and families in work/family conflicts. Some of the impact these issues have on the corporate world are discussed but are explored in greater detail in a separate volume, *A Corporate Perspective on Work/Family Conflicts*, which is forthcoming.

Chapter 1 provides an overview of the issues so that the reader can understand their magnitude. It is no longer appropriate to think of work/family conflicts as just "day-care" problems. Chapter 2 offers the framework for a better understanding of today's work/family environment. Work/family issues are examined at four levels: individuals, families, corporations, and governments. Some of the salient changes, conflicts, and impacts at each level are discussed. Chapter 3 contains a historical analysis that highlights the development of work/family relations over the past several centuries. Chapter 4 presents the findings of the Boston University Balancing Job and Home Life Study, one of the first large-scale studies conducted within a corporation on employees' attitudes and behaviors associated with balancing work and family responsibilities. This study provides a research base for many of the discussions about families throughout the book.

The next three chapters discuss work/family conflicts from the perspective of today's American families. Chapter 5 looks at the stresses experienced by family members, and Chapters 6 and 7 offer some insight into two of the most visible work/family conflicts, child care and elder care.

Chapter 8 identifies some of the mega-conflicts being experienced by society. Chapter 9 outlines the types of initiatives that have begun, especially in the public sector, in response to these conflicts. The final chapter looks at the challenges ahead of us—the possibilities of pulling together and following a vision of a society in which work/family issues are embraced and addressed.

Moving beyond current work/family conflicts demands that society does not fall into the trap of simplistic understandings. I hope that quick and easy solutions, often offered as political "satisfiers," will not be expediently substituted for more meaningful approaches to integral change. The future health of families and the quality of working life require the rejection of such superficial and overly simplistic analysis. Rather, the restructuring of family and work life necessitates policies that are deliberated with serious commitment accompanied by a sense of urgency.

ACKNOWLEDGMENTS

It is a humbling experience in writing a book such as this to realize how much others have contributed to its creation and birth. Dianne Burden, a colleague at Boston University, collaborated on the initial research. Her indefatigable labors were a source of inspiration, and her decision to switch careers left a vacuum difficult to fill. Without Marcie Pitt Catsouphes' labors this book would be at least another year in the making. In addition to authoring the two chapters on child care and elder care, she has thrown herself into locating and abstracting literature, reshaping many of my drafts, and serving as a true collaborator through the dreary tasks of getting the manuscript to the publisher. I also thank a number of graduate students, who put up with my chaotic work style and managed to pull together tremendously helpful material for this book, including Amy Zwieman, Shelly Steinrod, Jennifer Cracknell, and Serena Shapiro.

I am especially indebted to the corporations who participated in the study reported in this book. At a time when it was not as fashionable for corporations to express an awareness of work/family issues, the people within these companies who had the vision and the courage to mount such a study deserve more credit than they realize. Unfortunately they have opted for anonymity, but I want to convey my thanks and appreciation to their leadership and work on this project. The financial support from numerous foundations, including the Rockefeller Foundation, the Boston Foundation, the Office of Human Development within Health and Human Services, and Coping with the Overall Parenting Experience (COPE), made the research and writing possible.

Closer to home, I want to thank Dean Hubie Jones whose constant encouragement and support has enabled me to find the time and the resources to write. His incredible vision and level of enthusiasm have made a real difference in my career and my life. Many of my collegues on the faculty have also provided me with inspiration, ideas, and a level of support rarely found in academic settings. On a more practical level I am also very much in debt to Louise MacLeod and Susan Barhawy, whose many drafts of this manuscript tested their patience and received in turn my eternal gratefulness. And finally I want to give due acknowledgement to Mary Gill and Oneila DiCenso, whose daily ministrations and thoughtfulness are always appreciated.

During this period I was fortunate to receive a National Kellogg Fellowship award, which, while futher complicating my own work and family lives, has opened up a fantastic opportunity for me to look at these issues in a broader context and has given me much thought about where to go in responding to the dilemmas discussed in this book. So to my fellows in Class IX and the staff at the Kellogg Foundation—thanks.

Finally, I too have a work/family life that has made this more of a real-life adventure than just another academic persuit. Ridgely has been more than patient with my isolation and absences over the last several years as I undertook work on this book. So too have Nicholas and Benjamin begun an early orientation to work and family conflicts as their father had to resort to barricading himself from time to time in order to keep to a writing schedule. To all three I dedicate this book and hope we can find ourselves living in a society that adheres to a more family responsive set of policies and in which corporations and public policy makers join the family in assuming a new set of roles and responsibilities in assuring healthy families and productive workplaces.

Chapter 1

OVERVIEW

The balance between work life and family life is not a new phenomenon, as we shall see in some detail in Chapter 3, but rather a reflection of the particular social, economic, and political forces that come together to shape a particular period of time. Working and living constitute the two primary pillars of existence, and every civilization and society grapples with the delicate relationships that support these two functions. In some instances the boundaries between working and living have been blurred and any distinction between the two have become minimal. In other periods, particularly beginning in the industrialized era, the boundaries became more rigid in terms of separating the two functions. In times such as these, the conflicts between working and living, between the workplace and the family, have become more intense, and the balance or tradeoffs in finding mutual co-existence more difficult. The particular circumstances of individuals in the later part of the twentieth century, shaped in large part by the unique set of social, economic, and political forces that have marked this landscape, form what many consider to be a "high conflict" period.

Many of the conflicts that will be examined throughout this book under the rubric of work and family can also be looked at within the context of private/ public relationships. What is the relationship of the individual and the family to the society, in general, and its government, in particular? As each society works out a contract between its organized whole and the individual and family, a series of formal and informal policies, laws, and customs emerge to support this contract. Jean Jacques Rousseau's "social contract" brilliantly captured this essential and enduring relationship between individuals and society. It is precisely within the context of such a social contract that we find ourselves reexamining the mounting conflicts of work and family and the changing nature of the contract itself.

As much as our cultural themes would like to romanticize the family as a warm, supportive haven buttressed from the cruel realities of the external world, the reality is that the family is not an independent, self-sufficient unit able to function autonomously. We cannot divorce a rich family life from corporate influences and government policies. How families function and to what extent they experience stress is not simply a product of psychological and family dynamics but also of the presence of social supports and economic and political policies. From several perspectives, one of the major roles of any government is to insure and safeguard the family, providing it with supports and necessary protection to allow its healthy functioning. This is at the heart of the social contract.

This later part of the twentieth century finds the state of the family in the United States, by most accounts, fragmented, fragile, and operating at high levels of stress. The many changes that have buffeted the family over the past several decades have resulted in a generation of harried and exhausted families, rushing to maintain a sense of togetherness and economic viability. In barely a generation the family has by necessity gone from a one earner to a two earner household just to keep up with inflation. Earnings of the average household have dropped significantly over this time and consequently the two-adult family now works an average of eighty hours a week outside the home instead of the forty hours a generation ago. It doesn't take too great an imagination to begin seeing the impact of such change on every day living and functioning—less time to spend with children on homework, taking mother to a doctor's appointment, finding time for community activities—the list is endless.

All of this has taken place in a society that has a social contract unique to the industrialized world. This is not West Germany where mothers are provided with a "baby year" that gives them a modest monthly stipend for a year and guarantees their position at work for the same amount of time. Nor is the United States Japan, which resembles the United States of the 1950s with mothers slavishly caring for children within the home. Neither is this China, which has a system of subsidizing grandmothers by offering early pensions to enable them to provide caretaking roles. This is the United States, which has no family policy, no parental leave, no child care, and no family programs offered by its government. Nor does it have a particularly responsive private sector. With a few notable exceptions, most American corporations operate as if the changes of the past several decades had not happened: mothers had not moved into the workplace, and there still existed a person at home to minister to the needs of dependent family members, not to mention the working husband.

The primary consequences of this current system are that families are expected to adjust, adapt, and bear the burden of the changing social, economic, and political scene. A peculiar combination of strong cultural messages surrounding the independence of the family and the "hands-off-the-family" policy of the government, along with a brand of capitalism that neither supports government social policy nor corporate family policy, has left the family scrambling to find a balance when in effect the seesaw has left them high and dry. Most families have juggled, pared back, and accommodated about as much as they can and still manage to stay afloat.

To capture some degree of the magnitude of the change that has enveloped the United States, it is useful to examine some of the characteristics of a prototypical U.S. family in 1950 and in 1990.

1950	1990
Three children	One child
Mother at home	Mother at work
Parents age 22 when first child born	Parent age 35 when first child born
Mother-father married 15 years	Parents divorced/father remarried
Grandmother lives in house	Grandmother in extended-care facility
Family eats out few times per year	Family eats out 3 times per week
Children/mother part of scout troops	Children participate in afterschool activities and lessons

It is almost unimaginable that these radically different families are but a generation apart. The world of the 1950s is distinctly different from that of the 1990s. Today's family is more mobile, less stable as a unit, and more dependent on other institutions, such as day-care centers, schools, restaurants, and elder service agencies, to carry out what were once family roles.

One of the most important transformations in the American family that has occurred during the past few decades is hidden in the profile of the Thurmonds. It was reasonably accurate to depict the 1950s family as having a working husband, a housewife, and a couple of children. However, within the context of work/family conflicts, one of the most challenging aspects of today's families is that they are so diversified that they defy stereotypes. In the 1980s families and households included dual-earner families, single adults living alone, roommates, elderly couples, and homosexual couples. Although the more colloquial terminology of "work/family" is used throughout this book, it is not the intention to restrict the definition of "family" to a nuclear family composed of a father, a mother, and children.

Despite this diversity, the term "family" still conjures up the 1950s family. The strong cultural archetype of "the family" continues to hold sway, partly because of wistful and romanticized notions of family life as portrayed by Disney and Rockwell and partly as a defense in the absence of a functional alternative to the external realities of today. There is a widespread reluctance to give up the image of the kids being picked up at school and brought home to freshly baked cookies and hot cocoa. The image of the husband—freed from the worries and responsibilities of the home—walking from the supportive family and crossing over a clearly marked boundary to the workplace continues to cling to the American lore.

With little preparation the baby boomers have found themselves in a world that is quite different from that of their parents in terms of expectations, attitudes, values, and roles. Some of these transformations are indicated by a recent Gallup poll.

Are Baby Boomers More Able Than Their Parents Were?[1]

	More Able	Less Able	As Able
To get a job with long-term security	36%	49%	8%
To afford a home that fits their expectations	31%	58%	6%
To be at home/have their spouse be at home with the younger children	14%	75%	7%
To afford a good four-year college education for their children	41%	46%	7%
To afford to save money for their old age	39%	47%	9%

Today's generation faces an environment in which uncertainties about jobs and careers predominate. Long-term security is less likely. The ability to realize the American dream of an affordable house is slipping from its grasp. The ability to save money for old age is diminished. We are living in the midst of some uncertain times, and by necessity new perspectives have been developed about fundamental issues that seemed well defined and set during the 1950s.

- Who in the family has the responsibility for securing outside income?
- How should our children be raised and by whom?
- How is the responsibility for household management determined and divided?
- How is the stability of the institution of marriage judged?
- How are gender roles and responsibilities differentiated?

THE NEW ERA FOR WORK

Changes in the American economy have caused inflation to rise and increased the cost of borrowing money. Even after adjusting for inflation, the median income of households headed by 25 to 34-year-olds is 6 percent less today than it was ten years ago.[2] In contrast to 1960, when 43 percent of all families were single-earner families, only 14 percent of today's families have just one income-earner.[3] Most American families need to have two incomes. It is difficult for them to live comfortably and maintain a lifestyle that includes home ownership with just one income. Without wives' earnings more than 15 percent of working-wife families with children would be poor and another two thirds would be below the "comfortable" level.[4]

Many economists and others have commented that the increased participation of women in the labor force is probably the most significant change in the American workplace.[5] The rise in the presence of women in the workplace is truly phenomenal. The number of women in the work force has increased 173 percent from 1947 to 1980.[6] By the turn of the twenty-first century, women are expected to constitute more than three fifths of the new entrants into the labor force.[7] Although the changes in female employment rates have occurred across all age groups, it is most notable among women who are in their childbearing and child-rearing years. Current estimates indicate that 80 percent of employed women are of childbearing age and that more than 90 percent of these workers will be pregnant at some point during their working lives.[8] As Sekaran observes, the workplace is just not the same anymore. "The number of two-career families, single-parent families, and unmarried working couples living together is steadily increasing. This population constitutes more than 90 percent of today's labor force. Organizations are already beginning to feel the impact of this new breed of employee."[9]

THE NEW ERA FOR FAMILIES

Families have changed in terms of both structure and function. The composition of families is more vulnerable to change as a result of increasing divorce rates. The "number of divorces each year is twice as a high as it was in 1966 and three times higher than in 1950."[10] Some social scientists project that half of all marriages that began in the early 1980s will end in divorce. So-called traditional families, in which the father is the sole breadwinner and the mother is a full-time homemaker caring for children, are a small minority of all households. This type of family composed just 15 percent of all households in 1980.[11]

The emergence of so many "new" family types (such as single parents) and the fact that most adults of preretirement age are now employed have resulted in a situation in which few adults are available to respond to family needs on a full-time basis. Families have adjusted as best they can. They have entrusted their young children to teachers and child-care providers, a process often marked by considerable ambivalence. Fewer homecooked meals make their way to the table. And many household chores simply do not get done.

One of the least discussed topics of work and family is that life in the United States has accelerated several ratches in the past decade. This phenomenon is cited by most working adults as their single greatest aggravation. Not only does it now take two adults to earn the equivalent of what one adult earned a generation ago, but also the amount of leisure time has dramatically plummeted. The increasing demands made by work and home on adults create a hectic quality that permeates most of their days. America can now be accurately depicted as the "rushed society." Few effective strategies have been discovered for slowing down this pace that affects the quality of life for all of us.

The changes manifested at home and at work are revolutionary, if not radical, in that they have struck at the core of social structures and social functioning. As the 1980s have unfolded, families have been progressively challenged by seemingly unresolvable dilemmas in their work and family roles. The norms, models, and roles by which they were socialized several decades earlier no longer serve as viable guidelines. Many families have struggled to manage and balance their work and home life responsibilities, but the conflicts have continued.

Demographic shifts, new values, and changes in expectations have suddenly thrown off balance the management of family and work responsibilities. A broader spectrum of families is now aware of a reality long recognized by minority and low-income communities: the presence of a woman in the home to manage the household and dependents is a luxury seldom enjoyed except by the wealthy. In just a few short years this ability to maintain a household on a single income has been significantly reduced, broadening the middle class and putting them in line with the economic and social constraints of the lower middle class and the working poor.

This issue is not a simple correlation between income, education, and work. Cultural attitudes also play a great role. A large number of families with limited to moderate incomes remain steadfast in their adherence to the model of the father as breadwinner and the mother as homemaker. Furthermore, some women may not possess easily marketable skills, so that it is not profitable for them to work in light of child-care costs. Although the more affluent suburbs empty during the day, as dual-career families predominate, a great deal of mother-child activity is evident in the more traditional working-class communities.

THE INTERRELATIONS OF WORK, FAMILY, AND SOCIETY

Although it should be obvious to even the most casual observer that the changes that have occurred in the workplace and in the family are connected, the resulting conflicts have been exacerbated because society tends to treat them as if they were separate.[12] In previous eras a social convention arose that considered the domains of work and home to be basically distinct and independent of each other. Wives acted as if they let their husbands do all the worrying about the money, and husbands functioned as if their wives could take care of all the family and household needs. Despite the fact that changes in both the workplace and the home have made it all but impossible to ignore the connections between work and family, the myth of separate worlds has prevailed. This has led to growing dissonance between these interdependent spheres, which in turn has slowed the process by which society confronts conflicts.

Understanding the complex dynamics of work/family issues is difficult at best.

The multiple dimensions of each sphere frustrate any attempt to compartmentalize and oversimplify. It is useful, therefore, to utilize some of the concepts associated with systems theories when considering the domains of work and family.

Perhaps the closest and most basic conceptualization is that of a set of interlocking, semi-independent spheres. These work and family spheres can be considered as "systems," each with its own set of functions, roles, and responsibilities. The family system, which may supercede a single household, exists to provide care (physical and emotional) and nurturance to its members. The explicit function of the workplace is to achieve a particular productive goal. In both systems members assume one or more roles that are associated with the continued existence of the system.

This systems conceptualization becomes more complicated when the factors internal and external to each system are recognized. Internally, each system is affected by the needs, behaviors, and ideas of individual members. There is an almost endless list of human "needs" that might be fulfilled either at home or at work, such as affiliation, achievement and competence, self-esteem, and independence or autonomy. The first two levels of work/family conflicts are, therefore, established:

1. A person may feel conflicts between his or her own work and family responsibilities that, in essence, compete with one another
2. Two or more persons in a given system may have roles and responsibilities that do not coordinate with one another

From a different perspective, each of the systems also is affected by larger, external systems, such as communities (geographical or associative, such as clubs and unions) and the society at large (typified by different levels of government). The influence of these external forces makes the "boundaries" of these systems permeable, so that the internal functions of work and family systems are influenced by external forces. Social, cultural, and economic forces all impinge on the unique spheres of family, work, and society. The domains of work and family do not exist in a vacuum and do not function autonomously. Thus two additional layers of conflict are added to the systems conceptualization of work and family:

3. The goals and activities demanded by work and family may compete with one another
4. The needs of institutions external to work and family systems may impinge on their functioning

Work, family, and society each occupy a discrete arena, as it were, each with its own set of functions and each interrelated to the other two. Although the larger sphere of society seems to be somewhat encompassing of the other two, it also can be seen as constituting a unique domain, with the government being responsible for defining and safeguarding the values and political decisions of the population. In essence, two of the primary responsibilities of the government are to ensure the optimal functioning of both the work and the family domains.

Looking at the institutions of work and family in isolation makes it difficult to appreciate the interconnectedness of these systems. On basic levels work and family cannot exist without each other. The family system cannot fulfill its basic caring function unless some of the members are productive (not necessarily paid) workers. Similarly, the work system cannot exist unless it draws on the family system for its labor pool. The theory of separate worlds of work, family, and society is grossly inadequate for explaining the patterns of interaction that exist for developing effective programs and policies to support families and to assist employers and society in defining their roles and responsibilities. And yet, as Kanter comments, "there has been remarkably little attempt to link the two, that is, to locate problems in the work-family intersection, to determine the extent to which one system contributes to the health or illness possibilities of the other, or to discover what variations in each system make it most vulnerable to problems from the other."[13]

A visual representation depicting some of the more salient features of the home and work systems is shown in Figure 1.1.

Although the overlap among the systems can be positive, neutral, or negative, the relations among the three are tenuous at best and marked by conflict. Each system focuses on boundary maintenance, becoming more interested in guarding its domain and safeguarding it from the intrusions of the others than in finding ways of mutual adaptation and cooperation. Families are perceived as the inner sanctum of society, to be kept pure from the ravages of the environments outside and preserved at all costs to provide the type of emotional and affective support necessary to preserve a sense of well-being. Likewise, the workplace is seen in functional terms, a place of economic support, preeminent over the family in terms of time allocation, and suspect of any governmental intrusion, which can only upset and derail the free-market economy that undergirds its operation.

Workplace and family systems traditionally have had competing interests. Families, for example, have posed a threat to the workplace in breaking down the loyalty and commitment of its employees. To the degree an employee is required or desires to expend time and physical and emotional energy outside the workplace, the possibility exists that less time and attention will be given to the productivity needs of the workplace. There is, after all, a finite pool of time and energy. What one domain (e.g., family) gains, the other (e.g., work) loses. From the perspective of the employer, a choice can be made between wanting the employee to channel time and creativity toward solving home dilemmas and having that same energy for the benefit of the workplace. Likewise, the family may think that the workplace threatens its existence because the employer demands loyalty, forces a sense of separateness from the family, and often drains the physical and emotional resources to the point where little is left for the family. The entry of women into the workforce has only compounded this problem by increasing the intrusion of the workplace into the family.

Figure 1.1
Work/Family Systems

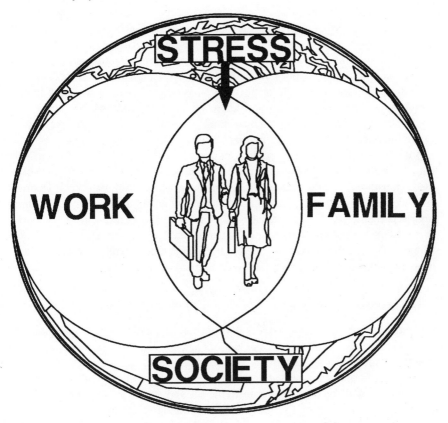

There are several perspectives on the intersection of the work and family systems. Some research has focused on the issues of spillover and compensation.[14] *Spillover* refers to positive and negative feelings, attitudes, and behaviors that might emerge in one domain and are carried over into the other. For example, a worker who has had a bad day at work might arrive home and be impatient with the children. On the other hand, a number of studies have documented a positive spillover from work to the personal lives of women. The physical and emotional health of employed women are frequently found to be better than the physical and emotional health of those who are at home full time. A second perspective centers around the concept of compensation, which suggests that people attempt to achieve a sense of balance and fulfillment in their lives. For example, an attorney who is involved in a lot of sedentary work might seek out physical activity after work, but a table waiter, who is standing for most of the day, might prefer to read or watch television at home. Ideas of spillover and compensation provide insights into some of the more "indirect" interactions between home and work.

Richter and Hall focus on the transition people make between work and family spheres as one way to study the intersections of these domains. They suggest that a person's "psychological availability" is an indication of the degree of conflicts between the two spheres. From this perspective, conflicts occur when the physical transition is not matched by the psychological transition. This unsynchronized transition might occur when a worker worries about a sick family member and just can't concentrate. Or when a worker comes home at the end of the day and needs some "time to think" before he can actively participate in the hubbub of family life at the dinner table. Richter and Hall state that "the major costs of . . . reduced (psychological) availability are *stress* for the individual and *reduced performance* for the organization."[15] Factors that might affect these transitions include characteristics of the work environment, such as pressure, degree of autonomy, occupational category, absorptiveness of occupation, time schedules, stage of career, and support system at work, and of the home or individual, such as age, family composition and presence of dependents, support system at home, values, gender, personality characteristics, family schedules, resources available, and emotional climate of home.

Implications of Change

People who are struggling to work out acceptable and satisfactory arrangements for balancing work and home roles and responsibilities are often caught in the middle of societal and institutional policies, programs, and attitudes that do not recognize and are unresponsive to life in the trenches. The disparities between the realities of daily life and the institutional and social policies that establish parameters for daily living lie at the heart of this conflict. If one was to freeze society at its current state to analyze this phenomenon, it would probably be captured by a classic struggle between the roles and expectations assumed by people that conflict with evolving institutional and social policies. Much of what is known about this phenomenon of change and its implications for individuals, families, corporations, and society is rudimentary—described more by conflicts than by accommodations or solutions.

Work/family issues affect just about everyone, so that one of the most compelling characteristics of work/family conflicts is their universality. Wives struggle to balance their traditional household and child-care responsibilities. Husbands are confronted with new behaviors and expectations at home. Large numbers of children spend increasingly long hours in the care of people other than their parents. Single parents are mapping out new territory of family functioning. Even the aging parents of today's working families are feeling the impact. And at the workplace, managers are struck by the growing level of infringement of family and home problems into the workplace. Corporations are finding that many workers are managing their homes from the workplace. In addition, managers are confronted by a changing set of employee values and worker expectations about the role the workplace should assume in response to work/family conflicts. All of this brings a new reality that challenges the relevancy and effectiveness of existing employee policies, benefits, and programs and, most important, the very organizational culture in understanding and meeting the needs of working families.

Despite the fact that work/family conflicts are really "everyman's" (and everywoman's) issues, there is still a widespread reluctance to deal with the conflicts and their implications for change. From just about every perspective the need for acknowledging and resolving work/family issues seems self-evident. The demographic realities are clear and not disputed. Employee and family stress are well documented. Expectations of employer response are growing. Global competition and the national drive toward greater productivity require a resolution of work/family conflicts as a primary strategy to maintain a competitive edge. However, the movement toward addressing these issues is limp and essentially leaderless.

The changes in our families and workplaces did not evolve out of some master plan or from economic or social policy established for achieving long-range goals for the common good. In fact, many institutions have been caught off guard by the changes, which has contributed to their slow reaction time. But institutional responses to change of this magnitude do not come easily. Society is stuck at a stage of high denial, even in the light of failed strategies, the increased level of tension and disintegration of the family, and compromises in the quality of life of its citizens.

Almost without exception, workplaces are still moored in a previous era, unresponsive to family needs and largely resistant to family-supportive policies. Corporations have continued to adhere to the myth of "separate worlds," which has allowed them to maintain firm boundaries that seems to protect the primacy of productivity. These organizations have become adept at denying ownership or responsibility for such problems experienced by individuals and families.

The impact of the changes has not been confined to families and corporations. Many establishments in the private sector have adjusted to a greater or lesser degree. Schools, stores, leisure and recreation facilities, and even churches have experienced the effects of changes in American society. The public sector, however, has largely ducked this issue, having become hopelessly mired by the complex ideological beliefs and controversies surrounding the creation of national family policies.

Consequently families continue to accept this issue almost completely as their own. Because of the immediacy of the issues they must face, families have been the most flexible and have been able to adapt more readily to many of the changes. Prevailing cultural norms place the burdens of dependent care and personal problems on the individual and the family, so that initial adjustments were made at this level. Of course, a cost was associated with these accommodations. For many people work/family conflicts are framed in a context of high pressure at home and at work. In contrast to a generation ago, when parents more or less trusted their own instincts as parents and were seemingly more tolerant of the unpredictable schedules of their children's development, today's parents strive to be superparents (and want their children to be superkids). The pressure also is present at work. Contrary to the predictions of two decades ago, people are working longer (not shorter) hours. Almost unrealistic expectations are set for performance at home and at work.

Although the magnitude of the shifts at home and work are sufficient to warrant institutional and social reform, these policy initiatives are slow in coming. Unlike the family, which has had to abruptly make marked adjustments, corporate and governmental institutions have responded in slow, incremental steps characterized by conflict and resistance. Perhaps this is not unexpected. For students of change one axiom supercedes all others: the more fundamental and universal the change, the more resistance can be expected. The phases of institutional transition stretch the system until it adjusts to the new realities. The current developmental stage of work/family change might be characterized as primary and elementary.

For all practical purposes, the primary conflicts surrounding work/family issues are perceived as first belonging to women and then to the family system. They are seen as women's issues because the primary concerns of dependent care have traditionally been relegated to and provided by women. Thus, the onus of change has been on women to accommodate their lives to any shifts necessitated by new lifestyles at home and at work—assuming that their new roles in the workplace did not mean abdicating their traditional roles at home. In fact, on entering the workplace, women seldom received relief from their household and child-care responsibilities. The concept of the supermom captured the inflexibility and resistance of many households to the radical change in the lives of women. Most men have not paid too much attention to these issues, since they have defined them and treated them as women's issues. From the corporate and government perspectives, work/family conflicts are seen as family issues that are not directly related to the responsibilities of either the workplace or the public sector. In fact, the strong cultural mandates to keep the government and corporations out of private family lives have served to maintain a hands-off policy and a denial of their roles and responsibilities.

Although work/family problems do not belong exclusively to women, or even to the family, current perceptions tend to define them as such. Because perceptions frame realities (whether real or imagined), the United States has not developed a true appreciation of the significance of these issues. It is extremely important to understand the relations between work/family issues and the domains of work and society at large, since no change will take place (and the existing conflicts will continue to worsen) as long as there is no significant ownership or "buy in" to work/family issues from either the government or corporations.

As great a gap as does exist between the universality and prevalence of work/family issues throughout society and the failure to address them, there is a revolution brooding beneath the surface. Like a fire smoldering within the walls of a building, the forces that drive the work/family issues are too pervasive and persuasive to ignore forever. Ultimately, the issue is too large and active to be penned up much longer. The motivation for change within the corporation is not driven by a newfound value on individuals and families, or an appreciation of their stress and struggle over balancing work/family responsibilities. The changes in policy, programs, and behaviors are primarily driven by the necessity of adaptation. If corporations do not recognize and accept the new demographics and values into their operations, they will suffer the same negative consequences brought on by a failure to adopt new technologies. Because women, dual-worker families, and single parents will continue to be permanent fixtures within the workplace, corporate policy and practice will have to take into account their needs. To the extent that spillover of family and home into the workplace impacts productivity, corporations will become sufficiently motivated to become involved in reasonable solutions.

As the interdependence between home and work have grown more acute, so have the conflicts between these two spheres. Some of the traditional norms and behaviors have bent to allow the new roles of working women and parenting to emerge. But a number of attitudinal, cultural, and organizational barriers have remained, and have created conflict for individuals, families, corporations, and society. In fact, conflict is at the center of work/family relations today.

Although a utopian future might envision a world of mutually beneficial trade-offs among institutions so that each system (family, work, and society) can maintain healthy and productive members, the reality is considerably different. Work/family relations are very much in a transitional phase, moving from the separate workloads of the old order toward the new configurations of the new workforce and the new family. This move toward the new order brings with it a series of growing pains as well as a potential to create structures and institutions that are responsive to the emerging needs of families and workplaces. Although change often appears to happen independently of any purposeful or well-planned policy, there is an increasing demand for leadership on all levels to assist in seizing and responding to the issues. Because interdependency increases the likelihood of conflict, forceful leadership will be at a premium in corporations, in government, and in the many fractured groups that speak for the American family. The rigid boundaries that have traditionally existed between these systems will have to be lowered to facilitate communication about common problems and solutions.

Certainly from a grass-roots perspective it is time to reexamine the balance, or, perhaps more appropriately, the imbalance, in current work/family roles and responsibilities. From most accounts the social contract is bankrupt or, at best, in need of serious restructuring if the American family is going to be able to return to a state of healthy functioning. Instead of relying exclusively on the family, we should turn to the political and economic sectors to assist in finding solutions to the current catalogue of work/family conflicts. The very recognition that these political and economic systems shape family choices and effect the overall health and functioning is a beginning. The fact that the necessity of restructuring the social contract between families and society is also essential to economic growth and survival only reinforces the urgency of this call for action.

In summary, the social contract has fallen apart. The existing fragments of such a contract are dysfunctional, harmful to the growth of families, and a yet to be appreciated burden on economic growth and global competitiveness. Unfortunately, as Machiavelli implied, there is no constituency for reform. Neither the public nor private sectors has provided any leadership in seizing this issue. Other constituencies such as unions have been too preoccupied with their own survival to lend any effective leadership. But the question that cries out for response as families flounder is: Whose responsibility is it to address these conflicts? Is it the government's, which has traditionally been seen in most societies as the base of family support? Is it the corporation's, who increasingly through its benefits programs has adopted a new welfare capitalism and in whose interest some resolution of this problem is essential? Or is it the family's, which has throughout time adapted and adopted to the environment around it? It will be the thesis of this book that all three have to assume some responsibility in working together to find better solutions. No social contract can be carved out by the public, private or family sector's alone. All three have a vested interest in finding solutions and, therefore, have to work together if any lasting solutions are to happen. Anything short of this partnership will result in fragmented solutions and increased conflicts.

It is the major premise of this book that work/family conflicts cannot be effectively understood or dealt with unless the principal stakeholders (the family, the corporations, and the government) are aware of one another's needs and interests. Further, and ultimately more important, no progress in resolving these conflicts can be achieved as long as there are fragmented approaches to the solutions. The history of government or corporations or families singularly attempting to resolve these issues has left a legacy of temporary solutions and outright failures. Until true partnerships are realized in which the intersecting spheres identify common ground and develop working models of cooperation and joint ventures, the stress and dysfunction resulting from work/family conflicts will continue.

The potential for resolving these conflicts has never been greater because the stakes are so high. It is to this end that this book examines the roots of the conflicts and begins to sketch the outlines of the exciting challenges of overcoming work/family conflicts.

NOTES

1. Whitehead, p. A–20.
2. Waldrop, p. 24.
3. Masnick and Bane, p. 7.
4. Ibid., p. 80.

5. Castro, p. 64.

6. *Work and Family: A Changing Dynamic: A Bureau of National Affairs Special Report*, p. 13.

7. Employee Benefits Research Institute, p. 2.

8. Stautberg, p. 278.

9. Sekaran, p. 95.

10. Mintz and Kellogg, p. 203.

11. Ibid.

12. Kanter, p. 8.

13. Ibid., p. 81.

14. Bronfenbrenner and Crouter, p. 70.

15. Ibid.; Richter and Hall, p. 8.

Chapter 2

DIMENSIONS OF WORK/ FAMILY RELATIONS

Trying to adequately understand work/family conflict is somewhat akin to picking up a jellyfish—it tends to be more allusive than manageable. There is a tendency to translate the work/family dilemma (no doubt exacerbated by media coverage) into simplistic segments. For example, both corporations and the government have most recently focused on day care for preschool children, not necessarily because it will resolve the most basic work/family conflicts, but because it is the most visible conflict and, at this point in time, represented by the most vocal groups. Never mind that this phase of day care covers only a five-year period. Why not focus on at least equal coverage on the next twelve to thirteen years, when the school day for children is considerably shorter than the work day (plus commuting time) for their parents? Or what about the problems of elder care? It now appears that the average American family will spend more time being responsible for an aging parent than it will being responsible for the 17- to 18-year-olds in its custody. Sometimes work/family conflicts are reduced to the confines of a child-care program, but this misses both the extent of the problem and the roots of the conflict.

The very fact that society has been slow to react to the range of the work/ family problems is some indication of the conflicts that surround work/family issues. Underneath these conflicts lie a series of social and cultural values, philosophical differences, competing economic theories, and institutional boundaries that seldom find their way to the playing surface or become linked to the discussions, but whose presence and importance cannot be underestimated. Any time the family becomes the focus of attention, deeply held values and beliefs become more important than the pleas of hard-pressed parents or supervisors.

To provide some insight into the complexity of work/family conflicts, it is necessary to examine the roles and interests of four primary stakeholders: the individual, the family, work, and society. Each of these stakeholders has a unique perspective on work/family issues. Dramatic behavioral changes have occurred at each of these four levels. Most of the changes are associated with alterations in values that directly affect the lives of individuals and families as well as the functioning of the business and government sectors. Many of the changes have, in turn, produced a range of conflicts that are related to alterations in old roles and structures and the emergence of new ones. Of particular significance are the impacts that the changes and conflicts have on each of the four major stakeholders. Indicators of stress are signs of negative impact, whereas increased well-being suggests the presence of positive impacts.

Table 2.1 outlines the dimensions of work/family change, conflict, and impact.

This chapter describes these dimensions of change, conflict, and impact. They constitute the backdrop and context for work/family issues and for individuals, families, corporations, and society. The information is presented in a structured manner for clarity and for purposes of analysis. The reality of the worlds of work and family is anything but flat and linear. The linkages and interdependence of one stakeholder to another binds them in a system. It is necessary to understand not only the four unique spheres of the system, but also the systemic linkages that tie one to the other. Without such a systemic understanding and approach, there is little hope for anything more than impulsive reactions and fragmented solutions to work/family conflicts that serve more as temporary analgesics than as long-term interventions.

INDIVIDUALS

Changes

Three generations of Americans are currently pioneering new lifestyles. As a group, today's children are the first to receive significant amounts of "child-rearing interactions" from child-care providers during the preschool years. Seniors have recently begun to examine and question different aspects of their prolonged years in retirement. And the baby boomers—composed of young and middle-aged adults—are struggling most directly with work/family issues. Virtually no one has been untouched by the aftermath of the sixties and seventies when the United States experienced a great deal of fundamental change resulting from shifting cultural and social norms, mores, and institutional structures.

The baby boomers are a unique group to study because they were coming of age during this period of marked change. They brought a new set of values to their young adulthood when they began to confront choices about marriage, parenting, and work. The baby boomers blazed new trails to the experience of adulthood.

The results of a 1983 American Council of Life Insurance Companies survey of one thousand baby boomers provide a glimpse into some of the changes in values related to work and family:

Table 2.1
Dimensions of the Work/Family Relations

	Changes	Conflicts	Impact

Individuals	- Adult Development
	- Adult Education
	- Career Development
	- Socialization of Children
	- Lifestyles for Elders
		- Role Strain
		- Role Overload
		- Identity
		- Role Cycling
		- Social Network
		- Expectations and Norms
		- Rising Expectations
		- Role Conflicts for
		  Children
		- Emerging Roles for Elders
			- Life Satisfaction for Adults
			- Adult Stress
			- Life Satisfaction and Stress
			  for Children
			- Life Satisfaction and Stress for
			  for Elders

Family	- Diversity - Family Time	- Family Identity - Role Blending - Role Strain - Marital Power	- Isolation of Nuclear Family - Strains on Marital Relations - Stress on Children as Family Members - Scheduling - Sense of Family Worth

Workplace	- Movement to a World
	  Economy
	- Technological Changes
	- Educated Workforce
	- Changing Demographics
	- Employee Attitudes and
	  Expectations
	- Increased Emphasis on
	  Human Resources
	- Decline in Preeminence
	  of the Workplace
		- Corporate Roles
		  and Identity
		- Corporate Conception
		  of the Family
		- Gender Conflicts
		- Dilemmas in Management
			- Scheduling
			- Decreased Productivity
			- Inadequate Structures
			- Employee Morale

Society	- Political Changes - Economic Changes - Diversity of Values	- Government Role - Lack of Consensus - Transmission of Values	- Crisis in Caregiving - Volunteerism - Impact on Institutions - Advocacy

- More than three quarters (76%) say an equal marriage in which husband and wife share work, child-rearing, and homemaking responsibilities is most appealing to them

- Fifty-six percent of unmarried adults living together

- Sixty-six percent would like to see less emphasis on money but not on work.[1]

The collective value systems, expectations, and beliefs are shaping American families and spilling over into today's workplace. These changes can be seen more directly in five specific areas.

Adult Development. Psychological theories of human development espoused before the 1960s reflected the life experiences of most adults at the time: the extended phase of adulthood (age 21 to death) was perceived as relatively static, and intrapsychic development was considered relatively complete (except for changes resulting from trauma or therapeutic interventions). There was a presumption that by the time a person became an adult, most of the developmental challenges should have been confronted, which would free up the adult to shift his or her focus to the next generation in the family. Education usually was terminated, a lifelong career identified, a lifelong mate selected. Except for the birth of children and the deaths of others, circumstances were expected to stay pretty much the same.

The life of the individual adult is distinctly different today. Central to this change is a new perception of self-realization in terms of self-development[2]. American adults, particularly in the middle and upper socioeconomic classes, have placed a great deal of emphasis on setting forth an agenda for their own development. This manifests itself in a range of personal expressions, from physical activities (e.g., aerobics and jogging) and life skills courses (e.g., stress management, health education, and parenting classes) to spiritual and religious journeys. There is now an almost universal recognition that personal development does not stop at age 21.

A number of indicators highlight the extent to which today's adults are placing a priority on their own development, rather than rushing to subordinate (and often sacrifice) their personal development for the next generation. Many young adults have explored options of postponing the assumption of family responsibilities, which has afforded them greater latitude in seeking out personal challenges:

- Young adults tend to postpone marriage. The current median age of marriage for men is 25.8 years, compared with 22.8 years in 1965. During the same period, the median age for first marriage for women also increased by three years, from 20.6 years in 1965 to 23.6 years.[3]
- The growth of single-person households (an adult living alone) has been explosive. This type of household increased 89 percent during the twelve years between 1970 (comprising 19% of all households) and 1982 (comprising 27% of all households).[4]
- More adults are remaining single for longer periods of time. In 1970, only 7.43 percent of all women between the ages of 30 and 44 years had never been married. It is anticipated that this figure will increase to more than 15 percent by the beginning of the next decade.[5]
- Women are postponing the birth of their first child. Whereas many mothers had their first child before they were 25 years old during the 1950s, by the 1970s a significant number of women delayed their childbearing until after age 30.[6]
- Women are having fewer children. The current fertility rate is approximately 1.8 per woman, in contrast to 1960, when it was 3.7.[7]

- Current projects indicate that as many as 40 percent of women baby boomers may remain childless or have only one child in contrast to 20 percent of the women in their mothers' generation.[8]
- An increasing number of young women are exploring ways to broaden their horizons; 52 percent of undergraduate enrollments in college are female.[9]

Adult Education. Except for a few stalwart people who attended night schools, most parents of the baby boomers considered themselves too old to attend school after they were in their mid-twenties. Reinforcing this perspective, most professional schools and graduate programs were hesitant to admit adults over age 30. What was once a rigid education-work continuum now looks more like education-work-education-work . . .

No longer is education reserved for the young. Adults of all ages have begun to participate in educational experiences ranging from workshops to degree programs. Community colleges and hospitals are just two of the institutions that are catering to the seemingly insatiable need of today's adults to continue their formal and informal educations.

- According to one report, the average age of students now enrolled in community colleges is 36 years, and this number is expected to rise.[10]

Career Development. The emphasis on self-development has created a new approach to work for many adults. Jobs are now careers, and work has become an expression of the adult. The potential for fulfillment in satisfactory work has been recognized. It is becoming more widely understood that people work for more than just the obvious economic reasons.

Because careers are seen as offering the potential for one arena of personal development, employees are more seriously evaluating whether a particular job with a particular company is the best match for them. In contrast to the adults entering work after World War II who may have stayed with the same company for a significant number of years, today's workers believe that it is worth the risk to change jobs if their current job is not satisfactory.[11]

- Within a single year, 8.3 million men and 6.9 million women changed their occupations, and within a single month, 3.3 million were looking for new jobs.[12]
- The results of a survey conducted in the San Francisco Bay area indicate that of those people placed in jobs by the U.S. Employment Service, 57 percent were not in that job thirty days later.[13]

Another indication of the attention being devoted to adult development is the increasing frequency of midlife career changes. In the seventies it would have been practically unheard of for a middle-aged engineer to go back to school to study to be a doctor or for a teacher to become an investment counselor. The social sanctions against this type of behavior would come from the family, who would advise against taking any economic risks, and from the workplace, which would be reticent about hiring someone who was showing signs of "instability." In the 1980s, new jobs in different fields often are perceived as opportunities to confront new challenges and develop new sets of skills.

Socialization of Children. Although many of the changes that have been occurring on the individual level impact most directly on adults, significant changes have been taking place with children. In contrast to the childhood experiences of their parents, today's children are socialized into a dramatically different world, both within and outside the family structure. A significant number of children experience the divorce of their parents, single-parent families, and often "blended" families after their guardian parents remarry.

- Between 1960 and 1975, the number of children per year whose parents became legally divorced more than doubled, going from less than a half million to more than a million per year.[14]
- Almost 60 percent of all children will live in a single-parent family for a significant period of time before they are 18[15].

The children of today witness some of the contradictions that are inherent to the transitional phase of the current changes in American families. On the other hand, traditional sex role stereotyping is becoming less distinct. They see Mom go to work and may have a Barbie doll who dresses for the office. Children raised in dual-income families may be expected to contribute to household maintenance and assume chores that are not assigned according to sex-stereotyped roles. Even though their fathers may be more involved in their upbringing than in previous generations, their mothers still assume the bulk of the household chores and family-nurturing responsibilities. Undoubtedly, this is confusing for some children.

One profound change that has occurred in the lives of young children is the amount of time they spend either alone or with an adult who is not their parent. A preschooler growing up during the 1950s whose mother was a full-time homemaker would typically spend almost all of the twelve waking hours every day with Mom (and perhaps with Dad on the weekends). Today's preschooler might have four hours with Mom or Dad each day. As a consequence, these children spend significant amounts of time with adults and other children, who add diversity to their early childhood experiences.

Lifestyles of the Elder Generation. Equally significant and often overlooked are the changes within the older generation. Although almost any discussion of changing demographics focuses on the baby boomers and the changing values of the new generation, there also are significant changes within the group often referred to as senior citizens. For most elders, their parents worked and then died. The concept of growing old gradually within a nonwork context is relatively new, and one that the current generation is piloting in terms of behaviors, roles, and norms. For example, many seniors are exploring the option of working part-time, a reflection of the difficult economic stress on many elders with inadequate or nonexistent pensions, as well as the testimony of the centrality and value of work in a person's life.

For many others, a relatively long period of leisure nonwork has resulted in migration to the warmer climates of the South and Southwest where socialization with large numbers of age peers creates a desirable lifestyle. The movement of elders into enclaves of retirement communities typically distances the elders from their adult children and other relatives, creating a more independent relationship between elders and their children.

- The results of a recent survey conducted by General Mills show that among the parents interviewed, 67 percent thought that their children should not feel any particular obligation to them when they become old.[16]

Conflicts

It is not surprising that work/family conflict is most deeply felt on the individual level. Although much of the conflict can be discussed under the rubric of work/family issues, the actual conflict often occurs within the individual. As the research findings presented in this book boldly attest, work/family conflict is both intense and widespread among individual employees. Some, such as working mothers, experience more intense conflicts than others, such as husbands with a wife at home. What is more remarkable than the gradations of conflicts, however, is the extent of the conflicts, which seem to be felt by just about everyone.

Role Strain. The concept of role strain typically refers to the negative interference resulting from a person's experiencing problems in one domain that affect the performance in a different sphere of life, a phenomenon termed "negative spillover." For some people, it is difficult to keep separate from work the emotional reactions to a family problem. An employee who is worried about a disabled family member might become distracted at work. Role strain also can move in the other direction. For example, the quality of family interactions can suffer when an employee is experiencing significant job dissatisfaction.

Role strain has become more common among working families as the demands and needs of both work and home seem to collide more frequently in the absence of corporate or societal support.

Role Overload. The management of multiple roles in two domains becomes difficult because of time and energy limitations.[17] It is as if responsibilities in the spheres of work and home compete for a person's time.

The strains that result from role overload can be experienced in a number of ways. For some, it is not being able to spend time with children because of work schedules and the demands of work. For others, it is having more roles and responsibilities at work and at home than the time allocated for such roles.

Working mothers in particular experience many of these conflicts because of cultural expectations for child-rearing and because home management remains largely relegated to them. Research by Catherine Ross and coworkers documented some of the depression rates that are associated with women who experience role overload.[18]

Some women attempt to reduce their role overload by focusing either on a highly demanding career or on the highly demanding early years of child-rearing, but do not attempt to do both simultaneously.

- As a recent cover story of *Fortune* magazine (August 4 1986) reported, one third of women with master of business administration degrees who were surveyed ten years after receiving their degrees had left corporations, primarily because of competing family demands.

Finally, without minimizing the impact of work/family conflicts on women, role overload is no longer just a women's issue. The results of recent studies at DuPont and the findings presented in Chapter 4 indicate that men are experiencing more conflict over career choices as they assume more responsibility for family.

Role Identity. People tend to internalize multiple identities that reflect some of the principle roles they assume. If adults believe that they are compromising one role in order to fulfill another, they may experience role identity conflicts. The adult son who sometimes arrives late at work because he has to check on his elderly mother may question his ability to be a good role model for his supervisees.

These identity conflicts arise when people need to establish some temporary sense of priority about which responsibilities to fill at a particular time. Guilt often accompanies these choices. A father who is late picking up a child at day care because an important meeting ran late may feel guilty because his behavior could suggest that, at that time, his work seemed more important than his son.

Role-Cycling Conflicts. Life at home and at work can be conceptualized from a developmental perspective. Within the "home system" an adult might proceed through different phases, including single adulthood, marriage, married with children, divorce, single-parenthood, remarriage, married with "empty nest," married with responsibility for the care of elderly parents, and widowed. Some of these phases are associated with intense family responsibilities, and others have a lower degree of demands.

In the domain of work, new employees with limited work experience who fill entry-level positions might find that the work challenges are limited, but there could be a lot of pressure to demonstrate potential. Promotions bring added challenges and may require extra effort during the initial phases of assuming the job. Renewed efforts usually are required by the employee when he or she changes employers (e.g., layoffs, firings, and voluntary terminations). In contrast, long-term workers who have mastered the job expectations and who have achieved their personal career goals might feel less pressure to perform.

Role-cycling conflicts can arise for a person when the developmental phases in the domains of work and family are not in synchrony with each other.[19] This might occur if there are intense developmental demands in both spheres simultaneously. An attorney in her early thirties may think that she must continue to demonstrate high output at work at a time when she also wants to increase her availability to her family after the birth of a child. A somewhat inverse dilemma might arise for a father in his fifties, after having reached some career goals, who wants to put some extra time into his family and discovers that his teenage children prefer to spend time with their peers and his wife is fully engaged in her career, having recently changed jobs.

Social Network Conflicts. Many working adults, especially those with intense family responsibilities, have a limited amount of time to establish and maintain social support systems. In contrast to the fifties when neighbors could be counted on to help with minor family emergencies, many working adults may be barely acquainted with their neighbors. Furthermore, most members of the support system probably work and have similar role overload conflicts themselves.

Geographical mobility exacerbates the problem. Work associates, friends, and neighbors move often, so that it requires a constant output of energy to establish new relationships. To make matters worse, even the grandparents may have moved to Arizona! Employees with dependent-care responsibilities (e.g., children, disabled family members, or aging relatives) may think that their social support systems are fragile and cannot be depended on for backup assistance. There may be no one to call if a parent's car breaks down on the way to pick up the kids at school.

Conflicts with Role Expectations and Norms. Conflicts that are related to established role norms usually are experienced as value conflicts. These conflicts can be "internal"; a person may have different values about appropriate roles that conflict with one another, or a person's values may be inconsistent with his or her behavior. "External" conflicts occur when one person's values conflict with those of another person who represents a different set of values. For example, a mother who rushes from work to pick up her sick child at school may receive a stern comment from the school nurse, who clearly disapproves of the child's having had to wait forty-five minutes for the mother to arrive. The message is clear: "Good" mothers are available to their children at all times.

One source of normative conflict is the clash between the values that people gradually develop during their childhood and the values that society may espouse when they reach adulthood. Baby boomers who grew up in the fifties are especially vulnerable to this "time-warp" in values. The values that their parents carefully taught them may not always be applicable during the eighties. Many of today's women carry with them images of the archetypal mother (who resembles their own mothers)—Mom at home, Mom cooking, Mom as scout leader, and Mom centering her life around the children during the day and around her husband at night. Although today's mother may try to emulate this parenting model, she is simultaneously faced with the new roles and expectations of the workplace.

Normative role changes also have affected men. The father of the husband of today came home at 5:30 P.M. each night, had a hot meal waiting for him, and after a relaxing transition period from the workplace said good night to all his freshly scrubbed children. The current reality includes a working wife and frequent meals at the local fast-food restaurant or pizza parlor with nights spent washing floors, and bathing kids and getting them ready for bed. The traditional role values that were taught to boys during the fifties did not prepare them for many of the roles they are currently assuming.

Rising Expectations. Rising expectations also shape and contribute to work/family conflicts. Added to these conflicts, the unrealistic expectations that some couples entertain about themselves can cause immense vexations and frustrations. The subgroup of baby boomers identified as Yuppies typify the self-imposed pressure felt by many young adults. Put simply, they "want it all now and in superior quality"—high-status/high-income positions, expensive and expansive well-maintained homes, meaningful marriages, and bright, creative, well-behaved children.

Although this personal pursuit of excellence can dictate fairly straightforward behaviors for work and economic goals, it becomes complicated in the arena of parenting. Parents simultaneously experience feelings of high expectations for their own parenting skills and strong achievement orientations for their children, potentially as a way to have tangible proof of the success of their parenting endeavors. Because meeting unrealistically high expectations is difficult, it is not surprising that various forms of guilt, based on an archetypal model of previous generations, seem standard fare for most of today's working parents.

Today's upper- and middle-class working parents may overcompensate for any perceived shortcomings in their abilities to raise their children. Although these children may have less direct access to their parents' time, they frequently have full schedules of extracurricular activities. Thirty years ago most parents thought that they were fulfilling their responsibilities to their children if the children were involved in scouts once a week and had some religious training, dance lessons for the girls, little league for the boys; and maybe a year of music instruction. Today's working parents, who may not be available for activities that require some parent involvement (e.g., community sports programs), want to be able to identify the best formal enrichment experiences for their children. These parents try to carefully assess the options for preschool or child care and make arrangements for their children to participate in an array of lessons that promote physical, artistic, and cognitive development. The list of such programs is almost endless in some communities.

Role Conflicts for Children. We have focused on conflicts of working adults, but in fact, these conflicts are manifested across the life cycle. Children experience some of the same types of role conflicts as adults. These conflicts are magnified because people in all age groups are entering uncharted waters.

Some youngsters exhibit signs of role overload. This can develop in children who are so busy with scheduled activities that they hardly have any time to socialize with their peers or to focus on some of their basic responsibilities, such as homework. In some families the addition of extensive home chores may make their daily activities seem overwhelming.

One of the significant psychodynamic challenges of childhood and adolescence is the development of a sense of identity. Under the best of circumstances, this can be a difficult task to accomplish. Children who live in families that experience intense work/family conflicts may find it especially hard to organize their perceptions of "identity." Children who fulfill some adult roles at home might find it complicated to simultaneously see themselves as children and as adults. Increased expectations for the achievements of children in some working families may make it more difficult for them to accept the fact that childhood is a time of life to make some mistakes and learn from them. It is tragic that some children who do not excel internalize their performance as a failure.

The problems that working adults have with the maintenance of a social support network also become conflicts for their children. In the short term, this is hard for children who believe that they may have to depend almost exclusively on their parents, who cannot always be available. These children also may not have had an opportunity to develop a long-term sense of trust in other adults (aunts, uncles, and neighbors). Furthermore, they may not be able to observe the interactions of their parents' support systems that develop at the workplace. A question can be raised concerning whether the conflicts about social support systems experienced by children today will affect their abilities to establish social support systems once they reach adulthood.

The state of flux of social norms can make it difficult for children to develop a basic understanding of their world. Part of this confusion may result from the diversity of families that has developed over the past two decades and from the fact that more people in addition to the parents are likely to be involved in rearing the children. The diverse experiences that children are exposed to during childhood may broaden their perspectives and enrich their lives as adults, but they can be confusing early in life. It is commonplace for working mothers to lament because their children complain that they aren't at home. On the other hand, mothers who are home full-time struggle with their children's criticisms that they don't "do anything."

Emerging Roles of Elders. To a great extent, the major challenge for many elders as they carve out the new territory of extended years in retirement is the creation of new roles.

Many seniors are exploring new interpretations of their roles and their responsibilities to their families. As the senior population continues to be more independent from the family unit (e.g., adult children and grandchildren), they are less available for the traditional caregiving and social support functions they have historically had in families. Consequently, the grandchildren often are not socialized with an intergenerational perspective, and the grandparents are not available to perform many small chores that can relieve young parents, such as baby-sitting, running errands, and acting as child-rearing advisers. Ironically, as we shall see in later sections of the book, this same separateness of the generations creates a different crisis when the elders cannot function independently and need the care and assistance of their adult children.

Another emerging role for elders is their relation to work. As society continues to acknowledge the talent and competence that many elders possess, additional options will be available for those seniors who want to maintain a role at the workplace. Some seniors will find volunteering programs such as RSVP (Retired Senior Volunteer Program) satisfying; others will want to become consultants in their fields of expertise; and still others will want to pursue part-time or full-time employment.

Impact

Freud indicated the necessity of blending work and love as the foundation for human behavior and life satisfaction. Seeking ways to find fulfillment at these most basic levels, most working adults struggle to integrate work and family into their lives. To the extent that neither corporations nor society assumes ownership of these issues, individuals and their families are left to bear the burden and pay the price that unresolved conflict brings.

There currently is no single index or assessment instrument that measures the total impact work/family conflicts have on the individual. Some indicators, however, provide information about the effect of these conflicts on a person's sense of well-being, life satisfaction, and wellness (physical, emotional, social, and productive performance).

Life Satisfaction for Adults. It is possible to conceive life satisfaction as the ability to pursue experiences in the realms of productive (but not excluding unpaid) work and of love (assuming that basic physical needs such as food, shelter, and clothing have been met). Although men and women may start from quite different economic, social, and cultural bases (i.e., norms, expectations, and boundaries), they both seek to carve out an acceptable life satisfaction level.

> • For women, job satisfaction has increasingly become an essential component
> of life satisfaction. Indeed, a large majority of women (76%) indicate that
> they would continue to work even if their income was not needed by their
> families.[20]

There is growing evidence that work functions as a positive force in the overall well-being of women. Women who work are typically less depressed and have higher rates of life satisfaction.

- Baruch and colleagues at the Wellesley College Center for Research on Women concluded that "a variety of well-controlled studies show significant mental and physical health differences that favor employed versus non-employed women."[21]

- In a recent study of caregivers of seriously impaired relatives, there was significantly less stress in those caregivers who worked in comparison to those who were at home full-time. This occurred despite the fact that the working caregivers spent almost as much caregiving time in addition to their work.[22]

Some adults report that their jobs are like a form of respite from the problems at home; thus, working makes their family responsibilities easier. This is corroborated in a study of employed and nonemployed spouses of alcoholic men in which employed wives found work to be a haven in coping with their husbands' alcoholism.[23]

Similarly, it is becoming more acceptable for men to develop their social and emotional capacities. Life satisfaction for men increasingly incorporates trade-offs in child care and home chores with career advancement.[24] Research indicates that men are becoming more involved with their families and are deriving increasing satisfaction from this role expansion. In contrast to the results of studies conducted during the sixties and seventies, Pleck has found that husbands of working wives are starting to invest more time in family roles than are husbands of non-working wives.[25] One social commentator has noted that men "too are tired of the old corporate attitude that deprives men of sharing the joys of active child rearing with their wives, the attitude that had allowed 90 percent of executive men to have families, but not a family life."[26]

As role boundaries break down, men and women are not forced to live within the narrower socially defined and accepted boxes of social and emotional behavior. The changes make it easier for all adults to explore the range of their talents and responsibilities rather than focus on just one aspect of their lives. Thus, work/family conflicts (and ultimately their resolution) have impacted the very nature of what constitutes life satisfaction and the degree to which individual employees can achieve what they perceive to be a satisfied work and home environment.

Stress constitutes a major impact of work/family conflicts on the individual. There is a significantly broad reporting of individual stress related to balancing work and home. Whereas a woman's home life tends to interfere with her work life, a man's work life has traditionally intruded on his home life.

Clearly, from every perspective, women are seriously impacted by work/family conflicts. Early in their careers women often are expected to bear the brunt of child-rearing at the expense of career. Out of economic necessity many women assume an increasing income-earning role that may take priority over their responsibilities for child care and household chores. The dual responsibilities of home and work are keenly felt by women. Pleck reports that women are much more likely to suffer from the stress of role overload than are their husbands.[27]

As cultural norms and expectations diverge from traditional ones, greater stress may occur for both men and women. This stress may manifest itself in increased depression, poor health, and a general lack of energy. It is quite likely that unresolved work/family conflicts will increase the stress for working adults as long as there are few family program initiatives, or organizational or social policies designed to assist these adults.

Life Satisfaction and Stress on Children. The most controversial impact of work/family conflicts centers on the effects on children. A number of demographics indicate that a large number of children in the United States are beset by problems.

- Since 1960 the high school dropout rate has increased dramatically, so that one of every four students do not graduate.

- There has been a 130 percent increase in the juvenile delinquency rate during the past two decades.

- The suicide rate for 15- to 19-year-olds has increased three times since 1960.

- The birthrate among white adolescent unwed girls has doubled in the past twenty years.[28]

It is irrelevant to ask whether work/family conflicts have contributed to this distressing picture of the life satisfaction of our children.

Questions are raised as to whether there are short- or long-term effects of having both parents at the workplace. Will these impacts be positive or negative? The arguments are heated on both sides, and the jury is still out. While one camp marshals data to argue the deleterious effects of mother's work on the child in terms of developmental achievement, security, and self-esteem, the other camp puts forth countervailing evidence that not only is the mother's employment not necessarily negative, but it may well have a salutary effect in terms of fostering independence, decision making, and responsibility in the child. Most meta analyses of this literature concluded that there is no overwhelming evidence to argue strongly on one side or the other of this issue. As the Panel on Work, Family, and Community, established in 1980 by the Committee on Child Development Research and Public Policy, stated, "Although we have identified no single overall effect on children that results from their parents working, we know that paid employment creates or adds to family income and decreased family time."[29]

It is possible to use theories of child development to surmise some of the impact work/family conflicts may have on children. Most theories propose that children's physical, cognitive, social, and emotional development proceed in a fairly linear manner, with each phase using the mastery of abilities associated with earlier periods as "building blocks" for more complex tasks. For example, many child development experts agree that one of the initial challenges for the human infant is to develop a sense of trust in human relationships as a result of consistent and supportive interactions with a "primary caretaker"—typically the mother. A little later in life more complex social challenges, such as separation and sharing, utilize the sense of trust developed during infancy.

New child-rearing models that depend heavily on the use of caretakers other than "Mom" may require that children confront relatively complex challenges earlier than previous generations of children. Years ago the extent of any sharing required by a 2- or 3-year-old was principally limited to play with a sibling or neighborhood child. Today it is expected that young children in group child-care situations will be able to acquire some rudimentary forms of these skills with an entire class for up to eight to ten hours at a time. These changes have altered public perceptions of what is developmentally appropriate behavior for children. Ten years ago kindergarten teachers expected that many children would show signs of separation difficulty during the first weeks of school. Today 5- and 6-year-olds who have separation problems seem a bit aberrant.

In many families the changes in adult roles and responsibilities at home and at work have resulted in a situation in which children are expected to grow up just a little faster. In some cases these expectations for maturer behavior result from lifestyle changes. Parents who eat relaxed meals at home may be more tolerant of squirmy youngsters who want to be excused from the dinner table. Children are more frequently being taken to adult environments, such as restaurants, however, and are expected to act grown up, not like children.

Some of the changes in the lives of children reflect their parents' rising expectations. There seems to be a marked increase in the achievement orientation of middle- and upper-income parents. For many of these parents it is no longer acceptable to have "average" children. There is an emphasis on providing the right combination of opportunities to children so that they can achieve certain objectives at earlier ages. An abundance of books are available that suggest methodologies for parents who want to tutor infants and toddlers on topics ranging from prereading skills to the identification of works by famous artists. Pressure starts early. Although many people laugh about parents who desperately try to get their children into the right preschool, this can be a stressful procedure for some parents (and for their children). This pressure to achieve may continue throughout the school years. Becoming average has become a negative attribute in our educational system.

Children also can feel the direct impact of the work/family conflicts experienced by their parents. Some working parents who have severe role overload problems may turn to their children, expecting them to assume some adult roles. Some of these expectations are associated with the fulfillment of household chores, such as cleaning and helping with meal preparation. For many children involvement in these tasks may define some concrete contributions they can make to the family. Having such a clear family role may support the sense of self-esteem and competence for some children. In some families teenage children may be asked to assume some financial responsibilities, such as contributing to savings for any higher education they might pursue.

A more controversial area of adult role assumption is the expectation that children can perform some roles that they are not emotionally or cognitively mature enough to handle. David Elkind, in his classic book *The Hurried Child*, raises poignant questions about the effect of this push toward maturity on our children. What is the impact on a 10-year-old when the single-parent mother discusses her romantic disappointments because she has no one else to talk to? What are the effects of expecting children to analyze and respond to situations as if they were adults when they are, of course, still children?

Children under 12 years who are expected to regularly care for themselves or for younger siblings may be in situations that challenge their capabilities. The concept of children fending for themselves has created a national scare in light of increased teen pregnancies, drug use, missing children, and the natural dangers faced by children coping on their own for significant periods of time during the day. At this point in time the family is left to struggle with this phenomenon and suffer the consequence in the absence of community programs and supports. The effects are highly debated, but it is the children who experience the loneliness, fear, and boredom cited by the Longs in their recent study of so-called latchkey children.[30]

On the brighter side, today's children may be better prepared for their adulthood than their parents were. The baby boomers, who are pioneering a range of diverse roles and lifestyles at home and at work, were socialized at a time when only one primary model existed: Dad went to work and Mom stayed home with the children. Today's children see their own parents and the parents of friends using different approaches to work and family responsibilities that might help them to identify some options for their own adulthood. Furthermore, today's children may not be growing up with rigid gender stereotypes, so that as adults they might be freer to actualize new work/family balances.[31]

A nostalgic view of childhood might include a lot of neighborhood-based activities: impromptu sports games, walks to the library, home-baked cookies, lazy summer days at the pool. Despite such reassuring memories, it has probably never been easy for most children to grow up. For the children of the eighties, however, the added work/family stresses felt by their parents might result in the fact that it's not much fun being a kid anymore.

Life Satisfaction and Stresses of Elders. The efforts of a number of advocacy groups have resulted in some tangible gains for America's seniors. Just a generation ago the primary work/family conflict for older Americans was the threat of insufficient money generated during the working years to cover the expenses of the postretirement years. Although many elders who live on fixed incomes still face daily battles with poverty, programs such as Social Security and Medicare have made substantial contributions to their lives. In addition, the increased emphasis on retirement planning might help some of tomorrow's seniors to maintain the desired "quality of life."

Elderly women today have a far higher rate of poverty than do elderly men. In 1984, 8.7 percent of elderly men and 15 percent of women age 65 and over had incomes below the poverty line with almost 90 percent of today's elderly poor women as single.[32]

Some of the lifestyle changes exhibited by middle-aged adults have also had a ripple effect on seniors. The opportunity to extend education through the adult years often is available to elders. One group, the Elder Hostels of America, promotes a wealth of exciting and challenging learning opportunities for seniors.

The passage of age discrimination laws and regulations has also provided some options for elders who want to maintain an affiliation with the workforce. For some elders this has meant a postponement of retirement. For others it may result in the elder's returning to work after retirement. In the past retirement was "for keeps." Today some elders are finding that it may be a time to start a new career.

FAMILY

Changes

"The family in its old sense is disappearing from our land, and not only our free institutions are threatened but the very existence of our society is endangered."

This quote could have come from President Bush's State of the Union Message, but in fact it is from the 1859 *Quarterly Review*. Much like the era of the preindustrial revolution, the 1980s experienced one of those rare cultural shifts as it began the gradual transition to a postindustrial society. No institution has had to undergo such dramatic and sweeping change in this process as has the American family. Like the changes that occur at the individual level, many of the measurable changes within the family reflect alterations in values and beliefs.

The changes in the American family over the past decade have not always been subtle or inconsequential. The rapidity of the change has been accompanied by new structures and new family behaviors. It also has led to significant cultural and social upheaval, creating in its path a series of conflicts.

Diversity. The most radical change in the structure of American families is the rapid movement toward diversity. Just a generation ago most families fit the model of "Dad goes to work, and Mom stays home to take care of the house and the children." At a time when the Kennedy family was charming the country from the White House and the media was bombarding society with cozy images of intact nuclear families, there was little recognition or understanding of families that did not "fit the mold." Within just two generations the standard and norm for the family structure have been considerably altered.

- In 1987 just 27.5 percent of all households comprised married couples with children under the age of 18 years.[33]

An increasing number of adults do not see marriage as a permanent relationship. The growing acceptance of divorce in our society reflects a change in some of the values associated with "family." Just one generation ago parents typically tried to preserve their marriage, even if this effort was "for the sake of the children." Today many adults believe that a destructive marriage has negative consequences for the children, and that a divorce might be a preferable arrangement for all family members. There is much less stigma associated with divorce than existed twenty or thirty years ago.

- There were twice as many divorces during the early 1980s as there were during the mid–1960s and three times as many as during 1950.[34]
- Between 1960 and 1980 the ratio of divorces to marriages virtually doubled from 25 percent to 50 percent.[35]
- Before the end of this century an estimated 20 percent of women in their thirties will be divorced, separated, or "spouse-absent." Only 13 percent of women in their thirties were in this group in 1975.[36]
- Some projections suggest that as many as two thirds of today's marriages will end in separation or divorce.[37]
- Commenting on today's adults, Cherlin and Furstenberg observe that "about nine out of ten will eventually marry; about one out of two will marry and then divorce; and about one out of three will marry, divorce and then re-marry."[38]

Families also are getting smaller, primarily because of changes in the child-bearing patterns of the baby boomers. Today's generation of adults is having their children later in life and are having fewer of them.

- Birthrates have gone from 3.8 children in 1958 to 1.8 per family in 1980.[39]
- About 50 percent of all family households in 1986 included no children under 18 years of age, up from 44 percent in 1970.[40]

A dramatic change that has received a lot of attention in the press is the rise in the number of single-parent families. These families are headed both by adults who have never married as well as by previously married parents.

- There were 8.9 million single-parent family groups in 1986, a significant increase from 1970, when there were just 3.8 million.[41]
- The number of single parents has grown to the point where a quarter of all families with children are headed by single parents.[42]
- The majority of households without a married couple are single-parent families—7.3 million.[43]

The remarriage of divorced adults, many of whom have children, has resulted in an increase in "blended families." These families include at least one step-parent and possibly stepbrothers and stepsisters as well as half brothers and half sisters.

- During the 1980s one out of every seven households with children involved a remarriage with at least one child from a previous marriage.[44]

An increasing number of men and women are pursuing relationships outside of marriage. During the 1960s it was considered somewhat radical for unmarried men and women to live together. An increasing number of adults now believe that "moving in" is part of a progression in a relationship.

- Since 1960 the number of persons of the opposite sex sharing living quarters has quadrupled.[45]
- In 1987 the number of unmarried couples who were living together totaled 2,334,000. This represents an increase of 745,000 couples since 1980.[46]

Perhaps the most dramatic demographic shift in the American household is the emergence of the single-person household. Young adults are opting to stay single. More widowed (and sometimes divorced) elders are choosing to live alone rather than moving in with their adult children. And divorced adults without children tend to establish independent households rather than move back home with their parents.

- There were approximately 25 million non-family households in 1987, 85 percent of which contained a person living alone.[47]

Taken together, the structural transformations above cannot be viewed as minor aberrations. They represent the manifestations of the underlying currents of social change.

Family Time. The conflicts that individuals are experiencing today have already altered many aspects of family life. Adults who are precariously balancing work and family responsibilities may respond to their personal time limitations by reducing family time, and thus limit experiences that families have together. Twenty or thirty years ago evening meals were a time for families to come together and share the events of their day. The entire context for dinner has changed for many families. The phenomenal rise of fast food is one of the more remarkable manifestations of how work/family changes have found their way into the mainstream of life. In one brief generation the rare event of eating meals outside of home has been changed. For many working families the fast-food restaurant represents one form of relief in trying to fulfill the multiple demands of work and home chores.

- The results of a 1985/86 Gallup poll that surveyed more than 1,500 adults revealed that more than one in three American adults eats at least one meal away from home each day. Approximately one third of these restaurant meals are dinners.[48]

This seemingly insignificant change in family behavior may be symbolic of other changes. Eating at restaurants makes it more difficult to maintain reasonably regular family schedules. Families that do not often have home-cooked food may not establish traditions associated with particular menus that could reflect the family's ethnic background. In many cases it is more difficult for families to establish nutritional standards. At home children may only get to choose from a selection of healthy foods, but at restaurants they see others eating foods such as french fries and high-sugar desserts. The commotion and activity in restaurants also may make it hard for the family to focus on being together.

In different ways other family times also are being sacrificed. Some dual-career families find that the best way for the parents to meet some of the child-care needs that occur during summer school vacations is for the mother and father to take separate vacations. Spending time together as a family is becoming a rare event for many working families.

Following the advice of many child development experts, many working parents are trying to squeeze in a half hour of quality time each day, so that they can maintain positive relationships with their children. Sometimes the family time takes a much lower priority.

Conflicts

It is not difficult to imagine the conflicts that beset the family, given the nature of the changes described above. Some of this conflict is cultural—much is pragmatic. The conflicts experienced by the family as a social unit, have a synergistic quality, so that the level of conflict and stress experienced by the family is in fact greater than the sum of the conflicts felt by each family member.

Family Identity. The changing nature of the roles and responsibilities assumed by today's adults calls into question the basic raison d'être of the family. Just one generation ago men and women got married to ensure that the couple could establish and maintain a close and intimate relationship, and that they could have children. The unspoken marital contract stated that the woman would provide the nurturance and emotional support to the family members and the man would provide the necessary financial support.

Today marriage is no longer a prerequisite to a long-term relationship between a man and a woman. Furthermore, some adults are challenging the belief that adults "get married and have children." Some couples are choosing to remain childless.

- In 1970, 16 percent of the women 25 to 29 years of age who had ever been married were childless. By 1981 this percentage had risen to 25 percent.[49]

Unmarried adults also are looking at issues of child-rearing from new perspectives. An increasing number of single adults are considering adoption or nontraditional methods of conception. And, of course, the number of children born to unmarried parents (especially teens and young adults) is rising.

- In 1986, 23 percent of all births occurred to unmarried women. Just six years before the rate was 18 percent.[50]

It might appear that the basic purpose of the family as an institution is threatened. Under the old order the family was seen as the emotional haven in a hard and demanding world. Men particularly—but all family members—could rely on the family to provide the basic emotional sustenance and support that serves to offset and compensate for the demands of the workplace and the external environment. As roles have shifted and work and family roles have blended, the family often has less time, energy, and resilience to provide this form of support.

It may be premature, however, to ring the death knell for the American family. The demise of the family may be a crisis in form but not in function. The reduction in the number of households that reflect the old family model based on the traditional nuclear family may not mean that homes are devoid of caring and love. Different types of families that are able to resolve some of the work/family conflicts also are able to offer a context in which family members have access to opportunities for emotional support, nurturance, and caring. Home can be a place where family members can share those aspects of their lives that they have in common.

Role Blending. The increased diversity of American families has directly affected the kinds of roles and responsibilities family members assume. Family roles have changed in two principal ways: (1) the assignment of responsibilities according to rigid gender stereotypes is becoming less common, and (2) with the entry of women into the workforce, often no adults are at home full-time to manage family and household concerns.

The compartmentalization of family roles that characterized previous generations is becoming an anachronism. The movement of wives and mothers into the workforce has introduced a realignment of the family system and a series of changes in relationships, roles, expectations, and behaviors. Spheres of responsibility that had been established as nonoverlapping have become blended. As women have entered the world of work, their roles and relationships at home have changed.

- During the late 1980s, 50 percent of women with children one year or younger worked; 75 percent of these mothers worked full-time.[51]

Yankelovich has observed that the cultural meaning of women working outside the home has undergone subtle changes. Up until 1960 the good provider theme defined a "real man." By 1978, Yankelovich reports, this definition had slipped from 86 percent to 67 percent. A decade later the distinction became close to meaningless. When women entered the labor market in the 1970s, this very act, instead of diminishing the mainlines of head of household, enhanced the status of women without adversely affecting that of men.[52]

The changes in women's roles ultimately required men to reexamine their concepts of their own roles. The results of a September 1986 survey of professional men conducted by Allied Van Lines suggest how some of the traditional roles have changed. In this survey 70 percent of the men polled said that they would be willing to move for their wives' career. A cultural attitude shift of this magnitude was unthinkable even a decade ago.

Role changes associated with income earning have changed more rapidly than the responsibilities for home life, principally the management of household chores and the care of dependent family members. The blending of roles has created a considerable degree of conflict between husbands and wives in dual-earner families. When the traditional family division of labor was rendered obsolete, there was no other appropriate structure to accommodate the new realities, leading to inevitable conflict over this division of daily labor. Pleck's masterful job of analyzing the existing research findings has resulted in his role overload hypothesis consisting of five propositions:[53]

1. Traditional sex role ideology is the major determinant of the division of family work.

   • Louis Harris comments that "when asked directly about the household chores today, 41% of all women report that they do, another 41% say they do a lot and their husbands help some, 15% report the chores being evenly divided, and 2% say the husbands do more."[54]

   • In 1976 Pleck found that men invested an average of ninety-six minutes a day (11.2 hours a week) in family work. In contrast, working women devoted 28.1 hours each week.[55] It is significant to note that in 1985 Pleck stated that the man's share of total child care and housework rose from 20 to 30 percent over the past two decades.[56]

2. The division of family work is inequitable, in that husbands do not do more housework and child care when their wives are employed, and that employed wives spend more time on the sum of their work and family roles than do their husbands.

3. Most wives want their husbands to do more family work.

4. Employed wives' role overload has negative consequences for their well-being.

5. Husbands are much more psychologically involved in their paid work role than in the family role.

   • According to Richter and Hall, "women who work outside the home and have families have psychological boundaries that are more permeable than man's in both directions." The women in this study also were less willing to stay longer at work but were willing to return to work issues at home, indicating that women often tend to be concerned with various aspects of their lives at the same time.[57]

These propositions underlie one of the most universal conflicts in American families: how to find an equitable distribution of roles and responsibilities for the working family, and prevent the consequences of role overload for those women who continue to bear the responsibility for children and house chores while assuming economic responsibilities outside the family.

Although mothers still assume the bulk of the responsibility for children within the context of the family, there have been dramatic changes in the ways families fulfill their child-rearing functions. The increased use of child-care providers results in mothers spending less time providing direct care and supervision to their children. The time-honored image of infants being cuddled and nurtured all day by mothers who spent their afternoons parading their carriages down Main Street and through the parks is now little more than a myth. Just drive through most suburban neighborhoods during the day and you will find more of a ghost town environment than the bustling neighborhoods of yesterday. Mothers of infants and toddlers constitute the fastest-growing segment of the labor force.

- In 1975 less than one third (30.8%) of wives with children under the age of 1 participated in the labor force. By 1988 this percentage had risen to more than half—51.9 percent.[58]

Use of child care provided by people other than the parents has resulted in a very different socialization process for children. Not only are today's children exposed to an increasing number of role models, but their own parents display a wider range of behaviors for them to imitate. There seems to be a greater social sanction for 3-year-old girls to pretend to ''go to work at the office'' and for boys to cuddle a baby doll because that is what they see their parents doing. The changes in socialization have already affected the expectations teenagers have for the roles they will assume as adults.

- The results of a national survey of more than 2,000 young men and women revealed that more than 90 percent of those polled believe that ''playing with the children'' should be a responsibility that is equally shared by men and women.[59]

Increased Role Strain. Work/family conflicts frequently precipitate role strain. Some research suggests that this stress may be associated with marital conflict.[60] When a father experiences tension at work, the stress may be expressed at home as a father–son conflict. A mother, on the other hand, who experiences stress at home may become less involved at work. The increase of role strain impacts the entire family system and the ability of the family to function as a unit. Although this may be severer at different stages of the family life cycle (e.g., when preschool-age children are present in the household), any heightened role strain can impact the general well-being of the family.

Marital Power. Role changes and role overload bring the issue of power to the fore. Employed wives' new found sense of independence and mastery at the workplace is brought into the marital relationship, often in the form of power. More and Sawhill cite a number of studies that suggest that employed wives exercise a greater degree of power in their marriages. Marital power is significantly higher among women who are employed full-time among those who are employed part-time or who have no income-earning role. By sharing in the role of acquiring financial resources for the family, the wife moves from the position of supplicant to that of contributor. This allows her to assume a bargaining position with which the husband has to contend. In essence, having both husband and wife in the work world changes the power relationship within the family.

When married women entered the workforce, the marriage often had to be renegotiated and the traditional assumptions and expectations of husbands had to be readjusted and, in some cases, changed. Some of the work/family stresses experienced by today's families have resulted from the couples' failure to discuss and renegotiate their roles and responsibilities.

Impact

The impacts of the conflicts experienced by the family extend beyond the difficulties of balancing multiple roles. A few of these outcomes are negative, and some are positive.

Isolation of the Nuclear Family. The time and scheduling constraints experienced by many working adults often translate into decreased interactions with members of their social support systems: relatives, neighbors, and friends. Over time the involvement of these adults can decrease, so that their families receive less emotional and practical support from people outside of the immediate household. Holmstron identified the isolation of the nuclear family as a significant barrier for the working family. It is ironic that the very supports of relatives and friends that could help to reduce work/family stress are distanced and cut off by the problem itself.

In a parallel manner working family members have decreased the time and availability that they can give to relatives outside their immediate nuclear family who need some care or assistance. The nation is facing a "provision of care" crisis. Families have typically provided the bulk of care needed by elderly and disabled family members. For example, estimates of family-provided care indicate that 80 percent of the home health services to the elderly; In addition 70 percent of severely retarded children live at home with their parents.[61] But today's families that do not have an adult home full-time may no longer be able to provide intense levels of care without assistance from outside agencies. "With the increasing scale of social dependence and the diminishing supply of family caretakers, the family's capacity to serve its dependent members has already been stretched close to the limit."[62]

Strains on Marital Relations. Conflicts that adults encounter as a result of their involvement in work and family spheres often affect the quality and the characteristics of interpersonal relations within the family. The strains of today's lifestyle on marriage are indicated by the high divorce rates. Marital discord can emanate from a number of sources, some of which may be associated with work/family conflicts, such as the changing expectations of roles, diminished time for interaction, and competition and power struggles.

- Data collected by the Bureau of the Census confirm the steady increases in the percentages of women who were divorced between 1950 and the late 1970s.[63] This increase occurred at a time when radical changes in family and work patterns were observed.

Some care must be exercised when interpreting the data on the American divorce rate. In part, the rapid rise in the number of divorces has resulted in external changes in society (such as the changes in divorce laws, including no-fault divorces). Furthermore, the greater number of divorces does not necessarily mean that there is more marital discord than previously existed. Marital stress may have been less visible for couples during the forties and fifties because they may have remained legally (but not necessarily emotionally or geographically) married. The rise in the divorce rate may be a temporary phenomena that is peculiar to the current transition era when individuals and families are experiencing such rapid shifts in their lifestyles. The divorce rate may diminish once families become socialized under the new set of expectations and values. The results of recent polls indicate that marriage, as an institution, may be making a comeback.

- Nationwide, the rate of marriages increased 3 percent during the early eighties. During the same period the divorce rate declined 5 percent. This decline is unprecedented in modern history.[64]

Perhaps only time will tell whether changes in the worlds of work and family have a cumulative effect of either supporting or weakening marital bonds.

Stresses of Children as Family Members. A significant part of the population attributes the growing number of problems associated with teenagers to the weakened family structure brought about in part by mothers who have entered the workforce.

- The results of 1986 Harris poll revealed that 55 percent of those surveyed gave today's parents a negative rating for their efforts to meet their responsibilities toward their children. In addition, nearly three fourths of the respondents thought that the problems that affect children today are worse than those that affected them when they were young. Significantly, parents and nonparents do not differ greatly in their assessments of the status of children.[65]

Some experts state that changes in the family structure and the decrease of direct parental involvement in the daily lives of children have deleteriously affected children. Bronfenbrenner, a respected family and child researcher, contends that the deterioration of the American family is responsible for the problems of today's youth.[66]

Other specialists suggest that the recent changes in family patterns may have had a neutral, or even a positive, impact on children. The scheduling problems experienced by working parents are forcing a greater independence and self-reliance on adolescents at the time in their development when they are agonizing over independence–dependence issues. This impact may counteract some of the intergenerational stress resulting from the society's prolonged period of childhood. Bettelheim suggested that the increased tension between parents and their adolescent children was the unavoidable consequence of the extension of the age of dependency.[67]

Changes in child-rearing patterns may have some other positive effects on the family. Many child development experts applaud the increased involvement of the father in child-rearing because his presence provides a male role model for the children. In fact, many social scientists in the fifties criticized the child-rearing model in which the mother assumed almost all the responsibility for the children. These critics contended that even though the fifties were supposed to be a "golden age" for children, the rigid separation of family responsibilities according to gender may have been deleterious to them. It was the critics' point of view that the virtual absence of the father from home activities meant that the children did not have much access to a strong male role model.[68]

As parents struggle to find time for themselves and for each other, a real and potential threat to the time they have to spend with their adolescent children is created. The impact on this vulnerable age group is not clear in the absence of credible research. Parents' employment status may not be as critical a variable as other factors, such as the teen's participation in structured activities such as work, sports, and afterschool volunteer work. Nevertheless, the increase in child neglect, suicide, and pregnancy points to a serious national problem at the doorstep of the American family.

Scheduling. When asked what is the most immediate challenge in trying to manage work/family responsibilities, time—or the lack of it—is the most frequently cited response. The harried lives of working single parents and dual-career families depend on creating schedules that allow them to manage their multiple roles and responsibilities. Married couples with children must juggle two jobs, two work schedules, school schedules, and the schedules of other institutions necessary for family existence. This calls for creative problem solving. The dilemmas of scheduling are acutely felt in those families in which shift work is involved or in which one or both of the parents work irregular hours. Other groups that experiences extreme conflict include families with multiple jobs, in which at least one of the adults must hold more than one job simultaneously in order to make ends meet. Also, families in which one or more members travel on a regular or extended basis often experience scheduling nightmares.

Sense of Family Worth. Not all the impact has been negative. With the multiple role changes, time constraints, and a realignment of power, there has emerged in many families a type of togetherness that comes with adversity. One result of this "pulling together" is an increased self-worth felt throughout the system. In addition, adults who have achieved some sense of balance to their work and family responsibilities may feel that this achievement supports their self-esteem.

The parents' increased confidence contributes to a positive emotional climate in the family.

Some families that experience role overload create expectations that each member will contribute to the overall welfare of the family. Children who are aware of their parents' pressures may become more willing to participate in the family as responsible members. They may clean their rooms and make their beds, not just because they will get their allowance, but also because they have identified concrete ways to participate.

Family members who realize that their contributions are important may have a heightened feeling of belonging, and the family identity is strengthened.

WORKPLACE

Changes

The United States emerged from World War II as the industrial giant of the world, a force energized to redefine industrialism. As the GIs returned home to man the factories and became educated through the GI Bill, wives left their machines and assembly lines and returned to the home to give birth to the baby boom. The image of the bustling workplace of the late forties provided the country with an archetype of a strong and resilient workforce that carried well into the eighties. Throughout the tumultuous times of the sixties the workplace— unlike the family, schools, churches, or the government—was one of the few institutions to escape relatively unscathed. Nevertheless, the economic roller coaster of the late 1970s and 1980s along with the broader cultural changes that buffeted our society have caused us to radically reexamine and, in rare cases, reorganize what had been a proscribed and somewhat rigid work world. The dominant social institution in which the majority of adults spend more time than they do in any other place or function, including sleep, is in the midst of intensive change on all levels, and by most accounts it is becoming ever more integrated and essential to daily life.

Although it is difficult to briefly describe the changes, a number of factors can be cited.

Movement to a World Economy. From a macro perspective the work environment of the 1990s is as different from that of the 1940s as night is from day. The vanquished of Japan and Germany have become the economic superstars, thanks in large part to U.S. economic assistance. Trade now takes place in a world community, and the rise of multinational corporations transcends nation boundaries or allegiances.

The world economy also has had a direct impact on the local level. Competition from abroad, particularly in the manufacture of cars, shoes, textiles, and electronics, has dethroned the supremacy of American industry, resulting in layoffs and job losses of millions, and has brought an intense questioning of the efficacy of the American workplace and the quality of the American worker. The image of manufacturing shoddy products that was tagged on Japan in the 1950s has ironically been reversed, with U.S. goods perceived as inferior in quality and craftsmanship. This change has resulted in a collective questioning of why the Japanese system works so well and what is wrong with our system. This in turn has led to an increased interest in quality circles and Quality of Working Life projects, and a slew of new books and gurus on better management.

Technological Changes. The image of the American worker packing his lunch and going to a workplace where goods were made or assembled dies hard. The assembly line, which was the prototype of industrialization, has practically vanished. The production of industrial products has been moved overseas, primarily to Third World countries where cheap labor is abundant. Today's workplace is much more likely to be an office than a factory. The number of blue-collar workers has declined dramatically, whereas white-collar and pink-collar populations have experienced explosive growth.

- The classicly alienating jobs on the assembly line now constitute less than 2 percent of all jobs in America.[69]

- Social commentators like Peter Drucker predict that by the beginning of the new century, blue-collar manufacturing jobs will follow the trends in agriculture and will constitute less than 10 percent of all jobs.

- Union membership has shrunk from 28 percent of workers to 17 percent.

- According to the Bureau of Labor Statistics, private sector unionization was just 15.3 percent in 1984, down from 38 percent in 1954. In just the three years between 1981 and 1984 membership in the AFL-CIO decreased by more than 10 percent.[70]

The postindustrial age has replaced the primacy of goods with services and information. Unlike the industrial era, it is not fueled by natural resources, but relies on high technology, brainpower, and a highly educated workforce. John Naisbitt's *Megatrends* aptly describes the new age as information-rich, decentralized yet global, and built on values of high tech–high touch, networking, participatory democracy, and self-reliance.

The changing technology has forced employers to rethink their management and organizational strategies. In this postindustrial era businesses will begin to focus on what Bell refers to as ''socializing'' (human welfare) functions rather than exclusively on ''economizing'' or profit-making functions.

Accompanying the technological revolution in American business is the explosive growth in the service industries. It is anticipated that during the next several years, service jobs will compose the major proportion of new jobs and will be responsible for increases in economic growth.[71]

Educated Workforce. Clearly, the strength of the postindustrial age is the talent, education, and experience of today's workers. To participate in this new and challenging world of work, employees are seeking to become better educated.

- The Bureau of Labor Statistics indicates that more than one fourth (26%) of today's labor force participants have had at least four years of college.[72]

It is becoming more difficult for less educated adults to acquire gainful employment. Many people who do not possess the education and skills necessary for many professional and technical positions look to the expanding service-oriented companies for employment. Businesses such as fast-food restaurants, security services, and residential cleaning services provide some support for today's adults who are trying to juggle their home and work responsibilities.

Changing Workforce Demographics. In many ways the changes in the workforce mirror the complex changes that have occurred within the family. A key characteristic in the workplace of today is diversity. The labor force of today is more reflective of the gender, ethnic, and cultural diversity of the population at large. In contrast to the management teams of yesteryear, which would typically be composed almost exclusively of white men, many high-technology working teams of today include women and minorities.

- From 1972 to 1982 there was a 59 percent increase in women managers and administrators, 61 percent in engineers, 100 percent in technical, life, and physical scientists, and 350 percent in lawyers and judges.[73]
- Women account for almost 50 percent of all workers today.

Although minorities still suffer from extraordinarily high unemployment rates and are underrepresented at the highest corporate levels, they are finding their way into and up through the corporation in numbers that were only dreamed of a few decades ago. Furthermore, immigrants represent the largest share of tomorrow's workforce since World War I.[74]

Changing Employee Attitudes and Expectations. Corporations also are facing a new breed of workers who bring with them a new set of attitudes and expectations that reflect the era in which they became adults. The baby boomers have nurtured new values, such as self-expression and self-fulfillment. Although sometimes characterized by the material quest of the Yuppies, the new values are inner-directed, and challenge both the traditional reward structure of the corporations and their management style. Yankelovich has characterized the New Rules as embodying personal freedom and responsibility. Postindustrial workers place great value on the degrees of control and discretion that they have over their own work. Technology has aided this development.

The new attitudes of today's workers have contributed to the need for corporations to adjust some of their approaches to management. Theories X, Y, and the newly emerging Z describe the differences and graphically demonstrate the challenge to management of understanding the new values of employees and incorporating some of these values into the corporate culture and management styles.

Increased Emphasis on Human Resources. The workplace has finally begun to realize that the needed "raw material" of the new workforce is people, specifically in an era of information and when knowledge, creativity, and initiative are highly valued. This recognition has translated into a new appreciation of the human resource function. What used to be called the "personnel department" was traditionally the dumping ground within the corporation, and anyone with dreams of upward mobility would stay clear of it.

The change to "human resources department" is more than a change in name because both the purpose and the function have been altered. This new term signals the corporate attention to the employee and the need to develop an organization that will nourish and support employee needs so that productivity can be maximized. The human resources department has moved into stress management, health promotion and wellness, career development, and employee assistance programs. It has introduced employee surveys and other vehicles to ascertain areas of employee satisfaction or dissatisfaction and other attitudes about work. These new activities are but one measure of the necessity for corporations to better understand and manage their employee needs, and to develop an effective climate and system for keeping valued employees and attracting new ones.

Decline in Preeminence of Workplace. Starting with the industrial revolution, the workplace literally pulled adult family members out of their fields and homes. The distance imposed between work and home was not just geographical and physical. In an effort to maximize productivity corporations began to strive to make the workplace distinct both psychologically and culturally. From the beginning of capitalism, work and family have been embroiled in the struggle for the loyalty, time, energy, and attention of their members.

In the latter part of the twentieth century corporations promoted the preeminence of the workplace as the norm. Whyte captured some of this philosophy in *The Organization Man*. During the fifties it was expected that the wife would support her husband as the income earner and would serve as a member of an adjunct family team employed by the company.

The dynamics between work and family changed radically during the sixties and seventies. The entry of women into the workforce resulted in one change: wives were no longer always in obedient readiness to support their husbands' careers. In addition, as roles blended and men began to reintegrate themselves into daily family activities, their loyalties became more divided. Increased family responsibilities and the desire of workers to pursue some avenues of self-fulfillment resulted in some men limiting their overtime, refusing transfers, and even not accepting promotions. Sekaran has commented: "The slow erosion of the work ethic, the changing success ethic, the social milieu that is creating a work and leisure ethic, and the increasing number of dual-career family members in the work system are all factors contributing to the reconceptualization of excellence."[75] Work will continue to assume a position of extreme importance in the lives of most adults, but as people strive to experience more "balanced" lifestyles that include some family experiences, work may no longer be all-consuming. The sacrifice may not be worth it.

Conflicts

The new workforce brings with it a range of personal needs and family responsibilities. These changes have produced a number of conflicts for the workplace.

Corporate Role and Identity. Without question, for-profit corporations are in the business of maximum profit. Although this basic purpose has remained the same throughout history, changes in today's employees and changes in society at large have made it necessary for many businesses to reexamine some of their functions.

Some firms are beginning to question whether they will need to assume "education" as a secondary function. Increasingly, American companies are confronting the fact that they have large numbers of newly hired employees who have not mastered even minimal educational competence. There is a lot of public debate about the causes of the deterioration in American school systems, but businesses are not able to wait either for change in our public education or for future employees who may be better prepared for work. Some corporations are beginning to step in and do part of the educational preparation themselves.

The need for training is not restricted to new employees. The rapid changes in technology often make it necessary for experienced workers to go back to school.[76]

- U.S. firms spend an estimated $60 billion on training each year and enroll approximately 8 million students annually.[77]

Recognition of the impact that an employee's personal and family life has on work performance has encouraged many firms to take a second look at the appropriate role of the corporation in these issues. Employers are beginning to see the degree to which "home matters" are brought to the workplace. Employees may have little choice but to use some work time to manage household affairs. For other workers, personal crises, such as a protracted divorce, make it difficult to leave emotional problems outside the office door. In addition, employees are beginning to ask their employers for assistance—in terms of services and benefits—with some of their family responsibilities.

As workers have become more vocal in their requests for corporate response to some home issues, the initial reaction of some business is "We are *not* social service agencies." However, on closer examination, it may be discovered that there is little difference between providing corporate-funded plans and public-sponsored dependent care assistance accounts. Similarly, it may not really make any difference to productivity whether the firm establishes a set number of days for vacation and for sick days rather than making these days available to the employee to use at his or her discretion to cover such responsibilities as the care of a sick child, the care of an elderly relative, and appointments. These concessions may make significant contributions to the overall morale of the employees.

In the final analysis the corporation has an enduring and central conflict. It can no longer afford to ignore the family needs of workers because they increasingly impact the goals and productivity of the firm. The conflict becomes even more poignant for companies when responses and solutions are contemplated. What are the boundaries for the problem, and will initiating action open floodgates? Where does their responsibility begin and end? How does this match up with the responsibilities of the workers themselves and of society in general? Because this is a relatively new conflict for American corporations, there are only scattered examples, models, and guidelines for them to follow that may offer some solutions. Most corporations have little expertise with which to address these problems, which further complicates what is an inherently sticky problem.

Corporate Conception of the Family. Despite the forces urging them to acknowledge the family needs of their employees' families, most corporations are tentative. One area of exception occurs with the provision of benefits.

Underlying the demand for social benefits was the growing belief that the employer had two obligations attendant upon his use of the workers' services: first to compensate workers adequately for the actual services they rendered . . . ; and then beyond this to assume certain obligations of a social nature essentially unrelated to production but existing because of the employee relationship. Those who hired the labor of others took on some social responsibilities pertaining to the needs of the man in his life off the job and in the society of which he was part.[78]

Gender Conflict. The new guys in the workforce are really the girls—or more appropriately the women—and there lies the rub. The work setting is faced with a multiplicity of issues as women have become prominent in the office and on the work floor. Some of these conflicts are physical, such as inadequate facilities to accommodate the needs of women. The majority, however, cluster around organizational and cultural problems. Issues of sexual harassment, open career advancement, potential discrimination suits, equal pay questions, and resentment by older male employees all underscore the gender issues that have surfaced.

A major consequence of the previous decades of separate worlds of work and home was a workplace developed and inhabited primarily by men. This was especially true in managerial ranks. Thus the culture that developed around most workplaces was a male-oriented culture, which, like the broader society surrounding it, has had a most difficult time assimilating women into its midst and cohabiting at work stations on an equal level.

Initial progress has been made. The workplace has witnessed some breakdown in the rigid traditional sex stereotypes associated with certain professions. In increasing numbers women are starting to pursue jobs that used to be exclusively filled by men.

• Women have moved increasingly into executive, administrative, and managerial positions. In 1975 only 22 percent of these positions were filled by women, but this rose to 34 percent by 1984.[79]

Although the focus of gender conflicts usually is centered on women, there also has been change with men, albeit more imperceptible. Women's roles, attitudes, and behaviors are not changing in a vacuum. Men have begun to adjust and react to these changes and have started to realize changes of their own. As a result of women entering the workforce in significant numbers, stereotypical attitudes and behaviors begin to break down around gender differences.

Despite the progress that has been accomplished, gender conflict continues to confront managers, legal departments, and equal opportunity officers. These conflicts ultimately affect overall morale and productivity.

Dilemmas in Management. Managers, particularly first-line managers who deal most directly with employees, face another set of conflicts. Many of these are related to the large number of single parents and dual-earner families in the workplace who are forced to manage their homes and their children from the office. In the absence of corporate policy, supervisors are left to interpret and set policy on an ad hoc basis. "Can I run home to let the insurance man do his damage assessment?" "I know I don't have any vacation days left, but can I take a sick day to take my child to summer camp?" What do supervisors do when parents are continually late because the day-care center opens only ten minutes before they are due at work? Does a supervisor sit down with an employee who has frequent telephone contact with his wife over home and child responsibilities? And if she does sit down with him, how does she handle the situation?

Often supervisors find themselves in an awkward position—caught between the real and felt needs of the parent employees and the productivity goals of the corporation. Few, if any, policies and procedures exist that can serve as guidelines to aide the supervisor.

Impact

The cumulative impact of the work/family dilemma on corporate America has been increased confusion. The realization that the family is going to be a permanent fixture in the workplace and that it will not leave its problems and responsibilities in the company parking lot is becoming clearer to chief executive officers, human resources departments, managers, and supervisors. Specifically, a number of immediate concerns can be highlighted.

Scheduling. What often is necessary or prioritized for corporations is not necessarily the same for working families. Thus when a computer team is working on a deadline to develop a new machine, the demands of personal and family life interfere with the round-the-clock schedule demanded by the product itself.[80] Scheduling conflicts exist on all levels and, as corporations are finding, the new values only complicate the issue. Companies whose employees work shift work and night work have always recognized these conflicts, and usually compensate workers financially as a way of overcoming resistance. The compensation and trade-offs are not as clear with working parents who have little discretionary time and feel even greater tugs from the family sphere.

Decreased Productivity. The image of an employee running home to a sick child, taking a half day to attend the school play, or taking a widowed mother to her monthly doctor's appointment and the daily routine of phone calls to spouse and children cause apoplexy among many managers. The impact of family management responsibilities at the workplace varies from minor inconveniences to severely impaired productivity. To imagine that family responsibilities, problems, and crises do not affect productivity is to wear blinders to today's workforces. As employees continue to witness the disappearance of supports and resources within their own families and communities, they are forced to use part of the work day to respond (albeit somewhat surreptitiously and informally) and care for some of their home and families responsibilities.

No extensive empirical studies have yet been carried out to measure productivity loss or drop off, but there is some documentation of the relation between family responsibilities and work performance. Emlen and Koren found in their survey of 8,000 employees in Oregon that parents with children under age 18 had significantly more days absent than nonparent employees in addition to behaviors such as coming to work late, leaving early, and dealing with family issues during work hours.[81] Fernandez reported that quality child-care arrangements had a direct impact on the productivity of employed parents. Women reported that this issue affected them in the area of dealing with family issues during working hours; men were affected through the impact on productivity in terms of missed work and tardiness.[82]

Anecdotal material about these problems abounds. For instance, many businesses report that corporate switchboards light up at 3 o'clock in the afternoon as parents and children communicate with each other after school. Stories such as these give some credibility to the research indicators that work/family conflicts affect productivity.

The productivity issue is a delicate one. First, it is difficult to measure. Second, the issue is much like America, Mom, and apple pie because it is difficult for supervisors to really be against parents who are looking after their children, their aging parents, or a disabled relative. Many of these employees would be neglecting their family responsibilities if they did not focus on them in some way while they were at the workplace. Corporations may think of their employees who have unfinished family responsibilities during work hours as "job abusers," but most of them do not view work/family conflicts in the same way as they view inefficiency and waste. One of the differences is that work/family conflicts are so universal that the corporate disciplinary options are minimal. Clearly, it would be impossible to remove all employees who have family responsibilities because this would leave a very small workforce.

The reasonable response of American corporations is to find the trade-offs and develop responsive policies and programs. Until this time, however, many companies are finding themselves tolerating this "deviant" employee behavior.

Inadequate Structures. Workplace structures had to undergo drastic changes in moving from the assembly lines of the industrial era to the work stations of the postindustrial information era. In a like manner, the new workforce of women, dual-earner couples, and single parents has created somewhat of a misfit between the old organizational structures and the needs of these populations.

Corporations have created many jobs that are inflexible, and incompatible with the needs of parents. The need for absolute beginning and ending work hours is efficient for the corporation, but incompatible with working parents' needs. Although travel schedules can constitute a third—or even a half—of an employee's job description, they do not take into consideration the desire and necessity of employees to carry out their roles of spouse and parent. Employees increasingly base their selection of places of employment and bid on jobs not solely on career advancement and financial incentives, but also on the degree of fit with their family roles and responsibilities. This presents the corporation with the problem of integrating the needs of production and organizational efficiency with the growing needs and demands of its employees. A series of new structures may be required to maximize the trade-offs between these two forces.

Employee Morale. The degree to which employees have unresolved work/family conflicts and the perceptions of workers about the responsiveness of their employers to these issues significantly affect employee morale. As employees with family responsibilities are beginning to look to the corporation for assistance in managing their multiple responsibilities, they start to compare the policies, practices, and benefits of their company with those of the company "next door." The roots of morale within a corporation often are difficult to pinpoint with any degree of accuracy because morale is a gestalt of many elements that can swing from a high to a low level because of a variety of internal and external factors. The work/family issues contribute to low morale as employees expect more of corporations, perceive little sensitivity by management, and become more stressed by the absence of community and social supports to assist in family needs such as child-rearing and the care of an aging parent. The converse also is true, and as we shall see later in this book, corporations can create positive images and high employee morale through relatively inexpensive but straightforward ways of expressing concerns. For those companies who ignore the growing conflicts or act as if the problem is transitory, lower employee morale, with its impact on productivity, is highly likely.

SOCIETY

Changes

The changes that have taken place in families and workplaces have, in large part, reflected broad social change. The currents of change were most evident in large-scale movements, such as for civil rights, the war on poverty, equal rights for women, and the sexual revolution. Regardless of the causative factors, society has undergone what has to be considered a major transformation over the past twenty years. In fact, the issue of work/family conflict would not be characterized in the same way if these fundamental shifts had not taken place. Most women would still be at home. Workplaces would be functioning with the same parameters as they did in the 1950s. Institutions such as schools and churches would reflect the social norms and values of a singular type of household: the man as the wage earner and the woman as the manager of the home. Society, however, as the context for both families and work organizations, has a significantly different set of values, attitudes, and norms than it did a scant thirty years ago. The new values were the result of the turbulent social forces that, once unleashed, would introduce fundamental change as it worked its way irreversibly into society. "These cultural, economic and political cross pressures cannot conceivably lead us back to the tidy status quo and sharply compartmentalized lives of the past. The plates of culture do not shift backwards."[83]

The analysis of changes in society could focus on changing norms and expectations. Because society acts as a stabilizing force for individuals, it accepts and institutes change slowly. This pace usually allows individuals, families, and social institutions enough time to acclimate to the change and adapt to a new set of realities. The rapidity of change over the past twenty years, however, seems to have outstripped many of these actors. The result is a set of social norms and expectations that has yet to be fully accepted and incorporated, creating a high degree of dissonance throughout society. Finally, it is important to understand that from a social perspective, even fundamental issues such as definition of family has little consensus. In the midst of this dramatic social change, political, religious, and economic forces continue to battle over family turf through arguing, advocating, and protecting a particular set of beliefs, thus preventing any coherent family policy or agenda from emerging.

Political Changes. During the past thirty years the United States has experienced a number of crises, including the assassination of President Kennedy, Senator Kennedy, and Martin Luther King Jr.; the Vietnam war (and the return of its soldiers); racial riots; Vatican II; Watergate; terrorism; Abscam; and the rise and demise of the Morale Majority. During these times of turmoil the American people elected leaders who espoused policies and programs that were at opposite ends of the spectrum. Is it really possible that within a single generation the country could embrace such differing creeds as the Kennedy-Johnson Great Society and Reaganomics? How can there be enthusiastic support for the war on poverty and the growth and support of social programs during the sixties and then popular acceptance of revenue-sharing and "getting the government off the backs of people" fifteen years later? These radically different conceptions of what role government should assume in shaping society and meeting the needs of its citizens underscores the magnitude of social change during this period.

The same phenomenon can be seen in the work/family field, where people of very different political persuasions are starting to take an interest in work/family issues. The impact of these issues on the government was perhaps most evident during the 1988 presidential elections. Both candidates, Bush and Dukakis, proposed child-care initiatives to help the working adults of the country be better able to cope with their multiple responsibilities. Both parties also have elevated the family onto the national agenda and addressed family issues in party platforms. These actions captured the national sentiment that the family deserves more attention and needs assistance in order to maintain a healthy level of functioning. Despite this public proclamation and debate over these issues, virtually no results have materialized. The paralysis surrounding these issues reflects the political sensitivity and the depth of the cultural roots that work/family issues bump up against. The political aspects of work/family issues are at last coming to the fore, and judging by these early incidents, there is a long road ahead.

Economic Changes. The economic climate of the country was on a similar roller coaster course. Periods of prosperity, inflation, and recession coexisted. The years of economic growth during the 1960s not only created many new jobs, but also demanded new sources of labor. The birth of the women's movement spawned, among other things, legal pressures to ensure equal access for women in the workplace. The spiraling rate of inflation brought scores of women to work out of sheer necessity and household survival.

The eighties brought with it the sudden realization of budget deficits. Government at all levels suddenly had to reckon with the fact that revenues are finite. Advocacy groups and legislative action have tried to respond by ''putting on the brakes.'' Even local government has experienced revenue limitations at a time when expenses continue to increase. School budgets have been slashed, and many community services (which help to alleviate the burdens in some families) have suffered damaging funding cuts.

It has become an almost impossible task for government leaders to prioritize societal needs when the needs of one ''deserving'' ground are pitted against another.

Diversity of Societal Values. Unlike in the fifties, which can be characterized as a time when most people held many basic values in common, society today is marked by considerable variation in social values. Although some factions of the population adamantly adhere to the more traditional values and lifestyles, many others are displaying new behaviors and espousing new values.

Many people have become eclectic about their personal values, picking some traditional ones along with others that are nontraditional. Attitudes about marriage often reflect this mixture of the old and the new. Despite some of the changing demographics associated with marriage, the prevalent societal norm has remained fairly stable. Most adults acknowledge and value the institution of marriage, and in fact marry at some point in their lives. The societal values regarding divorce have changed radically, however. Getting divorced or occupying a divorced status no longer carries with it negative social sanctions. Consequently, getting divorced does not stigmatize people, and the norms for staying in a married relationship have changed, reflecting the high rates of divorce and remarriage.

The social norms for having children also reflect this change. Whereas it was almost unthinkable during the fifties for married couples to want to remain childless, couples today feel much freer in electing not to have children or to postpone having them until their careers have solidified. Similarly, the norms for family size have changed to a point where the large family somewhat romanticized in the fifties is not highly valued today and even subject to negative sanction.

Conflicting values are associated with women's participation in the workforce. Not long ago mothers who ventured into the workforce cast a negative light on that family, particularly the husband, who was viewed as deficient in carrying out his responsibility as a good provider. Today cultural shifts and economic necessity have contributed to the incidence of women working outside the home. The changing expectations about women's employment has revolutionized not only the American family and workplace, but also society itself. Some societal values have changed with the behavior; women's right to self-fulfillment and economic independence through employment is now widely regarded as acceptable and desirable.

Society, however, still identified the family as being primarily responsible for child care. When women's labor force participation conflicts with the perceived needs of family members—especially those of young children—the dissonance in values becomes apparent. Immerwahr, commenting in the results of a 1982 Public Agenda Foundation Survey of attitudes about women's employment and child care, summarized some of the salient aspects of this ideological dilemma facing our nation.

When the issue of child care is not raised, then there is overwhelming support for women working, even when there is no economic necessity for them to do so. But, at the same time, there is a tremendous consensus in American society on the importance of taking care of children. . . . When the issue of work is not raised, then nearly all Americans endorse the duty of women to take care of their children. What is so difficult about the child care issue is that it pits these two fundamental issues against each other, apparently in a no-win situation. If women do work, they may, in certain cases, jeopardize their fundamental duty to their children, but if they do not work they may be giving up on their own rights. As long as working and child raising are considered in isolation, we find consensus and agreement. But as soon as they are placed in opposition with each other, public opinion becomes polarized.[84]

Conflicts

The degree of the conflicts experienced in society around work/family issues is associated with the resistance to change experienced at the societal level. The slow and incremental pace of change has made it difficult of the government to adjust and react to the dramatic changes that have occurred at the individual, family, and workplace levels.

Role of Government. The conflict that society experiences over work/family issues is similar to the conflict experienced by corporate institutions: To what extent should the government get involved with and become responsible for assisting families in reducing work/family stress? The answer to this question can only be addressed in the context of existing social policy and the conceptualization of the role of government in society. The United States, as has been stated on many occasions, is the only industrialized nation without a family policy. This is not accidental or an oversight on the part of insensitive lawmakers. Rather, it reflects the reality of a government based on the preeminent rights of individuals, one that adheres to an approach that emphasizes a role of minimal intrusion in individual and family spheres, reflecting the laissez-faire form of capitalism that stresses a free-market system. The basic values and economic principles that underlie these realities emphasize independence and self-reliance, placing the family at the core of society in a highly esteemed but relatively isolated and unassisted (except in the rare circumstances of disaster) position. Consequently, as the family struggles with the stress of working and fulfilling home responsibilities, society comes under increased pressure to become more involved in relieving families of that stress.

Unlike corporations, whose incentive for change is based on the self-interest of competition and productivity, society's impetus for change is driven more by the negative consequences of a large number of working families: What should society do about the number of infants who need day care? How should society respond to latchkey children? Does the government have a role in supporting families so that they can function more productively, for themselves and ultimately for society? Society is caught in a kind of time warp because traditional values drive policies and practices that permit little family assistance outside the "safety net" concept. Growing needs, however, are pressuring the government to do more.

In addition to the ideological barriers that have impeded the nation's progress toward the development of policies and programs designed to alleviate some of the work/family conflicts, many of the parameters for the government's role in work/family issues are determined by budget considerations. Families, corporations, and government leaders continue to raise the question "Who will pay?" The inevitable expense associated with a more active role in work/family dilemmas has slowed the expansion of direct government involvement.

These role conflicts arise because the boundaries between family and government are as murky, nondefinitive, and overlapping as those between work and family. Some attempt to define areas of responsibility has resulted from the private-public partnership models. This has been espoused at the national level as a way for the government and the private sector to work together to address the ills that continue to befall the American family. To date, the rhetoric is more convincing than the actual results.

Society, then, is caught in a bind of shifting values, changing norms, and expectations. Family stress could contribute to an overall weakening of society, but the insufficient support, inadequate policies, and inability of the government to own some of the responsibility for responding to these situations have not improved the situation for most families.

Lack of Consensus. One of the problems with the development of any government family policy is that the pluralism that contributes to the strength of the democratic system also makes it difficult to reach consensus (or compromise) about issues so central to American life as work/family conflicts. There is a tendency for work/family issues to polarize people into political and philosophical camps: Democrats versus Republicans; liberals versus conservatives. Nowhere is this polarization more evident than in the debate over family triggered by the political/religious issue. Those attached to the so-called Moral Majority have seized on the family as a cause, articulating a highly proscribed and dogmatized conception of family structures, values, and norms. This has clashed with the competing positions of the family, and resulted in a societal trade-off—a paralysis of consensus around family norms. Consequently, instead of forging ahead with a commitment to family policy, the United States has developed isolated programs that respond to a few of the more visible signs of work/family conflicts.

Transmission of Values. One of the essential roles that any society has for its own survival is the transmission of key values from one generation to the next. During times when values are changing rapidly or there is high values conflict, society must decide which values are in its own best long-term interest. The importance of the transmission of values creates one of the points of intersection between the family system and the society system. Society depends on stable families to transmit its values and culture. If the family becomes excessively stressed or relies too heavily on day-care centers or television, the socialization process is considerably altered. Together, families and society must decide how the young should be socialized.

A pivotal change in American society is associated with values pertaining to self-fulfillment. "The self fulfillment search is a more complex, fateful and irreversible phenomenon than simply the byproduct of affluence or a shift in the national character toward narcissism. It is nothing less than the search for a new American philosophy of life."[85]

The cultural revolution that swept the sixties and seventies brought with it a new set of values that markedly influenced what is referred to as the "me generation." The new music, pot-smoking, and sexual freedom were but manifestations of a new generation that, while not totally overthrowing their society, espoused a new set of values that were less authoritarian and "other" driven. The search for self-fulfillment accompanied by a heightened degree of self-centeredness and self-indulgence was a turning away from the perceived rigidity and shallowness of the old order and a rejection of the old rules, and an eager embrace of the new.

Examine the results of a Gallup poll of baby boomers' attitudes. Compared with their parents, are baby boomers:

More able to lead a fulfilling life?

More able	45%
Less able	29%
As able	19%

Better off with respect to the freedom to do what they want to with their lives?

Better	77%
Worse	13%
Same	8%

More able to place emphasis on doing interesting things in their lives?

More	68%
Less	8%
Same	23%

More able to place emphasis on pursuing satisfaction in a career?

More	60%
Less	13%
Same	27%

More able to place emphasis on caring for their parents?

More	45%
Less	5%
Same	46%

It could be posited that the current work/family conflicts are tied to the unresolved value conflicts brought on by the changes of the past several decades. This transitional period makes any resolution unlikely, since the major differential over values prevents a social response that is politically acceptable.

Impact

If government is unable to offer assistance in reducing work/family conflict and does not assume some leadership to strengthen both the social and the economic institutions affected by these conflicts, society is affected by both short- and long-term impacts. If no new policies or programs are adopted, and if the conflicts continue, several negative impacts can be identified.

Crisis in Caregiving. Families have traditionally, been and continue to be the bastion of caregiving to dependent family members, including children, disabled people of all ages, and elderly relatives. Although they have not altered the love and concern that is shown for these dependents, families are increasingly unable to continue to provide routine assistance and supervision for them.

Because working families are no longer able to bear the total responsibility for care, the private market has responded to these conditions and attempted to fill a growing need to help families with their family and household responsibilities. For example, child-care centers, nursing homes, home-cleaning services, supervised recreation programs for children, and information hot lines have been developed and marketed to working families. The cost of using these professional services instead of relying on family-provided services is not simply a financial one. There are many important dimensions of the substitution of paid care for family care. How does the depersonalization of care affect the delivery and the quality of services? Is this going to lead to more lawsuits and higher insurance costs, so that some private-market services will be too expensive? Already some summer camps, family day-care homes, and recreation programs have been confronted with excessive liability insurance or cannot obtain any insurance coverage. In some cases this has caused these vital services to shut down.

Some of the needs are being addressed by a combination of programs either developed by the private market or sponsored by government, but the needs clearly exceed the capacities of these programs. Unless society can support the care given by families, the nation may soon be facing an even greater crisis in caring. As we approach the new century, society has yet to confront many of the urgent dependency needs that exist among such populations as latchkey children, elders, and disabled people, who are now forced to either rely primarily on families or somehow make it on their own.

Volunteerism. Much of the highly touted private/public partnerships rely on volunteerism, in which people devote their spare or leisure hours to worthy causes. A large part of society, from the United Way campaigns to hospital staffing, depends on volunteerism. Because many of the tasks have largely been performed by women, their exodus to the workplace seriously threatens this foundation of American society. If the volunteer movement continues to falter, not only would those institutions and groups that depend on them be affected, but the very essence of the American way of life might be seriously threatened as well.

Impact of Other Institutions. Although the government is the most visible institution representing society, others also are affected by work/family conflicts. As people's work schedules, eating habits, shopping patterns, and leisure time activities change, virtually all institutions feel the impact of these changes.

Consequently, the lives and behaviors of working parents affect, for example, the schools, vacations, resorts, banks, supermarkets, and insurance policies. The attempt by society to face the problem of working parents cannot be focused on the need for a day-care center. The more fundamental structural institution and cultural changes serve as the real foci for meaningful change.

Local institutions are closer to the work/family conflict issues and are, therefore, more impacted. Schools, for example, have to deal not only with the ramifications of latchkey children, but also with parents who have an increasingly difficult time attending school functions. It is also the schools that must contend with the problem of having inadequate resources available for children with moderate, acute illnesses who are members of working families. These children may come to schools with colds or other symptoms because parents have to go to work, and there are no other options for the child.

Social service agencies have had to shift their operating hours to accommodate the usual nine-to-five work day of most of their clients. They also are finding that they need to develop the capacity to help their clients cope with work/family conflicts by developing new patterns of relationships, both with other people and with the outside world, if they hope to resume normal functioning.

Advocacy. On the societal level many work/family issues are associated with social injustices. Women encounter gender conflicts at home and at the workplace; minorities face discrimination, which intensifies work/family conflicts; the working poor are unable to meet even the basic needs of their families. If the conflicts continue to be unresolved, people with high degrees of work/family stress will intensify their advocacy efforts and their drive for equal rights.

Comparable worth cases currently being considered by the courts are a good example. These cases address problems of comparable worth—equal pay for men and women for jobs and skills that are roughly equivalent. The wide disparity between men's and women's salaries continues to constitute a glaring contradiction in a society built on equality. Despite the professional gains made by women, their wages were just 65 percent of those of men in 1986.[86] Society will have to pay either the social costs of this inequity or the cost of equalizing the pay where appropriate.

In summary, the impacts of work/family issues on society touch on the most basic issues of who we are and what type of society we want to live in. The current misfit between working families and existing social policies, or lack thereof, poses a genuine threat to the health of families and their ability to grow and develop within healthy environments. There are even greater threats to the nation from an economic perspective, since the current arrangements place the United States on an increasingly disadvantaged competitive basis within the global economy. Trying to compete with Japan and Europe, which have recognized the need to support families through public services for productivity gains, will continue to put the United States at a disadvantage within the global economy.

NOTES

1. American Council of Life Insurance, p. 1.
2. Mintz and Kellogg, p. 205.
3. United States Bureau of the Census, *Current Population Reports*, Households, Families, Marital Status, and Living Arrangements, p. 20.
4. Norton, p. 17.
5. Masnick and Bane, pp. 27, 129.
6. United States Congressional Committee on Foreign Affairs, p. 43.
7. *Editorial Research Reports on the Changing American Family,* p. 8.
8. Masnick and Bane, p. 40.
9. Hodgkinson, p. 16.
10. Ibid.
11. See Barton.
12. Ibid, p. 74
13. Bolles, p. 137.
14. United States Department of Health and Human Services, p. 7.
15. Hanson and Sporakowski, p. 16.
16. *Editorial Research Reports on the Changing American Family,* p. 8.
17. Sekaran, pp. 5–6.
18. Ross et al., p. 809–823.
19. Sekaran, pp. 5–6.
20. Hoffman, p. 378.
21. Baruch et al., p. 133.
22. Petty and Friss, pp. 22–26.
23. Googins and Casey, p. 47–66.
24. Ferree, p. 290.
25. Pleck, *Married Men: Work and Family*, p. 2.
26. Reynolds, p. 44.
27. Pleck, *Working Wives/Working Husbands*, p. 30.
28. Mintz and Kellogg, p. 219.
29. Kammerman and Hayes, p. 313.
30. See Long and Long.
31. Robinson et al., pp. 18–19.
32. Sidel, p. 158.
33. United States Bureau of the Census, *Current Population Reports*. "Households," p. 3.
34. Mintz and Kellogg, p. 203.
35. Gilbert, p. 254.
36. Masnick and Bane, p. 34.
37. Furstenberg, p. 20:3.
38. Cherlin and Furstenberg, p. 9.
39. Abel, p. 5.
40. United States Bureau of the Census, *Current Population Reports*. "Households," p. 4.
41. Ibid., p. 1.
42. Ibid., p. 8.

43. "Room for Diversity in Household Definition," p. B1:1.

44. Mintz and Kellogg, p. 227.

45. Ibid., p. 204.

46. United States Bureau of the Census, *Current Population Reports*, "Martial Status and Living Arrangements", p. 1.

47. United States Bureau of the Census, *Current Population Reports*, "Households," p. 1.

48. Harris, p. 22.

49. Blumenstein and Schwartz, p. 31.

50. Furstenberg, p. 20:3.

51. Mintz and Kellogg, p. 223.

52. Yankelovich, p. 100.

53. Pleck, *Working Wives/Working Husbands*, p. 23.

54. Harris, p. 98.

55. Pleck, *Married Men: Work and Family*, p. 2.

56. Pleck, *Working Wives/Working Husbands*, p. 146.

57. Richter and Hall, p. 21.

58. United States Bureau of the Census, *Historical Statistics of the United States: Colonial Times to 1970*, "Labor Force Participation Rates of Wives," p. 386.

59. Harris, p. 101.

60. See Piotrowski and Katz.

61. Gilbert, p. 254.

62. Ibid.

63. Masnick and Bane, p. 30.

64. Harris, p. 86.

65. Ibid., p. 113.

66. See Bronfenbrenner.

67. Bettelheim, pp. 5–10.

68. Mintz and Kellogg, p. 196.

69. See *Work in America*.

70. Hecksher, p. 3.

71. Johnston, pp. xii–xiv.

72. "Education Really Does Matter in the Job Market," p. B1:1.

73. Sekaran, p. 94.

74. Johnston, p. 76.

75. Sekaran, p. 98.

76. See Eurich.

77. May and Ingols, p. 15.

78. Allen, p. 26.

79. "Employment Trends," p. 2.

80. See Kidder.

81. See Emlen and Koren.

82. See Fernandez.

83. Yankelovich, p. xvii.

84. Immerwahr, pp. 34–35.

85. Yankelovich, pp. xvii–xviii.

86. "Women Gain Ground in Wages, Study Shows," p. C:11.

Chapter 3

A SURVEY OF THE PAST

Work/family conflicts have existed throughout American history, but the nature and specific characteristics of these conflicts have changed over time. We tend to examine the issues of work/family through the lenses of the present and the immediate past. Although this practice draws on what we know best and are most comfortable with, it provides a narrow perspective. The past two centuries have witnessed significant shifting of work/family arrangements, many of which will come as a surprise to those of us who are myopically mired in the present. Work/family arrangements have evolved out of the delicate and constantly changing relations between the three most central institutions in our society: the family, the workplace, and the government. An examination of the state of these institutions in earlier periods provides some fresh insights into the arrangements between these three spheres in the context of historical developments.

This chapter examines these changes over time, not for the sake of historical analysis per se, but for the insight such an examination may provide for the underlying conflicts of work/family in contemporary America. This march through time captures some of the changing dynamics of workplaces and families as well as the intricate relations that tie these two in an ever-evolving dialectic. Because families and economic organizations are at the core of our society, we cannot afford to ignore the lessons of history, and are advised to reexamine the past for a deeper appreciation of the enduring conflicts that have beset each generation. The many iterations that work/family relations have gone through over the past three centuries serve to underscore the centrality of this issue to every society. This chapter touches down within those eras and lifts out the lessons of the past so that they might provide some much-needed insight into the dilemmas and conflicts our society is experiencing over resolving its own work/family conflicts. Thus the current struggle is not an end point, but yet another phase in what can best be termed an ongoing evolution. (See Appendix.)

In the early 1990s it appears that the latest manifestation of work/family conflicts may be a revolution in social values and demographic shifts. Indeed, there may be such a revolution, but it still must be seen in the context of the past 300 years in which roles and responsibilities within families and workplaces have experienced other radical changes. As one compares the similarities and differences between the historical periods, it is easier to appreciate the fact that individuals, families, and institutions (including work) have gone through many prior dramatic changes. Not surprisingly, the upheaval of the current work/family issues is not the final stage; they will continue to change.

It is risky to compare and capture work/family configurations across generations and ages, since there are numerous intervening variables. This is especially true of a relatively brief overview such as this in contrast to some of the fine historical analyses written by Brandes (1976), Mintz and Kellogg (1988), Seward (1978), and others. Because our purpose is to provide a backdrop and not a comprehensive analysis, material easily becomes oversimplified. Take the issue of class for example. Often the discussion of work/family takes place as, if there were one class, or as if the issue impacted all classes equally. In reality, there are a number of important differences between work/family arrangements and conflicts among higher socioeconomic groups and lower ones. These distinctions are largely passed over to provide the general sweep of history.

COLONIAL TIMES

The period from 1600 to 1770 saw the first European families arrive on the American continent. They came with high hopes, ideals, and strong commitments to the search for religious freedom. Because the existing communities of North American Indians did not impose their cultures on the new settlers, the first white immigrants saw themselves as true pioneers in the middle of a geographical and cultural tabula rasa—a blank slate on which they proceeded to form a new society. Although they brought with them the family and work models from their homelands, the colonists arrived in a new country that did not require adaptation to preexisting institutions. People often arrived with deep religious convictions, though there were no organized churches. There was no government for the European immigrants. Opportunities for education and leisure were not structured. Typically, there were not even employers as we know them unless the new arrivals came as indentured servants or as slaves.

What was being germinated in these early colonialists was the beginnings of the American culture—independence and rugged individualism. Most of the settlers had fled from oppressive governments and societies, and they brought to the new land passionately held beliefs in religious freedoms and the opportunity for the individual to hew out his own existence. These beliefs undergirded by the values imbibed by the protestant ethic, the principles of Darwinism, and the familiar cultural themes of the survival of the fittest. It is interesting to note that most of these themes have been transmitted through the generations, and have influenced the development of the family and its relation to other institutions, particularly the government and the workplace.

Many of the salient characteristics of the work/family relations during colonial times were a direct result of the type of rural existence experienced by most people. The vast majority lived on farms during all of the seventeenth and most of the eighteenth centuries. By necessity, most households were practically self-sufficient. The settlers' major goals were to gain a foothold on the land and to meet the basic needs on a subsistence level. Families and small, loose-knit communities banded together to overcome harsh weather and land that often was unreceptive to agriculture. In addition, many settlers lived in a constant state of vigilance and warfare, first against some of the native Americans and later against the French and the British.

The context for both work and family experiences during the colonial years was that of a premarket, agrarian society. Family and community economics were largely based on a combination of self-sufficiency and barter. The use of currency for labor and the purchase of goods was limited; work was seldom considered "employment." Survival was the goal for each day's work. With the occasional respites for religious observances, almost all activities focused directly or indirectly on work. Most families could not depend on any long-term economic security.

In such a precapitalist society the family was the economic unit, and all able-bodied members—adults and children—contributed to the production. Thus the family constituted a cooperative economic enterprise, perhaps the precursor to the family business of today. All members, including women and children, made a necessary and important contribution to the enterprise. This family "business" orientation to work provided the structure whereby trades were learned and apprenticeships undertaken. Each family enterprise principally competed not against other economic forces, but against the elements.

Desegregating housework from economic work was a distinction not understood within this framework. Work was homebound and essentially family-defined. The family was constituted in such a way that it was almost impossible to separate work and family. Men and women spent long, hard days working the land together; life in colonial times was nothing like that depicted in some romanticized accounts. Families were true working families, and children were socialized into roles at an early age, which contributed to the economic vitality of the family unit.[1] In their role as assistants to their parents, children were considered economic assets.[2] As with most agrarian societies, the more children there were in the family (especially boys), the more robust the family would be economically. The low age of life expectancy and the high rate of mortality during infancy and childhood caused considerable upheaval in families, much of it focused around the need for available labor.

Even the household space was not all that distant from the work space. Little of the house was set aside for what we would call family space, such as a family room or a living room. Work was performed within the living structure, and it was not until the mid-eighteenth century that the craft shop that was separate from the home began to emerge.[3] The fact that apprentices and laborers often resided at the house of the master craftsman heightened the high degree of integration of work activities and household activities. The inseparable nature of work and family during the colonial era resulted in a curious phenomena; conflicts about work were typically with relatives: "There undoubtedly were . . . pervasive conflicts: between sons anxious to take over the family business and fathers holding onto parental authority; between husbands and wives; between brothers and brothers-in-law and cousins. Yet such conflicts were not between work and family."[4] During the colonial era, work/family conflicts were family conflicts.

The absence of formalized community institutions meant that the family unit not only was responsible for the survival of its members, but also had to fulfill additional functions in response to the needs of family members. The interconnectedness of all aspects of life was significant; any separate existence between family, and economics, law, politics, and religion was simply unimaginable. For all practical purposes, the family was the only social institution, a place where the child was educated, the elderly and infirm were cared for, values were transmitted, skills and crafts were taught, and goods were produced. "The family (and its structure) was a central force for maintaining economic, social, and political stability."[5]

The family, in effect, filled the void that existed because other institutions had not yet come into existence, and served as the foundation of society. There were many unfortunate consequences of the lack of a public "safety net" during this period. For example, there is evidence that dependent elders, who were no longer economically productive, often struggled desperately. The concern that some elders had for their own care (or care for surviving spouses) during their senior years is indicated in some of the wills. It was not uncommon for aging family members to stipulate in their wills that any inheritance was contingent on the beneficiaries providing care for the elderly parents. The absence of institutions that might have provided services to the elderly often resulted in older people—especially those without kin—"living on the fringe," much like today's homeless.[6]

The absence of developed infrastructures of society not only raised the importance of the family, but also fostered family cohesion, mutual aid, and support. The isolation of the geography and the tenuous nature of the emigration from an "established" society in Europe reinforced the interdependence of family members. The family system bore all responsibility for whatever needed to occur to survive and prosper in the new world. There were no other institutions to help the family in its endeavor—only the resources found within the family and kin system. The family was society, and the obvious overload resulting from such a sparse support system took its toll. In fact, it was almost 150 years into this period, right before the Revolutionary War, when communities began to accept some of the responsibilities that families had previously assumed. Alms and housing for widows, indigent families, orphans, and the mentally ill began to be established.

For most, family was the beginning and the end of the community. In contrast to the emphasis on nuclear family in today's conceptualizations of family, the family system extended to include a broad range of relatives who were considered kin. Although it was not common for more than two generations of a family to share a residence,[7] families typically lived in communities in which there were other members of their kin system, related by birth or marriage. Continuing patterns of immigration built on this kin network. In most cases kin could be depended on to provide vital assistance and support to individual nuclear families. Kin was of central importance to the social, economic, and political life in the community, and responsibility to kin was emphasized over ties to spouse—quite a reversal from the society of today.

The composition of the family and household size were influenced by a number of factors. Family size varied according to the mortality rates, birthrates, use of apprentices and employment of help, and age of marriage. The life expectancy data reveal a curious phenomenon; people who survived the dangers of infant mortality or maternal death could expect to live a relatively long life. For women the fear of death as a result of bearing children was very real; about one of every thirty births resulted in the death of the mother.[8] The survival of young children was also uncertain. In seventeenth century New England one of every ten children died before their first year in so-called healthy regions and one in three died in less healthy areas. This mortality rate can be contrasted with today's rate of 14 for every 1,000, which is the highest for the industrialized countries.[9]

Despite these rather grim statistics, the tales of the long-lived Adamses, Jeffersons, and Washingtons were not all that uncharacteristic of some of the colonies. For those who did not succumb to childhood diseases or death from childbearing, it was not unusual for men and women to last into their seventies. Variations in longevity existed among the different colonies. Although the image of the long-lived Yankee of New England is borne out in death records, residents of other regions experienced considerably shorter life spans. For example, a man who reached age 20 in the Chesapeake could expect to live only another twenty-three years. Few made it over age 60. Half of the women living in this region failed to see their twentieth birthday.[10]

The heavy dependence that most families had on the economic contributions made by children usually translated into a high fertility rate. Although the fertility rate varied significantly from one colony to another, it was common for a family to have from five to ten children.[11] Most women would have at least six children in fairly regular intervals of twenty to thirty months.[12] This high birthrate contributed to the high maternal death rate resulting from childbirth. Given the need for labor and the relatively crude state of health care and medicine, this cycle was hard to break. Childlessness was rare, with only one in twelve women occupying this category.[13]

Despite the high fertility rate, the average household size was only 5.8 persons because of the mortality rate and the variable definition of "family members" in the records.[14] The death of mothers, fathers and siblings was a common occurrence. The ramifications of these deaths, beyond the emotional turmoil, were most directly felt by families in the loss of labor. In communities of close-knit families adjustments were made along a number of lines to ensure both the survival of the family unit and the instruction of surviving children in skills and trade.

Marriage was viewed within an economic perspective. From today's perch the union of husband and wife was narrowly prescribed, tightly bound, and left little room for change or negotiation. In most instances it was more like a business contract than a relationship based on primary bonds between two equals. Marriage often was a contract of property negotiated primarily between the couple's parents. Although the marriages were not arranged in the manner practiced in other parts of the world at that time, the hand of the family in drawing up the union was quite evident.[15] In many cases the marriage was viewed in terms of both the economic potency of the relationship and the skills that would allow successful economic enterprise. From another perspective, the future of the family property had to be carefully considered. It was quite usual for parental consent to be given, so that the parents could reach satisfactory agreement over the distribution of family property.[16] Interestingly, the age of marriage was relatively late. Despite the prevailing myths of early marriages, the average age of marriage was approximately 25 years for men, and few women married before the age of 20, although this varied greatly among the colonies.[17]

For all but the very wealthy, marriage was an economic necessity. In the absence of government support a person could not survive on his or her own; single adults almost never lived alone.[18] "There was little place in colonial society for the unmarried. . . . For a women, marriage was deemed to be the only honorable state. . . . Bachelors were suspect, and in most of the colonies were heavily taxed and kept under close surveillance."[19]

Even the death of a spouse did not lead to households populated by widows and widowers. Remarriage (or a move into another household—usually that of kin) was most often necessitated again by economic conditions.[20] Whereas today's "blended families" typically result from divorced spouses and their families coming together as a result of second (or subsequent) marriages, during colonial times blended families were created when adults remarried after the death of their spouses. The remarriage of spouses often led to the rearrangement of families, and the blending of children from previous marriages was not uncommon.[21]

It was not until the end of colonial times, with the emergence of the revolutionary spirit in the mid–1770s, that marriage and the family were free from being a quasi-economic relationship. During the years when the Sons of Liberty introduced a new sense of freedom and independence to the colonists, ideas of liberation associated with marriage and the family began to spread throughout society. One indication was the rise in the number of women who petitioned for divorce. During the early colonial years, it was virtually unheard of for a woman to seek separation from her husband. According to records, the community of Plymouth did not experience a divorce until 1661, some forty years after its settlement by the colonists.[22] Although formal divorces were almost impossible to obtain before the 1800s, the end of the colonial era began to witness an increase in the number of separations. Notifications of separation allowed the dissolution of the marriage without going through the divorce petition, which violated social and religious norms. In eighteenth-century Massachusetts there were only 220 divorced couples, but 3,300 notices of separation were printed in the newspapers.[23]

The colonial times were reflective of a patriarchal society, and not surprisingly, there were quite discrete roles for men and women, especially within the marriage contract. Single women, before their marriage, were actually quite liberated in contrast to the bond that they assumed in marriage. For example, before marriage these women had the right to conduct business, own property, and even represent themselves before court. After marriage all of these rights and roles were abrogated to the marriage contract.[24] "Long term land deprivation imposed a heavy burden. It deprived women of economic independence, control of a household, and political influence. Without these advantages, colonial women, as a group, remained at the mercy of fathers and husbands or government authorities."[25]

Despite the involvement of all family members in carrying out the business of working and living, there was little equality between the genders. The household was still the male domain. Community laws and church doctrine supported the principles of patriarchy, in which it was the duty of women, children, and servants to submit to the authority of the father. Although men, women, and children often worked the fields together, traditional roles such as cooking and meal preparation fell to women.[26] Sets of roles evolved in which men worked the land and the trees and women took care of the animals and the farm chores. In nonfarm households the women often acted as salespeople, bookkeepers, and business managers, leaving the crafts to the men. Although the Puritan communities recognized the contributions made by women, the role of the wife was clearly secondary to that of her husband.[27] Above all, women were the bearers and keepers of the children and the guardians of health for the family. These roles were essential for the survival of the household. Many of the tasks assigned to women were those that could be carried out close to the home, such as tending animals and cultivating crops, so that the women could keep their eyes and ears on their charges.

Children constituted a critical dimension of work/family issues during colonial times. The care of children often was subordinated to other family interests, particularly economic survival, and child-rearing was not seen as the primary function of the family. Interestingly, child-rearing practices often were seen as the role of the father. Whereas the mother was expected to assume the daily routine of child care, the father was responsible for shaping the values of the child. In fact, most of the child-rearing books that were available during that period were written for the father, as he was to instill the moral and spiritual guidance in the child.[28] The disciplinary function of the father in early colonial times was seen in rather rigidly authoritarian households, where the father's rule was absolute, and control over family behaviors and decisions rested solely in his lap. Although these standards and practices tended to loosen over the succeeding generations, as economic independence served to free the family members from such control, up until the Revolutionary War this closely controlled family system was the norm.

The absence of a formalized institution of school during this period relegated children's education to the family. Some of the religions mandated education to the family. Others from the upper classes either brought in tutors or sent their children to Europe for schooling. The great majority of colonists, however, tried to fit in some form of education at home in the middle of a busy working schedule. Toward the middle of the eighteenth century schools began to become commonplace as homesteads began forming communities.

It was not unusual for children to spend only a few years within the nuclear family. By the time they reached their teen years they would be farmed out to other families for training or as extra hands. Likewise, if a family did not have enough children, they would bring in children from families who had surplus labor to be loaned, and for whom this surplus labor represented an economic hardship. Children in this circumstance would live in quasi-servitude in another family until such time as they would be able to gain their own independence or return to their natural family. The apprentice system was seen as a prevention against parental failures, pauperism, and economic dependence on the community.[29] From the perspective of twentieth-century child-rearing practices, the apprenticeship system seems harsh and strange, but given the importance of the child to the economic functioning of the families in colonial times, this approach to child-rearing was pragmatic and sensible.[30]

It was quite usual for colonial families to exert a great deal of influence over the children through the control of inheritance. Inheritance practices, along with the father's control of the family farm or business, served to keep children economically dependent well into their adulthood, delayed marriage, and encouraged sons to remain near their fathers during their lifetime.[31] Few boys moved far from the family homestead as they began their independent lives and even after they married. This began to change as the colonies matured and as the second and third generations became more acclimated to the newly developing society. In succeeding generations it became impractical to continue dividing land among the sons at the death of the father, and the inheritance issue played less of a role in determining family functioning; greater economic independence from fathers became possible and allowed occupations other than farming to be pursued. This accelerated as the semblance of villages and towns emerged from the scattered settlements of the early colonists.

By examining changing child-rearing practices the subtle and not so subtle changes in families and workplaces that occurred as this period approached the Revolutionary War can be seen. During the first years of colonization the children began as laborers. By the time the country was fighting the Revolution children began to evolve toward a more independent existence. Furthermore, the rigid 1600s perspective of children as the embodiment of sin had been transformed into an image of innocent children who needed molding.

By the end of the 18th century children were increasingly viewed as special creatures with unique needs. One sign of this new sensibility was the proliferation of books and games and toys aimed specifically at children. . . . The practice of fostering out children became less common. [During adolescence] sons were allowed temporarily to hire out their labor during the fall and winter months, thereby helping them to achieve a measure of financial independence while still in their teens or early twenties. Daughters, too, received new opportunities to attend school and to work outside the home.[32]

It was during this era that the first separation of work and family began to emerge. The growth of the market economy reinforced the distinction between work and family. In addition, the growing independence of adult children who were not so closely tied to the family farm or to the inheritance bondage that characterized the first few generations of colonists brought an even clearer distinction to work and family domains.

PREINDUSTRIAL

The next major historical era existed roughly from the War for Independence through the Civil War (1770–1880). This period represented a "settling in" of the country and was a recognizable change from life in colonial days. Many of the political philosophies associated with the American Revolution, such as participatory democracy, began to serve as a framework for daily lives at home and at work. After the country had gained its independence, people started to explore the meaning of freedom from a personal perspective: life, liberty, and the pursuit of happiness. Children became less and less necessary to the economic survival of the family. Workplaces became more distinct from homes. The nuclear family assumed a position of priority within the kin system, the concept of romantic love reconstructed marriage, and the role of women became a hotly discussed topic.

During the preindustrial period, the country began to expand and grow geographically, politically, and, especially, economically. The growth of town centers brought with it a further development of crafts and trades, such as woodworking, tanning, and milling flour, that had until then been part-time tasks that took place on the farms. Although the farming industry continued to dominate this agrarian society, the preindustrial shops began to form, and by the turn of the nineteenth century a fairly sizable and prosperous merchant class had formed in the large cities. Between 1820 and 1860 the proportion of non-farm workers rose from 28.2 percent to 41.1 percent.[33] In the early decades of the nineteenth century the family as a largely self-sufficient economic unit began to disappear.

During this period a number of inventions were brought to the United States. One of these was the ability to produce whole cloth more cheaply in factories than at the loom at home. This would not only create new industries, but also significantly liberate women from spending the hours and hours that it had taken to produce the family's clothes. Women and children began to enter the wage labor force, often working at home producing such items as finished clothing. Despite the pull and tugs of cultural imperatives around child care, women had unprecedented opportunities to work outside the home in fledgling grist mills and woolen mills that were seeking labor.

The increase in independent shops and business enterprises brought with it a growing separation of work and family functions. Unlike in the colonial times, the creation of business enterprises took men out of and away from the home. The existence of a separate place of work came to be a fairly common phenomenon. Even before industrialization the market economy of the eighteenth and early nineteenth centuries began to be characterized as impersonal. The very concept of specialization began to take hold in terms of crafts and business in general, which had spillover into the home and affected work/family relations. The experiences of apprentices began to evolve from a family-oriented situation to more of a business relationship with the master craftsman as the apprentices moved their residences out of the master's houses into boarding rooms.[34] Although the rapidity of this shift from the home to a workplace external to the home would find its completion during the next century of industrialization, the stirring in the beginning of this preindustrial period had grown significantly by the time of the Civil War. During this later period the term breadwinner emerged, thus formally recognizing the fading of the old model in which men and women worked side by side in and around the family homestead.

Changes in the structure of work and work locations were carried over into the family. As a result of the identity of a workplace separate from the home, the reorganization of home and work tasks began to be discussed. In the home these changes were reflected by the introduction of the concept of the home as the nurturing environment for emotional development and for self-fulfillment. As noted by Alexis de Tocqueville in 1831, the American family had undergone a transition from the rigidly prescribed "father as authoritarian" style to the "democratic family" that reflected the popular views of "individualism."[35] The isolated family of colonial times whose members worked closely together for survival was economically emancipated with the development of independent business enterprises. Relieved of some of the immediate economic subsistence needs, the family could afford to devote more attention to the rearing and education of their children and the women could have a life freed from many of the economic functions once solely relegated to the home. Thus not only was the father's role changing, but the mother's and the children's roles as well.

The concept of the family tied to kin in the earlier period now was rapidly changing to reflect the increased independence of the family in society. The extended-family model no longer fit in a society in which the economic sphere was becoming increasingly separate from the home and that, in many instances, constituted a life unto itself. Although kinship bonds made sense in an extended family with the proximity of each other's farms, the new family would more often be centered in what was termed the nuclear family. Isolated families began to replace the rather extensive kin networks that had brought families and society through the first two centuries in the new world. This shift, although not abrupt by the hindsight of history, nevertheless was a dramatic upheaval that transformed the social and ideological support that undergirded the family and the new society. The adjustment to the world outside of the farm and the economic bonds that held the family together brought with them a number of costs in terms of conflicts and personal unhappiness.

Expectations for marriage changed significantly during the preindustrial period. Romance, rather than rigid financial considerations, became the impetus for courtship. The use of dowries became unusual.[36] Husbands and wives were seen as having some responsibility for the emotional well-being of their partners.[37] By the mid-nineteenth century it was no longer considered sufficient if the husband provided only for the economic welfare of the family. Love in marriage was fostered in part by the escape from servitude to the land. The newly changing economic order allowed the household and the marriage contract to transcend the basic necessities of eking out an existence, and the new prosperity of both technological advances and changing work/family culture allowed the marriage relationship to develop along more emotional lines. The nineteenth century in particular saw the rise of the romantic view of "home and family," which were perceived as moral retreats from the outside world.[38]

As expectations for marriage and family life were expanded to include personal fulfillment, there seemed to be signs that people were increasingly disappointed that the home life did not meet the new range of needs being articulated. This can be seen in the relaxing of divorce laws in many states in the mid-nineteenth century, which in part acknowledged both the changing nature of the marriage relationship and the shift from an economic to an emotional contract. "Already the family was beginning to acquire an overload of expectations that it often proved incapable of meeting—a failure apparent in the gradually rising divorce rates."[39]

This shifting nature of the family was not all hearts and flowers. One underlying source of strain lay in the disparity between women's rising expectations for self-fulfillment and the isolation of married women within a separate domestic sphere. Young women were raised in a society that placed a high value on independence. On marrying, however, a woman was to sacrifice her independent pursuits to her family duties. She was expected to derive her deepest satisfactions from homemaking, childbearing, and child-rearing. There is some speculation that for women, the disparities between the emphasis on achievement during their childhood and the priority placed on assuming nurturing roles as adults contributed to personal turmoil that was sometimes manifested in the symptoms of hysteria commonly observed during this era.[40]

For many women the changing family and their relation to it represented a loss of power. In colonial times men and women were economically dependent on each other, thus providing women a certain leverage within the family. In the changing family of the nineteenth century the loss of economic functions by married, middle-class women eroded their power base. Although women were increasingly employed outside the home in textile mills and other factories, most married women tried to maintain their presence in the home. During this preindustrial era differences among economic classes began to emerge. The affluent young women remained at home until they married. It was seen as desirable for these women to adopt many of the attributes of the English nobility, developing social graces and creating a lovely home. In contrast, young women from families with limited economic resources went to work in the factories, hoping to get married and return to the home full-time.[41]

Although opportunities for women to work outside the home increased, some historians believe that many of them did not do so because of their deeply felt cultural traditions surrounding child care. "It was not industrialization that kept women in their homes in the early nineteenth century, but the deeply ingrained tradition of women's primary responsibility for home and child care."[42] These responsibilities for child care demanded long-term attention from the women, who often continued to have these responsibilities right up until their death.

The role of women was clearly changing, not only within the marriage, but also within society at large. In New England in particular the weakening of Puritan law and the emergence of English common law created a less equal footing for women. Whereas the Puritan laws had given women considerable rights—at least up until they married—the English law brought with it the dominance of the husband as the master of the household and the family. Women, in effect, were "dead" in the law. Not only were they not permitted to vote, but they could not be granted custody of their own children.[43]

Despite these circumstances, women made tremendous gains in furthering their own lives and their influence in society. The ability to obtain an education took a dramatic turn during this period. In the beginning of the 1700s four-fifths of the women could not write their names. By the end of the century four-fifths were literate.[44] In the broader concerns of society women—even without the vote—were extremely involved, and provided leadership to the significant social movements of the day, notably the temperance and the antislavery movements. This tradition of participation in social issues continued well into the twentieth century.

Many changes that occurred in American society significantly affected attitudes toward children and child-rearing. Whereas the Puritans had inculcated the concept of children being born in sin, the mothers during this period were being socialized into a quite different paradigm. Some of the ideas of European philosophers such as Locke and Rousseau began to filter into nineteenth-century America, and parents began to reconceptualize child-rearing. Childhood was recognized as a distinct stage of life with its unique needs, and parents saw children as innocents, to be protected from the potential evils and harmful effects of the world around them. This enlightenment period brought with it a tendency to support the goodness and natural tendencies of children.

This new view of children also was possible in that they were no longer so essential to the production needs of the family. As the family's work began to extend beyond the farm economy, children were fast becoming nonessential labor. By the end of the eighteenth century children were not expected to contribute substantially to the income of the middle-class family. This supported the goal of educating children at a time when the demands for a skilled labor force began to increase. Children were encouraged to become independent and responsible youngsters who would eventually develop into productive and functioning adults.

As children began to decrease their economic contributions to their families, they became more dependent on their parents. They spent more time away from their parents, however, in contrast to previous generations, who had worked alongside their parents from an early age. This combination of economic dependence and distance (in terms of time spent together) planted the seed for the generation gap.

Changes in work/family functions and structure led to lower birthrates. Although more than one third of households during this era had seven or more members, the average household size (which might include paid laborers, servants, and other nonfamily members) was just 5.79 persons[45] The causes for this drop in fertility rates are complex. In part it can be seen as the growing realization among parents that in an increasingly commercial and industrial society, children were no longer economic assets; in fact, they had become liabilities, and required significant investment. At the same time, the death rate remained high. In New Bedford, Massachusetts, for example, between 1808 and 1822 more deaths occurred among those children who were younger than 4 years than among people even in the old age cohort of 40 to 69 years.[46]

In contrast to the colonial days, expectations for family and work during the preindustrial era were quite different. During any time of significant change there usually is a great deal of negative reaction to such change. For some the change is too radical and too rapid, whereas for others the change may not be sufficiently broad or may not go far enough. This was apparently the reaction of different groups in late-eighteenth- and nineteenth-century America to the changes in the family that occurred during the preindustrial era. During the 1840s and 1850s a number of groups began to experiment with "alternative communities" (many resembling communes) in response to their "belief that the nuclear family posed a threat to harmonious society."[47] Some of these communities were "reactionary"; they thought that families had drifted from the strict doctrines of the church, and decided to pursue spiritual goals through community living. At the other end of the philosophical spectrum were groups that espoused "enlightenment" ideas such as recognizing that the nuclear family could limit the potential for self-fulfillment for women. Some of these alternative communal societies proposed that monogamous marriages distracted people from their broader social obligations; they also believed that children would benefit from frequent contact with more than two parents (i.e., multiple role modes).[48]

INDUSTRIALIZATION

From the end of the Civil War to the early decades of the twentieth century the United States experienced a period of explosive growth that was to transform and revolutionize all aspects of American society. The industrial revolution propelled the nation from a newly founded frontier land to a world class industrialist in the space of a few decades. Blessed with an abundance of raw materials and inspired by a national spirit of adventure and entrepreneurship, a greased industrial machine was created that would be the envy of the world.

It is important to locate the beginnings of this new era. The United States was still reeling from the aftermath of the Civil War, which had literally torn the country asunder. Tremendous social costs had been exacted. The havoc that was realized in both the North and the South during the war seemed to pale at times in comparison with the deep depression that settled in the land during reconstruction. Thus the much chronicled industrial expansion that occurred toward the end of the nineteenth century startled the country out of its social and economic woes and put it back on its feet again. The rise of the new capitalism did not occur without significantly altering the very fabric of the country. A vast land—a rich, sleepy country—was turned into a sprawling, dirty, industrial machine with all the social and environmental ills that inevitably accompany such metamorphosis. The Jeffersonian ideals of the landed citizen directly clashed with the evolving nature of American life, and the new capitalist era was a test to determine whether these two philosophies could coexist.

Many basic characteristics of American communities changed drastically during the industrial period. The growth of factory towns moved the United States from a principally rural country that depended heavily on agriculture as its economic base to a more urbanized nation. In 1870 seven out of every ten towns had populations of less than 2,500.[49] During 1860 nearly 60 percent of the labor force earned their living as farmers. By 1910, however, less than one third of the labor force was engaged in farming.[50] The years of industrialization were times of urbanization and the creation of teeming, crowded cities, inventing the new phenomenon of slums.

The ethnic and cultural backgrounds of communities also became more diversified during this era. The hope for employment in the newly industrialized cities and towns contributed to dramatic increases in immigration rates. Hordes of immigrants came to the United States from Europe seeking freedom, opportunity, and a piece of prosperity. These groups were desperately needed by the industrialists to fuel the unprecedented growth and success of industrialization. But it was these same groups that would settle in the cities, bringing with them their unique customs, religions, languages, and traditions, all of which had to be blended into the mainstream of America.

Not surprisingly, distinct variations in lifestyles between people of different economic classes became more exaggerated during the industrial era. Those on the lower ends of the economic pyramid bore the costs of the turmoil of the transition to industrialization. This marks the first time in history that families with limited economic resources needed to have as many family members as possible working outside the home. Throughout this era most of the U.S. population was considered working class. Industrialization kept most of these families a shade above poverty but not much more than that. Even before the depression years over half of all American families had incomes that were at or below a basic subsistence level.[51]

Up until World War I, working class Americans—who earned a livelihood in the nation's steel mills, railyards, textile and clothing factories, coal mines, and farms—made up a majority of the nation's population. . . . Most working class families moved frequently. . . . Full-time year-round employment was a rarity. . . . At a time when most middle class families had only one breadwinner, relatively few working class families could support themselves without the economic contributions of other family members.[52]

During this period most families found that factory employment did not provide for the economic welfare of their families. Employment often was sporadic, and even during times of regular employment when the worker toiled for long hours, it often was impossible to make ends meet.

In Homestead, a typical family of a mill worker lived below the poverty line, spending eight dollars a month for one or two rooms in an alley residence. After budgeting for food and deducting for clothing, fuel, and insurance, the family was left just forty-one cents at the end of the month—a sum that had to cover health care, furniture, education, recreation, church contributions, and savings. To supplement their weekly paychecks, families took in washing or boarders (who contributed an average of a quarter of the family's income) and depended on the earning of older sons who typically contributed nearly a third of the family's income.[53]

There is no doubt that the changes resulting from industrialization were not limited to the factories, but also significantly impacted the surrounding communities. Consequently industrialization added an overlay of social problems to the difficulties of postwar recovery. America was to repeat the horrors of industrialism in England in which the land and its people were ravaged by the relentless march of the capitalist machine. What emerged was widespread misery, cruelty, disease, slums, child abuse and exploitation, poverty, insecurity, and degradation.

The doubled-edged sword of progress took its toll on the cities, on families, and on working men and women. In effect, this era of industrialism created the cities and defined the working environments, labor/management relations, and, ultimately, the relationship between employer and employee. Capitalism took on its form and developed in the middle of tough, often unprincipled times. Jane Adams in the late nineteenth century championed the plights of tens of thousands of Chicagoans and described the failures of industrial expansion that had these people working in sweat shops, exploited in every aspect of their lives in the worst tenements, with little relief facilities.[54]

But perhaps more profound than at any time in the evolution of life in the United States, living and working during the industrial era would transform society and in its wake reshape every institution, value and custom associated with work. During this period work became employment. Men routinely accepted jobs away from their homes.

Factory life in the industrial era captured the shift from work to employment. The workplace would now be defined by the factory, which would capture a large group of citizens and introduce the workday, work structure, and work habits that would mold the common perceptions about work in America. Although there were dramatic differences between the early work enterprises, much of the industrial capitalists' rush to build on the remarkable growth in technology necessitated the creation of efficient production organizations. This growth was accompanied by the development of assembly lines and monotonous, repetitive piecework that would characterize the industrial era. The life of a factory worker, closed off from the outside, tied to a production schedule, and often routinized by the partialized task or role, was in great contrast to that of his father's generation, which was independent, "master of the earth," and close to the family. It should be kept in mind, however, that in addition to men whose families had been in this country for a few generations, the sprouting of factories provided out-of-home employment for other newcomers to the market labor force: women, immigrants, and emancipated African Americans.[55]

Factory life also entailed a growing sense of impersonalized relations as the size and nature of the factory developed. Corporations adopted strategies that reflected concepts of "scientific management" (e.g., personnel policies and antinepotism practices). In many respects scientific management served to eliminate connections between the family and work, a process that continued throughout the remainder of the twentieth century.[56] In this way industrialization resulted in separating the family's work from home, although many families continued to work together for many decades.

This development led to a sense of isolation and increasing distance between employer and employee, which ultimately resulted in broken communications, mistrust, and hard feelings, all of which are the grist of labor unrest, and led to the rise of unions. But in the early years of this period the enormous growth of the industrial machine took on a life of its own, charting its progress by instinct, the rush for profit, and with little thought of the social consequences in the process of industrialization. This inevitably led to many of the problems that continued to plague the industrialists in their quest to balance the rise of industry with their ability to create and maintain a stable and productive workforce.

The shifting meaning of work also played a large part in the necessary transition into the industrial age. The replacement of craft work by the assembly line was a difficult transition for those whose fathers and grandfathers had taken pride in their crafts. This image of the skilled craftsman was difficult to reconcile with the largely unskilled, routine, dirty, and monotonous work of the factory. In subtle and not so subtle ways the very nobility of work was slowly eroded as the role of the employee in the industrial venture took hold and the rewards of one's labor were less directly associated with the individual worker's initiative.

In establishing separate workplaces capitalism also established work as a central institution within American society. Although capitalism had always flourished in the trades and crafts of the early colonists, the advent of the factory brought into existence the autonomous institution of work organizations and with it the influence and power of economic enterprise. This quickly evolved into the earlier forms of bureaucratic institutions, which, over the ensuing decades, reshaped work in America. Whereas work and family life had been almost synonymous during the first two centuries of the country, the industrialists of the late nineteenth century needed to establish the predominance of the workplace. This in turn brought into existence the need for a well-ordered and structured work setting that exacted disciplined employees who were loyal to the organization and that inculcated them with the spirit of capitalism.

All of this set the tone for shifts in work/family relations that not only reshaped these relations in ways that were quite different from those of the past, but also in effect redefined the very relationship between work and family. Industrialization transformed some of the roles and functions of the family, and in fact resulted in the family's restructuring its life in order to better meet the needs of the workplace.

Thus it was over this period that genuine conflicts arose between families and the workplace as well as between the workplace and society over the neglect and costs of industrialism. It took almost sixty years after the beginning of industrialization for the enactment of regulations that began to improve working environments. Not until World War I were there any factory codes that required proper ventilation and sanitary appliances, workman's compensations on contract labor, restrictions on child labor, regulation of prison labor, and the enactment of the ten- and then the eight-hour workday. The entire period of industrialization progressed without the creation of a federal department of labor. Most of these benchmarks of progress resulted not out of the country's sense of social responsibility, but were responses to the heightening of labor unrest and the formation of unions.

A unique characteristic of the industrial period was the movement that had been labeled welfare capitalism, or social betterment. The conflicts between the two major institutions of work and family greatly intensified as the workplace came into its own. The new industrial capitalists were faced with creating the workplace as a distinct institution in which adults would not operate from their homes, but rather would come together to produce a product. Early industrialists needed a healthy, orderly, well-behaved, and loyal workforce. The uneducated immigrant or rural American, however, was unsocialized to norms of the new workplace, and often adjusted only marginally to an urban existence. Although most of these industrialists would have preferred to pay a wage and let the social order develop, social problems, from acculturation to housing and even serious alcoholism, all required their attention. The problems of employees invariably impinged on their enterprise, demanding their active involvement if business were to be successful.[57] Many of the employers of the time conceptualized corporate welfare programs as being designed to address perceived weaknesses in the family.

In order to meet these problems the owners of the largest businesses began to institute a series of programs and services to address them. From roughly the beginning of the post–Civil War industrialization through the Great Depression, there was established a host of programs aimed at creating a working and community environment that would ensure healthy and productive employees while ameliorating the potentially disruptive conditions that undermined successful business. During this period housing was built for employees and their families, schools were established, churches were constructed, medical care was provided, pension funds were introduced, recreation centers were established, magazines were published, and profit sharing plans were introduced. In fact, programs corresponding to today's elaborate social welfare system were set up in just about every area. Even child care was introduced during this period. In some companies education began as early as six to eight weeks after birth, in company nursery schools—a convenience to mothers, as it freed them to work in the mills. "Taken together these practices compose what is known as welfare capitalism: by definition any service provided for the comfort or improvement of employees which was neither a necessity of the industry or required by law."[58] For many managers it was a pragmatic approach to ensuring that the goals of the workplace were carefully met by socializing (others would use harsher language) these new employees to the workplace. For some this required getting the laborers used to new habits of the workplace, to working inside, and to operating machines, which many workers feared would replace them. For others the challenge was to create a new order, and the programs and services were inspired by this philosophy.

The connection of work and family was not lost on the industrialists. By ignoring the family the industrialists could have been faced with a competing unit whose loyalty and energy could undermine the goals of production. The threat to family viability was equally feared. As Brandes points out, this focus of welfare capitalism on the home was not incidental.

Welfare strategy derived in part from a theoretical estimation of the root cause of distress in industrial society. The source of unrest, business believed, was the disruption of family life. They found evidence which indicated that as women and children swarmed to the factories in the early twentieth century and began to contribute to family support, husbands lost some of their viability as masters of the household and family bonds weakened. The results were likely to be upsetting to all concerned, including the employers.[59]

Through the activities of welfare capitalism, businesses attempted to circum-vent these growing realities and tried to co-opt the employee and the family to create one big, happy corporate family, united together at the workplace. The employer was trying to design strategies to organize and maximize labor and, at the same time, create an environment that was conducive to profits and productivity. Thus it was not surprising that some of the early capitalists found the family image so appealing; the factory was simply an extension of the family where employees would spend their productive time. For instance, a worker entering the employment of the Endicott Johnson Company received a booklet, the "E. J. Worker's First Lesson in the Square Deal," which declared, "You have now joined the Happy Family," and then went on to describe the nature of benefits and services that composed the contract of this square deal.[60] Like many other capitalists, Johnson tried to instill a sense of family in the business enterprise—an image of harmony, security, authority, and stability, values highly cherished by the company and ones it was eager to instill in its employees. It was a powerful metaphor, both a confining and a comforting image, one that promoted the internal resolution of conflict. The transposition of the employer into a father figure was aimed at making industrial protest and rebellion the equivalent of patricide. Seeking actively to cultivate the symbolic merge of family and firm, publications directed at workers were replete with pictures of families, children, babies, and homes.[61]

As one strategy for fostering the family image, many companies developed clubhouses, churches, libraries, and recreation facilities—all of which would provide some alternative to what was a dingy life for most factory workers. Social workers were hired to visit homes and attempt to remedy home and family problems. Some were like home economists, providing advice on how to keep the home and how to confront the problems of home life. Others would dispense such services as extending the convalescence of those who might be carrying a communicable disease or tracing the causes of a physical illness to social prob-lems. Some industries provided concrete goods such as food and fuel to tide a family over a rough period.

For a rapidly industrial and urban society corporate welfare often was all that existed in the absence of government programs, which had not yet been devel-oped. Because the extended family was unable to provide all that would be needed to get the industrialized family through difficult times, the company filled the role and brought relief and care to those in need. It is important to understand, however, that the development of industrial welfare programs resulted not from concern about the deleterious effects that factory life had on the workers and their families. Rather, industrialists of the time instituted these programs to address the perceived inadequacies in the existing labor force, which was not meeting the needs of the factory. Furthermore, social programs were conceived as one way to capture the loyalty of workers and their families, which could help to ensure the dominance and preeminence of the workplace. "By injecting itself into the private home and health lives of its employees, the company reinforced the bonds between family and firm and further strengthened the collective identity of the corporation."[62]

Welfare capitalism marked the beginning of a formal recognition of the relationship between the family and the workplace. To tame and socialize the family, and especially to avoid the rise of unionism, early industrialists believed that it was necessary to quickly set up the services and assistance that would facilitate the fulfillment of household functions compatible with the needs of industry. Welfare capitalism set the stage for what continues to be the struggle of balancing work needs and household needs.

Welfare capitalism reached a peak during the 1920s, when the nation was experiencing significant prosperity. A number of factors contributed to its demise, including the negative reaction of workers to the paternalism and control that their employers exercised over their lives, the rise of labor unions, the expansion of community services provided through the private sector, and the increased accessibility of the automobile, which enabled the worker to more easily commute to work from neighboring communities rather than live directly in factory towns. Welfare capitalism primarily met its demise, however, because of the downturn in the economy, the rise of unions, and the onset of the Great Depression.[63]

There were a number of changing dimensions in work/family relations during the period of industrialization that had an immediate impact on the family. In contrast to previous eras, the family was no longer the principal economic unit. The kin system, so critical to the survival and growth of families during colonial times, came under increasing strain as the workplace appeared to be deleterious to family systems. For most immigrants family ties became an essential resource for survival and facilitated their adaptation and integration into their new homeland. Often the kin system was the primary resource for families encountering such crises as the premature death of a family wage earner, lack of employment, and the inability of the family to earn sufficient income to cover basic needs.[64] Despite the radical changes in the activities of daily life, kin ties were essentially maintained. There is ample evidence that a high value continued to be placed on family needs, which often took precedence over personal needs. For example, it was not uncommon for one daughter to remain unmarried to ensure that someone would be able to care for aging parents.[65]

Many factories reinforced kin networks and used them for recruitment purposes. In the early days of capitalism it was typical for employees to find jobs for family members. This recruitment avenue was common among members of the immediate family, whereby parents would find jobs for their children, as well as for more distant relatives, and supervise them in quasi-apprenticeship arrangements.[66] Employees quickly bought into this system, since employment preferences shown by shop supervisors gave them a vested interest in employment opportunities for their kin. Almost all workers became convenient employment conduits for other relatives.[67]

The nuclear family experienced changes in its composition and structure during industrialization. Fertility rates declined during these years. One factor related to this decrease was the growing realization that young children, who need the attention and supervision of an adult who might otherwise obtain paid employment, were "expensive" to have. Before the 1800s, women typically experienced childbirth every two years between the ages of 23 and 42 years, having 7 or 8 children. By 1850, the children were farther apart in age and the mother might raise 5 or 6 children. By 1900, the mother might raise 3 or 4 children who were once again spaced closely together. Within one century, the emphasis had shifted from child bearing to child rearing.[68]

Family size was affected by mortality rates as well as by birth rates. Mortality rates for children continued to be high even in the beginning of the twentieth century. One out of every five children died before the age of marriage. During this era, over one-third of the households experienced the death of a parent before all of the children established independent homes.[69] Despite these grim statistics, the overall mortality rates began to show a decline beginning in 1850. Improvements in living and working conditions coupled with advances in medical technology produced dramatic reductions in mortality rates beginning at the turn of the century.

During this era it became the custom—at least among the wealthy class—to delay marriage or to remain single. For example, a 1914 survey of the prestigious women's colleges in the Northeast showed that fewer than 40 percent married. Similarly, of the male graduates of Harvard at that time, nearly a third were still single between the ages of 40 and 50.[70] The turn of the century brought with it new expectations for marriage. The movement away from the purely functional contract of colonial times continued. The rapid changes in the family and work roles for women affected the orientations of both men and women toward courtship and marriage; the importance of emotional and sexual fulfillment increasingly found its way into marital expectations. Courtships became more liberal, and mores about sexual behaviors more relaxed. Similarly, changes were observed in the expectations for the sexual relationship between married couples.[71]

A significant rise in divorce rates occurred during the industrial period despite the difficulty in obtaining such divorces. Census Bureau information indicates that among the 37 million Americans living in 1867, there were slightly less than 10,000 divorces. At the turn of the century the population had doubled, while the number of divorces rose by 500 percent to 55,751.[72] In response to this rising divorce rate there were a number of legislative efforts to make divorces harder to obtain at the turn of the century. "Despite their intent these restrictions made surprisingly little difference in the prevalence of divorce proceedings. In

the half century between 1870 and 1920 the number of divorces granted nationwide increased fifteen fold. By 1924 one marriage out of every seven ended in
divorce."[73]

The transitional nature of work and family roles during the industrial period
resulted in a situation where it was quite common for women to be either at
home, on the farm, or in the factory. Although the roles on the farm were
familiar, it was novel for women either to become paid workers or to be full-
time housewives. But many women did go off to work because low wages made
it necessary for as many family members as possible to seek employment. In
1870 women constituted 14.8 percent of the total labor force. This percentage
rose to 18.3 percent by 1900.[74] At the turn of the century 5 million women (20%
of all women) were in the labor force.[75] From 1880 to 1900 the number of
employed women doubled. From 1900 to 1919 the number increased by 50
percent. During the beginning of industrialization it was primarily the single
women who worked in the factories until they could marry.[76] For example, in
1900 just 6 percent of married women worked outside the home, but a third of
all widowed and divorced women were working.[77] Family economic conditions,
however, increasingly caused married women to join the labor force. By 1919
more than 25 percent of all women in the workforce were or had been married.[78]

Despite the need for extra income, most households still needed at least one
adult at home because the demands of the external worksite made it difficult for
most employed mothers to tend the children and manage the household responsibilities. In families where both parents worked child care was typically casual
and haphazard, and often was provided by older siblings, grandparents, or any
other relatives who were in a position to offer it. During this era there was a
decline in the number of households that retained servants;[79] these were out of
the question for working-class families. Some families responded to the need
for an adult at home by establishing three-generation households, and between
1850 and 1870 there was a rise in the number of extended families.[80]

Other families sought boarders, which brought in income and sometimes made
it possible for the mother to remain at home. Many women who were full-time
housewives earned extra money by accepting work that could be done at home
but that was sold in the market economy (called "outwork"), such as piecework
and laundering. As industrialization progressed, the older children (who became
principal family wage earners) tended to remain in the family residence for
additional years rather than establish an independent household.[81]

Regardless of their employment status, women continued to have significant
responsibilities for the management of the household. As households became
more separate from the workplace, a new concept of higher standards for cleanliness developed, often instilled by the industrialists. These new standards required a significant amount of time because the technological innovations
developed during this era did little to reduce the amount of time needed to do
housework. At the turn of the century a typical housewife spent six hours a day
on two principal tasks: preparing the meals and cleaning the house.[82] Even at

the end of the industrial era most families needed someone at home to take care of the house and the dependent family members. Because only families with sufficient economic resources could afford for the mother to be a full-time housewife, this evolved into a position of status for most women—something to strive for. Although women who were full-time housewives no longer participated in production and earning family income, they assumed a new role: consumers of economic goods.

Women's roles also began to expand beyond home and work as they assumed leadership roles in the community. It became acceptable for women to attend college. The political arena saw the widespread presence of women as they became involved with the social movements of the day. This expansion of women's roles reinforced the tendency for lower birth rates. In retrospect, the end of the industrial era marked the beginning of the women's movement. It was a time of a sexual revolution that resulted in changes in morals, dress, and behavior. It also signaled a new era for women as they began to fight for voting rights and equality. Women began to openly question the limitations of the roles that society had assigned them.

The feminist political philosophies of the time focused on the relationships between the home and work roles of women. Catherine Beecher was one of the spokeswomen who promoted the so-called haven strategy, which espoused the desirability of having women in charge of suburban homes. August Bebel was one of the proponents of the Marxist industrial strategy, which stated that the discrimination of women would end as they began to enter the workforce in increasing numbers. A third political approach, the strategy of material feminism, was articulated by Melusina "Fay" Pierce. This ideology identified the fact that women needed to establish new relations with household responsibilities and with work. Pierce suggested that women control and market their own labor, which could focus on the needs of the household. Experimental cooperatives were organized that accomplished the tasks of laundry, baking, and child care. These women tried to socialize housework and child care and then adapt it to the capitalist system by selling these services.

As the home increasingly became the exclusive domain for women, customs related to child-rearing changed. The time that fathers spent with their children continued to decrease, and they had little involvement with the rearing of their children. Mothers were given almost total responsibility for the children.[83] No longer were fathers seen as the routine disciplinarians of the children. Society did not hold the fathers of this era responsible for the moral development of children; mothers were now credited with the successes and failures of their offspring.

As was the case for their parents, the daily lives of children were markedly different for those living in working-class homes in contrast to those living in households with some economic security. Mothers in middle-and upper-class homes increasingly nurtured the developmental needs of their children and supported their growth and development. Encouraged to devote time to their education, teenagers spent an increasing number of years living in their parents' households. Working-class children often were loosely supervised. Although day care and nurseries were introduced to the United States during the years of industrialization, they were accessible only to a small number of families. Most families used this institutional care only as a last resort before they had to place the children in a home for children or abandon them. Some of the negative reactions to day care in today's society can be traced to these early origins when day care was designed for the poorest of the poor and families with overwhelming social problems.[84]

Children in many working-class families toiled in the factories. Although social reformers such as Jane Addams fought bitterly to overcome the laissez-faire economic principles that allowed the marketplace to override the unwritten contract that society has to protect its children, it was not until the World War I era that legislation regulating child labor was enacted. Child labor was certainly evident during previous historical periods when children on farms and in craft shops had worked alongside their parents and relatives. What was new was the environment of the factory, which introduced unusual, tragic burdens for working children. As large numbers of children were exploited and abused in factories, the atrocities associated with child labor became more visible. Furthermore, the employment of children conflicted with the growing recognition of the developmental needs of children. The end of industrialization marked the end of the economic functions assigned to children, who began to be free to grow and learn in preparation for their adulthood.

There was some irony in the impact that factory work had on teenagers and young adults. In previous eras many farm families with limited incomes were forced to apprentice all sons except the oldest, who would inherit the farm. With the advent of industrialization young adults had the option of staying with their families and continuing to contribute to their families' economic welfare. In contrast to most teenagers in subsequent historical periods, these young people had a significant economic role in the family. Studies of household budgets in the 1890s indicate that the earning of industrial workers peaked when the employee was in his or her thirties. The family income, however, continued to rise until the father was in his fifties, primarily as a result of the contribution of teenagers living at home. In those homes where the economic contributions of the children were essential, young adults often were expected to defer marriage, and did not establish independent households until their early 30s.[85] Young adults who assumed this financial responsibility typically sacrificed their education, and thus were confined to the laboring class for their own adult lives.

By the first three decades of the twentieth century the basic values related to work and family were being questioned. New ideas were being considered about ways to promote the fulfillment of men, women, and children.

By the beginning of the twentieth century, middle class families had been shorn of many traditional economic, educational and welfare functions. The family's role in education, in health care and in the care of the aged, poor and the mentally ill had increasingly been assumed by specialists and institutions outside the family. At the same time, however, the family had acquired new burdens and expectations. The middle class family was assigned primary responsibilities for fulfilling the emotional and psychological needs of its members.[86]

Even the existence of World War I did not seem to stem the tide away from this experimental attitude toward assuming work and family responsibilities. The next several decades, however, were to serve as a dampening force on this road to fulfillment and the balancing of work and family. The economic upheaval of the Depression and the social upheaval associated with World War II brought a sobering end to experimentation in these spheres of life. The new rules of the game of work and family had switched dramatically by 1950, and most of the more radical approaches to lifestyles went underground until the mid–1960s.

The role of government was introduced into the equation for the first time during this historical period. Up until the twentieth century the government had in effect been a silent partner in the effort to let the activities of the marketplace proceed without interference. In addition, the government's role was shaped by the desire to limit the intrusion of society into the sanctity of the family. But the downside of the industrialization process and its ravages on the family forced government to become a third force in the work/family equation. "The changes which took place in the realm of family law during the early years of the twentieth century constituted a revolution in public philosophy. The nation's courts and state legislatures declared that government had not merely a right but a duty to promote family welfare."[87]

The relationships, struggles, and conflicts between workers and employers and between families and the workplace grew out of this era. The period of industrialization served as a forerunner to the work/family conflicts that intensified in subsequent years.

DEPRESSION AND WORLD WAR II

The advent of the Great Depression, followed shortly afterward by World War II, constituted yet another chapter in the history of work/family dynamics. Just as this was a highly stressful and highly unusual period of time for the nation as a whole, so, too, it was an unusual happening for families and workplaces. The anomalies of these years make it a time of exception rather than of rule. People have always been willing to experiment during times of extreme stress. Clearly, people do what they have to survive.

Although this was a relatively brief period, it is separated out in this chapter both to understand the particulars of this era as well as to understand it as a precursor to the next era. It would be difficult to understand the 1950s and the reactionary characteristics of that time unless the effects of life during the depression and World War II are understood. In fact, the lifestyle of the fifties may have at least in part occurred in response to the economic and emotional hardships suffered during the thirties and early forties that exploded traditional work/family patterns. It is as if the generation moving into the 1950s needed to reassure themselves by massaging family life and insulating it from the outside world.

Depression Years

The depression was a disaster that did not respect traditional economic class boundaries. In previous eras poor and working-class families constantly struggled against the elements. Their economic future was almost always insecure. The needs of their children were secondary to the economic survival of the family, so the children typically worked, contributing what they could. In contrast, families with some economic security during the three centuries after colonization had gradually developed the luxury of experimenting with lifestyle alternatives that allowed family members to pursue self-fulfillment.

The aftershocks of the depression changed everything. The wealthy and the poor struggled together. The great promise of the industrial revolution to bring the good life to one and all had failed. The high costs of industrialization, with all of its trade-offs, had been made with a vision of continuous improvements in living standards for working men and women. But the gains of the previous era came tumbling down into this crucible in which men, women, and children all scurried to attain some economic survival of their families. The 1930 census indicated that one third of all American families had more than one wage earner and that one fourth had three or more household members bringing in needed revenue to the household. Part-time jobs for children supplemented their fathers' income as well.[88] A study by the Brookings Institution analyzed the income and savings of families in 1929, and found that almost 6 million families—21 percent of the population—had annual incomes of less than $1,000. In a situation in which income levels were so low, savings were next to impossible. In fact, 40 percent of the population had no reserves to fall back on when the depression hit.[89]

The scarcity of jobs created some unsettling developments at the workplace in terms of competition for employment. The newly developing roles for women were particularly affected as the job scarcity increased. In fact, female workers and racial minorities were the first to be fired or laid off during the depression of 1932.[90] The question of working mothers and wives became even more controversial, and found its way into print on more than one occasion. The following announcement, printed in the *Workers Daily Page*, provides one example:

If they [married women] were relieved of their duties, there would be steady employment for others. I am not unmindful of the fact that machines have changed much of our manner of working; one machine in many cases doing the work which three or four men formerly did. But what about the woman who works so that she may enjoy luxury? This is not considering the social side of the question—the matter of divorce, children roaming the streets, locked out of their homes when their mother is engaged in gainful employment. It is no wonder that our youth are responsible for so much crime today. The lack of adequate homelife has caused much of the crime among our young people. But I was only going to consider this problem from an economic standpoint. If the wife and mother were not working, the head of the house would of necessity have more steady work, and better pay. On the other hand, it has been my observation after years in the E.J. factory that the man who has a working wife does not do his best.[91]

Many working women during the depression were in a no-win situation. Their income was so desperately needed by their families, and they often were able to keep their jobs because, in comparison to men, their wages were depressed. These women, however, were subject to strong negative sanctions because they were seen as responsible both for taking jobs away from men and for a wide range of social problems.[92]

The depression not only upset the workers' contract with this new industrialization (which had pulled them off the farm and from foreign lands, away from their families and their agrarian life), but also overthrew the faith in the economic system on which the whole society was built. The adjustment to the workplace and then the subsequent absence of employment significantly altered the perceptions toward work and capitalism.

During the years of the depression a new player entered the work/family arena—the government. Although the government had started to assume some traditional family responsibilities during the early 1890s (e.g., juvenile delinquency programs and institutional programs for the disabled), these were designed only for the "less fortunate" members of society. The New Deal programs, which along with the war would pull the nation out of the depression, were the first social services provided by the government that supported the "average" American family.

Just as this period ended the nation was beginning to reassemble the pieces of the collapsed economy, but then another, equally traumatic event exploded on the American worker and his or her family—World War II.

World War II

The seemingly distant World War I was no model for the experience the United States would undergo during the first half of the 1940s. The mobilization of the nation with all of its resources, the fighting of a war on several fronts, and the building of the great American war machine were to transform the nation, its economy and workplace, and its people for the remainder of the Twentieth Century.

Whereas the quibbling over women working a decade earlier had placed questions about gender roles into the forefront, the war shifted the issue once again. Because the majority of able-bodied men were off to war, America's industries anxiously turned to women as the only available supply of labor. Thus, out of necessity, women in large numbers took on a range of new roles and responsibilities. Almost half of all women held a job outside the home at some point during the war. More than 6 million women were employed between 1940 and 1944, which represented an increase of 50 percent.[93] The taboo against a working wife that had been picking up a great deal of support during the previous decade, now gave way to practical patriotism. It is interesting that despite the obvious need for women to work, official government statements communicated society's ambivalence about working mothers and wives. For example, a 1942 statement issued by the U.S. War Manpower Commission reaffirmed that the first responsibility for women during these years of war was to their families and homes.[94] Despite this conflict in values, "Rosie the Riveter" became an important symbol.[95] In some way this change in women's roles altered forever the cultural prohibitions against women as part of the labor force.

This was a time of great stress for families. Whereas the previous generations had struggled with the migration of the husband and father from the land to the factory, the war brought with it a new type of separation, one that would occur for a significant period of time and that often had a severe impact on the family.

During the war, one-sixth of the nation's families suffered prolonged separation from sons, husbands and fathers. Four to five million "war widows" had to cook, clean laundry and bear children alone. Wartime migration added even greater stress. Wartime families faced a shortage of adequate housing and a lack of schools, hospitals and child care facilities. Frequent movement from one community to another weakened kinship ties, generated a sense of impermanence, and created severe problems of social and psychological adjustment. The widespread employment of women and teenagers and the relaxation of social constraints made familial stress an inevitable by product of the war abroad.[96]

Long periods of separation resulted in low rates of marriage and birth during the war years.[97]

The employment of women brought with it a need to care for children while the mothers were at work and the fathers were at war. A few child-care centers were established by the private sector in large companies. The response of the government, however, was mixed. Although the federal government spent more than $51 million on child care (matched by more than $26 million from state governments), it was estimated that only 40 percent of the children in need participated in these government-sponsored programs.[98] For the most part women had to scramble to make arrangements with grandparents, relatives, or neighbors for the care and supervision of their children. Other children were left to fend for themselves, harbingers of the modern-day latchkey children.

This largely maternal home and workforce was seen as a natural outcome of the discrete roles for men and women during wartime; women's dual roles of managing the household and employment were their contributions to patriotism. In contrast to many of the governments of U.S. allies, the U.S. government did little to acknowledge or assist these working women. In Britain the government was quite active in establishing public day-care centers, central kitchens, and rural retreats for working women and their children. Even employers in England were required to provide one afternoon per week off of work so that women workers could conduct the family shopping.[99]

The image of the patriotic mother and wife doing it all for her country exacted a toll. There were some documented signs of strain. Women in the large cities changed jobs twice as often as men, and were absent from work twice as much.[100] This may well reflect the stress in balancing their job and home life demands and the single parent role, which most of these women occupied. Families, mostly wives, were left to fend for themselves and to own these stresses as part of the war effort.

After the war and the return of men to their homes and to the factories, life abruptly changed again and a new definition of work/family relations was developed. Men walked back into both the home and the workplace as if nothing had changed. Women were urged to leave their jobs to make room for the returning veterans. Employers, however, found that some women wanted to retain their jobs, even if they were demoted to lower-paying positions, and that a new work ethic felt by women was emerging.[101]

Not unlike the alcoholic family adjusting to sobriety after years of disruption, the family members were under severe stress and strain; their return to previous roles and expectations was difficult at best. This was reflected in the explosion in divorce rates immediately after the war. From 1940 to 1944 the divorce rate rose from sixteen per one hundred marriages to twenty-seven per one hundred marriages. By the end of the war another 500,000 marriages ended in divorce, and by early 1946, with only half of the soldiers having returned home, another 200,000 were involved in divorce proceedings.[102] "By 1950 as many as a million GIs were divorced. When combined with a relatively high number of divorces among Americans who had not gone to war, the result was an epidemic of divorces unprecedented in American history. Whereas in 1940 one marriage in six had ended in divorce, by 1946 the figure worsened to one in four."[103]

The end of the war marked the transition point for GIs and their families. The marriage boom instantly created large masses of newly established families. Housing was extremely scarce and cramped, so that many young couples lived with relatives and doubled up as a coping device. As husbands joined the workforce (and attended universities courtesy of the GI bill), the family was firmly established as a nurturing environment—seemingly separate from the harsh world of business.

Postwar Era

The 1950s are thought of as a time of high conformity. To some extent this was true, since at least on the surface everyone seemed to be doing much the same thing. If one were to have driven up and down the streets of Levittown during this time, one would have seen families becoming the quintessence of the nuclear family: Dad heading off to work, and Mom standing in front of their track house waving a fond farewell and then stepping inside to continue her busy day of raising the children and making sure the household was well managed (and impeccably clean). This scene was repeated up and down the street and across the country. It seemed as if this was really the only possible lifestyle.

People who were young adults during this era belonged to age cohorts that suffered unusual stresses during their lifetime. As young children they witnessed, directly or indirectly, the impacts of the Great Depression. They and their family members fought—and died—in World War II. Having survived these two cataclysmic events, this generation was looking for some respite, and tried to create a haven within which it could insulate itself from life's cruelties. The advent of television reflected these times quite well. The hits of the day, such as "Leave It to Beaver," "Ozzie and Harriet," "Father Knows Best," and "Donna Reed," all featured safe and secure families whose little problems could always be solved within twenty-five minutes and whose resolutions returned them to the tranquility of life in their homes.

The desirability of suburbia was central to this idealized and standardized life for the middle class. Young families literally flocked to newly built towns from which the fathers could commute to the cities and in which the children could be left in their yards to play safely. During the postwar period of 1948 to 1958, 13 million homes were constructed; 85 percent of these were in the suburbs.[104]

The creation of the suburban family, which was one of the hallmarks of this era, helped to reinforce the appearance of separate worlds of work and home. By 1960 as many people would live in the suburbs as lived in the central cities. This marked a radically new community structure, one that also reflected the growing affluence in the nation. The suburban lifestyle delineated during the fifties solidified the concepts of the separation of work and home according to gender that had begun to develop early during the process of industrialization. The availability of GI loans finally made it possible for many people in the rapidly growing middle class to simultaneously own a home and be able to support the family on the earnings of just the husband.

Even though the fifties are notable for this so-called traditional lifestyle, it was not traditional at all from a historical perspective. A quick glimpse at just a few demographics indicate just how much this time period differed from the patterns established in the historical eras that preceded it. Counter to longstanding trends, young adults got married younger, established independent households sooner, had their children earlier and had more of them, lived further away from relatives, and moved more frequently. Although it may have seemed that everything was in a "steady state," the fifties actually represented a quiet revolution because in effect it did not resemble anything of the past.

Until the 1940s fertility rates had been constantly falling and marriage rates had begun to fall off, while divorce, employment and household formation rates had been constantly rising. Had the 1940s and 1950s not happened, today's young adults would appear to be behaving normally. Their family formation would reflect a continuation of historical trends. However, when the benchmark chosen to judge the family pattern of today's young adults is that of their parents' generation, those born since 1940 do appear deviant. . . . But it was the parents' generation that deviated from historical trends."[105]

Life during the postwar years is characterized by increased social mobility, rising incomes, consumerism, and noticeably more leisure time. In an effort to succeed at work and to accept promotional transfers young families were more receptive to moving away from family and friends. The long-awaited dream of a home finally became a reality, came within reach for most of the rapidly growing middle class.

Even though the worlds between work and home appeared to be quite separate, the world of Whyte's classic text on the organizational man spoke directly to the power and influence of the American corporation in socializing the family into corporate life. What was good for General Motors was not only good for the country, but it was good for the family as well. The nuclear family constituted an essential support system for the male breadwinner and the company. Its role was to be ever ready to bend, sway, and adapt to whatever the company needed for its operational efficiency.

The apparent separation of work and home during this postwar period made it possible for many people to deny the existence of work/family conflicts. "Although the tension between work and family life has been recognized for some time, it could be masked, at least in part, when each family had two adults and one, the woman, was expected to be at home. With both parents working outside the home, the tension between the two domains has become more visible. When there is only one parent, and he or she is in the labor force, the tension may be overwhelming."[106]

Despite the fact that life at work during the fifties proceeded as if it had no relation to the family, it was during this era that U.S. corporations began to tentatively acknowledge the existence of the employee's family with the establishment of benefits. Although these benefits had been created during World War II as a means to circumvent the constraints of wartime and postwar wage freezes, they became an important link in work/family relations.

Family structure and marital behavior also were to undergo changes. The age of marriage, for example, fell to a record low. The 1950s experienced dramatic shifts from the previous eras when men would postpone marriage until their late twenties and women were typically in their midtwenties when they wed; however, the average age of marriage during the 1950s dropped to 22 for men and 20 for women.[107] A small minority of women (just 4%) were not married during their childbearing years.[108] By the late 1950s 70 percent of all women were married, compared to 42 percent in 1940 and 50 percent today.[109] During the postwar years marriage was "fashionable"; the rush to the altar was a major contributor to the baby boom that occurred during the next decade.

Just like the other demographic profiles of this era, the divorce rate deviated from long-term historical trends. The divorce rates in the fifties represented the lowest rate of increase during this century, and were in dramatic contrast to the leaps in the rates during and immediately after World War II. Despite this leveling off of divorce, not every home experienced continual marital bliss during these years. In fact, between one fourth and one third of all marriages that were contracted during the fifties ultimately ended in divorce.[110] In addition, because the stigma of divorce was exceptionally strong during this period, many marriages unofficially dissolved. Nearly 2 million men and women lived apart from their spouses, and many of those who lived together were unhappy. Public opinion polls reported that about 20 percent of all couples rated themselves "unhappy in their marriage" and another 20 percent reported only "medium happiness."[111] Despite the popular and romanticized image of the fifties family exaggerated by the newly discovered media of television, the reality was that life was not completely satisfactory for many people.

Family size began to grow during these years; high fertility rates produced the baby boom. Data from the Census Bureau indicates that in 1935, the birthrate for women between 15 and 44 years of age was 77.2 live births per 1,000 women. By 1955 this rate had increased to 118.5.[112] The baby boom reached its high point in 1957—a year when 4.3 million babies were born.[113]

It should be noted, however, that household size (in comparison to family size) continued its downward trend during the fifties because of a new and growing phenomena: the emergence of one-and two-person households. Even the dramatic increase in the number of families having four, five, or even more children did not offset the trend toward small household sizes.[114]

There was a growing tension between the fifties ideal of women's central role in family life and employment. Although women had begun to work once again in increasing numbers as the decade progressed, they were typically reluctant to develop any significant attachment to their work. In this sense, middle-class women would almost apologetically state that they did not have to work, but it provided them with a little fun money. This attitude prevailed despite the fact that almost 25 percent of all wives worked in 1950; nearly 12 percent of married women with preschoolers were in the labor force during the beginning of this decade.[115]

Women's roles, not surprisingly, stood in stark contrast to those of the war years, and in fact to those of all previous eras. The place of the wife in the home contributed to this unique family configuration. Behind the ideal, however, there was considerable conflict. For example, the Kinsey Report of 1953 offered one insight into the discrepancy that existed between the public image of women and the private reality. It reported that one half of the women had had intercourse before marriage and 25 percent had had extramarital affairs.[116]

The discontent of women also was reflected in their limited career choices. Despite often having similar educational backgrounds as men, women were not given the same opportunities for employment options. Most of the women who did work were restricted to such jobs as teacher, nurse, household help, clerical worker, and saleshelp.[117] A woman's place was in the home; studies showed that the housewife of the fifties spent more time on housework than either her mother or grandmother had. This was particularly true for women in metropolitan areas. A 1945 survey revealed that although the typical farm housewife spent sixty hours a week on housework, her big-city counterpart averaged more than eighty hours a week.[118]

Suburban life seemed especially well designed for the needs of young children. This era was the time of Dr. Spock, and many homes tried to develop an environment appropriately matched to the needs of their growing children. The postwar period accelerated the trend of focusing on the developmental needs of children and providing them with quite prescribed norms for their socialization.

By the end of the fifties 70 percent of U.S. households were families like those portrayed on television, with the father as breadwinner, the mother as housewife, and the children present in the home. Over the next two decades such dramatic shifts and changes took place within society at large that less than 15 percent of the households fit this fifties family type.[119] Even by the early 1960s twice as many women were working outside the home as there were before the war in 1940. These were not career-driven women, but wives and mothers who more than likely worked part-time to help supplement family income and put children through college. This trend was supported by the inflation of the 1970s, which compelled many wives to join their husbands to keep the real family income at the same level. The end of the two decades of the fifties and sixties saw the quickening of the two-earner families and the breakdown of the stereotypes of Dad as breadwinner and Mom as housewife.

As the necessity for dual-earner couples increased, there was no parallel movement within other social institutions to help families and their children adjust to the new realities of work and home life. It was not until well into the 1980s that the crisis in caregiving was fully appreciated as the rush for child care confronted both families pressed for economic reasons and companies struggling to attract and keep employees in an increasingly competitive labor pool. In addition, the full range of dependent-care issues became even more pronounced as long-term care of the elderly and the care for giving parents came up against the absence of caregiving daughters in the home. The men and women of the eighties not only had to unshackle themselves from the roles and socializations of their past, but also had to struggle to create effective vehicles for meeting their family and economic needs. This marked the entrance into the current era in which conflicts between the home and the workplace, put in the context of the larger society, continue to bump up against outmoded policies, insensitive institutions, and, in general, a society that is neither equipped nor willing to acknowledge ownership and deal with these conflicts.

CONCLUSION

The conflicts of work and home, although present throughout the history of the country, now begin to confront both the needs of the family and the demands of an increasingly competitive marketplace. Whereas the early colonists were able to work out conflicts at home, and the industrialists created services, programs, and policies to control the problems of the new workers, the later decades of the twentieth century are struggling with the roles and responsibilities of three independent, but interrelated sectors: the family, the corporation, and the government. It is the delicate interrelations between these three that will determine this era's response to this perennial problem. How these sectors will respond is yet to be seen. In an attempt to avoid costly and stressful work/family dissonance, it will be necessary to untangle the complexity of values, roles, and responsibilities—many of which have longstanding historical roots.

The focus of work/family relations in the 1990s is unique in that the longevity of people has resulted in a situation in which we currently have three generations of adults living who grew up in totally different worlds and who lived as young adults under very different circumstances. One might expect that the values and lifestyles of these three generations can be quite different. By the time the baby boomers have reached their midlife adult years, it might well seem to their parents and their grandparents that the sense of order in work/family relations (with which they had been familiar) had turned to chaos.

Three very different generations of adult Americans are now exerting their force simultaneously to pull and tug at the very foundations of traditional family and household structure. The older generations, born 1920 or before and age 60 or over in 1980, survived the Great Depression. Most have been through two world wars, many were immigrants or sons and daughters of immigrants, and all were born at a time when over half of the U.S. population was rural. They married late, had small families, and today many live alone. The middle generation, born between 1920 and 1940 and age 40 to 59 in 1980, entered adulthood during a period of optimism and affluence . . . Its members married early, bought large cars and houses, gave witness to civil rights, and had babies. Many in this generation are now in the empty nest stage of their lives and many are divorced. The younger generation is made up of the babies born during the "boom years" that began in World War II. They have begun to settle down in the central cities and small towns, two areas abandoned by their parents. More of the women have put independence and work before marriage and childbearing, and men and women are better educated than earlier generations. In these and other ways this younger group of adults stands in sharp contrast to its parents and grandparents.[120]

To achieve a sense of balance between work and family creative solutions will need to be developed that match the current social realities with changing family and corporate needs.

APPENDIX

Some of the changes in work/family relations that have occurred within specified time periods were outlined in Chapter 3. Many significant changes span several eras and can best be identified as historical trends.

Population Characteristics

The longer life spans experienced by today's Americans has resulted in an increase in the median age of the general population. Today the median age is 30 years, but in 1800 it was almost half of this, just 16 years.[121] The steadily increasing longevity of Americans has indirectly affected a number of dimensions of work/family roles and relations.

Because people are living longer, there has been an expansion in some of the developmental phases of their lives. Childhood has been lengthened, adolescence as a unique phase of development has emerged, young adulthood is now perceived as the entire decade of the twenties, the middle-age years have an expanded span of thirty-five years, and, perhaps most obviously, the senior years often last for two decades rather than for just a few years, as during colonial days. This flattening out of the human development cycle has caused a delay in some of the milestones of life. For example, the age of marriage and the age when the first child is born are postponed. In addition, the activities associated with each developmental phase are attenuated. Children are spending more years in education, adults are spending more years as workers, and the number of years that people spend in retirement are increasing.

Household Size

One of the most visible signs of change in American lifestyle is the decrease in the number of people per household. It is interesting to note that this is the continuation of a long-term trend, started as far back as 1790, when the mean was 5.79 persons. The mean in 1900 had declined by about one person to 4.76. By 1940 the mean had further declined to 3.67. By 1978 the average household had less than three persons (2.81).[122] Whereas very large households of seven or more persons were common in 1790 and comprised more than one third of all households (35.8%), they became an anomaly by 1970, with only 5.1 percent of all households having this many members.[123]

Perhaps more significant is the increase in the percentage of one-person households during this period. In 1790 only 3.7 percent of all households were one-person households. One hundred seventy years later, in 1960, this had increased close to 10 percentage points (13.1% of all households). During the next eighteen-years (1978), however, the proportion of one-person households had increased to 22.0 percent.[124]

Household Composition

Many of the work/family conflicts that emerged during the eighties are related to the fact that the adults in the household simply do not have sufficient time to get everything done. The fact that adults are precariously balancing both work and home responsibilities is exacerbated by the fact that there are fewer adults in the typical household in comparison to homes of the past. Even as recently as the turn of this century it was common for children to grow up in homes in which adults other than parents would be present, including boarders, servants, adult siblings, relatives, and even family friends.[125] In 1900 one of every ten households employed domestic help. By the 1980s this number diminished to one of every one hundred households.[126] In contrast, one or two adults in the household now assume full responsibility for home tasks.

Marriage

Up until the seventies it had been the trend during the twentieth century for both men and women to marry at earlier ages. From 1890 to 1950 the age of marriage for men had declined from 26.1 years to 22.8 years and for women from 22.0 years to 20.3 years.[127] The increase in the median age for the first marriage during the past two decades has been a deviation from this trend.

Perhaps a more dramatic statistic associated with current American Lifestyles is the number of adults who remain single. The rate of unmarried women between ages 30 and 44 is projected to rise to 15.2 percent by 1995. This seems quite high in contrast to the low 1970 rate of 7.49 percent.[128] Data documenting the long-term historical trends associated with adults who remain single provide a context for understanding today's rate of unmarried adults. Despite the media attention paid to the burgeoning numbers of a single adults, this is not the only time in history when there has been a high rate of adults who are not married. During 1890, for example, 15.15 percent of women aged 30 to 44 were never married, representing a rate similar to that of today.[129]

It is important to point out that the causes for remaining single have varied throughout the ages. During the industrial era some women elected to remain single so that they would be available to care for aging parents. At other points in history high rates of single women follow war years. Furthermore, the lifestyles of single adults varied during different historical periods. Before 1950 single adults of all ages were less likely to establish independent households, and more likely to share residence with some relative.

Today there are some relevant questions associated with prolonged single life. Are today's young people placing a higher value on work than on the family? What is the quality of life of an adult who does not have the experience of marrying and establishing a family? What are the effects of the more temporary, intimate relationships established by adults outside of marriage?

Divorce

There has been a great deal of public debate about the dramatic rise in the U.S. divorce rate in the past two decades, which had increased only slowly in previous historical periods. Without minimizing the importance of understanding the impact of divorce on members of society, it is interesting to use a historical perspective to consider the extent of today's disrupted marriages. In 1890, for example, the marriages of 23 percent of all 14- to 34-year-olds were disrupted by either death or divorce (with death accounting for nearly all of these).[130] It becomes apparent that throughout America's history, families have had to make adjustments to marital disruptions.

As recently as 1940 barely 1 percent of all men and women experienced divorce, and by 1970 less than 3 percent of women and 4 percent of men had been involved in a divorce.[131] Close to two thirds of all marriages that occur today will end in separation or divorce. "Between the late '70s and early '80s, the proportion of marriages that broke up within 5 years rose by about 5% for first and by more than 10 percent for second marriages."[132] Today significant controversy exists over the effects of divorce on the adults, the children, and the family system at large. It is becoming clear tht divorce also can impact the workplace, since workers under stress may suffer productivity losses. In addition, some employers are becoming more visible actors in divorced families as they comply with court orders to set aside parental earnings for child support payments.

Children

Much attention has been paid to the phenomenon of today's women postponing their families or, in some cases, choosing not to have children. This stands in stark contrast to their parents, who produced the baby boom. It is consistent, however, with the behavior of their grandparents and with long-term historical trends toward smaller families. A white woman in 1800 typically had more than seven children; her counterpart in 1900 had half that—3.56 children. The birthrate decreased by another third by 1929.[133] The high fertility rates of the baby boom years were inconsistent with this trend toward decreasing the birthrate rather than today's low rates. "[Forty] percent or more of . . . women born in the 1950s may end up childless or with only one child. This figure compares with 20 percent or less for the high fertility mothers of the middle generation, and 43 percent for women born 1906–1910 who represent the older generation is low fertility."[134]

Labor Force Participation

A glimpse at historical statistics shows not only that increasing percentages of women have been part of the labor force over the past one hundred years, but also that the change in participation rates has most significantly affected married women. For example, whereas 40.5 percent of all single women were in the labor force in 1890, this percentage increased just 10 percentage points to 50.9 percent by 1970. Only 4.6 percent of married women in 1890 reported employment. By 1970 this had increased tenfold to 40.2 percent.[135] Just ten years later employment rates for married women had jumped again to nearly 60 percent.[136]

NOTES

1. Groves and Groves, p. 157.
2. Seward, p. 64.
3. Mintz and Kellogg, pp. 21–23.
4. Zussman, p. 338.
5. Axinn and Levin, p. 18.
6. Steinmetz, pp. 170–171.
7. See Seward, pp. 44, 52.
8. Mintz and Kellogg, p. 13.
9. Ibid., p. 2.
10. Ibid., p. 37.
11. *Editorial Research Reports on the Changing American Family*, p. 12.
12. Mintz and Kellogg, p. 12.
13. Ibid.
14. *Editorial Research Reports*, p. 12; Seward, p. 50.
15. Seward, p. 57.
16. Mintz and Kellogg, 19.
17. Seward, p. 54.
18. Demos, p. 133.
19. William Kephart in *Editorial Research Reports*, p. 12.
20. See Cowan, p. 165.
21. Demos, p. 133.
22. *Editorial Research Reports*, p. 13.
23. Groves and Groves, p. 149.
24. Mintz and Kellogg, p. 61.
25. Alice Kessler-Harris in Sidel, p. 49.
26. Cowan, p. 165.
27. Sidel, p. 49.
28. Demos, p. 133.
29. Axinn and Levin, p. 20.
30. Ibid.
31. Kett, p. 245.
32. Mintz and Kellogg, p. 23.
33. United States Bureau of the Census, *Historical Statistics of the United States*, "Labor Force, Gainful Workers, by Age, Sex, and Farm-Nonfarm Occupations," p. 134.
34. Mintz and Kellogg, p. 50.
35. Ibid., p. 43.
36. *Editorial Research Reports on the Changing American Family*, p. 13.
37. Mintz and Kellogg, p. 56.

38. Calhoun, p. 109.
39. Deetz, pp. 121–122.
40. Mintz and Kellogg, p. 63.
41. Sidel, p. 49.
42. Epstein, p. 95.
43. *Editorial Research Reports on the Changing American Family,* p. 13.
44. Mintz and Kellogg, p. 56.
45. United States Bureau of the Census, *Historical Statistics of the United States,* "Annual Estimates of the Population," p. 42.
46. Kett, p. 232.
47. Mintz and Kellogg, p. 64.
48. Ibid.
49. Mintz and Kellogg, p. 96.
50. United States Bureau of the Census, *Historical Statistics of the United States,* "Labor Force, Gainful Workers," p. 134.
51. Mintz and Kellogg, p. 135.
52. Ibid., pp. 84–85.
53. Ibid., p. 84.
54. Wilinski and LeBeau, p. 28.
55. Sidel, pp. 51–52.
56. Mintz and Kellogg, p. 95.
57. Brandes, p. 2.
58. Ibid., pp. 5–6.
59. Ibid., p. 34.
60. Zahavi, p. 20.
61. Ibid., p. 46.
62. Ibid., p. 49.
63. Kamerman and Winston, p. 152.
64. Hareven, "The Dynamics of King in an Industrial Community," p. 73.
65. Mintz and Kellogg, p. 88.
66. Harevan, *Family Time and Industrial Time,* p. 2.
67. Zahavi, p. 69.
68. Mintz and Kellogg, p. 51.
69. Ibid., p. 104.
70. Ibid., p. 110.
71. *Editorial Research Reports on the Changing American Family,* p. 14.
72. Ibid.
73. Mintz and Kelloggg, p. 109.
74. United States Bureau of the Census, *Historical Statistics of the United States,* Gainful Workers, "Labor Force," p. 134.
75. Abel, p. 7.
76. Mintz and Kellogg, p. 111.
77. United States Bureau of the Census, *Historical Statistics of the United States,* Marital Status of Women in the Civilian Labor Force," p. 133.
78. Mintz and Kellogg, p. 111.
79. Ibid., p. 124.
80. Seward, p. 106.
81. Ibid.

82. Mintz and Kellogg, pp. 89–90.
83. Cowan, p. 166.
84. Sidel, pp. 118–119.
85. Owen, pp. 92–93.
86. Mintz and Kellogg, pp. 107–108.
87. Ibid., p. 128.
88. Sharf, pp. 147–148.
89. Axinn and Levin, p. 176.
90. Fernandez, p. 7.
91. Zahavi, p. 74.
92. Sidel, p. 55.
93. Ibid., p. 56.
94. Ibid., p. 119.
95. Fernandez, p. 8.
96. Mintz and Kellogg, p. 174.
97. *Editorial Research Reports on the Changing American Family,* p. 15.
98. Sidel, p. 119.
99. Mintz and Kellogg, p. 164.
100. Ibid.
101. Fernandez, p. 8.
102. Mintz and Kellogg, p. 171.
103. Ibid.
104. Ibid., p. 183.
105. Masnick and Bane, p. 2.
106. Kamerman, "Meeting Family Needs, p. 1.
107. Mintz and Kellogg, p. 179.
108. *Editorial Research Reports on the Changing American Family,* p. 15.
109. Mintz and Kellogg, p. 179.
110. Ibid., p. 194.
111. Ibid.
112. United States Bureau of the Census, *Historical Statistics of the United States,* "Birth Rate-Total and for Women 15–44 Years Old, by Race," p. 49.
113. *Editorial Research Reports on the Changing American Family,* p. 15.
114. Masnick and Bane, p. 19.
115. United States Bureau of the Census, *Historical Statistics of the United States,* "Married Women (Husband Present) in the Labor Force, by Age and Presence of Children," p. 134.
116. Mintz and Kellogg, p. 201.
117. Sidel, pp. 60–61.
118. Mintz and Kellogg, p. 195.
119. Ibid., p. 203.
120. Masnick and Bane, pp. 10–11.
121. United States Bureau of the Census, *Historical Statistics of the United States,* "Median Age of Population, by Race, Sex, and Nativity," p. 19.
122. Masnick and Bane, p. 19.
123. United States Bureau of the Census, *Historical Statistics of the United States,* "Households, by Number of Persons," p. 42.
124. Masnick and Bane, pp. 18–19.

125. Ibid., p. 24.

126. Owen, p. 110.

127. United States Bureau of the Census, *Historical Statistics of the United States*, "Median Age at First Marriage, by Sex," p. 19.

128. Masnick and Bane, pp. 27–29, 129.

129. Ibid.

130. United States Bureau of the Census, *Historical Statistics of the United States*, "Marital Status of the Population, by Age and Sex," p. 20.

131. United States Bureau of the Census, *Historical Statistics of the United States*, "Marital Status of the Population," p. 20.

132. Furstenberg, p. 20:3.

133. Mintz and Kellogg, p. 110.

134. Masnick and Bane, p. 40.

135. United States Bureau of the Census, *Historical Statistics of the United States*, "Marital Status of Women," p. 133.

136. Mintz and Kellogg, p. 204.

Chapter 4

JOB AND HOMELIFE STUDY

The major purpose of this chapter is to present the findings of one of the first research projects to examine work/family stress from within the corporation. Although much has been written about the work/family issues in the public media, there has been relatively little empirical data to support the anecdotal material that increasingly is found in popular journalism. As things had begun to dramatically change in relation to household composition, the influx of women into the workplace, and the emptying out of geographical communities, work- places were just beginning to address the phenomenon. In fact, when the idea of carrying out this research was first broached with one of the *Fortune* 100 companies in 1984, it was most revealing that the company had no experience in examining the changing workforce or future trends. These findings are now more than five years old, but they still represent a broad-scale picture of 1,600 employees who responded to a lengthy questionnaire that covered much of their work/family interactions, issues, and conflicts. The focus of the study was to examine how work and home lives interact with each other in the context of two major corporations. Earlier research had focused almost exclusively on either the home or the workplace, with the prevailing assumption that the two sectors were separate spheres, one having little to do with the other. What research that did exist usually took place outside of work environments and with the primary focus on how work impacted home life. The later investigation expanded the research question to look at how family factors influence work life as well as how work influences family life. This interactional dynamic reflects the struggle of most families today.

Much of the data in this chapter was first reported in a monograph, *Boston University Balancing Job and Homelife Study,* Dianne S. Burden and Bradley Googins, Boston University, 1986. A full description of the study design and methodology can be found in this monograph.

STUDY SITES

Two corporations were selected for the study to better generalize and compare findings. The two sites represent quite different workforces and work cultures, but both were *Fortune* 500 companies, and thus representative of large, corporate workforces.

Company A was a large public utility located in the Northeast and had a cross section of white-collar and blue-collar employees. It had a number of active unions, and at the time of the study had neither policies nor programs relative to dependent care.

Three work sites were selected for the study. Site A was a site in which primarily professional staff and managers were employed. Site B was a sales and clerical site, and site C, a site of blue-collar craftsmen and semiskilled technical employees. A total of 1,249 employees were provided with a questionnaire, of whom 711 returned usable questionnaires (response rate = 57%).

Company B was a high-technology firm with worldwide operations. Sites in the Northeast were selected in two states. It had a heightened interest in dependent care, but no policies or program initiatives at the time of the study.

Five work sites were studied. Two of the work sites were primarily managerial and professional, with a number of skilled engineers and financial personnel. Many of these employees had a great deal of travel responsibility, which was one of the reasons this site was selected. The other three sites were primarily blue and pink-collar sites. All three were responsible for customer service and had large warehouse facilities as well as telephone operators. A total of 1,280 questionnaires were sent out, and a response of 854 usable questionnaires were returned (response rate = 67%).

FINDINGS

Workforce Demographics

The respondent populations for both companies were full-time employees who were representative of the total company populations in most demographic characteristics. Tables 4.1 and 4.2 summarize respondent characteristics. There was a slightly larger percentage of female respondents than the percentage of women in the overall corporation population. This would not be true if the study were conducted now. The so-called service industry has brought a significantly higher proportion of women into the labor market, and in both these companies new employees hired even in the few years since the survey has been conducted has significantly increased the number of women employees.

The respondents' educational levels were slightly higher than the national average. This was primarily because of the respondents in Company B, where the high-technology environment tended to attract a significantly higher proportion of employees with college and graduate educations. The percentage of

Table 4.1

Breakdown of Study Respondents by Gender, Age, and Marital Status (Response Rate = 63%)

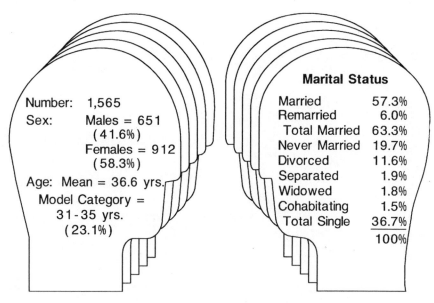

Number: 1,565

Sex: Males = 651 (41.6%)

Females = 912 (58.3%)

Age: Mean = 36.6 yrs.

Model Category = 31-35 yrs. (23.1%)

Marital Status

Married	57.3%
Remarried	6.0%
Total Married	63.3%
Never Married	19.7%
Divorced	11.6%
Separated	1.9%
Widowed	1.8%
Cohabitating	1.5%
Total Single	36.7%
	100%

nonwhite respondents, although lower than the percentage of nonwhites in the population, was somewhat higher than the percentage of nonwhite employees in each corporation. This represents a glaring weakness of the study. Although the study population does reflect both regional and corporate data, it does not represent the national workforce in this particular regard. A second study is now in the developmental and planning stages to expand and partially replicate the study by conducting the survey in more geographically and racially disperse populations of the company. The percentage of managers was significantly higher than one would expect within a corporation because of the purposive sampling strategy utilized in site selection (i.e., two sites were chosen specifically because they were management and professional sites).

When managers were assessed by gender, more than half the men but fewer than one-third of the women were managers. This differential reflects the imbalance found throughout most corporations in the proportions of men and women in decision-making positions.

The study was particularly interested in examining differences in work/family issues among marital and parental status categories (see Table 4.3) Respondents were divided into six categories according to whether they were married or single, male or female, or parents or nonparents. For purposes of the study the category for parents was determined to be those employees with children 18 years or younger. Those with children over age 18 were put in the nonparent

Table 4.2
Breakdown of Study Respondents by Education and Ethnicity

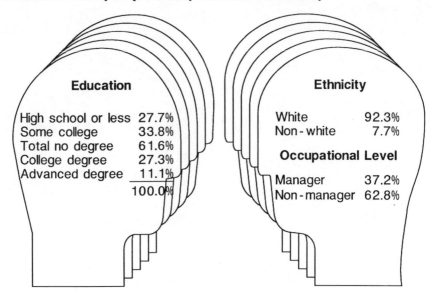

Education	
High school or less	27.7%
Some college	33.8%
Total no degree	61.6%
College degree	27.3%
Advanced degree	11.1%
	100.0%

Ethnicity	
White	92.3%
Non-white	7.7%

Occupational Level	
Manager	37.2%
Non-manager	62.8%

Table 4.3
Marital and Parental Status Categories

	Percent of respondents
Married Female Parents	15.5%
Married Male Parents (Spouse employed)	14.0%
Married Male Parents (Spouse non-employed)	8.7%
Single Female Parents	6.8%
Single Male Parents	2.6%
Married Female Non-Parents	15.8%
Married Male Non-Parents (Spouse employed)	6.8%
Married Male Non-Parents (Spouse non-employed)	2.3%
Single Female Non Parents	20.3%
Single Male Non-Parents	7.2%
	100.0%

(n = 1,565)

category. This arbitrary cutoff was made to assess the impact of work/family on parents who had primary dependent care responsibilities rather than on those who exclusively had older children whose maturation required less dependent care activity. It could be argued that this period might be even more stressful for some parents, but for this study it was important to examine employees whose children were of school age. Thus the artificial definition. Married men were further divided into subgroups according to spouse employed or nonemployed.

The ten marital and parental status categories that resulted appear in Table 4.3. This unit of analysis is referred to throughout the book.

This breakdown by category provides graphic evidence of the changing demographics not only of the workforce, but also of the American family. The so-called traditional household of the father at work and the mother at home with the children is anything but typical in these workforces. Reflecting the national trend data, married employees with spouse not employed constituted only 11 percent of the sample. The vast majority of employees at both companies are from dual-earner families (52%). Although the data on dependent care other than child care is minimal in the study, it is clear that most employees have to deal with the multiple responsibilities of job and home. Solely from the perspective of child care, 47 percent of the employees have children aged 18 years or younger.

The single male parents are men who have custodial responsibility for their children. Because this is a relatively rare phenomenon, they are a very small group, although they are distinct from the other categories and thus are reported here. Because their numbers are not significant enough statistically to make comparisons with the other categories, sometimes they can be misleading in terms of drawing firm conclusions. Nevertheless, they will continue to be reported, but without inferences beyond their numbers.

As the analysis of family characteristics of the workforce indicated repeatedly at all sites, only 11 percent of the workforce are married men with wives at home, and only 8.7 percent are the traditional family of married male *parent* with wife at home. The great majority of employees are either dual-earner couples or single. Most workers are, therefore, faced with the demands of balancing job and home responsibilities. Results also indicated that the small minority of married men with wives at home are disproportionately represented in upper-management, high-salaried positions (see Table 4.4). In other words, those making the management decisions and setting human resources policy for the workforce may have little firsthand knowledge of the lifestyles and multiple job and home life responsibilities of the great majority of their employees.

There is great speculation driven by a hopeful optimism that corporate managers whose behaviors and decisions shape corporate culture and the programs and policies, such as those of dependent care, will experience radical changes as the next generation takes over the corporate reins. Because their wives represent the dual-career and working wives model, these managers will be socialized and influenced by a different set of normative guidelines. At least that is how the thinking goes. There is more optimism than research findings to fuel this contention.

Survey Results

To best maximize the research findings, the data are organized under four major headings. These constitute the heart of the findings, and are formulated

Table 4.4
Salary Levels

F = 70.43   P < .001

Males: $36,829
Females: $24,296

Category	Salary
Married Male Parents Spouse Non-Employed	$43,582
Married Male Non-Parents Spouse Non-Employed	$42,917
Married Male Parents Spouse Employed	$39,128
Single Male Parents	$35,431
Married Male Non-Parents Spouse Employed	$33,364
Single Male Non-Parents	$26,049
Single Female Non-Parents	$25,200
Married Female Non-Parents	$23,927
Single Female Parents	$23,704
Married Female Parents	$23,675

0   10,000   20,000   30,000   40,000   50,000

to assess the work/family interactions of employees and the impact of these interactions. The headings are as follows:

1. How are employees handling family responsibilities?
2. How are family responsibilities overlapping into the workplace?
3. What is the impact on employees of balancing work and family?
4. What is the impact on corporations of work/family conflicts?

Question 1: How are Employees Handling Family Responsibilities?

Hours in Work Week. As indicated in Table 4.5, men of all marital and parental status categories work slightly more hours per week than do women of all categories (all respondents were full-time employees). The greatest discrepancy is between male parents (mean = 44 hours) and female parents (mean = 40). The greater number of hours worked by men partially explains salary differentials between men and women. This figure does not include commuting time, which adds an average of another hour and a half to two hours per day, or seven and a half to ten hours per week. It is not surprising that the average adult working full-time spends more time on work and work-related activities than on any other single activity, including sleep. It is also noteworthy that the projections of a decade ago that society would experience decreased work time and increased leisure never materialized. Americans are working longer hours than ever. The traditional forty-hour work week that allowed millions to enter the middle class on one income has practically disappeared as employees are working longer and more varied hours than in previous decades. The men and women in this study group reflect this trend. The hours (if commuting time is combined with actual work time) reflect national trends. One private national survey indicates that the average work week has grown from 40.6 hours in 1973 to almost 47 hours a week. For professional workers not covered by wage-hour provisions the work week is now reported to be sixty-two hours. Louis Harris surveys also confirm this trend, and add that the movement toward longer hours is unmistakable and accompanied by a drop-off in leisure time from 26.2 hours to 16.6 hours.

The findings in leisure time are remarkably consistent with the employees in this group. In Table 4.6 the hours for parents fall between thirteen and twenty-one hours. This is in sharp contrast with the non-parents, who in many cases have twice the amount of leisure time of parents. Not unexpectedly, the amount of leisure time is inversely related to the amount of time spent on family responsibilities (see Table 4.8). It is easy to dismiss these findings as the cost for parenting, but in light of tighter economics, in which it takes more and more of disposable family time to achieve economic security, and in light of rising dependent care responsibilities in new areas such as aging parents, the scarcity of available leisure time and its impact on individual and family stress cannot be minimized.

Table 4.5
Hours in Work Week

F = 26.27   P < .001

Total Mean Hours: 41.92

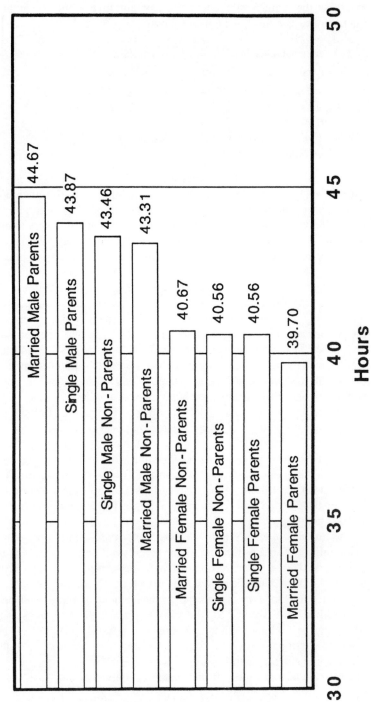

Married Male Parents — 44.67
Single Male Parents — 43.87
Single Male Non-Parents — 43.46
Married Male Non-Parents — 43.31
Married Female Non-Parents — 40.67
Single Female Non-Parents — 40.56
Single Female Parents — 40.56
Married Female Parents — 39.70

Hours

30   35   40   45   50

Table 4.6
Leisure Hours per Week

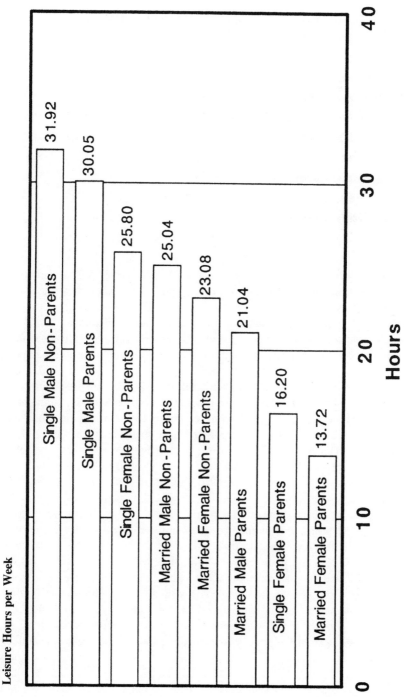

Single Male Non-Parents — 31.92
Single Male Parents — 30.05
Single Female Non-Parents — 25.80
Married Male Non-Parents — 25.04
Married Female Non-Parents — 23.08
Married Male Parents — 21.04
Single Female Parents — 16.20
Married Female Parents — 13.72

Hours

0   10   20   30   40

Table 4.7
Responsibilities for Home Chores by Marital and Parental Status

	I Have	Share Equally With Spouse	Spouse Has
Married Female Parents	56.5%	42.2%	0.4%
Married Male Parents	5.5%	55.9%	38.6%
Married Female Non-Parents	43.4%	51.8%	4.9%
Married Male Non-Parents	5.1%	71.0%	23.9%
Single Female Parents	97.9%		
Single Male Parents	91.4%		
Single Female Non-Parents	94.5%		
Single Male Non-Parents	92.1%		

Responsibility for Home Chores. As indicated in Table 4.7, a discrepancy in the perceptions of male and female respondents arises when they are asked who in the family is responsible for home chores. The home chores list includes alternating traditional female and male tasks. Respondents are asked who is responsible for jobs like keeping track of money and bills, plus planning and arranging for all that needs to get done. Married men are more likely to perceive that they share equally with their spouses than are married women. Married men appear to be at an advantage in the workforce when compared with all other categories, as almost none of them report full responsibility for home chores.

Although married men are likely to report that they share home chores equally with their spouses, when they are asked how many hours per week they and their spouses spend on home chores, a different picture emerges. As Table 4.8 indicates, married men report that their spouses spend twice as many hours per week on home chores as they do. No significant difference is found between married men with employed wives and those with nonemployed wives on hours per week the husband spends on home chores (about twelve hours for both groups). The primary difference between single-earner and dual-earner couples is that the employed wife spends considerably fewer hours per week on home chores than does the nonemployed wife, thus reducing the overall amount of time the couple spends on home chores per week. Having an employed wife apparently increases the family income without much cost to the husband in terms of increased time he must spend on home chores (see Table 4.8).

Although much of this can be analyzed from a gender perspective, it also brings into question the very nature of home chores and the responsibility for them in households in which all adults are working. As women employees become more removed from the socialization they received from their largely nonworking mothers, the standards for adequate home functioning or cleanliness

Table 4.8
Hours per Week Spent on Home Chores

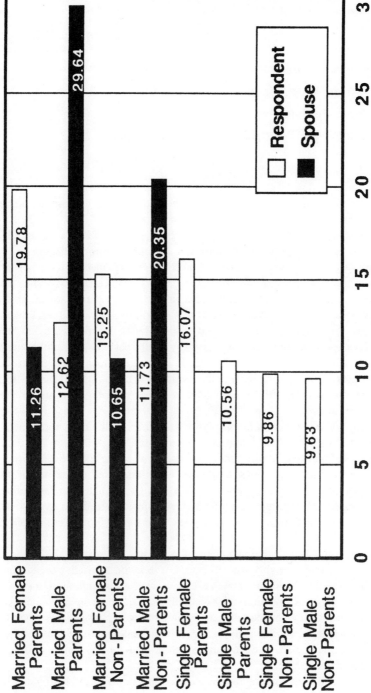

Table 4.9
Responsibility for Child Care by Marital and Parental Status

	I Have	Share Equally With Spouse	Spouse Has
Married Female Parents	54.0%	39.5%	6.5%
Married Male Parents	2.1%	27.7%	70.1%
Single Female Parents	96.7%		
Single Male Parents	53.8%		46.2%
	(n=7)		(n=6)

become redefined. Dust balls under the bed may not be quite as bothersome to dual-earner households.

Responsibility for Child Care. When the respondents were asked about responsibility for child-care activities, a different pattern of discrepant perceptions emerged. Here female parents are more likely to perceive that they share equally with their spouses (39.5%) than are men (27.7%) (Table 4.9). When asked about hours per week spent on child care, the women's perception of sharing is not supported. Married women report that their husbands spend ten fewer hours per week on child care than they do (Table 4.10). Married men report that their wives spend more than twice as many hours per week on child care than they do, despite the fact that 69 percent of married men come from dual-earner couples. Child-rearing apparently continues to be a woman's responsibility, even if she is working full-time outside the home and earning a major share of the family income.

Combined Work and Family Responsibilities. Combining hours spent on work, home chores, and child care presents an interesting snapshot of the main ingredients of working family time. Because most of these three categories are compartmentalized, or at least treated so when discussed in the media, the totality reveal quite different patterns for men than for women, and for parents than for nonparents. For parent employees, for example there is an average of an additional twenty to thirty hours per week than the for nonparent employee (Table 4.11).

Although female parents spend the greatest number of hours on combined activities (about eighty-four hours per week for married women and seventy-nine for single women), male parents as well are spending almost twenty more hours per week on family responsibilities than are nonparent male colleagues. The discrepancy between men and women lessens considerably when nonparents are considered by themselves. Parenthood appears to be a major factor in increasing hours spent on combined work and family responsibilities for both women and men.

Three other interesting findings are presented in Table 4.10. First, when single-

Table 4.10
Hours per Week Spent on Child Care

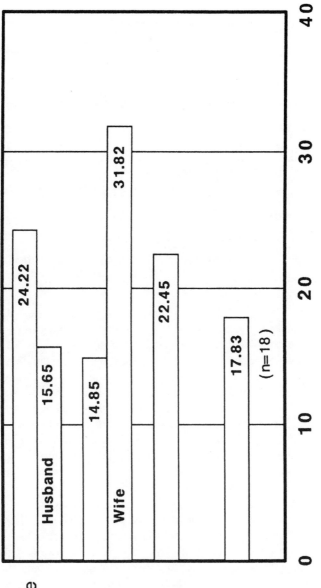

Table 4.11
Hours per Week Combined Work and Family

	Work	Home Chores	Child Care	Total
Married Female Parents	39.70	19.77	24.22	83.69
Single Female Parents	40.56	16.07	22.45	79.08
Single Male Parents	43.87	10.56	17.83	72.26
Married Male Parents	44.67	12.62	14.85	72.14
Married Female Non-Parents	40.67	15.25		55.92
Married Male Non-Parents	43.31	11.73		55.04
Single Male Non-Parents	43.46	9.63		53.09
Single Female Non-Parents	40.56	9.86		50.42

Do You Hire Anyone From Outside to Help With Chores?
Yes   9.7%   (n=143)

male parents and married-male parents are compared, little difference is found in the number of hours per week they spend on child care, even though the single men are noncustodial parents. Married men who are living with their children do not appear to spend more time with their children than do single men, even if the single man is not living full-time with his children. This finding supports studies that suggest that the most important impact of divorce on children is not father absence, but mother absence. That is, children may not have much less contact with their fathers after the divorce than before. However, because the mother may have to spend many more hours working to make up for the lost income and may have less time for the children because of reduced emotional support from another adult in the family, a child may have considerable less contact with the mother after the divorce.

A second finding is that married-female parents, not single-female parents, spend the greatest number of hours per week on combined work and family responsibilities. The presence of a husband in the home does not appear to reduce the workload for mothers. To the contrary, single-female parents seem to have the advantage of spending less time per week on both home chores and child-care activities. This advantage of increased discretionary time may be offset by other factors, such as the considerably higher family income of married-female parents, virtually all of whom are in dual-earner families.

A further observation centers on the small difference in the total number of hours between married-female parents (83.6%) and single-female parents (79%)—a difference of about four and a half hours per week. It appears that given this difference between single and married categories, marriage takes only about four and a half hours per week. Although cynics of marriage might rejoice, this does provide sobering findings on the distribution of home-based roles and responsibilities.

A third finding of note was that few employees are hiring anyone from the outside to help with family responsibilities (9.7%). Even the increased income and reduced time available to dual-earner couples do not seem to result in employees hiring others to take care of home chores. When the managers' responses are contrasted to hourly employees, the percentage never gets beyond 12 percent. Either people prefer to do their own home chores, or they think that they cannot afford to hire someone to help. Whatever the reason, the image of the two-career family who hires a housekeeper to take care of the home appears to be more myth than reality.

Question 2: How Are Family Responsibilities Overlapping into the Workplace?

As dual-earner and single-parent families have become the norm, the spillover of their household responsibilities into the workplace becomes more frequent and extensive. Precisely because this is a relatively recent phenomenon, little empirical data have been collected to determine the arrangements and impacts of this workplace management of the home.

To assess the overlap of family responsibilities into the workplace, employees were asked about (a) their child-care arrangements, (b) the impact of child-care responsibilities on work activities, and (c) the support networks they utilize to help manage their job and family demands.

Child-Care Arrangements. As can be seen in Table 4.12, relatively few employees utilize formal day-care arrangements. When all parents are considered, spouses provide child care for the 40 percent of married-male parents who have nonemployed wives. For other employees formal arrangements are reported frequently only for preschool-age children (day-care centers 14%, licensed day-care homes 11%). Most children are cared for through informal arrangements (with 17.8% of preschool children in unlicensed day-care homes).

These findings might act as a cautionary red flag for corporations contemplating appropriate responses to child care. This tendency to rely on informal arrangements reflects an interesting dichotomy between the assumed need for child care and the corporate rush to provide child care, and the attitudes of parent employees. Few employees either desired or utilized formal day-care services. Furthermore, only 11 percent indicated that they were dissatisfied with their current arrangements. Given the current crisis in child care, it is important to consider that the solution may not always be in the direction in which policymakers may be moving. For these companies to invest considerable resources in constructing child-care centers may be inappropriate and misguided. It may be that the strategy of financial or informational resources, combined with structural issues such as flex time, would be more critical than the selection of on-site day care.

Another perspective on this item was the high incidence of children who are

Table 4.12
Child-Care Arrangements

	Overall	Children 0 - 5 (n=166)	Children 6 - 12 (n=174)	Children 13 - 18 (n=152)
Child takes care of self	35.8%	2.4%	30.5%	74.3%
Spouse	30.6%	42.2%	40.2%	20.4%
Day care home (unlicensed)	10.4%	20.5%	8.6%	2.6%
Day care center	8.1%	15.7%	4.6%	0.7%
School	7.6%	7.8%	11.4%	3.9%
Child checks in with neighbor or relative	7.0%	3.6%	12.1%	6.6%
Someone comes to home	5.2%	9.0%	5.7%	0.7%
Day care home (licensed)	4.5%	9.0%	3.4%	1.3%

left to care for themselves—latchkey children. When the categories of child-takes-care-of-self and child-checks-in-with-neighbors-or-relative are combined, almost 43 percent of school-age children (ages 6 to 12) and 76 percent of teenagers (ages 13 to 18) appear to lack structured supervision after school.

This is particularly noticeable for children who range from under age 1 to age 5. The percentage is small, but nevertheless it is a disturbing piece of data that indicates that a group of children under age 5 are on their own during the workday. Although this may well be a reportable child abuse situation, it should always be remembered that some parents *perceive* that they have no alternative. Just recently a chief executive officer, in discussing why he initiated a child-care program at his company, related this event. A security guard passing through a parking lot outside the company heard crying coming from inside a locked car, and discovered a young infant in a car seat. On further investigation he found that both the mother and the father worked for the company, but on different shifts. There was about a fifteen-minute interval between the time one parent went in and the other was released. These parents saw this temporary drop-off as the only strategy open to them. It may be easy to criticize, but it is important to realize that many individual employees and employers (such as this executive) are ignorant of possible options as well as of dilemmas parents face.

The situation of being left alone may seem more questionable for younger children than for teenagers, but the social desirability of leaving teenagers completely unsupervised for four or five hours every afternoon also may need to be considered. When such problems as teen pregnancy, drugs, and suicide rates are considered, the issue of afterschool supervision or planned activities for children of all ages may warrant increased attention.

For as much attention as is given to child care, virtually little attention is given to sick care. Finding child care that is appropriate, affordable, and secure is difficult. No institutional arrangements have been created to assist parents with caring for sick children; consequently these occurrences fall between the cracks. Although parent employees appear to be coping with their regular child-care arrangements, no formal arrangements were reported when children are sick. Because of either formal or informal backup, many parents resort to a variety of patchwork devices and are left with situations that can only engender fear and worry. Note, for example, that even with children under age 1 to age 5, in the categories child-stays-by-self, respondent-checks-in-by-phone, and other-child-cares-for-sick-child, more than 12 percent of these children are at some form of higher risk than most parents would prefer (Table 4.13).

The strategy usually relies on either the respondent staying home or the child being left home alone. As indicated in Table 4.14, married-women employees are far more likely to stay home with a sick child (66%) than are married men (21%). Even though only 40 percent of married men have nonemployed wives, 76 percent report that their wives stay home with sick children. The likelihood of women staying home with sick children greatly increases absenteeism rates for women when compared with male parents, thus becoming a major factor in

Table 4.13
Child-Care Arrangements When Child Is Sick

	Overall	Children 0 - 5 (n=166)	Children 6 - 12 (n=173)	Children 13 - 18 (n=288)
Spouse stays home	48.8%	60.2%	52.6%	39.1%
Respondent stays home	47.5%	46.4%	45.1%	42.4%
Respondent checks in by phone	20.6%	9.0%	20.8%	35.1%
Child stays by self	18.0%	1.8%	14.5%	41.7%
Relative cares for child	10.2%	10.2%	12.1%	7.3%
Babysitter cares for child	8.9%	14.5%	8.1%	1.3%
Other child cares for sick child	4.7%	0%	4.0%	10.6%

Table 4.14
Comparison of Male and Female Parents Staying Home with Sick Child

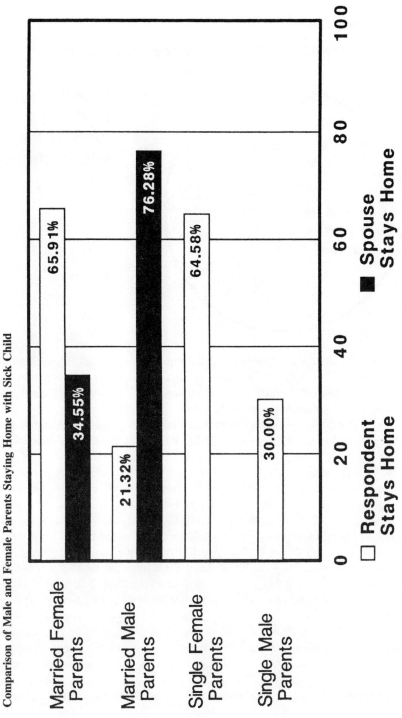

Table 4.15
Worry About Children

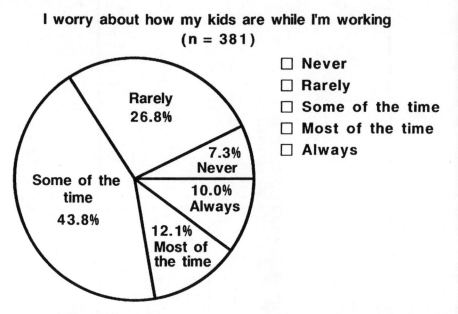

I worry about how my kids are while I'm working
(n = 381)

☐ **Never**
☐ **Rarely**
☐ **Some of the time**
☐ **Most of the time**
☐ **Always**

keeping the absenteeism rates for male parents low. In fact, there is almost a direct correlation with the difference in days absent for women and days absent for men, with the difference reported between men and women of staying home to care for sick children (see Table 4.28).

Impact of Children on the Workplace. Parent employees were next asked a series of questions to assess the overlap into the workplace of concern about family demands. As indicated in Table 4.15, a considerable number of parents (24.7%) are worrying about their children while they are at work either always or most of the time. Although it is not unusual for any parent to be worrying about their children from time to time, the fact that one out of four parents report worrying about their children either all or most of the time is significant. Put in terms of impact on productivity, it would mean that at any point in time a quarter of parents are not able to realize their full productive capacity. To what extent this impairs productivity cannot be determined from this data. It would be hard to imagine, however, that productivity is not impacted. The lack of adequate child-care arrangements may be a major factor contributing to this overlapping concern of parents.

An unanticipated child-care option emerged during the course of the study—bringing the children to work. Researchers noticed that when they visited work sites, particularly on school holidays or snow days, the sound of children could be heard in the background. They began to ask managers whether it was common for employees to bring children to work. At one site, for example, a warehouse

Table 4.16
Bring Children to Work

Have you ever brought your child to work because of lack of other arrangements?

location where primarily male employees loaded trucks all day, the plant manager reported that children at the work site were once a problem during working days on which schools were closed. At one point there frequently were thirty to forty children of employees running around the warehouse. There was no supervision, and an unfenced pond was behind the warehouse. Once the company realized the liability implications involved, children were banned from the work site. According to the plant manager, the problem was solved.

To determine the scope of bringing children to work, parent employees were asked in follow-up interviews whether they ever brought their children to work with them because of lack of other child-care arrangements. As indicated in Table 4.16, 41 percent reported that yes, they did bring their children to work during work hours, and 46 percent reported that they brought their children to work during nonwork hours. Of these, half reported this occurring more than once during the year. Bringing children to work appears to be an emergency child-care option used with increasing frequency by employees. Companies may be providing informal child care whether they intend it or not. The alternatives appear to be increased absenteeism of employees and increased worry among parents about leaving children home alone. Innovative company policies for emergency child care may be a necessity in the future.

Work/Family Stress. A simple, one-item question was devised to obtain a generic sense of work/home life stress. Most interesting was the small differential between the responses of men and women. Despite the fact that women spend more time on combined work and family responsibilities, follow-up interviews with fifty-one parent employees indicated that male parents are as likely as female parents to report that they experience a lot of

Table 4.17
Work/Family Stress

To what extent do you experience stress in balancing work and family responsibilities?

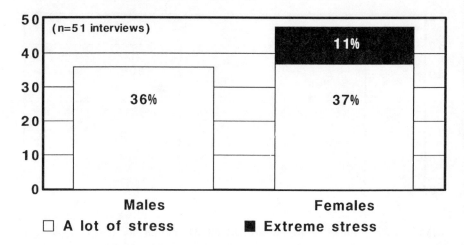

☐ A lot of stress   ■ Extreme stress

stress in balancing work and family responsibilities (36% of men and 37% of women; (Table 4.17). Only female parents, however, report extreme stress (11%) in balancing both roles. Although work/family issues and conflicts usually are seen as women's issues, and indeed are perceived as such within corporations, the data provide some fragmentary evidence that this may be changing. That an equal number of men are experiencing and reporting stress may be a bellwether of changing male roles and responsibilities.

The next set of questions examined support networks that employees utilize to help them balance their multiple demands.

Support Networks. To determine the role of social supports in the work/family equation, the respondents were given a list of thirty persons and agencies and were asked which of them were helpful in enabling the respondents to manage their many job and family responsibilities. Who did they turn to for assistance and help of any kind? The list included family, friends, and work colleagues for the informal social supports, and churches, doctors, clubs and organizations, and company resources for the formal supports.

The most striking finding of the analysis of informal and formal support networks of employees is the differences between male and female responses (see Table 4.18). A major difference in male and female support networks underlines the importance of marriage to men in providing support for the workplace. Their informal system clusters around spouse and work colleagues. Women, on the other hand, appear to derive somewhat less support from mar-

Table 4.18
Informal Support Networks

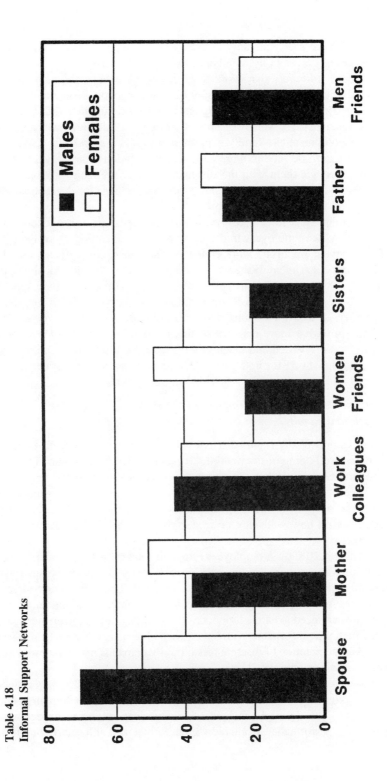

riage, and have a considerably broader field of support from their network of women friends and family members.

The fact, however, that work-related support people are mentioned more frequently than friends in the measure of formal support networks suggests that work is becoming the new friendship and extended-family network. Four of these highest-rated experts were work-based (Table 4.19). With few people left at home to coordinate the family support network and social life activities, employees seem to be relying more and more on relationships formed in the work setting to provide them with the sustenance to manage their multiple demands. The workplace, therefore, increasingly becomes a locus for decreasing isolation and gaining friendship and support.

The implications for employers of this change in support networks may be profound. When employers transfer workers, for example, more than just the job is changed. Important work colleague and friendship networks may be disrupted, to the detriment of the work setting as well as the individual employees. Similarly, the importance of work and marriage to men becomes apparent. If one or both of these supports are terminated or severely disrupted, the result may be serious loss of emotional and social support for the man involved. Women may be somewhat more resistant to this disruption, as their support networks tend to be more varied and extend into stabler friendship and family networks. The trend, however, for both men and women appears to be greater reliance on informal and formal supports provided in the workplace.

Question 3: What Is the Impact on Employees of Balancing Work and Family?

This section of the report discusses the impact on employees' physical and emotional well-being of the multiple demands of work and home. To determine at the outset how well they thought they were doing in the two domains of work and home life, respondents were asked to assess their job performance. Because there is no measure of family performance per se, they also were asked to rate themselves on how well they do in carrying out their role and responsibilities as parents.

As Table 4.20 shows, employees rate their job performance much higher than family performance (86% unusually good or good at the job versus only 59% unusually good or good at family responsibilities). This differential suggests that employees may be putting greater effort into the job than into the family because of the primary need to earn a living; or it may simply reflect the greater specificity with which job performance can be assessed. Job demands may be measured by successful completion of discrete tasks; family demands may be viewed as open-ended and never completed.

This differential between job and family performance also was reflected in the in-depth interviews. For most parents not only is the job domain boundaried by policies, job descriptions, and relatively clear employee expectations (reviewed by performance evaluation both formal and informal), but it also is

Table 4.19
Formal Support Networks

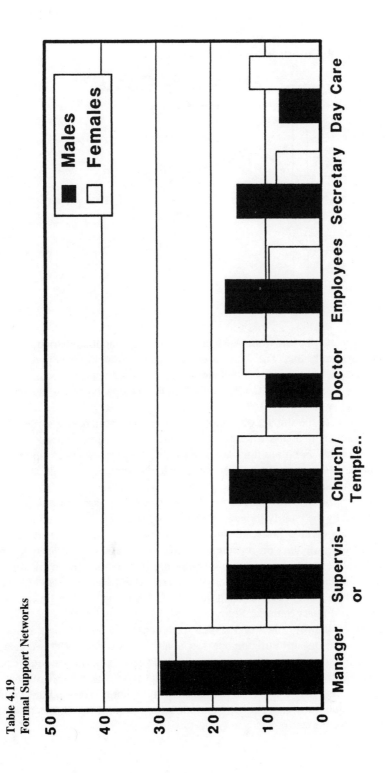

Table 4.20
Rating of Job Performance vs. Family Performance

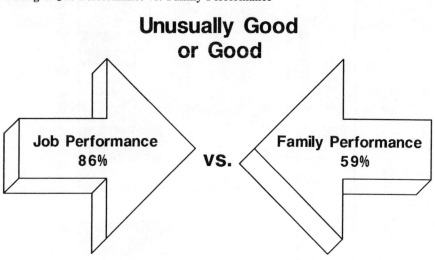

somewhat of a haven from the seemingly endless, nonboundaried, and erratic nature of family life. The feelings of inadequacy brought on in part because of the inevitable comparisons with their own parents often seem to occur in isolation, as if they were the only family feeling such inadequacies about the family and household environments.

To measure the impact of combined work/home demands, a series of scales were utilized to assess affective, cognitive, and behavioral responses to the stresses of managing multiple responsibilities. Measures include job/family role strain, depression, health and energy, financial support of single parents, absenteeism, problems with drinking, and job satisfaction.

Job/Family Role Strain. Job/family role strain was assessed utilizing a scale developed by the Family Impact Seminar Study at George Washington University (Bohen and Viveros-Long, 1981). It was originally used to measure the impact of flex-time programs on reducing work/family stress. The scale measures internal emotions and concerns about fulfilling both family and work roles. It is a thirteen-item scale with an internal consistency reliability of .78 (Cronbach's alpha). High levels of concurrent validity and construct validity were found in the Family Impact Seminar Study.

Mean job/family role strain scores were compared among eight marital and parental status groups utilizing one-way analysis of variance. The two categories with the highest role strain were married-female parents and single-female parents (Table 4.21). The two groups, therefore, that have the greatest responsibility for home chores and child care, spend the most hours per week on combined work and family responsibilities, and have the fewest leisure hours also exhibit the greatest amount of job/family role strain.

Table 4.21
Job/Family Role Strain

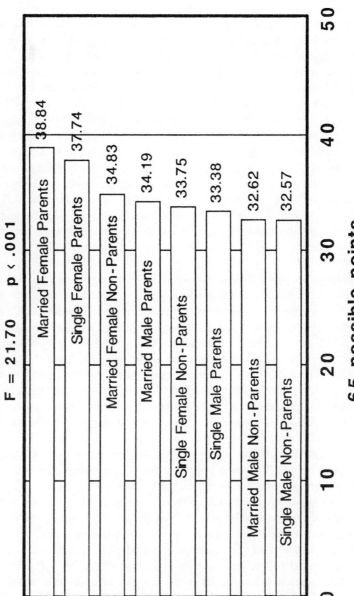

(Hi score = hi strain)

F = 21.70   p < .001

65 possible points

Most Difficult Problems. When asked to rate the degree of difficulty of a series of job/family management activities, respondents reported that the most difficult were those that required time to maintain social contacts and community relations (Table 4.22). The most difficult activities, particularly for parent employees, were to participate in community activities and to help or visit neighbors or other friends. These responses illustrate the results of the support network analysis that suggested that employees are turning more and more to the workplace for support, as they no longer have the time to spend on traditional community and friendship support activities. With the majority of both men and women in the workforce, few resources remain for community volunteer work and social functions. This confirms the earlier findings of social support networks, in that the geographical and kin communities are the areas that become slighted when time forces cutbacks. It appears that these traditional forms of social supports become expendable, and new systems of support are created in the environment where most adults are spending the majority of their time—the workplace.

Similarly, when asked which problems they *felt* were the most difficult, parent employees in particular reported that inadequate time was the major stressor. Most frequently mentioned feelings were "I wish I had more time to do things for the family" and "I feel I have to rush to get everything done each day" (Table 4.23).

Depression. Employees' emotional well-being was measured in part by the Center for Epidemiological Studies Depression Scale, designed to measure depressive symptomatology in the general population (Radloff, 1977). This scale contains twenty statements of feelings or behaviors expressed both negatively (e.g., "I felt depressed") and positively (e.g., "I was very happy"). Respondents were asked to indicate how often they feel that way.

One-way analysis of variance comparing depression scores of the eight marital and parental status groups indicated that single-female parents have the highest levels of depression and married men (both parents and nonparents) have the lowest (Table 4.24). Again, the importance of marriage as a support system for men appears evident.

When depression was assessed using multiple-regression analysis, a different picture emerged. The most important factors predicting depression among employees are job/family role strain, salary, and job satisfaction. High role strain and low salary are predictive of increased depression. In other words, women are not more depressed because of their gender per se or because of their marital status, but because (a) women have greater job/family role strain because of primary responsibility for home chores and child care in addition to working full-time; and (b) women have lower salaries than men. The least depressed groups, married men, also have the lowest job/family role strain and highest salaries. Men who experience the same family responsibilities as women react in exactly the same way as women, that is, with increased job/family role strain and depression. As family responsibilities become more equally divided between

Table 4.22
Job/Family Management: Most Difficult Problems

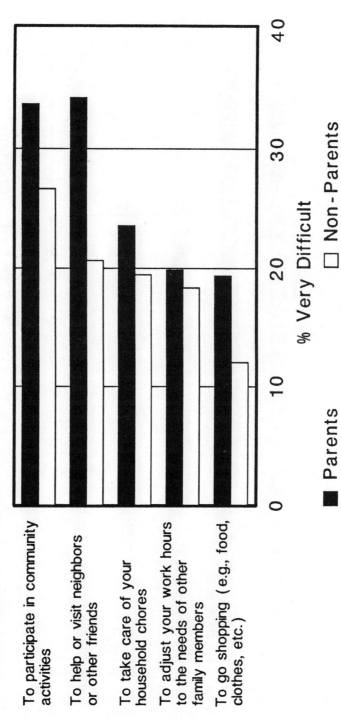

Table 4.23
Job/Family Role Strain: Most Difficult Problems

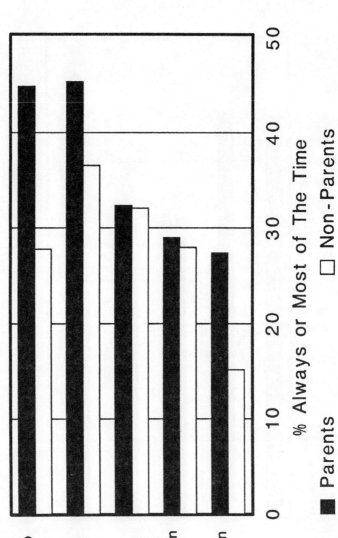

% Always or Most of The Time

■ Parents   □ Non-Parents

Table 4.24
Depression

(80 pt scale - hi score = lo depression)
F = 10.50   p < .001

Category	Score
Single Female Parents	63.93
Single Female Non-Parents	65.06
Married Female Parents	66.86
Single Male Non-Parents	66.88
Married Female Non-Parents	68.85
Single Male Parents	68.92
Married Male Parents	70.30
Married Male Non-Parents	70.79

men and women in coming years, gender differences on measures of well-being also should disappear.

Health and Energy. Similar results were found when physical well-being was assessed on a two-item scale utilized by the Quality of Employment Survey at the University of Michigan Survey Research Center (Quinn and Staines, 1979). The scale measures both perceived health and perceived energy levels on ten-point scales (Cronbach's alpha = .69). Similar to the findings for depression, multiple-regression analysis indicated that the most important factors predicting reduced levels of health and energy for both parents and nonparents are job/family role strain and days absent from work (Table 4.25). Parenthood by itself also is a predictor of reduced health and energy. Job satisfaction again emerges as a mitigating factor. Employees with high job satisfaction also are likely to exhibit greater health and energy. Again, gender and marital status fall out of the equation. That is, even though it may appear that women employees (particularly parents) have lower levels of health and energy, this result is not due to their gender or marital status, but to the increase in family responsibility that gender in particular entails. Men with similar responsibilities react the same way, with reduced health and energy.

Single Parents and Child Support. Since salary emerged as such an important factor in predicting depression, and since single-female parents were the most depressed of all marital and parental status groups, a further analysis was conducted into the financial situation of single-female parents. Two key facts emerged: (1) the salary levels of single-female parents are among the lowest of all categories at all work sites studied; and (2) to compound their already pre-

Table 4.25
Health and Energy

(20 pt scale - hi score = hi health & energy)
F = 6.43   p < .001

Category	Score
Single Male Parents	15.68
Married Male Parents	15.64
Married Male Non-Parents	15.30
Single Male Non-Parents	15.18
Married Female Non-Parents	14.81
Single Female Non-Parents	14.68
Married Female Parents	14.24
Single Female Parents	14.04

carious financial position, more than half of the single-female parents who have custody of their children report no financial assistance from their children's fathers. This finding is consistent with national studies on noncompliance with, or nonexistence of, child support orders—noncompliance that cuts across all socioeconomic classes.

Life Satisfaction. The measure of well-being that did appear related to marital status was overall life satisfaction. Life satisfaction was measured by a three-item general scale on life satisfaction and happiness utilized by the Quality of Employment Survey, along with an additional item measuring satisfaction with marital status (Cronbach's alpha = . 70 for the married respondents' version, and .78 for single respondents).

One-way analysis of variance comparing life satisfaction scores among marital and parental status categories indicated that married employees of all categories scored higher than single employees (Table 4.26). Most satisfied were married nonparents, both male and female. Least satisfied were single-female parents and single-male nonparents. The stress of parenthood combined with singleness appears evident in reducing life satisfaction for women. More surprising was that single-male nonparents, the group that has the greatest amount of leisure time and the least job/family role strain, also has the second lowest life satisfaction. Again, study results seem to underline the importance of marriage to male employees' well-being.

In addition to affective and cognitive measures of well-being, behavioral indicators were assessed to determine employees' overall well-being.

Absenteeism. The first behavioral measure of well-being assessed was absen-

Table 4.26
Life Satisfaction

(10 pt scale - hi score = hi satisfaction)
F = 13.29   p < .001

Category	Score
Married Female Non-Parents	7.72
Married Male Non-Parents	7.66
Married Male Parents	7.62
Married Female Parents	7.29
Single Male Parents	7.25
Single Female Non-Parents	6.89
Single Male Non-Parents	6.79
Single Female Parents	6.48

teeism. Respondents were asked to report how many days they had been absent from work during the previous year. As reported in Table 4.27, married-female parents and single-female parents have the highest absenteeism rates of all categories. Single-male parents and married-male parents have the lowest. As has already been suggested in the discussion of child-care arrangements, it appears that mothers may be subsidizing fathers by staying home when children are sick. This family decision enables fathers to have low absenteeism rates at the cost of high absenteeism rates for mothers. The possible consequences of this trade-off for the careers of the parents involved were not directly addressed by this study. As will be discussed later in this report, however, parent employees, particularly men, agree that family responsibilities have a negative impact on career advancement. Increased absenteeism of mothers may be one of the components of this perceived outcome.

Alcohol as a Problem in the Family. Employees were next asked whether drinking had ever been a cause of trouble in their family. Overall, 22 percent of respondents, or about the national norm, said yes. As with life satisfaction, however, major differences emerged between single and married respondents. Single employees of all categories were considerable more likely to report drinking as a problem in their families than married employees (Table 4.28). Single men reported the highest incidence, and married men the lowest. More than half of single-male parents reported drinking as a cause of family trouble. The study did not assess, however, whether drinking is a cause or a result of family trouble. It could be speculated that marital status is somehow associated with alcohol as

Table 4.27
Days Absent from Work During Last Year

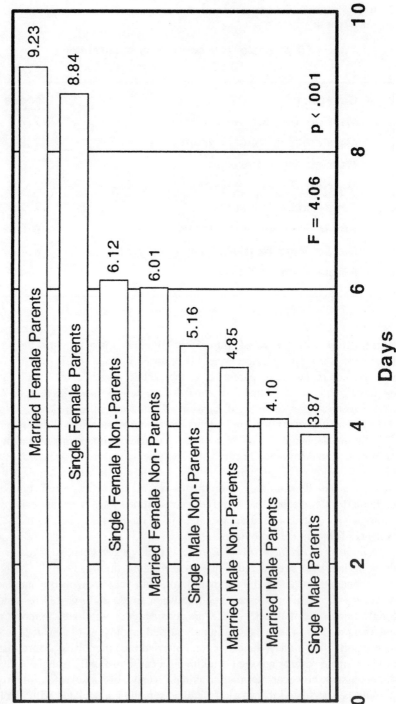

Table 4.28
Has Drinking Ever Been a Cause of Trouble in Your Family?

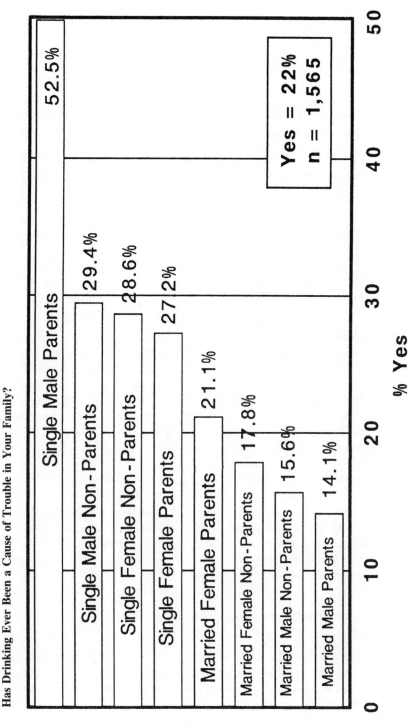

Table 4.29
Job Satisfaction by Marital and Parental Status Group

F = 2.78 P = .007	(35 possible points)
Category	**Score**
Married Female Non-Parents	20.26
Married Female Parents	20.08
Single Female Parents	19.84
Married Male Parents	19.59
Single Female Non-Parents	19.55
Married Male Non-Parents	19.13
Single Male Non-Parents	18.76
Single Male Parents	18.56
Total Mean Score:	19.65

a problem in families; but whether alcoholism leads to singleness, or singleness leads to alcoholism is not addressed by the study.

Job Satisfaction. Job satisfaction emerged as an important factor in the well-being of employees. As indicated in the multiple-regression analysis, high job satisfaction is predictive of reduced depression and high levels of health and energy. Job satisfaction becomes particularly important as a mitigating factor when it is considered that married women (both parents and nonparents) and single-female parents have the highest job satisfaction of all categories (Table 4.29). Although high role strain and low salaries may have a negative effect on well-being for women, women's higher levels of job satisfaction appear to counteract some of the negative effect. In other words, regardless of the heavy work and family demands placed on women parent employees, the job appears to be worth it to them. Their increased role strain and lower salaries may be at least partially compensated by their satisfaction with being in the job world. A competing theory would account for the high degree of job satisfaction in the workplace as a haven. Women in particular find the workplace a refreshing alternative to the unending demands of the household, and find their adult network of work colleagues as their new community and source of social supports.

Question 4: What Is the Impact on Corporations of Work/Family Conflict?

Given the incidence of work/family stress in the workplace, what is the impact on employers? What are some of the future trends developing in the workforce, and what can employers do to anticipate these trends to meet the current and future needs of their employees?

Table 4.30
Attitudes Toward Employed Mothers

$$n = 1,511$$
$$F = 19.78 \quad p < .001$$

It is much better for everyone involved if the man earns the money and the woman takes care of the house and children

1 = Strongly Disagree   5 = Strongly Agree

Married Male Non-Parents (Spouse non-employed)	3.42
Married Male Parents (Spouse non-employed)	3.10
Married Male Parents (Spouse employed)	2.42
Married Male Non-Parents (Spouse employed)	2.28
Single Male Parents	2.28
Single Male Non-Parents	2.18
Single Female Parents	2.14
Married Female Non-Parents	2.07
Married Female Parents	1.95
Single Female Non-Parents	1.91

Behaviors and attitudes often are at odds in the face of fundamental social or individual change. Although behaviors can appear to change on the surface, it is really the attitudes that lurk below the behavior and operate at the core of the individual or work organization. Fundamental change cannot take place until attitudes change. Thus if you want to understand the nature of the work/home life dynamic, it is instructive to examine underlying attitudes.

One issue that became clear through a series of questions exploring attitudes toward women at work is that traditional attitudes are still deeply rooted in the workforce, particularly among men. For example, men of all categories agreed more than women that it is better for the man to earn the money and the woman to care for the family (Table 4.30). Similarly, when attitudes were examined about the impact on children of working mothers, men and women had significantly different perspectives. Again, men were more likely than women to disagree that a mother who works outside the home can have just as good a relationship with her children as a mother who does not work (Table 4.31). Married-male parents with employed spouses had the most liberal attitudes of all male categories. Married men with wives at home had the most traditional attitudes. These findings suggest a significant polarization by gender within the workforce that could be cause for concern.

A more complex set of attitudes emerged when probing the impact on careers of family responsibilities. As indicated in Table 4.32, 71 percent of men perceive that family responsibilities negatively impact on their careers and their ability

Table 4.31
Attitudes Toward Employed Mothers

$$n = 1,511$$
$$F = 21.56 \quad p < .001$$

A mother who works outside the home can have just as good a relationship with her children as a mother who does not work

1 = Strongly Disagree   5 = Strongly Agree

Married Female Parents	**3.81**
Single Female Parents	**3.57**
Single Female Non-Parents	**3.51**
Married Male Parents **(Spouse employed)**	**3.38**
Married Female Non-Parents	**3.36**
Single Male Non-Parents	**3.03**
Single Male Parents	**2.90**
Married Male Non-Parents	**2.87**
Married Male Non-Parents **(Spouse non-employed)**	**2.44**
Married Male Parents **(Spouse non-employed)**	**2.37**

to advance in the company compared with 54 percent of women. This difference in perception can be viewed in two lights. First, it could be viewed as significant that more than half of all employees report family responsibilities to impact careers negatively, thus reinforcing the widespread perception of conflicts between work and family. The responses also could be interpreted as another indication of traditional values. That is, men may overwhelmingly believe that family responsibilities should be taken care of by their spouses so that their (the men's) careers will be unfettered by such responsibilities.

These and other related questions reflect an attitudinal backdrop that is vital to examine before work/family conflicts can be fully understood and resolved. Social and cultural changes occur slowly, and the traditional values that have underpinned the family adjust even more slowly to new roles, structures, and realities.

Corporations, like family members, also react slowly to new demographic realities, such as dual-earner couples and single-parent employees. Table 4.33 suggests that those employees at *highest risk* for work/family stress (married-female parents, single-female parents, and married-male parents) believe that their companies are *least sensitive* to their needs. With the exception of the small number of single-male parents, most of whom do not live with their children, a polarization exists between parents and nonparents concerning perceptions of company sensitivity. Corporations have not yet had to deal full force with the

Table 4.32
Family Impact on Career

Family responsiblities negatively impact employees' careers and their ability to advance in the company.

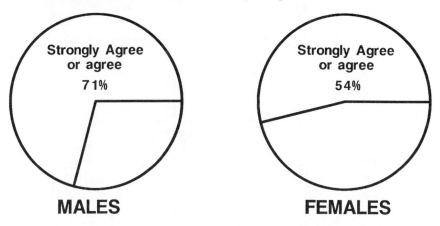

MALES   FEMALES

spillover of parents and their problems into the workplace. Judging from the data, parents may be beginning to express dissatisfaction with lack of company recognition and support of their difficult situations. What is equally intriguing is that this differing perspective of parents and nonparents disappears when employees are asked whether their supervisors are sensitive. In both corporations surveyed parents and nonparents alike rated supervisors significantly higher than their companies in sensitivity toward employees. This finding may indicate that as creators of ad hoc policy in the absence of formal company work/family policy, supervisors reflect a sensitivity toward their employees on a day-to-day basis that is greatly appreciated. This situation raises additional questions about the potential for increased supervisor stress as supervisors are forced to make individual decisions in the absence of corporate policy. "Can I leave early to prepare my child's birthday party"; "I know I am out of sick days, but my child was just sent home from school." Supervisors must deal with dilemmas such as these on an increasingly frequent basis.

What is most striking is the differential response that emerged between the two corporations. Almost twice as many respondents in Company B as in Company A considered the corporation sensitive to their needs (Table 4.34). The striking differences in employees' perceptions of the two companies cannot be explained by better benefits, more enlightened policies toward parents, or day-care programs; both companies are similar in these respects. At the time of this research neither company had any benefits, programs, or policies that addressed

Table 4.33
Company Support of Employees

n = 1,520

Do you feel the company is sensitive to the needs of a working person like yourself?

$F = 3.40$ $p = .001$

Category	Value
Single Male Parents	3.65
Married Male Non-Parents	3.39
Single Male Non-Parents	3.33
Single Female Non-Parents	3.31
Married Female Non-Parents	3.31
Married Male Parents	3.26
Single Female Parents	3.11
Married Female Parents	2.99

Total X = 3.25

1 = Very insensitive   5 = Very Sensitive

1   1.5   2   2.5   3   3.5   4

Table 4.34
Corporate Sensitivity to Work/Family Needs

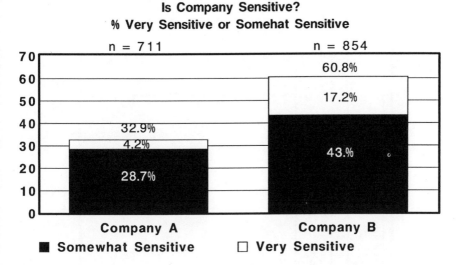

Is Company Sensitive?
% Very Sensitive or Somehat Sensitive

dependent care. In fact, there were strikingly few differences between the companies on a number of variables. Both were desirable places to work and in the upper levels of corporations in terms of salary and benefits. What is different is a more intangible set of messages that are transmitted through the corporate culture that in one company communicates a sensitivity and in the other more of an insensitivity. This finding suggests, in part, that overall management and corporate policy and style can go a long way in projecting concern and sensitivity to working parents. Thus before jumping to specific programs for child care or policies on flex time, it might be wise to examine the broader management climate and corporate culture.

Corporate Responsibility. What should or could the corporation do to lessen work/family stress? Employees recommended a number of programs, benefits, or structural changes, most of which are neither novel nor unexpected (Table 4.35). Policies that address greater scheduling flexibility were most frequently mentioned. Suggestions for work conditions improvement entailed primarily increased company attention to work/family conflicts. Although day-care benefits were mentioned third most frequently overall, they were mentioned first in recommendations of policies to make parent employees' lives better. The day-care benefits suggested included not only on-site programs, but voucher systems, contracting to off-site centers, cash benefits, and flexible-choice benefit packages as well. These recommendations suggest a more active role for corporations in family support.

Another series of questions sought responses on employees' perceptions of social problems. Table 4.36 reports societal problems of greatest concern to

Table 4.35
Things the Company Could Do to Make Work and Homelife Better

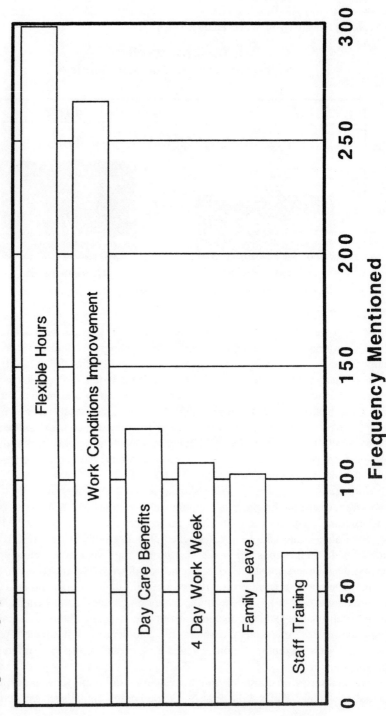

Flexible Hours

Work Conditions Improvement

Day Care Benefits

4 Day Work Week

Family Leave

Staff Training

Frequency Mentioned

0   50   100   150   200   250   300

Table 4.36
Respondents' Societal Concerns

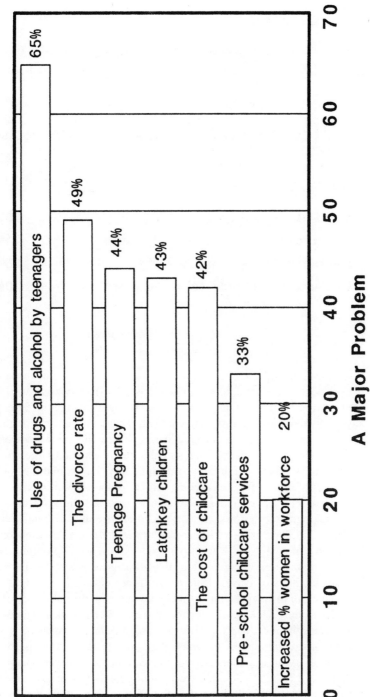

(1 = no problem; 5 = a major problem)

A Major Problem

Use of drugs and alcohol by teenagers — 65%
The divorce rate — 49%
Teenage Pregnancy — 44%
Latchkey children — 43%
The cost of childcare — 42%
Pre-school childcare services — 33%
Increased % women in workforce — 20%

Table 4.37
Responsibility for Solving Societal Problems

Who has the responsibility for helping parents and families deal with the problems of balancing work and home,

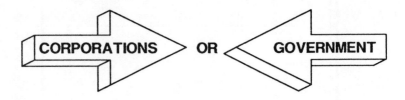

Each has equal responsibility	43%
Corporations should take the lead	41%
Neither has any responsibility	16%
Government should take the lead	0%

(n = 51 interviews)

respondents as indicated in follow-up interviews. Not coincidentally, most of the problems mentioned, although not caused by the advent of working parents, are nevertheless tied to that phenomenon. Teens who are alone after school may have fewer social supports and controls, and thus may run higher risks for problems such as drugs and teen pregnancy. Research has not yet been conclusive on this topic. The issues for younger children are centered more around absence of parents (latchkey children) and affordability and availability of child care. Shortages of child care are reaching critical proportions in many locales.

Interestingly, none of the respondents perceived the government to be the sector taking the lead in issues such as child care and work/family arrangements (Table 4.37). This is a striking contrast to attitudes of a previous generation in which government was the primary mover in most social programs such as child care. Thus the Reagan revolution of getting government off the backs of the people may have succeeded if these results are viewed in this light. The not-so-good news for the corporation is that in the retreat of the public sector, employees are increasingly looking to their employers to help with the issues. This has long-lasting implications for corporate policy, and responsiveness to both employees and communities in which they operate. Expectations are a powerful variable in trying to understand corporate response to these issues.

Emerging Trends. Although work/family conflict is already an area of stress for employees, particularly in the area of parenting, study results suggest that the conflict may intensify in coming years as family support demands increase. Emerging areas of stress raised, but not explored thoroughly, in the study include the following:

• *Care of aging parents*. Forty-three percent of respondents currently take some responsibility for care of aging parents. For 6 percent this caregiving responsibility is a major problem. As the population ages and the birthrate declines, fewer adult children are available to provide family care; this pressure on the workforce is likely to increase.

• *Time spent on second jobs or at school*. To maintain adequate incomes and to increase chances for advancement, 12 percent of respondents work an average of thirteen hours per week in a second job outside their full-time job. Almost 23 percent of respondents attend school outside of work for an average of six hours per week. These employees, all of whom are full-time, are clearly taxed to the limit of their available time. Increasing housing, day-care, and education costs are likely to further the need for supplemental income from second jobs.

• *Spouse employed by the company*. Almost 25 percent of married respondents reported that their spouses were employed by the same company. With the average age of first marriage increasing, and the incidence of divorce and remarriage increasing as well, it is now more likely that future spouses will meet at work than at school, social, or neighborhood settings. The work setting may be rapidly replacing the friendship network in the support system of employees. The implications for management of larger numbers of married couples in the workforce may be numerous, and have yet to be considered in any systematic way.

• *Projected childbearing*. As indicated in Table 4.38, almost half of all respondents report that they plan to have children in the future—19 percent within the next year and 53 percent within two to four years. Clearly the issue of parent employees and resultant work/family conflict is not one that is going to disappear soon. Because the fastest-growing segment of the workforce is married women with children under age 3, it is evident that women are no longer taking long periods of time away from work to raise children. Even if they did, employers would find it necessary to entice them back to work because of resultant labor shortages. The potential work/family conflicts within the workforce appear evident and growing.

CONCLUSIONS

All these facts point to the changing nature of both families and workplaces. They also underscore the need to examine the attitudes, behaviors, and policies that hinder successful resolution of these complex roles and functions. The nearly 1,500 employees who participated in this research existed along a continuum of dependent-care providers. All of them are struggling and will continue to struggle with their particular issues in regard to work and family or household. What comes through from the data is a genuine anguish among these employees and their families, and a series of contradictions between the needs and expectations

Table 4.38
Projected Childbearing

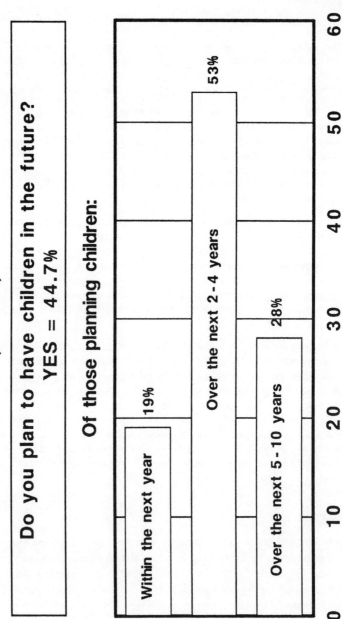

(n= 443)

Do you plan to have children in the future?
YES = 44.7%

Of those planning children:

Within the next year — 19%

Over the next 2 - 4 years — 53%

Over the next 5 - 10 years — 28%

%

0   10   20   30   40   50   60

of corporations and society toward working families, and the families' ability to carry out their roles and responsibilities. The remainder of this book builds on these findings in better understanding both the factors that contribute to work/family conflicts and the elements and components necessary for resolving them.

Chapter 5

CONFLICTS WITHIN THE FAMILY

For the vast majority of Americans, work/family conflicts have become an identifiable part of daily life. The problems generated by these conflicts increasingly impact families as they struggle to carry out their roles and responsibilities. This chapter explores the dimensions and salient characteristics of work/family conflicts that directly impact family functions.

WHAT IS A FAMILY?

There are some problems using the generic term family when designating the entire personal-family-home domain of one's life. At first glance the term family may seem too restrictive because some of the conflicts either occur at an individual level or center around household management tasks (which may be semi-independent of family relations). Furthermore, the term family tends to conjure up the 1950s image of a nuclear family with Mom, Dad, and at least a couple of children at home. At that time the prevailing concept of family was the Ozzie-and-Harriet-type, intact nuclear family that was aggressively marketed by the primary social institutions (e.g., schools and religions) and the media. Despite the growing diversity of household types in the United States today, this unidimensional archetype of the American family persists.

Thus the discussion of work/family conflicts begins with the definition of what is family. This struggle over the definition of family is not simply an academic exercise: the fluctuating conceptions of family reflect the changing values and cultural upheaval of our society. A major initiative of Jimmy Carter's presidency was the convening of a White House Conference on the Family. Much of that effort was mired down in intense debate over what was and was not a family. Although it is not the intent of this chapter to get into the specifics of that debate, which is fueled by complex religious and cultural issues, it is important to note that the very nature and definition of the family are hotly contested and cannot be separated from the work/family sphere.

Using the term family itself creates controversy, since its traditional meaning overlooks and ignores the newly emerging family types. Because the narrow and simplified notion of a single American family type is no longer appropriate, discussing today's "family" requires a number of qualifiers and modifiers to get a true picture of the family. Even the field of studies that this book addresses— work/family—constitutes an erroneous conceptualization of the population it studies. Although a significant number of households cannot identify with the term family, they nevertheless share many of the work/family conflicts.

The term household may better capture the population's living arrangements. Although the Census Bureau has long recognized this term in their surveys, the public has been socialized to the term family. Unfortunately expanding the concept of "family" to "households" has its own drawbacks. A significant problem with this more liberal term is that family responsibilities often extend beyond a person's own household, as in the case of adult children providing care to a dependent elderly parent who resides in his or her own home. In addition, the term family connotes the emotional and interpersonal dynamics that play such an important part in work/family conflicts. In contrast to the term household, family is ingrained in our culture, and evokes a concept more familiar to those outside academia. Consequently the more colloquial term family is used in this book, despite its limitations.

THE EXPERIENCE OF CONFLICT

The universality of work/family conflicts is manifested by the following items:

- *Fortune* magazine, in its study of 400 men and women with children under age 12, found that 37 percent of the fathers and 41 percent of the mothers indicated that their jobs interfered with their family responsibilities.[1]

- Among the 1,200 employees surveyed by the Work and Family Resources consulting firm, 60 percent of the men indicated that family concerns impacted their career goals, such as not considering promotions and transfers that would decrease their availability to their families.[2]

- A third of the employees who participated in the 1977 Quality of Employment Survey indicated that the responsibilities of work and family interfered with each other. An analysis of this survey data found that work/family conflicts were negatively correlated to family adjustment, job satisfaction, and a personal sense of well-being.[3]

- Thirty-nine percent of the working mothers who participated in a survey of 5,000 employees thought that the dual roles of work and family responsibilities were more than a "minimal problem."[4]

- One third of the workers who participated in the 1979 Quality of Employment Survey indicated that work schedules (including excessive hours or inconvenient schedules) interfered with family life.[5]
- The research of Piotrowski indicates that at least for some women, the quality of their work life is related to the quality of their family relationships.[6]

CONTEXT OF CONFLICT

Family conflicts reflect, in part, an environment in which families are forced to deal with multiple roles and responsibilities. These environments or contexts shape the family's work life arrangements and directly contribute to and exacerbate these conflicts.

Values

Although family composition and roles have changed during the past two decades, Americans have not, by and large, devalued family. The 1981 Catalyst survey found that among the employees who participated, 58 percent of the women and 60 percent of the men thought that family was their most important concern in life.[7] Other recent studies have provided some insight into the satisfaction that family life continues to provide to its members: in one survey two thirds of the married adults were "very happy" with their marriages and nearly three fourths of the children interviewed described their families as being "close and intimate."[8] It would appear that despite the stress of work/family conflicts, many families continue to play an essential part in the lives of their members.

However, with the vast number of dual-earner families that emerged during the seventies and eighties, many American workers began to experience a disquieting dissonance. All of a sudden adult family members were expected to focus almost exclusively on work during the day, which in many cases seemed as if a higher priority was being placed on work. Many adults were confronted by a culture and a value system that reinforced the notion that they had to choose between their commitment to work and their commitment to home.[9] This "forced choice" put many working family members in a situation of psychological turmoil because their values dictated that family was of ultimate importance, but their behavior suggested that work was more important.

Another factor that has exaggerated the conflicts experienced by many working families is that the changes in societal attitudes and values often lag behind the adaptive changes that people make in their behavior. Because deeply held cultural values are so integrated into family life, changes in family roles that are in consistent with traditional norms add a significant overlay of distress. For example, the concept of wives going out to work when there are children at home is not an accepted value, despite the fact that this is a reality throughout the country. Participants in the Balancing Job and Home Life study were asked to respond to the statement "A mother who works outside the home can have just as good a relationship with her children as a mother who does not work.'' The statement evoked a considerably negative response, particularly among the men.[10] This would imply that there are certain cultural family types that serve as quasi-normative, in that they are highly valued and aspired to, at least by some significant portion of the population. The divergence from this ideal type brings with it dissonance and, therefore, stress and conflict in trying to fit the existing demands and realities into the prevailing cultural norms. For many families this divergence spills over into role conflicts between household members and into intrapsychic stress in terms of guilt and feelings of inadequacy, leading either to the supermom syndrome or to increased feelings of guilt.

Gender and Role Expectations

At the heart of family conflicts lies the dichotomy between gender-related roles and expectations and the inability of current working and home-care arrangements to fit with these previously accepted norms. Buried more deeply behind the mundane conflicts over who does the dishes and who gives the children their baths is a more profound family struggle over gender equity, power, and mutual satisfaction of psychological and developmental needs. It is, therefore, not surprising that many aspects of work/family conflicts have been popularized as a battle in the war between the sexes.

The dissonance between value systems and daily life is most acute for women. Despite the significant role many women play in securing economic resources for the family, our society continues to convey the following messages:

- Women belong at home.
- Women should take care of the needs of the household.
- The healthy development of children depends on the quality of their relations with their mothers.
- Women who work will no longer care as much about their families' needs for nurturance and emotional growth.
- Women's first priority should be their families.
- Men cannot successfully compete at work unless their wives are taking care of the house and the children.
- Marital discord will result from men and women socializing at work.
- Men's sense of self will be threatened when they are no longer the sole source of family income. This is intensified when their wives earn more than they do.
- As women are able to support themselves (and their children), they will be less committed to entering or sustaining their marriages.

These are but a few of the fears and existing cultural values and norms that add to the family conflict over working and taking care of the home front.

Nowhere is the gender conflict more obvious than in the traditionally stereotyped roles of household tasks and child-rearing. Much of the division of labor within the family is grounded in the functionalist views of Parsonian systems theory. Instrumental and expressive activities are viewed as the unique responsibilities of men and women, respectively. Because many of the women's roles arise out of the biological acts of childbearing and nursing, men are exempted from these roles and turn to instrumental roles.[11] Although there is considerable criticism of that school of thought, it is clear from the review of the literature on family labor and from the data presented in this book that household tasks are often sex-typed and that women do most of the work.[12]

Gender role conflicts manifested at home tend to revolve around three issues: (1) the amount of time working men and women invest in home/family responsibilities; (2) the types of tasks assigned to family members as a result of sex role stereotyping; and (3) the comparative degree of accommodations made by family members in support of men's and women's careers. Gender conflicts usually arise because the family system has not adapted sufficiently to the change in women's role outside the home. Although it is collectively apparent that some of the family roles must be renegotiated when women are at work and no longer available full-time to respond to family and home needs, other family members often are reluctant to pick up additional responsibilities.

Gender role conflicts that occur at home can appear in many different family types, including the traditional married couples, people of the opposite sex living together, and dual-career couples. Although these conflicts are typically expressed between adults of the opposite sex sharing a residence, other family members also can become involved in gender role conflicts. Surprisingly, single parents may not be exempt from these conflicts because they may encounter expectations about "appropriate" sex role stereotypes from their children or from their parents. In a similar manner, working single women who assume responsibility for the care of an aging parent may have to resolve some gender conflicts with adult male siblings who are not sharing the burdens of elder care. As women have taken on new roles they typically feel the most poignant impact of the resultant conflicts because household management and dependent care have traditionally been ascribed to the female.

There are some significant differences in the work/family conflicts experienced by men and women. For example, some recent studies indicate that among women, family-related stress—although typically lower than work-related stress—is more strongly associated with negative mental health indicators such as depression. The opposite is true for men; however, family stress was associated with physical problems for men.[13] A number of studies suggest that in comparison to men, the overall well-being of women is lower.

The mental health of wives was lower than that of husbands. And whereas husbands derived their senses of well being from both work and non-work situations, wives derived their sense of well being basically from the satisfactions derived from the nonwork spheres of their lives and by experiencing less interrole conflict. Thus the evidence again indicated that wives experience greater role conflict than men do and as a consequence their mental health suffers.[14]

Although wives' conflicts often are manifested in high stress, husbands may tend to function as if they were well insulated from their wives' stress. There is a strong correlation between men who spend long hours at work and high work/family conflict for themselves as well as for their wives. Longer work hours for the wives, however, predict only role strain for the women, not for their husbands.[15]

A 1984 study of 5,000 employees found that, overall, 60 percent of the men (in contrast to 28% of the women) reported that they had "no problem" with child-care issues.[16] This study found a significant gender gap among men and women with respect to the stress felt about child care and work/family conflicts. The research surmised that working mothers, who assumed the bulk of the child-care responsibilities, were in essence functioning as single mothers.[17] Furthermore, whereas 39 percent of these working women believed that their dual roles created some stress at home, only one-third that proportion (32%) of men reported this stress.[18]

There is conflicting data about the relation between a woman's experience of stress and the number of roles she assumes. The results of some research suggest that professional wives, especially mothers, experienced less well-being than their husbands because they felt a greater sense of frustration trying to assume multiple work and family roles simultaneously.[19] There also is evidence, however, that there can be a salutory nature for women who fulfill both work and family responsibilities.[20] Marks argues that involvement in multiple roles enhances, rather than drains, energy.[21] Barnett and Baruch have reported similar findings with respect to wives' employment, contending that the more roles these women hold, the better off they are.[22] It is possible that involvement in multiple roles can offer women several different social support networks to which they can turn for assistance. This potentially positive benefit of multiple-role assumption was suggested by the recent substance abuse research conducted by Googins and associates (1989). In that study the workplace tended to act as a haven or buffer for employed wives of alcoholic husbands. The working role, in essence, enabled them to offset the dysfunctional and depressing environment of the household and to develop a countervailing positive support within the workplace. This benefit to women of assuming multiple roles also might explain the high level of job satisfaction among married women and single parents found in this study's data, despite the high levels of job/family role strain exhibited by the same groups.

Their own socialization has contributed to work/family conflicts for many women because they were raised to believe that they should be able to independently cope with family issues.[23] Women who maintain this belief system are less likely to ask their husbands for some assistance because they see the need for support as a sign of failure in their role as a woman/wife/mother. These women, who try to fulfill expectations as superwomen, put themselves at risk for role overload. Women who are employed outside the home tend to assume two jobs. Role overload received much attention during the 1960s as women began moving into the workplace and yet maintained their household and family responsibilities.[24] This type of role overload is associated with physical and emotional exhaustion. Indeed, some research has found that among women, employment is associated with improved mental health only if their spouses share the family work.[25]

Because socialization is such a powerful cultural determinant, it is not surprising that the effects of socialization are very much a part of the conflict, and serve as barriers to reducing gender strain. The multiple roles of working and parenting or householding are new to both men and women, since they have no previous socialized models on which to organize and relegate these multiple responsibilities. This is particularly true of housework and child care, which have traditionally been set according to gender, a system strongly endorsed by our normative social system.[26] Some of today's career couples are experimenting with role interchangeability and a varying day-to-day allocation of domestic responsibilities that reflects career demands.[27]

Some women may anticipate the difficulty of resolving some of the almost inevitable work/family conflicts and make a choice: among women business executives, one fifth have never married and an additional 20 percent are either separated or divorced. Less than half of these women have children. In contrast, 99 percent of their male counterparts are married and an almost equal proportion (95%) have children.[28]

As discussed in the ''Household Management Role and Parenting Role'' sections of this chapter, there is abundant evidence that men are not providing much more assistance to their working wives in this arena than they did when their wives were at home full-time. One study found that although working husbands typically use their wives as a source of help, working women are more likely to depend on other relatives.[29] This reality has been on the agenda of the women's movement, and the resultant gender discord has surfaced in feminist literature.

Despite the fact that men might not be investing much additional time in family/home responsibilities, they are feeling stress when they perceive that these needs may not have been met. The 1987 Boston University Balancing Job and Homelife study data described in Chapter 4 found nearly equal percentages of men (36%) and women (37%) reporting ''a lot of stress'' related to their attempts to balance home and work aspects of their lives. Research conducted in 1981 found that among the male engineering graduates surveyed, approximately half indicated that they experienced work/family role conflict.[30] Finally, a Minneapolis-based research firm reports that more than 70 percent of the fathers under age 35 participating in their study stated that they had serious concerns about how they were managing work/family conflicts with their wives.[31]

Dramatic changes in women's roles occurred during the sixties and seventies; we may be witnessing comparable changes in men's roles over the next several decades. During these times of transition some interesting changes have occurred among men. Pleck reports an increasing participation of men in housework and paints a more egalitarian picture emerging in what he terms the ideology of sharing.[32] He indicates that there is some evidence that the discrepancy between husbands and wives associated with the performance of household chores is related to education, whereby husbands with higher education are more likely to share in these responsibilities (unless the family structure reflects the more traditional model in which the wife is a full-time homemaker). This may be reflective of the *Fortune* survey, in which slightly more than half of both men and women reported that fathers and mothers equally share in child-care responsibilities.[33] Despite the possible changes in gender role conflicts that might occur in the United States, women continue to be torn between the expectations of work and home. Sekaran, referring to her 1985 research, observes that "wives, irrespective of their level of competence, felt uncomfortable when they spent more of their time on career activities than on family ones. They seemed to be constantly in the throws of a dilemma as to whether careers could or should be given the same attention and priority as the family."[34] Because women keenly feel their responsibilities to both work and family, they tend to experience psychological overlap between these two domains. The permeability of the boundaries between their work and home results from their dual sets of demands. Thus it is not unusual to find women who leave their geographical home to enter the workplace, but who are psychologically attached to the home in terms of management tasks, guilt, and a feeling of inadequacy in meeting their own expectations of what a good wife/mother should be.

One interesting twist has occurred as women attempt to sort out their roles during different stages of their life cycles. After having trained and prepared themselves for their careers, they may find it difficult to pursue their professions full-time when their children are young. Some women who even temporarily pull back on their career commitments and focus on their families believe that they have copped out. There is almost a sense that these women feel a need to explain themselves to their professional associates.

As women have assumed their working roles they have most often done so within a social and cultural framework that lacks adequate models for the integration of women's multiple responsibilities and offers insufficient support for women's roles. It is seldom supported or accepted for a woman with a family to throw herself into her work with the same abandon and commitment of time and energy that a man does. Strong sets of norms and social expectations produce a high degree of stress and uncomfortability for women. "All in all, indications are that even though husbands and wives might perceive their careers to be equally important and see their work and family worlds in more or less the same way, the wives encounter impediments in experiencing high levels of satisfaction at the workplace and enjoying a sense of well-being."[35]

Women are experiencing unique forms of work/family conflicts. They have been tantalized, challenged, and excited about their jobs and careers. At the same time they are frustrated by their inability to "have it all" without considerable sacrifice. On the other hand, no one asks men—nor do they ask themselves—how they can "have it all." Cultural and social constraints have made it difficult for women with family responsibilities to allocate sufficient time to ensure career mobility and success. The functions assumed by women tend to subsidize the careers of their husbands, but they are not likely to receive the same kind of support. Working women tend to pay a high price for their multiple roles, which is often not fully appreciated by men and certainly not by corporations and society.

Institutional Rigidity

A third dimension of the context of work/family conflicts that are manifested at home is the rigidity of outside institutions. Instead of serving as supports for working families, they can actually exacerbate and contribute to the conflicts. Although the majority of adults have become involved in the operations of the workplace, institutions such as schools, health facilities, corporations, and numerous service operations still operate as if the family is in the home during the working day and is easily able to fulfill responsibilities of homemaker and care providers. Remaining focused on their own institutional needs, most organizations have not been able to shift and adapt to the working families of today to any great extent. The family is primarily left to its own devices in terms of getting the washing machine fixed, taking care of a sick child, and taking an aging parent to a doctor's appointment. It is as if the demographic changes associated with the fact that most adult family members are now participating in the workforce have gone unrecognized by both public and private institutions. Consequently the family continues to bear the brunt of responsibility for getting it all together.

Within the private market there are a few examples of potential changes that can help to alleviate some of the stress experienced by many working families. Some physicians who live in competitive regions are starting to offer early morning, evening, and weekend hours. Home shopping (by way of catalogue, television, and telephone) has proliferated. A few organizations, such as health clubs and larger shopping malls, offer some child-care services. But these adaptations are the exception. Consider the situation of a working family interacting with the local branch of the U.S. Postal Service. The family receives a notice that a postal worker attempted to deliver a registered letter (such as a new credit card), which requires the signature of the addressee. The notice left at the home indicates that the letter will remain at the post office for three days, after which it will be returned to the sender. It is quite possible that the working family will not be able to get to the post office during working hours, and will have to wait until Saturday, but that might exceed the three-day period. Consequently the letter is returned, and the process starts all over again.

Unlike families in most other industrialized countries, families in the United

States can expect little institutional response and support to their caregiving roles to children, parents, and themselves as family. The inviolate sacredness of the family precludes governmental and corporate interference and perpetuates the now dysfunctional relations between the institution of the family and the institutions of work and society.

CONFLICT IN ROLES

Several roles assumed by adults occur in a variety of family/household types, including income earning, parenting (or providing care for another dependent relative), managing of household, assuming responsibility for spousal (or its equivalent) relationship, and attending to personal (e.g., physical, intellectual, spiritual, and social) needs. Of particular interest to this book are the problems that arise because of the difficulties adults experience when they try to accomplish their responsibilities as income-earners while simultaneously fulfilling other primary roles associated with family life.

As mentioned in Chapter 2, there are several aspects of role conflicts. Role overload results from having too much to accomplish. Role strain is associated with problems of competing roles. Adults often experience this dilemma when they cannot "be in two places at one time" (either geographically or psychologically). Another factor in role conflict is that different roles often require different skills, and it can be difficult for people to make the transition from one role to another. In contrasting typical work and family roles it is not uncommon to find that work roles are associated with control, set schedules, paid work, and intellectual/cognitive outputs, whereas family roles often are characterized as being less controlled and more informal relative to scheduling, unpaid work, and having emotional outputs.[36]

Role conflicts cannot be conceptualized as if they have a singular effect on different people. For example, the perceived quality of the role mediates the effect it has on a person. A parent who is satisfied with the development of his or her children and with the care they receive is likely to have a minimum of parental stress. Similarly, a worker who receives a lot of satisfaction from different aspects of the job (including consistency with career goals, sense of autonomy, pay, supervisory style, and manageable work load) is likely to experience less work-related stress than a worker who has a high level of dissatisfaction. The following observation by Hoffman is particularly relevant.

Although some writers expect employed women to have higher morale because of the satisfactions of outside employment, and others expect them to be stressed because of work overload, there is agreement that satisfaction with one's employment status—whether one is an employee or a full-time homemaker—will have a positive effect on family relations, mothering behavior, and child outcomes. A number of studies support this prediction (Birnbaum, 1975; Farel, 1980 . . .). As has often been pointed out, however, the casual direction involved in these studies is not clear, for satisfaction could be the consequence of the happy outcome as well as the antecedent.[37]

Thus discussions of role conflict need to acknowledge that differences occur that result from the qualitative characteristics of these roles as perceived by individual adults. Four roles in particular can be examined in some depth.

Parenting Role

The challenges of the parenting role to working adults have symbolized work/ family dilemmas for the past decade because these two roles (working and parenting) often are seen as the most difficult and most demanding.[38] Many theorists in family development identify the roles associated with children and work as the two primary factors that account for the transitional challenges confronted by families.[39] The balancing of parenting and working is a reality for many adults. The proportion of mothers with a child under age 18 who are working full-time grew from 29 percent in 1975 to 41 percent in 1986, with the largest increase for mothers with children under age 3.[40] Research findings suggest that work/family role strain is associated with the number of children in a family and with the presence of preschool-age children.[41] Furthermore, they seem to compete most directly with one another. Although the two worlds of parenting and working are not mutually exclusive or inherently incompatible, the demands of each are sufficiently rooted in different arenas and make quite different emotional and logistical demands that can result in conflict for the working parent. Although parents who are new to the dual roles often find the conflicts most intense, the feelings of stress are evident throughout the whole range of family developmental stages.

Because the parenting role has captured much of the attention of work/family conflicts, this aspect of dependent care will be highlighted as a primary family role that can compete with work responsibilities. However, different forms of dependent care (e.g., elder dependent care or care of a disabled family member) can result in similar stresses for working families. A working parent whose mother needs a great deal of attention because of her isolation or because she has a prolonged illness can trigger the same type of conflicts that working parents with dependent children experience.

Working parents who are exploring alternative ways to meet their work and family obligations are confronted with some strong (and typically "traditional") value system directives associated with their parenting roles. Historical context, ethnic background, religion, and regional lifestyles all produce specific "culture of the environment" that can dictate certain parameters of the parenting role. The disparity between ingrained sets of cultural norms and the reality of the demands put on the new family structures creates stress and guilt.

Many working families are saddled with feelings that they are not really satisfied with their performance at work or at home. These working parents are confronted with role ambiguity.

Because . . . women describe both fulfillment and disappointment in paid work and house-work, their responses are most aptly characterized as ambivalent. This ambivalence shows up in conflicting feelings, inconsistent opinions and even the desire to be in two places at the same time. For example, at one moment they say that they are sure their jobs are good for their children; and at the next moment they say they feel guilty about their work. . . . To develop an unqualified preference for either paid work or housework would require the individual to deny the real problems in one and the real rewards in the other.[42]

These pioneering parents have divided loyalties: when they are at work they worry that they are not providing sufficient attention to their children, and when they are at home they worry that they are not able to put sufficient time and effort into their jobs.

A significant number of working families have children at home. In 1986 the proportion of mothers who were employed full-time and had a child under age 18 rose to 41 percent (from 29 percent in 1975), and the greatest increase was among those mothers who had children under age 3.[43] Despite the fact that many of these working families with children—especially those with preschool youngsters—use some form of child care during the parent's or parents' working hours (see Chapter 9), these parents still perform an almost endless number of parenting tasks. It is perhaps surprising how much time working parents are able to condense into their nonworking hours. One study of preschool-aged children who attended a nursery school found that there was no difference in the amount of time the working mothers devote to direct interaction with these children, although they did have less "indirect time" (time when the child and the parent were in the same room but involved in different activities) and less "available" time (when the mother was within calling distance of the child but not engaged in the same activity).[44]

It can be especially exhausting for parents to come home from work and then try to compress activities and interactions into the evening hours and the weekends. Many of these parents, and children as well, want to devote this time to "special time," when parents and children can share with each other. And yet many parents (and many children) are just plain tired at the end of the day, and dinner needs to be prepared, and the wash needs to get done, and the house needs to be cleaned, **and** the boss wants a report completed in the morning. It is understandable that many studies find that work/family conflicts are heightened when the families contain children, especially young ones.[45]

Some of the conflicts experienced by parents have to do with the ease with which they become socialized to the corporate culture that dictates the primacy of work. Workers who are open about their commitments to their families, which sometimes interfere with work demands, are somehow judged as being "less committed" to work. Working parents often feel that the energy that they must devote to work detracts from their abilities to be good parents and, similarly, that the time and emotion focused on family matters somehow decreases their capacities to focus sufficiently on work responsibilities.

Studies that compare parent and nonparent employees have demonstrated higher levels of stress in the parent populations. Holahan and Gilbert observe that their research supports the notion that the addition of the parent role appears to complicate the life situation of the couple, making dual career pursuit more difficult to maintain.[46]

Research has found that among working women there is a correlation between their dissatisfaction with the fulfillment of their parental roles and depression.[47] It is possible that working women simultaneously feel a number of emotions associated with their parenting: love, responsibility, lack of control, guilt, concern . . . setting the stage for depression.

The parenting role is particularly notable because it is almost relentlessly demanding and a role for which most adults are minimally prepared. The results of some studies suggest that parenting is associated with high levels of stress, especially for the mother.[48] In fact, a study by Barnett and Baruch found that the role of mother was associated with high levels of role overload and role conflicts, but this was not the case in connection with women's assumption of the roles of spouse and wage earner.[49] Some research suggests that work may actually offer women a respite and a buffer from the emotional and psychological demands they experience at home.[50] This ameliorative effect of work may be more common among women who are experiencing spousal problems, but work may make them more likely to suffer stress as a result of the problems that working mothers perceive in their parenting role.[51]

Gender differences in the amount of responsibility assumed for child care can intensify some of the work/family conflicts manifested at home. A study of 285 parents conducted in 1987 found that the mother's dissatisfaction with the father's participation in child-care activities was a significant predictor of her work/family stress. These results were not duplicated among the fathers.[52]

Many of the effects of parenting on working mothers are manifested on a personal level. Some research indicates that although working mothers make an effort to fulfill both their work and their parenting responsibilities, they make extensive personal sacrifices, including insufficient sleep and rest, limited free time, disrupted eating, diminished time on self-care, and reductions in social activities.[53]

And yet, despite the toll that parenting can exact, it is a powerful statement that among middle-aged parents who participated in a recent survey, 88 percent said that they would choose to have children again.[54] There seems to be almost a consensus parenting can be the most challenging role many adults ever assume, but it also can be wonderfully fulfilling.

Spousal Role

Today's marriages are subject to strains from a number of sources, as is evidenced by the high divorce rate. Half of all U.S. marriages begun in the 1980s will end in divorce, in contrast to those begun in the 1960s, when divorce was still a relatively uncommon occurrence.

One of the highly recognized challenges for today's working families is the problem associated with adult's tight schedules. It often seems as if every minute of every day is taken up by an unrelenting multitude of tasks. Working adults are becoming efficiency experts and, by necessity, are devising ways to make every second count. It is almost an art to being able to do more than one thing at a time. Time spent in the car may no longer be just driving time: some people use this time for office dictation; parents may devote this time either to conversations with their children or to educational games; many drivers compose mental lists that help them to better organize the rest of the day.

Many working families with children try to squeeze every unscheduled minute, so that parents can spend more time with their children. One of the roles that tends to get relegated to the bottom of the list is time spent on spousal relationships. By the time many working adults have put in a full day's work, spent time with the children, and completed a few necessary household chores, they are exhausted. There often is little emotional or physical energy left to relate in a meaningful way to a spouse, and many adults find that they are simply unable to devote sufficient attention to their marital relations. Time together becomes scarcer both during working days and during nonworking days. Trips to the movies or out to dinner together become less frequent. The weekend without the kids often doesn't even get on the family agenda. On a more daily basis the decreased frequency of sexual relations and practices also reflects this time squeeze, getting postponed because of exhaustion and inattention to each other. There is an abundance of anecdotal data indicating that the time crunch experienced by working families contributes to work/family conflict. Rather than being opportunities for emotional support, interactions with spouses can become an additional responsibility that seems to take more energy than the adults have. It is significant that in the Balancing Job and Home Life Study, married working women reported more job/family stress than even single mothers.[55]

Stress in the marital relationship also can result from the changes that occur in the wife that are unmatched in her husband. The dissonance in the personal development of marital partners is likely to produce some conflicts for the married couple. There are several scenarios for this development mismatch. Some couples may have had years of their relationship structured according to the husband as breadwinner/wife as homemaker model. The dynamics of this relationship are bound to change if the wife enters the workforce and develops a strong affiliation to her career. Other couples may have spent the first years of their marriage in a more egalitarian manner, with both spouses working and sharing in the home responsibilities. These couples might change their expectations for their relationship after the birth of a child. Regardless of the circumstances, the personal and professional development of one spouse seldom occurs in tandem with the personal and professional development of the other, and this can contribute to work/family conflicts. Out of these conflicts can come opportunities for growth.[56]

Commuter marriages, in which married couples live in different geographical areas close to their respective jobs and "commute" to be with each other on the weekends or during other nonwork time, are an extreme example of how work can intrude on marital relations.

The relation between marital stress and work/family conflicts is bidirectional. Unresolved work/family conflicts, such as disagreement over the division of household work, can contribute to marital (or its equivalent) discord. Understandably, it is unlikely that this one dimension of a relationship, in isolation, will be the primary cause of serious marital problems. But unresolved work/family conflicts can be the expression of other dysfunctional aspects of a relationship, such as poor communication or insufficient response to the personal needs of one's spouse. At least one study has found a relation between the failure of the husband to adequately share in the home chores and the wife's indication that she was considering divorce.[57]

Household Management Role

There are several dimensions to the interference that work imposes on the management of household tasks. At a basic level, many working adults experience some stress over the question of whether or not the chores will get done. As a by-product of the role overload experienced by so many workers, it seems like there is never enough time to accomplish everything. And if household tasks are done, it often seems that a certain standard has been compromised because things are completed in a haphazard manner. Unlike in the homes of their parents, the beds may not be made every morning, the laundry may not get folded as soon as it is taken out of the dryer, and the house is not vacuumed daily. Another component of work/family conflicts is associated with scheduling problems: the plumber says he can come but can't make a specific appointment, so workers may be forced to stay home all day and wait for him or her to appear.

Like parenting, household management has traditionally been assigned to women and is, therefore, a significant manifestation of one of the gender conflicts. Gender discord around family issues obviously goes far beyond sharing the housework. Nevertheless, the research that focuses on housework represents an interesting bellwether of work/family conflict in general. Disparity and inequality arise as women attempt to gain an equal foothold in the workplace and at the same time try to gain equality in the division of labor at home. The stresses, strains, and struggles of wives and husbands around household and child-care responsibilities constitute an extremely sensitive predictor of poor family adjustment as well as overall well-being.

A particular point of contention for many working women is that spouses of working wives do not invest much more time in housework than the husbands of wives who are at home full-time. A number of studies confirm this reality.[58] Pleck estimates that the amount of time men contribute to household duties is one fourth to one third of the time contributed by women. He notes that the rising proportion of time contributed by men to the total volume of home and family tasks largely results from the fact that women are devoting fewer hours, not that men are putting in more time.[59] The Balancing Work and Home Life study (Burden and Googins, 1987), for example, found that women spend about sixteen more hours each week on combined home chores and child care than their husbands do. Of further interest are the perceptions of the husbands about the sharing of housework and child care, which differed dramatically from those of the wives. Whereas 42 percent of the wives said that their husbands shared housework tasks equally, more than 56 percent of the husbands thought that they did.

A great deal of other research confirms the inequities. Horschchild's recently published book, *The Second Shift,* states that among the working families interviewed, 70 percent of the men did less than half of the housework.[60] Many working women look toward their children—rather than to their spouses—to help with the housework.[61] Wives may not have expected their husbands to invest equally in household chores.[62]

The division of household tasks may vary according to the proportion of the total family income that the wife contributes. Some studies suggest that women who earn higher proportions of the family income are more likely to receive some assistance from their husbands.[63] In addition, when wives' jobs require extra effort, such as overtime or travel, husbands tend to invest more time in household and family activities.[64] This phenomenon may occur because in some families a woman's status and power is associated with her earning power. In these cases the rationalization that the husband works harder and should, therefore, be excused from household tasks is no longer tenable. It also is possible that some families arrange to have the woman either work fewer hours or at a less demanding job, so that at least one adult has some energy left to attend to some of the household chores. The gender conflict here becomes apparent because it is almost invariably the woman who assumes this role in the family.

Income level also may affect how spouses prioritize work and family responsibilities. In contrast to men with higher incomes, working-class men typically place their families above their jobs in terms of importance and satisfaction. These families may have few economic alternatives other than having all family members contribute to the performance of household chores. Because the working-class family may depend on the wife's income, the husband may be more willing to contribute his fair share to household tasks. In contrast, more affluent professional men can treat their wives' income as unnecessary and inconsequential, and often can maintain a belief system that it is the wives' responsibility to make arrangements for household chores by either staying home or paying for the services of someone else.[65]

One interesting change is that although women continue to carry the bulk of the responsibilities for child care and home management tasks, there may be less traditional role assignment. It is no longer "deviant" for men to prepare dinner, vacuum, and bathe the children. Many families are devising a more flexible conception of who will attend to which needs so that the priority tasks get completed.

Role of Individual Self

As mentioned in Chapter 3, there has been an increasing recognition of the importance of responding to adult developmental needs. Within the past two decades our society has developed a greater awareness of the benefits of adults nurturing themselves physically, emotionally, creatively, and intellectually. It is no longer considered selfish for adults to devote some time to exercise or to social interactions because, in the long run, everyone gains when adults feel "renewed" and "self-actualized." These adults have more energy to devote to work and greater emotional reservoirs for their families. Unfortunately this personal role is the one that often is most vulnerable when working adults begin to search for ways to reduce work/family stress. Holahan and Gilbert found that the most significant role conflict among dual-career couples was between their professional role and their personal-self role.[66]

There is some evidence that working families who do not have an adult available at home on a full-time basis experience stress associated with limited recreational experiences and social isolation.[67] Today most working adults have responsibility for the equivalent of one and one half to two full-time jobs when the hours devoted to home and family responsibilities are added to their paid work hours. Not surprisingly, the 1986 research conducted by Sanik and Mauldin indicates that mothers in working families (both two-parent and single-parent) devote less time to recreation and personal care activities compared with those who are home full-time.[68] The absence of an adult available to manage the home makes a significant difference to full-time workers, especially in those families where one of the family members needs dependent care (e.g., child, aging relative, or disabled family member). It is difficult for these working adults to find the time to relax after work or on the weekend because of the many tasks that require immediate attention. Many families are forced to readjust their expectations of what can be accomplished. Working families with children may consider it a good week if the shopping gets done, the clothes are laundered, basically nutritious meals are prepared, the children are bathed, and some time is devoted to activities with the children. Everything else, such as reading the newspaper, is seen as extra.

One of the reasons for this role overload problem is that work takes up more and more of a given worker's day, a phenomenon that accentuates the time limitations in families where no adult is home full-time. During the sixties it was a popular notion among futurists that the U.S. work week would gradually decrease to perhaps thirty-two hours (which would increase the time available for leisure). Some sociologists anticipated that toward the end of the twentieth century, adults in the United States would face a challenge in deciding what to do with all their free time. Just the opposite has occurred. Since 1973 working America has increased the median hours of work by 15 percent, and the amount of leisure time has decreased by one third.[69] A recent survey conducted by *Time* magazine found that nearly three-fourths of women and half of the men felt that they had too little leisure time available to them.[70] It is becoming common once again for adults to work ten-hour days, six and seven days a week. According to one national survey, one third of all workers experience problems with "excessive or inconvenient hours" that interfere with their family life.[71] One journalist has commented that the fundamental problem with work/family conflicts is that "Americans have become prisoners of work."[72]

Some of the intrusion of work into potential personal time has been supported by communication technologies such as car phones and beepers. Many workers feel as if they are always on call. Some companies have offered to provide computer systems for their employees to use at home, with the stipulation that the employees spend the regular workweek at the workplace and use the "office at home" for unfinished business. Although the new technologies offer the potential for employees to have some flexibility and control over their work hours, they also facilitate the intrusion of work into the home.

One problem associated with role overload is that working men and women may not have sufficient time to devote to the development and maintenance of a social support system. During the fifties the wife typically was at home full-time and was able to frequently interact with neighbors, friends, and relatives. She had the time to entertain and to plan social events. Out of necessity working families tend to sacrifice their social identity.[73] A network of family and friends may provide working adults not only with potential of affiliation and recreation, but also with some assistance that can mitigate against some of the work/family conflicts. Unfortunately, as shown in the research conducted by Googins and associates (1989), time constraints make it difficult for working couples to cultivate and strengthen their social support networks, which ironically are needed even more when the negative effects of role overload begin to affect working families. Consequently these resources are not there when the families need them the most.[74]

CONFLICTS IN DIFFERENT FAMILY STRUCTURES

This section examines the particular impacts on different family or household types, including dual-earner families, single-parent families, working families with disabled children, blended families, families with unusual work schedules, and single-person households. This typology is by no means an exhaustive categorization of families and households, and some of the distinct concerns of many family types (e.g., minority families, intergenerational families, and gay families) are not directly addressed. This rough cut of family types is useful, however, in identifying some of the more salient work/family conflict issues manifested at home.

The main purpose of this framework is to identify the unique conflicts directly experienced by the variety of families and households that constitute today's working families and communities. The secondary impacts of work/family conflicts on dependent family members (e.g., children and elders) are discussed in later chapters.

Dual-Earner Families

Of all the changes that have occurred in American families, the emergence of dual-earner families reflects much of what has occurred in our society. Some observers of the increasing prevalence of dual-earner families, speculate that this change is a sign of the structural alterations and value shifts in contemporary society that emphasize an increasing partnership in family life and results in more equity between husband and wife and more collaborative decision making. The dual-earner family typifies the dramatic move from a traditional wife-at-home household to a household in which both spouses work.

The selection of labels for families in which both spouses work has been given considerable attention in the literature. A number of authors have attempted to make a distinction between dual-career and dual-worker or dual-earner households. Most social scientists define the dual-career family as one characterized by "equal distribution or division of labor in family functions and by the spouses' strong commitment to personal growth and increasing levels of responsibility in their respective careers."[75]

In contrast, the terms dual-worker and dual-earner families describe the employment status of the spouses but do not specify the degree of their career affiliations or their orientation to family and home roles. There is an implication in making this distinction that the former group has careers (rather than jobs), that they adopt professional pursuits (rather than more common front-line jobs), and that they have a certain level of economic security (i.e., work is part of their self-actualization, not merely a means to an economic goal).

Some considerations that reflect the potential socioeconomic differences between dual-career and dual-earner families need to be addressed. The lifestyles of the two groups, to cite one example, may be quite different. Another difference may be the attitudes that the spouses have toward their dual-earner status. Dual-career couples who consciously choose this lifestyle may cooperate with each other in anticipating and resolving work/family conflicts because their lifestyle is, to some extent, voluntary, and both spouses may feel some commitment to it. In contrast, dual-worker families who cannot support themselves without two incomes may feel more trapped by the necessity of having both spouses work. As the results of the 1979 research conducted by Holahan and Gilbert suggest, it is also possible that dual-career couples have value systems that enable them to explore and accept nontraditional solutions to work/family issues.[76]

It is important to keep in mind while reviewing the dual-earner literature that the vast majority of families in which both the husband and the wife work are not the stereotyped yuppie, two-career couples', but rather couples who perceive their jobs not as "careers," but as "jobs." Benenson, in his recent critique of dual-career family analysis, observed the following findings that typify dual-earner couples:

- The number of married women in elite professions is insignificant relative to all married men.
- The elite dual-career pattern reproduces traditional spousal inequalities.
- Women in elite professions are more likely to be single or divorced or to have no children if married as a consequence of career involvement.
- The largest concentrations of professional women are in the low-paying fields of nursing, education, and human services.
- The most significant occupational development since World War II has been the growth of women employed in clerical, lower-level professional, and service jobs. The working class and middle class are increasingly characterized by a two-worker family, and the poor working class by a sole female provider. The motivation for employment is economic, rather than self-actualization.
- These classes of dual-worker couples do not have sufficient income for domestic help or child care, and they rely on their social support systems.[77]

The distinction between a career person and a worker hints at the relatively ignored class distinction that exists among working couples. Not unlike many social problems, the social acceptance of an issue as a problem usually occurs when significant numbers of the middle and professional classes become affected. This was true with most of the illegal drugs, such as marijuana and cocaine, that were present in urban, low-income communities for many decades, but were seldom perceived as a social problem until the drugs became visible in the middle class. The same evolution is certainly true of dual-earner families. Although the combination of staggering rates of inflation during the late sixties and seventies, the women's movement, and the growing quest for labor brought the dual-career concept into prominence, the experience of having both husband and wife work was not new to lower socioeconomic groups and to minorities in particular. Throughout the late nineteenth and the twentieth centuries it was necessary for both adults (and children) in families with limited incomes to work to remain economically viable. Although this chapter does not dwell any further on the class issue, the attention that has been generated around this "new phenomenon" of the dual-earner couple is not news to the lower economic classes in our society. Perhaps the real difference rests not so much in the work/family conflicts as in the different approaches to the resolution of these conflicts. The relatively higher economic status and standard of living of dual-career families afford them access to resources that can minimize and eliminate some of the work/family conflicts. Dual-career couples may be able to consider employing an *au pair* to assist with child care and a house-cleaning services to help with some of the home management chores. Dual-earner couples with more limited incomes may have to limit their choices of resolution of work/family conflicts. Although these families are not as likely to purchase expensive services, they may have easier access to a familiar neighborhood sitter or a relative who can help with some of the family responsibilities.

One of the problems with focusing on the differences between dual-career and dual-worker families is that it tends to emphasize class differences among women, which can distort and misrepresent their experiences. Many discussions of the dual-career model indicate that career commitment holds a central position in women's lives and contrasts paid work with nonpaid family and household responsibilities. This framework compares the attitudes of working-class women—not with working-class men—but the limited number of women in those professions results in a framework that closely conforms to that of male professionals in their career orientations and commitment. Working-class women's financial reasons for seeking employment are directly contrasted with the personal reasons given by dual-career professional women. Financial need often is taken as excluding personal motivations; women who "have" to work are seen as not wanting to work, rather than as disliking aspects of their current jobs.[78] This model of dual-career couples, which dwells on the class differences among women workers and juxtaposes their career orientations, creates an illusion that the work/family orientations of dual-career women and women in dual-worker families are as different as night and day.

Dual-earner families share many common experiences and conflicts, regardless of their income levels or occupational orientations. Consequently, for the purposes of this chapter, the more encompassing terms dual-earner and dual-worker are used, rather than the more narrowly defined dual-career couples.

The entry of married women into the workforce has been referred to as the "subtle" revolution of this century. As wives have entered the labor force, nearly every member of the family system has been forced to adapt. These changes have taken place on a large scale, and thus the universal phenomenon of dual-earner couples.

- According to the Conference Board, today there are about 47 million men and women in dual-career families, up from 900,000 families in 1960.[79]

- Nearly two fifths of the U.S. workforce is composed of spouses in dual-earner households.[80]

- More than half of all married couples (51.8%) were dual-earner couples in 1981, in contrast to 23.6 percent of married couples in which the husband was the sole income-earner.[81]

With more than half of all American families adopting this lifestyle, dual-earner families have emerged as much more common than the traditional husband-as-breadwinner model.

AREAS OF CONFLICT

Family System Adjustments

The family system needs to make major adaptations when no adult is available to attend to family and home needs on a full-time basis. The role overload problem quickly becomes a family problem because the family does not have access to the time necessary to accomplish everything in exactly the same way it was done during the fifties when the mother could almost exclusively focus on these responsibilities. The movement of wives and mothers into the workforce resulted in an inevitable modification of the role division in marriage toward greater symmetry of responsibility for breadwinning and, to a lesser extent, homemaking.

Most working adults would find it beneficial to have another person (or people) support their careers by attending to home and family needs, freeing the employed adult to focus on work. Before the advent of dual-earner households the wife usually served in the capacity of propping up the husband's career.[82] Her contribution to the economic vitality and upward mobility of the family lay primarily in the support she offered to her husband. When considering the dual-earner family it can legitimately be asked, "Who is available now to prop up the family?" and "Whose career does the family prop up?" Many of the work/family conflicts experienced by dual-worker families reflect the fact that family structures are not able to adequately provide the necessary supports for two working adults.

The fact that two spouses now share (at a minimum) two roles each (worker role and family role) complicates the dynamics of organizing and coordinating functions. The complexity of interactions becomes apparent when the roles of the dual-earner family are contrasted to the traditional family model. In the traditional family structure the wife's home/family role affected the husband's worker role, and the inverse was true when the husband's worker role affected the wife's home/family role. The combinations of interactions are multiplied in the dual-earner family in which the wife's worker role affects her home/family role (and vice versa), the wife's worker role affects her husband's worker role (and vice versa), the wife's home/family role affects her husband's worker role (and vice versa), and the husband's worker role affects his home/family role (and vice versa).

This expansion of the roles of wife and mother not only shifts some of the traditional responsibilities of other household members, but also makes it necessary for families to reexamine many of the deeply held values that undergird the social and cultural constructs of the family system. The structure of the dual-earner family contrasts dramatically with the traditional nuclear family of the fifties in which the assignment of roles was simple and clear (one adult taking primary responsibility for the management of the household and the care of children and any other dependents and the other person focusing on the economic well-being of the family unit). The need to redefine family roles, especially those that had been rigidly conceptualized as gender-specific, constituted a social upheaval for many families.

This failure of the family system to readjust as the wife left the home has continued to smolder as a source of conflict up to and including the present day.

Gender Conflicts

The decision of spouses to adopt the dual-worker lifestyle can be, in itself, conflict-generating. For many couples the adoption of a working role outside the home for the woman conflicts with the strong cultural theme of the man as the good provider. This can set up resentment among some men who internalize their wives' employment status as a commentary on their inadequacy as bread-winners. During the years when large numbers of dual-earner families began to emerge the Holmstrom study identified the cultural definition of masculinity as "superior" and the need of men to retain this gender advantage as one of the barriers encountered by these couples.[83]

The dual-career family faces two gender-related challenges: How might women's needs (e.g., economic, physical, cognitive) be accommodated (rather than subordinated to family needs)? and How can women compete within a workplace or career when the constraints of home and gender role expectations put them at a distinct disadvantage? Men's work often is structured around the assumption that men have minimal direct-care responsibilities for their homes and families. In fact, they can be expected to bring work home and allow the demand of the workplace to supercede the needs of the family. However, when both spouses work it is seldom possible for both of them to allow work to take precedence over home and family needs during nonwork hours.

The growing stress experienced by dual-earner families was reflected in the literature during the seventies and eighties. Note the titles of some articles during that time: "Dual career—A Family Killer"[84]; "The Stress Check: Coping with Stresses of Life and Work"[85]; "Management and Marriage—Push and Shove"[86] and "More Working Wives Expose Their Hubbies to the Joy of Cooking."[87] Much of this conflict between men and women in dual-worker families results from the role conflicts engendered by the new family structure. The disappearance of the separate spheres of work and family may have occurred more successfully outside the family than inside.[88] Whereas the workplace was increasingly aware of the spillover of family into the workplace, much of the traditional roles and expectations that existed before the expanded numbers of dual-worker families did not significantly adjust to the new family structure. Even husbands who express attitudes congruent with those of their wives on the appropriateness of wives working do not evidence appreciable changes in their own behaviors, such as significantly increasing their contributions to housework and child care. Indeed, the results of a recent study indicate that those husbands in dual-earner families who invested more time in housework and child care reported higher marital dissatisfaction. For some families the restrictions that result from gender stereotypes can create no-win situations.[89]

Parenting

On the one hand, dual-earner couples are likely to find that they experience many of the same role difficulties and adjustments as other working parents, as discussed earlier in the "Parenting Role" section of this chapter. Sometimes, however, there are unique challenges faced by dual-earner couples who were able to maintain a fairly egalitarian marriage before the birth of a child. Couples tend to fight more about the division of labor at home after the birth of a child.[90] Spouses in dual-worker families may also find that they are in competition with each other for time with their children. Evening time may be "father's time" in those families where the mother is available to the children during the day. In single-parent families that parent typically is the only parent who interacts with the children during nonwork hours. However, the small window of time that constitutes nonwork hours in dual-earner families must be shared by both parents. Working mothers who experience some ambivalence and guilt about their employment status may feel protective of the time she can share with her children. In some cases the father is squeezed out.[91]

Some working mothers also feel ambivalence about the father's participation in child care. Working mothers who feel guilty about leaving their child during working hours may want to reassure themselves (and prove to their husbands) that they are still the "experts" in child care. These factors may result in situations where the mother criticizes the father's attempts to help with child care. The father may then become decreasingly interested in participating in these activities.

Pleck's research on the changing patterns of work and family roles found that the very desire of the wife for her husband to do more child care had, over and above its direct effects, a powerful conditioning effect on the relation between the employed wife's level of child care and her family adjustment and well-being. "The more child care she does, the better her adjustment if she is satisfied with her husband's child care participation, but the worse her adjustment if she is not satisfied."[92]

Developmental Priorities

Another set of conflicts often experienced by dual-worker couples occurs around what Sekaran and Hall have termed asynchronism, a concept that describes the phenomenon of conflicts that the spouses feel either with each other or between work and family. Asynchrony is an incompatibility of the work/family interface among dual-earner families. This conflict results from the couple's attempts to meet their work and family responsibilities. "Many of the strains inherent in the two-career relationship can be traced to the attempts of the two parties to deal successfully with the normal tasks and transitions of adult life."[93] Because each partner has now assumed both working and family roles (often including parenting or some form of family dependent care), the developmental stage of their career and their personal and family life cycles often seem at odds with each other. In fact, it is probably quite uncommon for both the husband and the wife to simultaneously deal with the identical life stage issues in the family and work domains.

Although Freud identified work and love as the primary tasks of adult life, working couples may well be focused on different stages of work and love and would, therefore, not necessarily be concerned about the same issues at the same time. Dual-earner families often experience some asynchrony when women temporarily disrupt their careers during childbearing years. The strain on the wife often is related to her career, potential damage to long-range goals, and confusing sets of expectations around career goals and parenting. For the husband, who may be at the most demanding stages of his career, the perceived threat of family needs and demands may conflict with work expectations. Another example of asynchrony is a husband dealing with the issues of midlife crisis while the wife is focused on developing her career identity. At a point in life when men may be turning their resources toward the family (affiliation), women may be turning their energies outward to career pursuits (assertions).

Life cycle issues such as the transition to parenthood, achieving midlife, and moving from parent to parent and worker roles are difficult enough to deal with in their own right. Put in the context of working couples, the dynamics of trying to understand and meet the needs of each other while maintaining other role responsibilities can contribute to overall levels of stress in the working family.

Thus relationship development and career development have to be addressed simultaneously in a relationship in which the needs of one partner may be quite different from those of the other.[94] Both adults in dual-earner families bring with them their own life phases in work and family domain that may not only be internally congruent, but also conflict with the life stage needs of their spouses. Issues such as career success are seldom discussed by spouses in dual-worker couples, partly because these adults may experience some confusion about the apparent conflict in personal/family goals and work goals. It is hard to specify what they really want out of life and when they want it. Couples who do not anticipate the experience of asynchrony may revert to traditional roles and gender-stereotypical behaviors.[95]

It is difficult to disentangle the multiple factors that contribute to asynchrony in dual-career couples. As discussed in Chapter 2, there is a need to continue to study work/family conflicts from a systems theory perspective. "What is missing is an investigation of the career cycle, the family cycle and the individual development and growth cycle of both partners . . . to determine the stages where the partners get 'out of sync.' "[96]

Career Competition

The level of women's career aspirations often is associated with the degree of work/family conflict manifested in a dual-career family. Not surprisingly, if career aspirations are high for both spouses, it becomes difficult for the family system to make sacrifices for both careers. Because the husband typically has been socialized into a focus on work and career and the wife into a more supportive role, conflicts can arise when the wife needs to compete for the family support to her career. Barriers to the wife's career mobility at work, especially in comparison to her husband's experience, can result in heated discussions and conflict at home. Holahan and Gilbert, in examining newly emerging patterns of career aspirations in women, found that high career aspirations were negatively related to role conflict for men, but positively related to role conflict in women.[97] These findings confirm the fact that men with high aspirations are performing in a manner congruent with societal expectations, while women's nontraditional aspirations are seen as dysfunctional in that they add to role conflict.

One of the factors that can contribute to this sense of competition between spouses is that the wife may feel a need to justify her decision to focus on her work, rather than be a full-time homemaker. It is as if by excelling at work, it becomes more apparent why she made that decision.

The careers of husbands and wives can compete in many ways. Sometimes, without even being aware of it, husbands and wives compete against each other in an unspoken race for promotions and salary increases. More than 15 percent of all working wives earn higher incomes than their husbands.[98] Some men who are willing to share the family income-earning role with their wives still want to be the primary income-earner, and find it disquieting if their wives earns more money.

The competition becomes more tangible when one spouse needs to make career sacrifices because of the work demands of the other spouse. Company transfers may set the stage for this type of career competition between spouses. If one spouse is relocated, this can have a deleterious affect on the career of the other spouse. Career decisions that tend to pit one spouse's career against the other spouse's career can ignite gender conflicts. "The findings [of career competition] often indicates, while there might be high commitment to both careers, at decision time when the two come into direct conflict (e.g., when offered a promotion requiring relocation), the husband's career usually took priority (Hall and Hall, 1979). The degree of mutual commitment to both careers and to family was found to be a strong correlate of marital happiness and often the family was required to make accommodations to the careers."[99]

SINGLE-PARENT FAMILIES

Throughout history single-parent families have existed as a result of the death of a spouse, separation, divorce, and child birth before marriage. From 1870 to

1970 there was a fairly constant rate of single-parent families who made up approximately one tenth of all families.[100] During the past two decades, however, single-parent households have constituted an increasing percentage of all households and of the workforce. Most of these families (90%) are headed by women.[101]

- Between 1970 and 1982 the number of female-headed families increased by 71 percent.[102]
- In 1984, 26 percent of all family groups were composed of single-parent households, which almost equals the 29 percent that consisted of married couples with a child under age 18.[103]
- It is estimated that as many as one third of American workers will be single parents at some point during their working years.[104]
- During the early 1980s approximately 8 million single parents served as heads of household for one fourth of the American families with children under age 18.[105]
- More than four fifths of single fathers and more than two thirds of single mothers are in the labor force.[106]
- Three fourths of single women with school-age children are in the workforce (in contrast to 57.9 percent of married women with school-age children).[107] Among these single-parent workers half work full-time, year round.[108]
- According to the National Institute of Child Health and Human Development, 70 percent of white children and 94 percent of black children born in 1980 will experience living in a single-parent family for some time before they are 19 years old.[109]
- Between 1970 and 1986 the number of children who live with their mother only increased from 10.8 to 21.0 percent.[110]

During the sixties single-parent households usually were perceived as women and children on welfare. Although the fastest-growing group of single-parent families are those that can be characterized as parents in the never-married category, most of today's single-parent families were formerly two-parent families.[111] The majority of these parents have experienced separation or divorce (69%), some were never married (22%), and a minority have been widowed (9%).[112] The dramatic increase in divorce in all income groups has led to the normalization of single parents and their presence in the workforce. In fact, it has almost become fashionable for single adults who want to have children to adopt them.

Although there has recently been a noticeable percentage increase in the number of single-parent households headed by men, these families still represent a small percentage of all single-parent families. Consequently the single parent often will be referred to as "mother" or "woman."

It also is important to keep in mind while discussing the work/family conflicts associated with single-parent families that many two-parent families actually function as if they were single-parent families. Thus it is not uncommon for adults whose spouses travel frequently, whose spouses are not present for long periods of time (e.g., hospitalization), or women whose husbands contribute negligibly to family and household needs to share some of the conflicts discussed below.

Just like any type of family structure, some single-parent families can function well and resourcefully, whereas others are fraught with stress and turmoil. Many discussions of single-parent families focus on the potential problems that can arise. In fact, although single-parent families may experience a range of work/family conflicts that should not be minimized, it also is possible for them to avoid some of the stresses endemic to other family structures. Without doubt, the sheer presence of two adults in a family does not ensure that there will always be domestic harmony. In some cases some of the arenas of conflict are eliminated in the single-parent family structure. Single-parent families are unlikely to confront the career competition between spouses that can develop in dual-career families. Similarly, the absence of a partner might, ironically, lessen some of the work/family conflict because there is one less role (spousal role) the working parent needs to consider. Instead of carrying responsibility for three distinct roles—worker, spouse, and parent—the single-parent might focus just on the worker and parent roles. Particularly in those families where the husband requires more "work" at home than he invests (e.g., the wife prepares the meals, washes the clothes, and cleans the home), single parents may feel that they have one less dependent person to care for. This can be a significant difference for those women who are married to men who set high standards for home management and are critical if the house is messy or if the meals are not prepared to their liking. In contrast, the single parent doesn't have to worry about pleasing another adult. Many experts agree that in the long run, children tend to benefit more from living in a nurturing and supportive single-parent family than in a two-parent family fraught with significant marital turmoil.

Despite the functional aspects of some single-parent families, they often face a high degree of work/family conflict. Burden reports that single parents are "at risk for high levels of job-family role strains and decreased physical and emotional well-being."[113]

Areas of Conflict

Income. Most single parents, particularly females, encounter intense issues related to the economic support of their families. A great deal of attention has been devoted to the documentation of the harsh lives of many single parents, borne out by their economic plight. Although single-parent families can be found in every economic group, most single-parent families experience significant financial struggles. According to the Census Bureau, more than half (56%) the households headed by women with children under age 18 had incomes at or below the poverty line.[114] Some of this poverty is associated with the income loss suffered by women after divorce. Female-headed households constitute approximately 15 percent of the population, but they account for more than 50 percent of the poor.[115] It is significant that after divorce, the income of the women and children decreases by 73 percent, whereas the income of the fathers increases by 42 percent.[116] This difference reflects the failure of many fathers to provide financial assistance to their children. Over half the single-female parents who have custody of their children and who are supposed to receive child support from the father, do not, in fact, receive the full amount of support.[117] This is especially disturbing, since many of these fathers have earnings that put them in the middle-and upper-income socioeconomic groups.

Almost 75 percent of children who live in a single-parent family for some time during their first ten years experience poverty, and among these youngsters, one of every five confronts this poverty for a minimum of seven years.[118] One seventh of women who had been in middle-and upper-income groups while married need public assistance after their divorces.[119] Although the poverty rates for female-headed households declined from 50 percent in 1960 to 19 percent in 1980, many single mothers face almost unsurmountable economic problems.[120]

Public attention on the feminization of poverty has increased our awareness that women and children are the largest (and the fastest-growing) group of poor people in America.[121] Female-headed households have half the median income in comparison to all types of households, and two-thirds less than married couples.[122] The income of single mothers actually declined 7 percent during the years from 1967 to 1984.[123] It is significant that the income of married couples increased by 14 percent during those years.[124] This situation can be desperate for single mothers whose average income in 1983 was less $10,000 per year (in comparison with more than $28,000 for married couples heading families.[125] Although this limited income level reflects the number of women who must rely on public assistance (more than half the female-headed households rely on Medicaid and food stamps), there also are large numbers of single mothers who struggle to support their families from the earnings of low-paying jobs.[126] Almost 40 percent of working single mothers are unable to earn sufficient income to place their families above the poverty level.[127] Among working women, single parents are more likely to hold low-paying jobs (such as service and blue-collar positions) and experience higher rates of unemployment.

Perhaps one of the most significant barriers faced by single mothers is whether to participate in the workforce. Three principal factors affect the decisions of these women. First, there is the problem of securing a job that can earn her a "family wage." Second, many low-paying jobs that might be available do not offer benefits. The potential lack of medical insurance is a frightening possibility for parents, so much so that many of them decide to stay on public assistance and be assured of coverage for their families rather than risk an uncertain job that does not provide for these needs. Finally, the cost of unsubsidized child care makes it economically unfeasible for many single women to go to work. Despite all these barriers, more than two thirds of single mothers are in the workforce.[128] All these factors are complicated by the fact that many single mothers are faced with the prospect of either looking for their first jobs or returning to work after a long absence from the job market.[129]

Some of the work/family conflicts confronted by single mothers are associated with the fact that many of them find it necessary to work full-time. Among mothers who are participating in the workforce, 54 percent of single mothers in comparison with 43 percent of married mothers, work full-time.[130] Although part-time work might help to ease some of the child-care needs and their associated expenses, part-time jobs typically do not provide the income or the benefits needed by single parents.[131]

Structure. The reduction from two adults to one adult in the household significantly decreases the resources to care for dependents and to serve as backups or substitutes if sickness, schedule conflicts, or other intervening event should interfere with the working parent's ability to carry out work and family responsibilities. Typically, two-parent families have at least the potential of more adult resources that can help to achieve some balance between work and family demands. Much of the role overload and role strain witnessed in dual-earner families is present in a more exaggerated form in single-parent families. Even two-parent households can find it difficult to manipulate their working schedules to attend to such family matters as going to a child's play, staying home with a sick child, caring for elderly parents, or spending extra hours at work; this can seem almost impossible for the single parent to manage alone. In many cases four hands are better than two, at least in terms of time-intensive tasks such as household management and child care. In comparison to their married counterparts, working single parents devote less time to household tasks.[132]

When assessing the structural aspects of single-parent families it is important to realize that the availability of resources affects the way an individual family functions. Some parents independently fulfill most of the parental responsibilities (with some possible assistance of child-care services). Other single-parent families receive support (e.g., financial, emotional, and practical) from the parent who does not reside with the family. Some of these families might receive child-support payments, and the children) may spend scheduled time (such as weekends or summers) with the "absent" parent. In other families another adult (relative, friend, or companion) might assume some of the parenting functions.[133] Some single parents must rely almost exclusively on their own talents, creativity, and energy, whereas other single parents are able to utilize the resources of additional adults. Many single parents look to their own mothers and to their children for needed support.[134]

Parenting. Even when there are two adults to share the responsibilities, parenting is a challenging role. Most single parents have just one child under age 18 although approximately 10 percent have three or more children.[135]

At least one recent study reports that single parents do not seem to experience more stress associated with parenting than married mothers.[136] Despite the logistical problems that single parents face in meeting their children's parenting needs, recent research suggests that single working mothers actually devote more time to child-care tasks each day than do married working mothers.[137]

One of the special problems many single-parent families experience is associated with the limited incomes single mothers have; they simply cannot afford quality child care, but this care is necessary for the parent to support the family.

Relations with Children's Other Parents. Although many single mothers assume most of the parenting responsibilities, the fathers of the children usually are living. The increasing popularity of joint-custody arrangements has increased the presence of both parents in the lives of their children.[138] Consequently, in a growing number of families, the custodial parent must interact with the other parent on some level. Ex-spouses (or the never-married fathers)—who might continue to have an adversarial relationship with each other—may need to communicate about the financial needs of the children (e.g., child support and medical insurance coverage), overall developmental progress, and the coordination of visits. The relationship with the ex-spouse's family (e.g., grandparents) also can be particularly sensitive.

Although the participation of the noncustodial parent can act as a potential resource for the single working parent who might seek some relief from the ever-present parenting responsibilities, this involvement clearly introduces added stress to the single parent's life. "Single parents often find the existence of the other parent to be more of a problem than a help. Increased concern for that person's rights may only exacerbate the already difficult circumstances of single parenting."[139]

The separation or divorce of parents can be a wrenching experience for the child, particularly in terms of the relationship with the father, who typically is not frequently accessible after the divorce. In a recent national survey about half the children aged 11 to 16 years whose parents had divorced had not seen their fathers in the past year; only one in six had seen their fathers once during the past week.[140] Other reports indicate that three years after divorce, half the children do not see their fathers at all.[141]

Discrimination. There are many anecdotal accounts of the kinds of discrimination confronted by single parents, both at home and at work. Some of this results from the stereotypes our culture has developed about divorced and never-married mothers. There are perceptions that these women have "failed" and are "unstable."[142] Their family structure, often referred to as a "broken home," is viewed in a negative light.[143]

These discriminatory attitudes may put single parents at a disadvantage on the home front. Single mothers often are seen as risks to landlords, who hesitate to rent an apartment to a woman whose income might be insecure and who has children who might damage the property. Single mothers also can encounter discrimination at work. These women may face pointed questions about their ability to work overtime or the reality of them being "committed" to their jobs.[144]

Family Transition. Family systems experience the stresses of change whenever there is a significant transition that affects one or more family members. Regardless of how the single-parent family comes into existence (e.g., birth of a child to an unmarried girl or woman, separation or divorce after marriage, death of a spouse, or adoption by a single person), the emergence of this family type signals major transition. In many cases the change into a single-parent family is accompanied by a lot of stressful emotions (e.g., loss, abandonment, anger, and resentment), and other changes such as moving to a new residence. The fact that the single mother may seek a new job (oftentimes after a long absence from the job market) also can require a lot of adjustment from the family. Furthermore, all family members may experience dramatic lifestyle changes as a result of income loss. These factors have lead one family theorist to comment that "all types of single parent families experience more and longer critical transitions between equilibrium stages (stages of stable numbers and growth of members) than two parent families."[145]

When the transition to a single-parent family follows divorce, the family adjustment period can be lengthy. Whereas the conventional wisdom surrounding divorce views the event primarily as a brief disruption of one or two years before adjustment to the new family structure, studies such as that of Wallerstein and Blakeslee found a quite different picture. Their research suggests that divorce typically continues to negatively affect at least one of the spouses for many years, and children can experience a prolonged sense of inner turmoil.[146]

Although divorce usually is discussed within the family context, it has a legitimate place within the study of work/family dynamics. It would be quite unusual for such a highly charged event to be carefully sequestered in the family and out of the workplace. The spillover into work no doubt has a real and significant effect on job performance, in much the same way it does within the family. Whereas for some the workplace becomes a welcome respite from the disruption within the family, for others the impact of loss and emotional stress are brought into the office. A number of companies, in recognizing this issue, have formed support groups for divorced employees to help them deal with some of their emotional issues. One *Fortune* 500 company formed a group for recently divorced male managers that continued for several years at the request of the group participants. In our culture men often internalize conflicts such as those experienced during a divorce, and divert them into outlets such as increased attachment to work or to drugs and alcohol. Support groups for divorcees can be helpful for these men.

Finally, the status of single-parent families often changes. Dependent children grow up, and the parent becomes a single-person household. The single parent may remarry, and the family becomes a blended family. Approximately three quarters of single mothers remarry within six years after a divorce.[147] As with all family systems, these changes throughout the family's developmental cycles necessitate readjustment.

Social Life. The social needs of the single parent frequently are unmet. Some recently divorced adults indicate that they were confronted with the need to establish new friendships, as the dynamics of former relationships (especially with friends of the ex-spouse) often change after a divorce. Limits on time, money, and child care also place constraints on the social lives of single parents. At some workplaces this can affect the relationships established with fellow employees when socializing occurs after work hours.[148]

Social isolation and loneliness can be major themes in the lives of single parents, and it is significant to note that single mothers report having the smallest social support systems.[149] A study comparing mothers in single-and two-parent families indicates that single mothers devote less time to personal care and to recreation.[150] Single fathers also appear to limit their social interactions.[151]

The stresses of single parenthood and the limits imposed on the accessibility of social supports may contribute to the emotional risks experienced by single parents. As a group, single mothers exhibit high rates of depression and anxiety in comparison with women in other marital categories.[152] Single fathers also are vulnerable to loneliness and depression.[153]

FAMILIES WITH A SPECIAL NEEDS CHILD

Although the combination of parenting and working roles is particularly stressful for many people, the conflicts, needs, and problems are exacerbated for those families with a child who has significant special needs. These parents (most often the mothers) typically spend a lot of time interacting with government bureaucracies, arranging for specialized programs, and implementing home-based interventions—all of which are extremely time-consuming and may be emotionally exhausting. Because our society focuses on the anticipated limitations of these children rather than on their capabilities, many of these parents expend a lot of energy trying to pry open doors of opportunity for their children.

Working families with a disabled child can be seen as families at risk. Krauskopf and Akabus suggest that "families with children with handicapping conditions will experience (more) serious imbalance."[154] Although these families can experience lifelong stress, certain developmental stages are likely to accentuate the conflicts: initial diagnosis of disability; preschool years, during which appropriate child-care placements can be difficult; adolescence; and young adulthood, when formal schooling may be completed and prospects for independent living considered.

It is important to understand that families with a disabled child often must confront other difficult situations. "Children with disabling conditions are disproportionately represented in single parent households, low income families and families with other handicapped children."[155] Understandably, there is a lot of family stress associated with the raising of a child with significant special needs. Although there is no evidence that these families experience higher rates of divorce than others, in some situations the stress associated with the care of a special needs child contributes to marital disruptions, and the parents either separate or divorce.[156] A single parent who is caring for a handicapped child is likely to experience compounded work/family stress. One study suggests that single parents, who tend to have less financial resources available to them, may have a more difficult time maintaining a sense of optimism about their child's situation and future.[157]

Emotional Stress

The parents of children who have significant special needs are often vulnerable to stress from a variety of sources and are at risk for both severe chronic illness and emotional problems.[158]

Like many working parents, the parents of disabled children can experience guilt about going to work rather than devoting their days to their children. This guilt can be intensified if the parents continue to have feelings of "responsibility" for their children's condition. Guilt can form a psychological barrier for working parents, who feel unable to devote undivided attention and commitment to work during their working hours.

Work

The decision about working can be complicated for the parents of a child who has a disability. Many families with a disabled member experience increased financial strain, owing to the magnitude of incurred medical and therapeutic interventions, and income may be a necessity.[159] Work also can provide essential medical benefits for the child. Some parents select a job according to the type of medical benefits provided to maximize the care that can be obtained for their children. Other families may find that the care required by their children makes it difficult, if not impossible, for the primary caregiver to maintain employment. The all-encompassing degree of care indicated becomes an insurmountable obstacle for those mothers seeking employment.

As mentioned earlier, work and the social support systems that may develop at the workplace can offer the parent respite from the constant worry at home. This can be a valuable "renewal" for the parent who can return home feeling refreshed and better able to give attention to the special needs child. Hirst reports that among the mothers of disabled children who participated in his study, those who were employed were less likely to report chronic ill health in comparison with those mothers who remained at home full-time.[160]

Like the parents of young children and the caregivers of dependent elders, employees with a disabled family member can experience some interference with their performance of work tasks. The disabled family member may be more susceptible to certain illnesses that necessitate parental supervision and lead to absenteeism from work. Other parents of special needs children may find that their worry or concern results in a certain level of distraction. Those parents who need to provide intensive care during off-work hours may not be able to consider jobs that entail overtime or traveling.[161]

Specialized Child Care

As discussed in Chapter 6, child care can pose some difficult problems for parents. The task of securing, paying for, and maintaining quality child care for a special needs youngster can be especially challenging. Few child-care programs and after school programs are able to respond to the special needs of a significantly handicapped youngster, and the spaces in specialized programs are limited.

Scheduling

The schedules of special needs families can become quite intricate. Often the parents must arrange for special diagnostic sessions, which may be followed by clinical interventions. Although some of these sessions may occur at school for school-age children, sometimes they are scheduled at other times. In addition, parents may need to attend conferences with teachers and specialists at a more frequent rate than is typical for most schoolchildren. Arranging time to go to these extra meetings can be difficult for the working parent.

BLENDED FAMILIES

Blended families are the result of the high divorce and remarriage rates. They are family units that consist of one natural or adoptive parent who is single (never married, divorced, or widowed) and who has remarried. In some situations the blended family consists of children from just one of the parents, but in other cases both parents have children from previous marital (or quasi-marital) relationships. The relationships can be characterized by a great deal of complexity. Thus, to take one example, Bill (48 years old) now lives in a household where his two children (aged 13 and 16) from his first marriage are with him on the weekends and one night during the week. He recently married Janet, who brings three children (aged 7, 9, and 14) from her first marriage. These children live with Janet and Bill during the week and spend every other weekend with their natural father.

In past historical eras blended families resulted from the remarriage of widows and widowers. Today the increasing proportion of blended families is associated with both the high rate of divorce and the high rate of remarriage (75% of divorced adults eventually remarry).[162] Among adults, "about nine out of ten will eventually marry; about one out of two will marry and then divorce; and about one out of three will marry, divorce and then remarry."[163] In the 1980s one of every seven households with children involved a remarriage with at least one child from a previous marriage.[164] It is currently estimated that one of every nine children under 19 (or one of every six to seven children in two-parent families) are living with one natural parent and one stepparent.[165]

From one perspective, the advent of the blended family gave new meaning to work/family dynamics. This household is captured by working families in which the schedules and responsibilities often exceed those of just one household. If balancing work and family issues is tough for dual-earner families, imagine the complexities and conflicts that can occur in a dual-earner blended family. The adults in these families often bring to the work place two sets of family issues.

Areas of Conflict

Transitions. For those blended families that have a constant number of family members who reside together, the transition into their new family composition can be seen as one stage in the family's development. After some period of initial adjustment, relationships can be forged between the children and their stepparents, the children and any stepsiblings or half siblings, and the spouses. Many blended families include children who regularly spend time at a different household (with the other natural or adopted parent). In these cases the transitional stages frequently can recur because the family system must readjust each time the composition of the family changes.

The blending of a new family can be difficult, especially if the previous families recently experienced divorce. In addition to the transitions associated with divorce, the members of the new blended family experience the stress of establishing a new marriage and an immediate change in the size of the family. The initial stages in the establishment of a blended family can be as problematic as the period after the divorce. Hill has identified the compounded changes associated with the establishment of a blended family as significant "structural disorder."[166]

The remarriage of divorcees who form a blended family may not be a permanent family structure. Although 80 percent of all divorcees remarry, 60 percent of these will divorce again.[167] The members of these families will once again confront significant transitions.

When considering the challenges to parents in blended families, it is important not to paint too gloomy a picture. Often adults who are involved in second marriages believe that these marriages are significant improvements over their first marriages.[168]

Relationships with Noncustodial or Shared-Custodial Parents. As is the case with single parents, many blended families maintain some level of relationship with their children's other biological parents to ensure child support and coordination of visits. This coordination is not always smooth. For example, it is possible that the mother may feel that the remarried father has too much visitation time allocated to him in their divorce arrangement. She might constantly resist him in terms of both time and flexibility when he needs to make alternative arrangements. In other families the custodial parent may resent the different lifestyle or child-rearing rules in the home of the blended family. The difficulty of interacting with a former spouse can complicate the dynamics of many blended families.

Sibling Relations. The integration of children from different families can pose many challenges to parents. In some families the children of one parent may not reside with the blended family but come only for visits. Other families have stepsiblings living together. The more long-term nature of these relations makes the resolution of difficulties more imperative. In other family groups the children may have only one parent in common.

The interactions between the children often are characterized by highly charged emotions. Children who have experienced divorce are apt to be angry with their natural parents and to feel rejected by their parents' new spouses. These feelings may be transferred to the stepsiblings. Blended families that include teenagers can face especially difficult challenges. Francine Klagsburn, who has written a book that discusses blended families, observes that in these families, "competition for parental attention and jealousy are the main culprits."[169] A further barrier often introduced into blended families is a wide disparity in age between the children in the families.

Compounded Schedules and Communications. In comparison with some other family structures, the blended family must function within severe time constraints. In addition to responding to the scheduling needs of children who reside in the home of the blended family, some of these parents must adopt a framework that integrates a schedule around specific days and times they must leave work to pick up children from a previous marriage. In these cases the working parents might experience less flexibility about overtime and work overflow to home. If a biological child is visiting just once or twice a week, they may be forced to have work fit this visitation schedule. Blended families that evolve from the divorce of two previous marriages, both of which produced children, find that their family schedules include the constant shuttling of children between two homes.

MOONLIGHTERS

There is one family structure that reflects an exceptional level of involvement in the income-earning role. In this structure at least one adult moonlights, that is, holds more than one full-time job simultaneously. Moonlighters can be found in traditional families where the wife is a full-time homemaker, in single-parent homes, in single-person households, and in dual-earner households. In the past decade the number of women who moonlight has more than doubled.[170]

What is common among moonlighting families is a concern about family income: the second job usually is just a way to make ends meet. Other than the occasional consultant who picks up interesting projects, few workers who moonlight would maintain that this is a desirable lifestyle.

Some of the conflicts experienced by moonlighting families are shared by those families in which one adult is both working full-time and attending school.

Areas of Conflict

Lack of Quality Family Time. Moonlighters often experience time constraints in a number of ways. The time that they must devote to work is time that they cannot devote to family/household or personal roles. Voydanoff indicates that there is a direct relation between the number of hours devoted to work and the degree of work/family conflict.[171] For some moonlighters the problems of role overload become a moot point because these people assume just one role: that of an income-earner. They may barely have time to eat and sleep. Sometimes achieving a balance between home and work is out of the question.

In some ways parents who work on different shifts (sometimes coordinated to resolve some child-care needs) face some of the same challenges to their marital relations as are experienced by moonlighting families because the spouses seldom interact with each other during the work week. This can put a lot of stress on a marriage. According to one report, one out of every six working couples with children under age 6 do not work hours that overlap.[172]

SINGLE-PERSON HOUSEHOLDS

A household type that is seldom recognized as a family but which constitutes an increasing proportion of American households is the single-adult household. Today non-family households (people living alone or with unrelated people) outnumber married couples with children. This group represents a marked break from the past era in that they are independent of a family that resides with them. Workers who live in single-person households have a great impact on the labor market today. The single-person household is evident in every age cohort. Although many single-person households are comprised of elderly individuals, 27 percent of households with adults 25 to 34 years old consist of these non-family households. Single-person households include adults who have never (or not yet) married as well as those who are separated, divorced, or widowed.

Adults who live alone may not be without some family responsibilities that can conflict with work. For example, some of these people might have children who principally reside with the other parent. Other single adults might assume some (or all) of the dependent-care responsibilities for an elderly relative or neighbor. Despite the fact that the lifestyles of single adults may differ from those of adults in other family structures, they, too, can experience agonizing work/family conflicts.

Areas of Conflict

Balance Between Work and Personal Life. The elusive balance between work and home life can be difficult for some single adults who try to include social experiences, recreational activities, and events of their personal interests in addition to career-related tasks. Rather than rushing home to take care of family responsibilities, some single adults become obsessive workers who fill up voids in their personal time with work. One manager at a utility company related that since he was divorced and living alone, he would work until eight or nine at night and then go home because there was nothing to go home to. By working late he thought that he could get a jump on the next day's work.

The willingness of some single adults to devote their lives to work feeds into the prevalent work ethic culture. This practice makes it more difficult, however, for other workers to convince their employers that it is in the best interest of the business to encourage employees to lead balanced lives.

Social Needs Met Through Work. Some of the conflicts of single, middle-aged adults who live alone revolve around issues of isolation and unmet needs for interpersonal relations. Some of these workers may be struggling to find Mr. or Ms. Right. The immediacy of this issue is dramatized by the media in stories that emphasize how poor a woman's chances are of getting married once she is over 30, or the running out of her biological clock in terms of bearing children. Aspects of the work/family conflicts of these adults also can be characterized by a desire to fulfill some of their personal needs on the job. To some single adults the workplace represents the major meeting ground for romantic relations. According to a 1987 study conducted by the American Society for Personnel Administration, more than half the companies who participated in this research indicated that it was common for coworkers to be "attracted" to one another.[173] Tensions can be created at work as these relations go through their normal ups and downs, especially if the work relationship between the two persons is close (e.g., members of the same working group or supervisor/supervisee). An additional complication is introduced when single and married employees become involved. From almost any perspective, office affairs can (and often do) get quite messy, creating short- and long-term conflict for the parties involved.

Preretirement Singles. Another segment of single employees living alone are older workers. They often face concerns about their future care. The spillover into work can be both direct and indirect. Those workers who are in their preretirement years may begin to pressure their employers (and society at large) to help them establish arrangements so that they can achieve some security about their postretirement life. As discussed in depth in Chapter 7, the working adult children of these older, single workers also may experience work/family conflicts as they anticipate the dependent care of their aging parents. This can constitute a significant distraction at work. Ironically, as society has tended to focus on the needs of the elderly in terms of both Social Security and long-term health care to the point where many have charged that the elderly gains have been at the expense of children, the case inside the corporation has been just the opposite. The need for child-care assistance has been made loud and clear. Corporate responses such as flex time and job-sharing have been designed with the young dual-worker families with children in mind. The needs of the older worker (and his or her working adult children) usually are ignored. Although the developmental needs experienced in later years are important and as worthy as those of the younger working parents, the political agenda focusing on elder needs has not yet succeeded in capturing the corporate attention in the same way as the issues of working parents.

CONCLUSION

The real and potential conflicts that exist around balancing home and work become more pronounced the longer it takes us, as a society, to begin to recognize the growing gulf between the characteristics and changing nature of our households and families, and their interaction with the workplace. The development of multityped households, the movement of most adults into the workplace, and the failure of the corporate and public sectors to adequately address dependent-care issues have left the majority of families and households living within outmoded institutions and structures, irrelevant to their needs and frustrating their ability to achieve a healthy and productive level of functioning.

Many of the conflicts experienced by working adults cut across all the household types discussed in this chapter. Others are unique to the particular needs of the household type. In any event it is clear that the proliferation of household types makes it difficult to define a typical family. Although this presents a formidable challenge to the solution, or at least the lessening of work/family conflicts, it makes an adequate understanding of the nature, degree, and extent of these conflicts equally problematic.

Many commentaries about work/family conflicts appear to have an implicit set of assumptions that treat household and even family responsibilities as "a drag," a necessary but severe impediment to healthy and happy work/family relations. Because the workplace has been so dominant, the negative overtones relative to household responsibilities and child care often frame them as "problems" to be solved to get the "right" balance. When seen through this lens, responsibilities for home and family appear to impinge on the "more important" adult task of work. More recently there has been an emphasis on the family component of work/family conflicts, and less attention has been paid to the degree to which work truly interferes with the acts of living and achieving a satisfying family life. As long as the roles and responsibilities for home care, child care, and dependent care are viewed simplistically, as burdens and impediments to productivity, the total work/family picture becomes biased and distorted.

The subtle coloring of the workplace as a more revered place implies that it has first-class status, and thus relegates the family to second-class status. Both spheres are equally important in contributing to healthy and satisfying adult lives.

There is a serious implication of defining family matters as interference in the domain of work. When family issues become trivialized, it becomes easier for institutions such as work and the government to place the burden of resolving work/family conflicts within the family sphere. At first glance it may seem that work/family conflicts primarily reside at the home. Because the family has historically been left to its own wits to adjust to, accommodate, and resolve these conflicts, society has developed a set of expectations that the resultant problems are the family's to solve. Only recently have a few lonely voices begun to suggest that the root of many of these conflicts are not simply an inherited legacy of families, but that they lie in a much more complex relation of a family to its work environment and its social contract. For the most part work/family conflicts continue to be perceived, defined, and treated as if the domains of the corporation and the government had little to do with these issues and even less responsibility for getting involved with solutions.

The winds of change are strong, however, and the work/family conflicts within the family are increasing and are appropriately being examined within the broader context of societal roles and responsibilities. Families will continue to struggle and suffer over balancing work and home life demands, but the stage for lessening family stress will rest on greater corporate and societal participation and partnerships with the family in achieving conflict resolution.

NOTES

1. Chapman, p. 35.
2. Trost, p. B:1.
3. Pleck et al., "Conflicts Between Work and Family Life," pp. 29–31.
4. Fernandez, *Child Care and Corporate Productivity*, p. 68.
5. Kamerman and Winston, p. 179.
6. See Baruch et al., p. 133.
7. Sekaran, p. 179.
8. Cherlin and Furstenberg, p. 7.
9. Ferree, p. 292.
10. Burden and Googins, p. 47.
11. Parsons and Bales, p. 23.
12. See Miller and Garrison.
13. See Baruch et al., p. 132.
14. Sekaran, p. 46.
15. Hoffman, p. 367.
16. Fernandez, *Child Care and Corporate Productivity*, p. 54.
17. Ibid., p. 60.
18. Ibid., p. 68.
19. Sekaran, pp. 45–46.
20. Burden, p. 37.
21. Marks, pp. 924.
22. See Barnett and Baruch.
23. Baruch et al., p. 132.
24. See Robinson; and Walker and Woods.
25. Baruch et al., p. 133.
26. Johnson and Johnson, p. 149.
27. Ibid., p. 149.
28. Levine, p. 31.
29. Kanter, p. 68.

30. Sekaran and Hall, p. 163.
31. Trost, p. B:1.
32. See Pleck, *Husbands' and Wives' Family Work, Paid Work, and Adjustment,* Chapter 7.
33. Chapman, p. 30.
34. Sekaran, p. 190.
35. Ibid., p. 47.
36. See Baruch et al., p. 131.
37. Hoffman, p. 377.
38. Burden, p. 41.
39. Hill, p. 21.
40. Cherlin, p. 47.
41. Voyandoff, p. 751.
42. Ferree, p. 296.
43. Zill and Rogers, p. 47.
44. Hoffman, p. 381.
45. Sekaran and Hall, p. 163.
46. Holahan and Gilbert, p. 465.
47. Cited in Baruch et al., p. 133.
48. Ibid., p. 131.
49. Ibid., p. 132.
50. See Googins and Casey, 1989; and, Baruch et al., p. 132–133.
51. Baruch et al., p. 133.
52. Hughes, p. 4.
53. Pond, p. xi.
54. Cherlin and Furstenberg, p. 7.
55. Burden and Googins, p. 32.
56. Hunt and Hunt, p. 194.
57. Reynolds, p. 86.
58. Cowan, p. 172; Haavio-Mannila, p. 198; Reynolds and French, p. 86.
59. Pleck, *Changing Patterns of Work and Family Roles,* pp. 3–5.
60. Cited in Reynolds, p. 86.
61. Hoffman, p. 374; White and Brinkerhoff, p. 206.
62. Sekaran and Hall, p. 68.
63. Ferree, p. 68.
64. Sekaran and Hall, p. 162.
65. Ferree, p. 290.
66. See Holahan and Gilbert, pp. 451–467.
67. See Fowlkes, p. 357.
68. Sanik and Mauldin, p. 55.
69. Gordon, "Work, Work, Work," p. 40.
70. See Gibbs.
71. Kamerman, "Meeting Family Needs," p. 14.
72. Gordon, "Work, Work, Work," p. 39.
73. See Fowlkes, p. 358.
74. Sekaran, pp. 184–188.
75. Leavitt, p. 1.
76. Holahan and Gilbert, pp. 451–467.

77. See Berenson, pp. 19–44.
78. Ferree, p. 291.
79. See Sekaran and Hall, p. 6; Sekaran, pp. ix, 94, 199.
80. Sekaran, p. 86; Place and Wise, p. 49.
81. Pleck, *Working Wives/Working Husbands*, p. 11.
82. Fowlkes, p. 358.
83. Holmstrom, p. 1.
84. See "Dual Careers—A Family Killer."
85. See Cooper.
86. See Combe.
87. See "More Working Wives Expose Their Hubbies to the Joy of Cooking."
88. See Kanter.
89. Stocker, p. 101.
90. Ibid.
91. Hoffman, p. 383.
92. Pleck, "Changing Patterns," p. 9.
93. Sekaran and Hall, p. 160.
94. Thomas et al., p. 513–521.
95. Sekaran, pp. 24–30.
96. Sekaran and Hall, p. 160.
97. Holahan and Gilbert, pp. 451–457.
98. Sekaran, p. 86.
99. Sekaran and Hall, p. 8.
100. Caple, p. 74.
101. Prince, p. 38.
102. United States Bureau of the Census, *Current Population Reports.* "Households, Families, Marital Status, and Living Arrangements," p. 6–7.
103. Hanson and Sporakowski, p. 3.
104. Burden, p. 38.
105. Prince, p. 38.
106. Norton and Glick, p. 13.
107. Burden, p. 38.
108. Amott, p. 100.
109. Ibid., p. 117.
110. United States Bureau of the Census, *Statistical Abstract of the United States: 1988*, p. 50.
111. Norton and Glick, p. 11; Caple, p. 79.
112. Melli, p. 31.
113. Burden, p. 39.
114. Pett and Vaughan-Cole, p. 104.
115. Mintz and Kellogg, p. 216.
116. Ibid., p. 227.
117. Grief, p. 87.
118. Sege, "Poverty's Grip on Children Widens," p. 20.
119. Caple, p. 86.
120. Mintz and Kellogg, p. 216.
121. Caple, p. 85.
122. Ibid., p. 86.

123. Amott, p. 118.
124. Ibid.
125. Norton and Glick, p. 15.
126. Caple, p. 86.
127. Amott, p. 99.
128. Ibid., p. 100.
129. Jones, p. 8.
130. Amott, p. 106.
131. Jones, p. 8.
132. Sanik and Mauldin, p. 55.
133. Caple, pp. 81–84.
134. Burden, p. 40.
135. Caple, p. 86.
136. Burden, p. 40.
137. Sanik and Mauldin, p. 55.
138. Melli, p. 33.
139. Ibid.
140. Cherlin and Furstenburg, p. 8.
141. Mintz and Kellogg, p. 227.
142. See Jones, p. 39.
143. Keith and Schafer, pp. 49–59.
144. Prince, p. 38.
145. Hill, p. 28.
146. See Wallerstein and Blakeslee.
147. Burden, p. 38.
148. Jones, p. 10.
149. Burden, p. 40.
150. Sanik and Mauldin, pp. 53–54.
151. Gladding and Huber, p. 15.
152. Jones, p. 9.
153. Gladding and Huber, p. 15.
154. Krauskopf and Akabas, p. 29.
155. Schilling et al., pp. 69–70.
156. McCubbin, p. 101.
157. Ibid.
158. Hirst, p. 291.
159. McCubbin, p. 101.
160. Hirst, p. 294.
161. Saltzberg and Bryant, p. 20.
162. Cherlin and Furstenberg, p. 8.
163. Ibid., p. 9.
164. Mintz and Kellogg, p. 227.
165. Norton and Glick, p. 11.
166. Hill, p. 28.
167. French, p. 61.
168. Cherlin and Furstenberg, p. 8.
169. Quoted in French, p. 61.

170. Reynolds, p. 25.
171. Voyandoff, p. 750.
172. See Sege, "Couples Working, Parenting in Shifts," p. 1.
173. Kantrowitz, p. 48.

Chapter 6

CHILD CARE

The 1960s witnessed the social and lifestyle changes brought about by the burgeoning women's movement. As women entered the workforce, the nation began to recognize the need for alternative child-care arrangements. Although the family typified in the fifties rigidly limited the horizons for most women, it did offer a fairly predictable system for rearing children. A certain amount of security was felt in this arrangement both by families and by society. At least in most middle-class families Mom was home to attend to the needs of infants and preschoolers. She was waiting at the door when her school-age children walked home from their neighborhood school. She could be easily contacted in case of illness or emergencies that occurred at school. She was home and available during school vacations and holidays. Furthermore, Mom would arrange for any extracurricula enrichment activities (e.g., dancing, sports, music, socialization, and religious education) that she and her husband thought were necessary. Without pausing to consider that the quality of this approach to child-rearing varied tremendously from family to family and was subject to the mother's individual skills in parenting, most homes were relatively child-centered. Society, as a whole, depended on this.

The consciousness-raising activities characteristic of the early days of the women's movement brought this child-centeredness into question. Some women proposed radical departures from their traditional roles, and suggested that if their intellectual and professional development required their full attention, perhaps they would make sacrifices and not have children. Other groups of women tentatively began to question whether they might not be able to "have it all." These women started to assess whether it was necessary to arrest their own development for the duration of their childbearing and the consequent child-rearing years. A Gallup poll taken in 1938 found that only 21 percent of the population approved of a woman's working if her husband was able to support the family. By 1978 this percentage had more than tripled to 72 percent in approval . . . as long as the need for child care did not come into the picture.[1]

In some ways it is unfortunate that the emergence of day care as a child-care option developed within the framework of society's response to the "women's right to work" issue, for it caused many people to confuse women's methods with their motives. Some people interpreted the mothers' desire to work as a sign that these mothers were placing the needs of their children in a secondary status. Research during the 1960s was already beginning to show that preschool experiences had a positive impact on children's development, and that nursery school was typically perceived positively because the parents chose it to meet the needs of the child. Despite this prevailing attitude toward early childhood education, some critics believed that child care was "harmful," viewing these arrangements as a response to the "selfish" needs of self-centered mothers. This approach to the issues of child care that pits the needs of mothers against those of their children distorts the realities of the options and their implications. It may be in the best interest of families (and therefore, society) that all parents have the option to utilize these child-rearing alternatives that maximize the development of all family members.

It is not surprising that child care has become one of the most emotion-laden work/family conflict issues. A number of widely held "American" values have been associated with the more traditional approach to child-rearing. It is as if "Mom, home, and apple pie" were inextricably connected to full-time parenting. Some people discuss child care provided outside the family as if it were the single most destructive force attacking "the family." These critics believe that if some of the child-rearing functions are taken out of the home, the entire family structure and its attendant values will be destroyed.

Undoubtedly, personal values have an indisputable effect on reaction to child care.

Discussions of child care at the leadership level have frequently become bogged down in a bitter dispute between family "traditionalists" and "modernists." At its core is a debate over the nature of the American family. Many liberals have welcomed the liberation of women from housework and see real advantages for children, both in terms of increased opportunity for children to interact with other children and increased educational opportunities for children from poorer families. Many conservatives . . . view the movement of women into the workplace and children out-of-home care as a sign of the destruction of the family; they see child care as only one more step in a broader movement to replace the traditional family unit with a variety of lifestyles.[2]

Regardless of expressed differences in values, most people genuinely want to do what is best for the children. The problem is, no one knows for sure—in either general or individual terms—what is best. As with any era of significant social upheaval, the entry of mothers into the workforce was precipitated by a complicated set of interrelated factors, including economic changes in the country and profound changes in values. There simply wasn't the time to conduct long-term studies of the effects of all these changes before they happened. Somehow working parents must satisfy themselves that the choices they have made are the best ones for their families. It may not be possible to assess the long-term impact of working mothers (considering the range of variables such as income, work schedule, type and quality of day care, ages of the children, and parental satisfaction with work) until the children of the baby boom generation are adults. Although the results of preliminary studies are reassuring and indicate that children of working parents are developing in healthy ways, there remains an experimental element to the utilization of day care and a certain degree of uncertainty that cannot be easily alleviated.

There is another way in which the issues of values enter into the discussion of child care. Not only are adults struggling with their own values, but decisions about child care also affect the context within which they socialize their children to their values. One of the most immediate dilemmas faced by many parents who utilize child care is that the transmission of family values may be diluted because their children will have other adults as models of potentially different value systems. It is quite probable that a parent and a child-care provider would react at least somewhat differently to a situation that raises questions of "values." The daily lives of children involve experiences that elicit value-context responses of their parents, such as use of "bad" language, aggression, and physical privacy. For example, a parent might respond to a child's nonmalicious "stealing" with some discussion, including some moral (maybe religous) comments on the situation, whereas a preschool teacher might react in a more nonjudgmental manner and simply state that the article belongs to someone else and needs to be returned.

Many parents put a high priority on the consistency of value systems between home and child care (or school) but find that although some of the espoused values of the child-care situation reflect those of the home, there also are inevitable differences. Parents who place a high priority on the health of their children may be careful to screen the child-care provider (and sometimes even other family members) for such environmental factors as smoking. Likewise, many parents are careful to express their desire for their child to have a healthy diet, and yet frequently the caretaker decides what constitutes a healthy diet. It can be frustrating for parents not to have direct control over the number of times each week their child might have cookies with snack or to be aware of the child drinking "regular" milk instead of lowfat milk.

Sometimes it's not the care provider but another child to whom the parents object. Parents of a 2-year-old might become concerned that their toddler will start having tantrums after observing another child who frequently exhibits this behavior.

There is probably no absolute right or wrong approach to these issues, but rather a variety of factors to consider, including the age of the child and the circumstances of his or her particular situation. Many families lament the fact that the use of child care may weaken the parents' ability to present to their children a relatively consistent set of values. Without a doubt, children may reject the values of their parents whether the parents are at home or employed. Furthermore, by the time children reach school age, they will be exposed to a multiplicity of values. Working parents may have to confront two tiers of value conflicts. The first results from using child care, which represents an approach to child-rearing that may seem to conflict with some of the parents' own values. The second level of conflict arises when the care provider's values seem to differ from those of the parents.

CHILD CARE: A PERVASIVE NEED

Is child care an important issue? There can be no doubt that in ever-increasing numbers, more and more families are needing child care, which reflects the fact that mothers of young children comprise the fastest-growing segment of America's workforce.[3] Consider the following:

- In 1950 the percentage of working women who had at least one child age 6 or younger was 12 percent; by 1984 this figure had increased to 52 percent.[4]

- More than one half of all children under age 6 (10.5 million) had mothers in the labor force in 1987.[5]

- More than half of mothers with children over the age of two were in the labor force in 1982.[6]

- During the latter part of the 1970s, 45 percent of women whose youngest child was between ages 3 and 5 were employed. By 1986, 60 percent of women with a preschool child as the youngest were participating in the labor force.[7]

- More mothers of younger children are entering the labor force. Currently more than half of all women with infants under age 1 are in the labor force.[8]

- In 1976, among working women who had had babies, 31 percent returned to work within a year. By 1984 this percentage increased to 48 percent.[9]

- The percentage of single mothers who are working is higher than the proportion of mothers in two-parent families who are working. In 1980, 59 percent of single mothers were working in comparison to 45 percent of mothers in two-parent households. Interestingly, the gap in the statistical difference between these two groups narrows for the mothers of younger children. For mothers of children under age 3, the labor participation rate is 47 percent, and it is 41 percent for mothers in two-parent families.[10]

A continuation of significant changes in the labor force participation of mothers is expected.

- "Nearly half of mothers with children under the age of 1 are in the labor force, a 95% increase since 1970. And by the end of this decade, there will be about 4.8 million more children with working mothers than in 1980."[11]

The numbers do not tell all the story, but they certainly confirm that there are large numbers of parents who are working and struggling to resolve issues of child care so that they can continue to work. Although some of the most dramatic statistics focus on the child care of infants, toddlers, and preschoolers, child-care needs do not end once children reach school age. After school and vacation also can pose problems for working parents.

One fact is indisputable. America's children are spending more time away from their parents and their home in the care of other adults.

CHILD CARE SERVICE ALTERNATIVES

To understand the role that child care plays in work/family conflict issues, it is necessary to establish some familiarity with the child-care system in the United States. Parents who need (or anticipate needing) child care also must gain some understanding about the primary characteristics of the different types of child care available. A basic choice for working parents is the determination of whether the care to be provided will be in the child's home or outside the child's home.

A primary advantage of *in-home care* is that it tends to be more flexible for the family and more individualized for the child. When the provider comes to (or lives in) the home, it may not be necessary for parents to tailor the child's schedule so that it meets their working schedules. The child's daily routine is thus less disrupted by the parents' working lives. For example, parents who use an in-home provider do not have to rush to be sure that an infant is dressed, fed, and ready to leave the house by a particular time (synchronized with the parents' arrival time at work) because the care provider can take care of these needs after the parents depart. In addition, because the care provider will focus on the children in just one family, the adult-child ratio is likely to be favorable. At-home care schedules and activities can be developed with the needs of just one (or perhaps a few) child(ren) in mind. The potential for highly individualized care often makes in-home care a good match for young children. The determination of the quality of the in-home care depends on the judgment of the parent because there currently is no certification or licensing process associated with in-home care. Furthermore, in-home care typically is expensive because the income of the care provider may depend on the fees charged to just one family.

Out-of-home care is a broad category that includes both family day care (offered in the home of the child-care provider who may or may not be a relative) and center-based care (e.g., preschools, nursery schools, and day-care centers). Most out-of-home care situations include children from more than one family, and therefore can provide potentially valuable socialization experiences for children. The licensing of out-of-home care usually is delegated to state governments, except in situations where federal money is allocated directly to child-care programs (such as Head Start, which has additional programmatic and other regulatory requirements). Consequently any assurances for even the minimum quality standards can vary considerable from state to state. Many states do not even require registration (which may not entail any care standards) for family day-care homes. In those states that do promulgate minimum licensing standards for these homes, the number of unlicensed "underground" homes proliferates. One recent estimate is that between 70 and 90 percent of all homes providing child care in states with regulation laws are unlicensed.[12]

Although much of the public debate about child care has focused on day-care centers, less than one quarter (estimates range from 15% to less than 25%) of the preschool children who have working mothers attend day-care centers. In contrast, two thirds of these children receive care in family day-care homes (licensed or unlicensed) and typically spend their days with relatives, neighbors, or friends of their parents.[13] The following chart specifies the types of child care used by working mothers with children under 5 years[14]:

In Child's Home

By father	13.9%
Grandparent	5.9%
Other relative	5.2%
Nonrelative	5.5%

Care in Another Residence

By grandparent	11.3%
Other relative	6.9%
Nonrelative	22.0%

Group Care

Nursery school	5.6%
Day-care center	9.2%

Other

Care by mother	9.1%
Other	0.2%

Much attention has been given to the utilization patterns associated with child care. One interpretation of the heavy reliance on family day care is that working parents prefer this more informal approach to child care for a variety of reasons. It may more closely resemble the child's own home (or what the home might be if the parents were available for full-time care) and usually is less expensive than center-based care. Family day care typically has more flexibility than the schedules established at child-care facilities. Furthermore, parents are more likely to have a personal relationship with the provider even before the child-care arrangement begins (e.g., with a relative serving as the provider). This apparent "preference" may reflect the fact that family day care is the parents' only viable choice because either there are no center-based slots available or the cost of center-based care and in-home care is not feasible. As the supply of child-care center services has slowly increased, greater proportions of working families with preschool children have decided to use center-based child care.

The outline of basic child-care service categories above is not intended to fully describe each service approach. Rather, it highlights the fact that there are some significant differences in the types of child care available. Working parents need to be aware of these differences to anticipate the effects of each approach on the child care provided. Equally important is the need for policymakers to understand these differences because it is their decisions that will affect the diversity of care that now exists.

AVAILABILITY

The most immediate conflict working parents encounter when they need child care is that its availability in most regions of the United States is limited. Estimates comparing the number of preschool children of working parents in New York City who need child care with the number of licensed slots available suggest that as few as 7 percent of these youngsters are participating in child-care experiences that meet even minimum government standards.[15] One study reported that 59 percent of female employees and 40 percent of male employees interviewed stated that they had difficulty finding day care for their children.[16] Stories about women putting their children's names on lists years before the care might be needed (sometimes as soon as the mother is aware she is pregnant) are becoming increasingly common. Waiting lists are the standard fare for most center-based care facilities, and many families find that they never make it to the top of the list. The results of at least one major survey indicate that approximately three quarters of all workers feel that the lack of affordable, quality child care is a problem.[17]

Projections about the future availability of child care do not offer hope that the supply of child-care services is likely to significantly improve. "Within the next decade, five out of every eight persons entering the labor force will be women. Less than a third of the families seeking day care find service readily available."[18]

The majority of working parents find that the problems associated with child-care shortages do not end once they have been able to locate care for their preschoolers. In many communities working parents discover that there are few spaces in afterschool programs, if these programs exist at all. For example, there are not formal afterschool programs in half the towns in Connecticut.[19]

Working parents may find themselves in a bind when they are not able to enroll their children in quality child-care programs because the supply does not meet the demand. Certainly it brings no peace of mind to working parents if they think that they have had to compromise on the care given to their children because there simply is not enough quality care available.

QUALITY

The overriding issue for parents as they consider child-care alternatives is quality. The results of a 1987 study portrays the struggles that working families have as a result of concern about the quality of child care. The participants in this study were parents who had contacted information and referral agencies to assist them in their child-care search. Among the survey respondents who stated that they felt they had to "settle for less than they wanted," compromises about quality issues (e.g., inadequate ratio of adults to children) often were mentioned by parents.[20]

One of the most frustrating issues for working parents is that it is difficult for them to adequately assess the quality of a particular program. Much of the quality of any program depends on the somewhat elusive nature of the interactions between the child and the adult care provider. As a result, even programs that meet the minimum standards and seem to offer a range of appropriate activities may not provide the kind of care that has a positive impact on the child's development.

The difficulties encountered in attracting competent personnel who have the required set of complex skills continuously erode the quality of child-care services. Simply put, child-care providers are poorly paid, which deters many people from considering this field. It is reported that 90 percent of all family day-care providers and 75 percent of child-care workers in centers earn less than the minimum wage.[21] Research conducted by the Women's Policy Institute discovered that nearly half (40%) of all full-time child-care workers earn less than $5 per hour. This compares with the fact that less than 18 percent of all full-time workers in the labor force have such low incomes. These statistics become especially disconcerting when we consider the fact that parking lot attendents, whom we pay to "watch over" our cars, get paid more than child-care workers, to whom we entrust our children.[22] Given this data, it is not surprising that the turnover rate among child-care workers is about 40 percent a year.[23]

COST

It is ironic that many of the very services (e.g., elder dependent care and child care) that are designed to ameliorate elements of work/family conflicts can actually generate more stress for the parent(s). Although the quality of these services is threatened because of the low pay, the labor-intensive nature of these services results in high costs, and working families can experience significant financial hardships as a result of paying for them. The cost of child care can be so high that many working parents find that they are not netting enough money after the expense for child care is calculated. Child-care costs usually exceed the cost of car payments, the family's food bill, and college tuition costs. Nationally, the average cost for full-time child care is $3,000 per year (approximately $62 weekly), and in many areas it is much higher.[24] Yet the income of working mothers often is a necessity for families either because they are the sole income-earner for the family or because their husbands earn less than $15,000 a year.[25]

Variations in the cost of child care reflect a number of factors, including the type of care, the age of the child, the number of hours of child care received, and the regional economic situation. Below are some examples of full-day child-care costs in 1983.[26]

	Family Home	Facility	Child's Home
Boston	$45–$160	$90–$150	$260–$340
New York City	$35–$140	$60–$150	$165–$300
Atlanta	$30–$60	$35–$70	$165–$230
St. Louis	$45–$50	$65–$80	$165 and up
Dallas	$50–$70	$60–$90	$165–$200
Denver	$65–$105	$65–$105	$165–$200
San Francisco	$55–$90	$90–$120	$165–$200

The costs of child care need to be put into the context of the mother's income. In 1983 the average annual salary for women was $12,758 ($245 weekly).[27] It is not a complicated calculation to determine that the average working mother of a preschool-age child spends between 10 and 25 percent of her earnings on child care.[28] Women with more than one child in day care are not likely to bring home a significant income.

Collectively, the amount of money American families spend on child care is staggering. It totaled $13 billion in 1985, which was a giant increase from the $5.5 billion spend just six years earlier in 1979.[29]

CONFLICTS WITHIN THE FAMILY

One of the signs of the changing of American lifestyles is that the issues of child care often affect all family members: mother, fathers, and children. Although it remains a top priority on the agenda of the women's movement, child-care issues have entered the arena of a "family issue."

Children

Speculation about the impact of child care on children is central to the emotional debates on child care. Two basic sets of questions are involved:

1. What is the effect of maternal employment on the development of children? Does the absence of the mother during work hours affect the parent-child relationship? Does

the mother's employment status affect her in ways that alter her interactions with her children?

2. What is the impact of child care on children? How does the experience of child care affect the development that occurs during childhood in contrast to the approach to child-rearing in which the child spends most of the time at home with his or her own parent?

Although the research into these issues abound, it is important to keep in mind that the experience of child care is complex with a multitude of variables that are hard to definitively isolate from one another. Consequently it is not always clear exactly how to interpret the research results. Some of the variables that can affect the outcome include socioeconomic status of the family, attitudes of different family members toward maternal employment, attitudes of the care-takers toward maternal employment, mother's affiliation and attitudes toward her job, degree of family stress, age of child, length of time child is in child care each day, group size, and, and the elusive quality of the child care provided (by mother or other care provider). The following caveat is important:

Studies that look only at the correlations with maternal employment at one point in time can be misleading in at least three ways: (1) the effects of employment at one stage in the child's life may only show up later; (2) a contemporaneous effect may disappear with time; (3) the traits that seem maladaptive at one age may develop into strengths as the child matures, or the converse may appear.[30]

A further complication when considering the results of research is that a number of questions are raised by child development experts about the validity of the instruments used to measure the effects of child care on children. Although some measurements depend on fairly objective observation-based checklists (such as counting the number of specific types of aggressive behaviors manifested during a specific time period), many people dispute the results of certain "stress" measurements.[31]

Maternal Employment. At the heart of the issues about the effects of maternal employment on children is the emphasis on the importance of children (especially those age 3 or younger) developing at least one "special" bond with a parent. Most psychologists believe that the ability to have a close and secure relationship with a parent affects the child's ability to form intimate relationships as an adult. During the past two decades, as mothers increasingly entered the workforce, many people began to question how the absence of a full-time mother (or parent surrogate) would affect child development. In other words, can parents (mothers in particular) establish the same kind of quality relationships with their children during nonwork hours as they would if they were at home full-time?

The results of some recent research have been fairly reassuring to parents. "Many researchers believe that mothers (or fathers) should take a leave of three to six months to ensure that proper bonding develops between infant and parent. After that, they see no reason why both parents can't return to work—if good day care can be found."[32] But, as might be expected, the results are mixed. Jay Belsky, professor of human development at Pennsylvania State University, summed up the studies last year: "A good deal of evidence now exists that extensive day care experience in this country seems to be associated with . . . an insecure attachment relationship, as well as increased aggression and noncompliance later on."[33]

The issues for working parents of older children are of a slightly different nature. If the parent (mother) is not available full-time to supervise the activities of the children, are children more likely to experience greater peer influence? Some parents are concerned about the academic progress of their school-age children who are involved in afterschool programs but might not be able to devote sufficient attention to their homework. Despite parents' fears, evidence shows that children are not adversely affected by this situation. "One . . . study, conducted over a period of five years by a team of psychologists in 38 states who interviewed 573 school-age children, found that children whose mothers work have higher IQs. In a similar study conducted in 1980 by the National Assessment of Educational Progress found that . . . children of working mothers were found to have significantly higher reading scores than did their classmates."[34]

The situation becomes more perilous for teenagers, who typically are less often involved in supervised activities. Working parents constantly worry about the involvement of their older children in drugs, sex, and neighborhood gangs. Ironically, few question how much influence full-time mothers actually have on these behaviors.

Child Care. Most recent studies have focused on the effects of child care on the development of children. The primary shortfall of these studies is that they do not follow a generation of day-care children into their adulthood. As a result, we currently are involved in a large-scale social experiment whose outcome no one can reliably predict.

Overall, there are mixed results on the effects of child care.[35] At Ohio State University, Hock compared 114 children whose mothers returned to work shortly after birth with those infants whose mothers decided to stay at home. By the time these children reached age 3 ½, there were no differences in measurements of intelligence, social behavior, achievement, or the teacher's assessments of their development.[36] A 1983 study conducted by Galambos and Garbarino of rural families found no differences among fifth- and sixth-grade children receiving care from their mothers or from a child-care provider as evidenced by measures including school adjustment, academic achievement, and attitudes toward education ("classroom orientation").[37]

Some studies suggest that children who have received child care since their infancy may experience negative effects, such as increased aggressions and less impulse control. As the research continues, the quality of the child care emerges as the overriding factor.[38] Ellen Galinsky of Bank Street College and president of the National Association of Education for Young Children comments: "The quality of day care is extremely important. . . . The absence of the mother alone is not a cause of insecure attachment."[39] At least for children over age 3, most experts seem to agree that quality day care does not negatively affect children. In fact, many researchers report that these preschool experiences may have measurable positive effects, such as the development of social skills.[40] The importance of the quality of the child-care situation is highlighted when children in "good" child-care situations are contrasted with children in situations that do not offer the same level of quality service. The results of research conducted at the university of California suggest that the development of infants in high-quality child-care situations at least equals that of children cared for by their mothers. In contrast, infants who recieved care that evidenced compromises in quality demonstrated the negative effects of this care later in their preschool years.[41] Studies that focus on slightly older children report similar results. For example, researchers at the University of North Carolina found that the absence of consistent, quality interactions with children in child-care centers affects the subsequent behavior of these youngsters.[42]

Although this research may help some working parents feel more positive about the child-care approach as a supplement to their parenting, many parents continue to worry whether their day-care arrangements provide the high-quality care they know their children deserve.

Parents

In addition to the immediate financial impact of child care, parents confront logistical and psychological conflicts related to child care.

The daily routine that incorporates child care can become complicated for working parents. Often it involves a frenetic morning pace focused on getting the child ready, preparing any necessary lunches, and dropping the child off. One problem faced by some families is that the morning drop-off time and the afternoon pick-up times do not coincide exactly with the parents' working (plus commuting) schedules. When the children in the family attend different day-care centers or schools, each with its own schedule, the logistic complications begin to multiply. Fortunately many families are able to develop a family schedule that can accommodate both work and child care. These schedules seem to function most effectively only when everything is running smoothly. Some children experience separation anxiety in the morning and protest when their parents try to leave, which results in the parents being late for work. An older child might discover that homework has been left at home and requests that the parent go back to retrieve it. Schoolchildren may miss the bus. These situations require that parents make extra efforts to be sure that interruptions, and consequent late arrivals at work, are kept to a minimum.

The use of child care by working parents means that a concerted effort must be made to ensure that there is an adequate amount of communication among all caretakers. During the fifties Mom directly observed all the behaviors and activities of her young children, and could make informed decisions about her response to the children based on this knowledge. She knew when her children had had a poor night's sleep and were likely to be cranky. She understood that her child might need some extra attention the day after a sibling's birthday. She was apt to identify the early symptoms of an impending illness. Today children who regularly spend time in child-care situations may have three or more caretakers (e.g., mother, father, preschool teacher, preschool assistant, and early drop-off or late pick-up aide) on any given day. One study conducted at Bank Street College in New York found that the respondents typically use 1.35 child-care arrangements (not including parental care) per child; nearly one third (30%) used two child-care arrangements.[43] Even in optimal situations where communication occurs regularly, it is impossible for each caretaker to fully understand what the day has been like for the child when another caretaker was in charge. The mother may forget to tell the teacher that the child had a fight with her brother before school. At pick-up time the teacher may not remember to tell the father that the child did not want to eat much lunch. And then the child gets home and is argumentative; without understanding what had precipitated all this, the mother loses her patience. It is hard for working parents to get a handle on the little things of a child's day that can make a big difference.

The continual need for communication can be encumbered by the fact that working parents often use the services of multiple child-care providers before the children are old enough to attend elementary school. Changing care providers can result from a number of situations: turnover in the child-care staff at a center, child's promotion to the next age-group in center-based facilities, parental dissatisfaction with the facility or care provider, changes made in the type of child care owing to the developmental changes that naturally occur in the child, and geographical moves made by the family. Certainly during these transitions attention needs to be focused on the adjustments made by the child. These changes also require parents to devote time and energy to developing relations with the new care providers. A Bank Street College study on the subject of child-care arrangements suggests that the factor of instability in child-care arrangements was a strong predictor of health problems among working mothers.[44]

Many parents find that they must be prepared to make a number of supplementary arrangements for their children even after the children are in a child-care program. Many of the child-care programs available in preschools do not offer services during school vacations or during the summer. This "school calendar" also is typical for many afterschool programs. Parents in dual-earner families may opt to "split" the parents' vacation time so that they can supervise their children because it is so hard to obtain quality child care that operates year round. One of the most difficult situations for working parents results from the illness of a child. This can pose a number of logistical problems because few resources are designed to meet this need. Most working parents find that their friends and relatives (who might otherwise be willing to help with child care) also are working. Those who might be home during the day are likely to be involved in the care of their own young children and are not likely to be able to care for a sick child.

Services are just beginning to develop that offer care for mildly sick children either in a group setting (e.g., at a child-care center, health maintenance organization, or pediatric floor of a hospital) or arranging to have a care provider come to the child's home. Some families are able to take advantage of these options if they exist in their communities, but other families have no choice except for a parent (or older sibling) to stay at home. In dual-earner families the need to care for a sick child may precipitate a discussion between the parents about who can most afford to miss work that day. All arrangements have to be made within a limited time framework if symptoms of the illness do not occur until the morning.

It is some of these psychological issues—especially the guilt—that are the most difficult for parents. The results of numerous studies indicate that perhaps the most prevalent reaction working parents have about using child care is guilt. The guilt seems to develop from several sources. In the first place, child care can seem to be an unfamiliar approach to child-rearing because this was not the way the parents themselves were raised. Parents also may harbor fears that the child-care provider may not adequately meet the needs of their child.[45] Some parents worry that they can't be sure what effects long-term child care will have on their children. And even those parents who are enthusiastic about their child-care arrangements and who are happy about their work situations sometimes feel that maybe they are missing out on something. The results of one study of women corporate officers revealed that the women felt that the biggest sacrifice they had made for their careers was that they did not have sufficient quality time with their children.[46]

Research suggests that "children and employers both stand to suffer as a result of the parental guilt and stress that may result from work/family conflicts."[47] It is likely that nearly half of all working mothers experience stress related to child care.[48] Furthermore, it is not just mothers who experience this stress. A study conducted by Stanford University on couples, in which both parents had master's degrees in business administration, found that anxiety about the children's well-being was actually higher among fathers.[49]

CONFLICTS AT THE WORKPLACE

Parental responsibilities can be felt so intensely and be so emotionally encompassing that it is easy to understand why child-care problems spill over into the work domains of employed parents. Working parents, especially mothers, more frequently report difficulty balancing home and work responsibilities than do nonparent employees. A University of Portland study found that whereas more than one third (38%) of women with children stated that they had some problems meeting the demands of home and work, only 9 percent of women who had no children indicated that they had these conflicts.[50] Unresolved child-care issues can affect workers in many ways. The birth of a child most often results in some type of leave for the mother and sometimes for the father. Incompatible schedules between work and child care or school (occurring either regularly or on occasion) can cause either tardiness or early departures from work. Caring for sick children often necessitates absences. And worry either about the child-care situation or the individual child can distract working parents.

For working parents a common source of work/family conflict is associated with the breakdown of the usual child-care arrangements. The sitter may call and say she (or one of her children) is sick. Perhaps child care is not provided during certain vacations or on particular holidays when the parent needs to work. Or the child-care provider announces that she has accepted a new job and will be stopping her services next week. A study of 285 working parents conducted by Bank Street College found that there was a strong, positive correlation between reports of work/family conflict and the degree of breakdown in child-care arrangements. Another interesting result of this research was that the rate of child-care breakdown was associated with psychosomatic complaints by the fathers.[51]

Research on work/family conflicts of parents that are manifested at the workplace has primarily focused on time missed from work (e.g., absenteeism, tardiness, early departure, and long lunch hours). As one might expect, parents experience higher rates of absenteeism than do nonparent employees (except for fathers whose children receive in-home care).[52] The type of child-care arrangement being used affects the parents' absenteeism rates, with in-home care proving to be the least disruptive and self-care being the most. The results of a study conducted by Hughes at Bank Street College suggest that more than one third (35%) of the working parent respondents had missed work at least once during the past year because of child-care problems. In addition, 57 percent stated that they had been absent as a result of their child's illness.[53]

Most studies indicate that child-care problems affect the work of women more than that of men because women seem to accept more of the daily responsibility for child-care arrangements. For example, in one study mothers in dual-earner families miss 50 percent more days each year than do the fathers.[54] Men with a child under age 12 in a second study averaged 9.4 days absent, whereas women with a child under age 12 were absent 11.2 days.[55] One study of 5,000 working parents at five companies found that 45 percent of the mothers, in contrast to only 17 percent of the men, stated that providing care for a sick child was at least somewhat of a problem.[56]

There currently is no hard data about the effects of child-care problems on the level of productivity of working parents. Other than anecdotal accounts, there is no quantitative understanding of how this work/family conflict impacts worker morale, ability to work up to one's potential, feeling of affiliation and loyalty to the workplace, worker effectiveness and efficiency, and the capability of employed parents to competently meet expectations on a timely basis.

SOCIETY'S CHILD

Except for educational activities, most sectors of our society accept the notion that child care and child-rearing is the responsibility of parents, and most decisions related to these activities are left to parental discretion. Other than in extreme situations, such as apparent child abuse, parents receive little interference and little assistance with child care from the public sector.

Although this philosophical orientation seemed to work adequately for most families during the fifties and sixties, the changing composition of American families has altered some of the "rules of the game." It can no longer be assumed that families are capable of fulfilling their obligations to their children independently. Working parents may need assistance to be sure that the supply of child-care services is adequate and accessible; they may need the expertise of specialists to ascertain the quality of child-care facilities; and they may need some financial assistance to help cover the costs of these services.

The lack of societal response has created a serious problem in the United States; there are increasing numbers of children who are in situations where they receive poor-quality care. This ultimately puts our children at risk—physically, cognitively, emotionally, and socially. It is at this point that child care, a significant work/family conflict for parents, becomes a critical societal concern.

Some social commentators are particularly critical of latchkey arrangements, and say that someone should do something for these families and these children because it should be the right of children to have a caring and responsible adult available to them to act as a buffer between them and the harsh realities of today's world. But despite the public attention focused on the phenomenon of children who do not have any adult supervision and take care of themselves, the number of latchkey children continues to rise.

The Children's Defense Fund, which actively advocates for a wide range of children's issues, estimated in the early 1980s that 5.2 million children under age 13 were essentially responsible for their own care for significant periods of time every day.[57] The U.S. Department of Commerce (1976) estimated that 1.6 million, or 13 percent, of children in the United States between ages 7 and 13 were without adult supervision before or after school hours. The U.S. Department of Labor (1982) puts the number of children age 10 or under who self-care at 7 million.[58] One study of more than 8,000 employees found that 15 percent of the men and 28 percent of the women used self-care by their children or care by a sibling for an average of fourteen hours each week. A startling one quarter of these latchkey arrangements made by these working mothers were for children under age 6.[59] A study in Oakland, California, found that 66 percent of 11 - to 14-year-olds had sole responsibility for younger brothers and sisters—10 percent on a daily basis and 25 percent between two and five days a week.[60] Contrary to some common misperceptions about the phenomenon of children's self-care, latchkey arrangements are not more prevalent among lower-income families; in fact, their rates increase with family income.[61]

Most people have strong reactions to the thought of latchkey children. The images of self-supervised children run the gamut from school-age children who sit in front of a television all afternoon so that they feel like they have some company, to young children who are terrified when the doorbell rings, to adolescents who have additional opportunities to experiment with drugs and sex. Indeed, most experts contend that it is unsafe to ever leave a child younger than age 8 alone.[62] Physical safety for these young children is the paramount issue. For example, it is suggested that as many as one quarter of all home fires are started by children who are left home alone.[63]

Empirical research about the effects of self-care by older children is mixed. Some child development experts, including Bronfenbrenner and Crouter (1982), purport that self-care tends to strengthen peer influence and weaken familial influence, which might contribute to lowered academic performance within particular population groups.[64] There also have been reports of increased rates of depression among poor and working-class children who care for themselves six or seven days each week.[65] Some studies, however, suggest that limited self-care may not be associated with negative effects for all children. Two studies of middle-class children did not uncover differences between groups of children who were supervised by an adult and those who cared for themselves in self-esteem, self-reliance, academic achievement, and measured levels of fear.[66] It is quite possible that the effects of self-care are mitigated by a number of other variables, including the amount of time spent in self-care, the age of the child, the child's level of maturity, characteristics of the community in which the child resides, and the nature of the parent-child relationship. Some people suggest that conclusive evidence of the long-term impact of self-care arrangements is not yet available.

It is too simplistic to place blame solely on the parents for not making suitable arrangements for their children. Most of these parents are forced to work in order to provide their children with the basic necessities of life. The majority of them would be happy to use quality, appropriate services if they were available and of reasonable cost. For some parents self-care may be the best choice in contrast to poorly supervised programs in which children are exposed to bad peer models. For other parents it is really their only choice. Society does have some responsibility to ensure that families have the opportunity to participate in quality care.

CONCLUSION

Many people see child-care issues as being center stage in the drama of work/family conflicts. This results both from the compelling nature of the needs of children and from the love and care that parents want to be able to extend to their children. One aspect of the conflict is quite obvious: at the minimum, children need some supervision round the clock (at least up until their preteen years), which conflicts with the relative unavailability of employed parents during work hours. Some care arrangements must be made.

Despite all the conflicts that child care presents to parents, the real story is the reluctance of either the private or the public sector to assume some ownership of the issue. Both corporate and government policymakers handle child-care issues very gingerly, offering some assistance when pressed as long as the major responsibility is kept out of their domains. Government's involvement either has been limited to families at risk or has assumed very low profiles, such as monitoring minimum standards or establishing tax benefits for those who can deduct their expenses. Although the workplace has begun to perk up around the child-care issue, it has not entered into any significant partnership with the family in resolving their common problems around child care.

In the final analysis the role of the public sector will determine whether and if the child-care issues get addressed in any meaningful manner. Despite all the activities that corporations may undertake to resolve the child-care problems of their employees, the child-care issue is too large and universal to be the primary responsibility of the private sector. Child care touches on some of the most fundamental values and cultural norms of our society, and failure to resolve such a fundamental issue as the care and development of our nation's children speaks as loudly as any specific policy. Because of the many changes confronting our society on social and economic levels, the question must now be raised as to whether child care should not be placed in the same category as education: a social obligation that is of critical importance to the family and the child, as well as to the broader society itself. Can the United States afford to continue its current policy of wrapping its child care within its minimalist economic philosophy, and still be competitive in an industrial and postindustrial world that has, for the most part, directly addressed its child-care issues through some type of social policy and supports?

Is the current policy a good investment in our society and our economy, and can we expect the problem to either take care of itself or be resolved through yet undiscovered strategies? The current drift and confusion symbolizes the broader set of conflicts surrounding work/family issues. Essentially, private issues are spilling over into the broader society and will require a drastic reorientation if the problems and conflicts are going to be resolved. If we, as a society, step back from our entrenched position and examine the multiple dimensions of the child-care problem, we may realize that a bold set of policy initiatives will have to be forged in the public sector if the health and development of our children are going to be realized, and if we are going to free our current workforce so that they can add to our economic competitiveness.

NOTES

1. Immerwahr, p. 32.
2. Ibid.
3. Place and Wise, p. 2.
4. Sekaran and Hall, p. 6.

5. H. Haygne, in Employee Benefits Research Institute (EBRI) p. 3.
6. Kamerman, 1983, p. 2.
7. Place and Wise, p. 2.
8. EBRI, p. 1.
9. Place and Wise, p. 2.
10. Hoffman, p. 379.
11. Gardener, p. 27.
12. Johnson, 1987.
13. Ibid.
14. *The Numbers News* p. 2.
15. Sen. Christopher Dodd (D.-Conn.), quoted in Place and Wise, p. 42.
16. Emlen and Koren, p. 5.
17. Fernandez, *Child Care and Corporate Productivity,* p. 30.
18. Glove Editorial, 3/20/89, p. 16.
19. Dodd, quoted in Place and Wise, p. 42.
20. Emlen, p. 5.
21. Dodd, quoted in Place and Wise, p. 42.
22. Hanafin, p. 8.
23. Chapman, p. 32.
24. Hanafin, pp. 1, 8; Place and Wise, p. 42; EBRI, p. 6.
25. Dodd, quoted in Place and Wise, p. 42.
26. Place and Wise, p. 18.
27. Place and Wise, pp. 18, 42.
28. Hanafin, p. 8; Place and Wise, p. 42.
29. Hanafin, p. 8.
30. Hoffman, p. 384.
31. See Bass, p. 30.
32. Ibid.
33. Ibid.
34. Berg, p. 93.
35. Mintz and Kellogg, p. 224.
36. Bass, p. 30.
37. Rodman, pp. 100–101.
38. Bass, p. 30.
39. Ibid.
40. Ibid.
41. Ibid.
42. Ibid.
43. Hughes, p. 5.
44. Place and Wise, p. 3.
45. Chapman, p. 30.
46. Ibid.
47. EBRI, p. 5.
48. Emlen and Koren, p. 7.
49. Place and Wise, p. 2.
50. Emlen and Koren, p. 5.
51. Hughes and Galinsky, pp. 3–4.
52. The following description incorporates some statistics that resulted from a large

study that included 32,000 working parents. "In a work force that overall misses about 9 days per year, on the average, men employees who have no children miss 7 ½ days. Add to that ½ day for being a father, 1 day for out-of-home care, or 5 ½ days if the kids are looking after themselves. The men are now up to 13 ½ days per year. Women employees, even without kids, start out at 9 ½ days, having lost a couple of days more than men per year probably because of a division of labor in which they assume more family responsibilities in general. Add 2 days if the kids are in care outside the home, or 3 ½ if they are looking after themselves. The mothers are at 13 days per year. . . . Add another 3 days if she is a single parent" Emlen, 1987, p. 3.

53. Hughes, p. 5.
54. Emlen, p. 2.
55. Emlen and Koren, p. 6.
56. Fernandez, "Child Care and Corporate Productivity," p. 2.
57. Immerwahr, p. 31.
58. Robinson, p. 4.
59. Emlen and Koren, p. 3.
60. Robinson and Coleman, p. 6.
61. Emlen, p. 5.
62. Bass, p. 29.
63. Immerwahr, p. 31.
64. Hoffman, p. 382.
65. Bass, p. 30.
66. Ibid.

Chapter 7

ELDER CARE

Although the major focus of work/family issues has been placed on children as dependents, a second stage has broadened family responsibility to include elder dependents. The changing demographics and graying of America present American society and American corporations with a major set of challenges: Who will provide the care and who will be responsible for meeting the needs of our elderly population?

A number of issues that are either directly or indirectly related to work/family conflicts affect elders. Although this chapter primarily focuses on the effects elder-care responsibilities can have on the employed caregivers, elders may experience other dimensions of work/family conflicts, such as seniors who are facing retirement or who have returned to work after retirement.

THE CHANGING POPULATION

The dramatic and far-reaching changes in the elder (age 65 or older) population in the United States have supported the elder advocacy movement popularized by the Gray Panthers. An unprecedented increase in the number of elderly people is projected. In 1980 there were 25 million persons over age 65. Less than ten years later this total had increased to 29 million. And the projections are for continued growth. It is expected that the number of elders will climb by 250 percent to 65 million in the next four decades.[1]

Elders also are rapidly becoming a much greater percentage of the total population. At the beginning of this century elders constituted just 4 percent of the total population. It took fifty years for this percentage to double (8% in 1950). By the mid–1980s the growth in the percentage of elders had accelerated to 12 percent. Demographers project that this growth rate will continue with the aging of the baby boom generation, so that elders compose approximately 17 percent of the total U.S. population by 2020 and possibly as high as 21 percent by 2030.[2]

It is not just that the numbers of seniors is increasing. Equally important is that our elders are getting older. Today approximately four out of five persons reach age 65. Of these, 50 percent have a chance of living past their 80th birthday.[3] As our population of elders ages there are increasing chances of these older seniors becoming part of the group of frail elderly who are at risk medically and whose dependency needs expand. In 1987 the number of seniors over age 75 was 12.2 million, which constituted more than one third (30 million) of those over age 65.

Perhaps even more significantly, the fastest-growing segment of our population is the group of people who are over age 85. Between 1960 and to 1980, the number of people age 85 and over rose 165 percent, and by 2020 the number is projected to climb by 500 percent.[4] The increase in America's elders will occur even in the very oldest population group. Among today's elders approximately one in eleven is age 85 or older. This ratio is expected to be one in four by 2050.[5]

These demographic changes in the U.S. elder population impact not only these seniors, but also their families. At the beginning of the twentieth century one of every four persons experienced the death of at least one parent before age 15. By 1976 this had declined dramatically to one of every twenty.[6] As recently as 1963, 25 percent of people over age 45 had at least one parent still living. In comparison, by 1980, 40 percent of people in their late fifties had at least one parent still alive.[7] Between 1900 and 1976 the proportion of middle-aged couples with two or more surviving parents increased from one in ten to nearly one in two.[8]

Unlike any previous historical era, today's "typical" married couple has more living parents than children.[9] Longer life expectancies have begun to change aspects of the relations between adult "children" (who may be elders themselves) and their elderly parents. In 1900 a woman typically spent nineteen years being responsible for the care of her child and approximately nine years being responsible for the care of her parents at the end of their lives. Today, "for the first time in history, we overlap 50 years with our parents' lives. Which means that we can expect to be responsible for our parents longer (18 years) than for our children (17 years)."[10] Because these demographics are reshaping our society, many of the factors now associated with elder care barely existed in previous generations.

It is important to remember that the change in elder dependent care is not just the significant increase in the number of years during which this care is needed. Despite the fact that a greater proportion of today's elders are perhaps in better health than people of the same age during earlier periods, the increased longevity experienced by large proportions of our population typically results in a longer phase of elder dependency at the end of one's life. Given that the fastest-growing segment of our population are age 85 or older, it is significant—but not surprising—to note that 20 to 25 percent of these elders were in nursing homes in 1987.[11] More than 50 percent of elders who are at least age 75 have some type of disability.[12] Among those elders over age 85, fully half require some assistance with daily living because of chronic illness or disability.[13]

Large numbers of noninstitutionalized elders must rely on assistance from friends, family, and any available services offered in the community. "For every disabled person who resides in a nursing home, two or more equally impaired elderly live with and are cared for by their families."[14] It is estimated that the number of functionally impaired elders who are not institutionalized (in hospitals or nursing homes) may be as high as 5 million.[15] The U.S. Department of Health and Human Services projects that this figure will reach 65 million by 2030.[16]

These statistics tell a poignant and direct story: greater numbers of Americans are living longer and need more years of increasingly intensive care assistance than ever before. "The elderly population is growing at a pace that threatens to outstrip the capacity of family and friends to care for them."[17] This sudden but indisputable shift in demographics has caught most families in our society at least somewhat unprepared. Almost without exception, elder dependent care issues that become work/family conflicts are initially experienced as family crises.

THE FAMILY—THE FIRST LINE OF DEFENSE

Most Americans find it comforting to think that their families will care for them in their old age. This notion is not just a nostalgic and Pollyanna fairy tale. In contrast to some of the proclamations about the demise of caring and nurturing families that foster meaningful and responsible relations among its members, research indicates that family members are at the forefront of the care provided to seniors. According to a study sponsored by the American Association of Retired Persons and the Travelers Companies Foundation, up to 7 million family members (75% of them women) are providing care for an average of twelve hours per week and have been doing so for at least two years.[18]

Despite the increased mobility of today's Americans (which includes elders as well as their adult children), a significant number of elders who have children still living are in contact with them regularly. Research indicates that an on overwhelming majority of elders who have living children visit with them at least weekly.[19]

Numerous studies have generated information about the fact that families provide the "overwhelming majority of services" to elders.[20] Family care frequently is estimated to be 80 percent of all care given.[21] Without a doubt, the extent of this family-based care involves significant numbers of families. Current estimates suggest that there are 2.2 million families responding to the needs of dependent elders who are not institutionalized.[22] When the care and attention provided also to institutionalized elders are considered, the number of adult children involved in elder dependent care doubles. "These findings suggest a very conservative estimate that over 5 million people are involved in parent-care at any give time."[23]

It is perhaps not surprising that caregivers are likely to be women, as attested to both subjectively and objectively in several studies.[24] Historically, our society has assumed that the woman will take care of most of a family's nurturing needs, including the care of elderly relatives who are dependent. This assignment of dependent care responsibilities by gender may rapidly become a thing of the past because there simply may not be enough women to take care of all the elder care needs. From a demographic perspective, we are beginning to witness a change in the ratio between the number of dependent elders who need care (whose numbers are increasing) and the number of adult children who are available to provide this care (whose numbers are decreasing with the reduction in birth rates). In addition, the pool of women who are potential caregivers is shrinking because of the unprecedented rise in the number of women who have entered the workforce. Projections suggest that 75 percent of all women between ages 45 and 50—prime years for having elderly parents who need some care assistance—will be in the labor force by the year 2000.[25] In comparison to their mothers, today's women will experience additional constraints on their caregiving capacities imposed by their work responsibilities. It is important to note that recently there have been some signs that an increasing number of men are beginning to participate in the care provided to both children and elders. Some of this change may be occurring as a result of social and political pressures, changes in values, and new expectations for the relations between men and women. In the near future it will become increasingly necessary for men to share both the joys and the burdens of elder caregiving simply because there will not be enough women available to respond to the needs of our country's increasing elder population.

The large number of families who are involved in the care of an elderly relative typically provide intensive levels of care, which places demands on time, energy, emotions, and financial resources. Perhaps one of the most easily obtained indicators of the intensive nature of elder care is the time families devote to this responsibility. On average, highly impaired elders who are not institutionalized receive twenty-eight hours of care each week from family members who reportedly spend an average total of forty hours each week with those elders.[26] This amounts to four hours every day of the week—equivalent to a part-time job—in addition to whatever other responsibilities the caregiver might have.[27] Families devote this time to provide the care recipient with a wide range of services that might include personal care (such as bathing and dressing), household chores (errands, cleaning, cooking), transportation, management of the elder's finances, arranging for and mediating contact with service providers, and companionship. In addition to these activities, many family members become critical to the provision of medical services to elderly family members. These services often can extend beyond straightforward scheduling and dispensing of oral medications. "Because hospitals are discharging elderly patients more rapidly than before, family members increasingly are expected to provide highly technological services as well as nurturant support. Some relatives are responsible for care that is more complex than that which licensed vocational nurses are permitted to manage in hospitals."[28]

The often intensive daily needs of dependent elders are typically of a long-term nature and usually increase with time. Years ago, although younger elders may have recuperated after serious acute illnesses or severe accidents, the frail elderly would probably have died. Today these medical emergencies may not so much affect the length of person's life span as have an impact on the number of years of dependency at the end of life. Elder care usually is not a short-term intervention after which the elder resumes full independence. The Long-term Care Survey (1982) reported that among the survey respondents, 44 percent of the caregivers had been furnishing assistance for between one and five years.[29]

Even when it is an act of love, elder care is a demanding family responsibility. And more and more adults are becoming involved in it. The family crisis—which so often ignites work/family conflicts—results from the fact that changes in individual, family, and community lives have assaulted the capabilities of informal caregiving networks.

WORKERS AS CAREGIVERS

Common sense might lead one to conclude that many of the social upheavals that occurred at accelerated rates during the past two decades (such as single-parent families and dual-career families) have strengthened women's affiliation to work so much that there is no one left at home to provide family-based care to dependent elders in the family. Although there can be no doubt that these changes have altered some aspects of caregiving, it is somewhat surprising to discover the extent to which employed family members continue to provide the needed care, typically at a cost to themselves. It may be analogous to working parents who do not abandon their parenting responsibilities or love their children less because their children attend school or receive child care during work hours. Just as these parents may try to offer "intensive/condensed" parenting to their children during nonwork hours, employed adult children somehow fit in their caretaking activities for their dependent elders. And just like working parents, when the need arises adult children usually are available to their elderly parents even during work hours. The family care network continues to function, having been stretched beyond a reasonable expectation of its capacities.

A number of studies have explored the incidence of elder dependent caretakers among worker populations, and have found that 25 to 30 percent of today's workers also are likely to be caregivers.[30] The preliminary results of the 1989 Health Action Forum Survey confirmed earlier studies and indicated that 28 percent of the employee respondents provided elder care.[31]

Although employed caregivers typically are middle-aged, they can range in age from their twenties to their sixties.[32] The incidence of caregiving is high among older workers, who are providing assistance either to their spouses or to their parents, who are likely to be frail elders. In 1986 Retirement Advisors, Inc., conducted a survey of preretirees (ages 50 to 68) and found that 28 percent were already involved with the provision of elder care and that an additional 9 percent anticipated assuming responsibilities for caregiving within the next five years.[33] The work/family conflict implications of these older workers as care providers is significant for the following reasons:

• They are likely to be experienced, valued workers
• They may have less physical energy to confront and resolve work/family conflicts within their immediate nuclear family than when they were younger
• They are at a point in their lives when they might be actively making retirement plans

A significant portion of working caregivers assume responsibility for the bulk of the care recipient's (typically the parent's) needs. An 1988 study at the University of Bridgeport revealed that not only are large numbers of employees involved in elder dependent care, but also more than 40 percent considered themselves to be the *primary* caregiver.[34] Among the employees who participated in the 1985 Travelers survey, nearly one half (48%) were self-identified as the primary caretaker.[35] Depending on the level of functioning of the elder, this caregiving can be a time-consuming responsibility that exacts physical and emotional stress.

Employees who are involved in elder care are not on the fringe of America's labor force. Several studies have explored the employment profiles of working caregivers, and have documented that many are long-term employees. It is common for people in this group to have twenty or more years of work experience and to have worked for their current employers for ten or more years.[36] These employees are probably able to make important contributions to their company, regardless of their particular position or job title. In fact, although the incidence of working caregivers is not more or less likely to occur among different descriptive employment categories, it seems that between one third and one half of employed caregivers hold management or professional positions.[37] Their contributions are valued, and yet their family responsibilities may interfere with their ability to perform up to their potential at work, or their work responsibilities may hamper their abilities to respond sufficiently to the elderly family members who depend on their assistance.

Despite the fact that most employed caregivers work full-time, they devote surprisingly large amounts of time to the needs of their elderly relative.[38] All employed caretakers (including those who share the caretaking responsibilities with others as well as the primary caretakers) commonly spend ten to twenty hours each week on caregiving tasks.[39] When one considers the fact that these workers have their own homemaking chores and obligations to other family members in addition to these caregiving hours—on top of work hours—the challenge simply in terms of juggling schedules is enormous. The challenge is more difficult for those who assume the role of primary caretaker. These employees report spending thirty or more hours each week on caregiving.[40]

Certainly one factor that greatly affects the frequency of contact between the caregiver and the recipient is the geographical proximity of their residences. Those who live in the same home are likely to spend more time on caregiving activities (especially companionship), but these "visits" are easier to arrange. For most employed caregivers the relationship with the elder requires some travel for any visiting. One national survey of 418 caretakers found that only one fifth shared a home with the care recipient; an additional 11 percent of the elders were in nursing homes and 69 percent were "in the community."[41] Other surveys have found a similar distribution of residences among its caregiving workers in relation to the homes of care recipients.[42] The results of the 1985 study conducted by the Travelers Corporation found that "fully 35 percent of the elders live a distance from the employee—adding logistic difficulty . . . to the stress."[43]

Despite the effort that long-distance visits entail, employed caregivers maintain regular contact with the dependent elder. Only 7 percent of the caregiver respondents in the Travelers survey visited their dependent relative less often than once each week; more than 75 percent visited "a few times a week or more," with a full 42 percent establishing contact each day.[44] A recent survey sponsored by the Health Action Forum corroborated the fact that employed caregivers incorporate visits as part of their nonworking schedules.[45]

Those who are unfamiliar with elder care might mistakenly assume that any work/family conflicts experienced by the working caregiver would be resolved by hiring someone (such as a home health aide) to take care of the elder during working hours. For numerous reasons, including cost, individual needs of the elder, limited availability of competent home health workers, and the resistance of the elder who wants to remain as independent as possible, this outside help is not forthcoming. Although employee caregivers do utilize more hours of paid help than caregivers who are not in the workforce, such services are not used by the majority of working caregivers.[46] The Travelers Company found in 1985 that only 15 percent of their caregivers used paid help as the primary care provider.[47] A dramatic finding by the 1987 American Association of Retired Persons (AARP) survey was that an overwhelming majority (86%) of the employee caregivers did not use any paid assistance.[48]

Like child-rearing, caregiving can be a long-term commitment. Many employees continue in this role for 3.5 to 6.5 years.[49] It quickly becomes obvious that employed caregivers may assume two demanding roles (as a worker and as a caregiver) for a significant portion of their working years. Assuming that the average person works for approximately forty years, if even just eight of these years are spend on caregiving, these two sets of responsibilities may compete for the worker's time, energy, and commitment for fully one fifth of the employment years.

Families and the workplace need to prepare for the complexities that arise when workers also become caregivers to dependent elders because this will affect large numbers of employees. According to the Health Action Forum, "the number of employees caring for elder relatives will increase substantially in the future. [Sixty-nine percent] of all respondents expect to provide care to an elder within the next five years."[50] Caregiving can affect and conflict with work, and work can conflict with and affect caregiving; this is a reality for today's American families.

WORK/FAMILY CONFLICTS MANIFESTED AT HOME

There can be little doubt that caring for an elderly relative is a stressful responsibility, even though it also can be a meaningful and rewarding experience. Research suggests that as many as one third of employed elder caregivers find that their elder-care responsibilities are a significant problem for them.[51] The emotional context of elder caregiving often is complex and replete with difficult personal issues. Adults involved in elder caregiving must confront the realities of the dependencies that usually remain the same year after year or grow more demanding. Illnesses often are part of this experience. And, for many, issues of death and mortality introduce significant sadness into the relationship. Some caregivers experience the beginning of a prolonged mourning process when their parents initially demonstrate the need for assistance.

Although many people compare some of the responsibilities of elder care with child care, there are some important practical factors associated with elder dependent care that differentiate the two types of caregiving. Unlike the birth of a child, which many parents are able to plan for to some extent, the need for elder care often comes on suddenly and without much forethought by potential family caregivers. Furthermore, although prospective parents may be able to estimate the approximate cost of the child care that will be needed during the years before entry into school, it is impossible to calculate ahead of time the level of care an elder might need or for how long the care will be necessary. Finally, the childbearing years and the early years of child-rearing (typically the most physically demanding period of child-rearing) occur when parents are somewhat younger and during a time of life when adults might have more physical fortitude than during the later middle-age years when the need for elder caregiving might be needed. Although adult children caring for their dependent parents (or other elderly relatives) could enjoy good health, they are likely to have less energy than they had even ten years earlier. In fact, in the case of caregivers who are preretirees who might be caring for spouses or parents, these workers might themselves be elders who are caring for "older elders."

The emotional relationship between the caregiver and the care recipient can develop complicated dimensions that were not present before the elder developed the need for care. Perplexing for many family members is the emergence of role reversals, which result from the adult child nurturing and taking care of the daily functional needs of the aging parent. The relationship between the elder parent and the adult child can become further encumbered when the elder expresses either ambivalence or outright rejection of the very assistance that is desperately needed. Many elders are reluctant to have family members provide aid with intimate personal care (such as bathing or dressing) because these tasks are perceived as injurious to the elders' sense of dignity, privacy, and independence.[52]

In some cases the (elder) parent-(caregiver) adult child relationship witnesses the resurfacing of unresolved differences that were experienced in the past—sometimes as long ago as the caregiver's childhood.[53] Historical familial tensions, stresses, and dynamics may become exacerbated and their impact on family members intensified by the experience of isolation that many families experience in the caregiving situation. The isolation of the caregiver and the care recipient not only can aggravate the relationship between these two family members, but also may extend to other filial relations. When either (or both) the elder or the caregiver begins to feel that "I am in this alone," resentment is bound to build up against other family members who might not be contributing as much to the overall care of the dependent elder.[54] This unequal distribution of caregiving tasks among family members is widespread. The 1987 AARP survey of employed caregivers found that 65 percent of the survey respondents did not get help from other household members (such as spouses or children of the caregiver), and 63 percent did not receive help from any other family members (including other adult children of the dependent elder—the caregivers' siblings).[55] When the ever-present work and concern about the loved one is combined with the stressful context of caregiving, the caregivers and the care recipients alike can become emotionally at risk.[56] In one study caregivers reported having symptoms of depression three times as often and feeling angry four times as often as the general population.[57] Other problems experienced by working caregivers include physical fatigue, stress, and anxiety.[58] "With less time to spend with their own families, interruptions on the job, postponed vacations and altered retirement plans, it's little wonder that caregivers suffer from depression, anxiety, frustration, helplessness, sleeplessness, and sheer emotional exhaustion."[59]

There are many ways family caregivers of the aged make sacrifices in their personal and family lives so that the needed care is available. For employed caregivers the tendency to make personal sacrifices is exaggerated because these caregivers may try to minimize any interference with work. When adjustments have to be made, most employed caregivers attempt to make the necessary accommodations "at home." There are several indicators of the personal adjustments that employed caregivers make in an effort to limit any impact on work. The 1987 AARP survey found that whereas only 5 percent of the respondents stated that caregiving "regularly" interferes with work responsibilities, three times that number (17%) felt that caregiving interfered with recreation or home activities, such as shopping, "often" or "most of the time."[60] Research conducted by the Travelers Corporation found similar patterns among the employed caregivers.[61]

As a consequence of these adjustments, caregivers give up vacations and social and leisure activities so that they can manage responsibilities associated with caregiving, other household or family needs, and the demands of work.[62] "Some investigators (Cantor, 1983; Horowitz, 1982; Long and Brody, 1983) have found that daughters who work continue to meet their responsibilities to their families, jobs and elderly parents who need help. When confronted with competing demands on their time and energy, they give up their own free time and opportunities for socializing."[63]

Some of the more tangible measurements of the sacrifices made by families involved in elder care are economic. The 1985 Travelers survey of its caregiving employees found that nearly one third (approximately 30%) provided financial assistance to their elderly family member.[64] Data suggest that as many as three quarters of nonspousal caregivers provide as much as one tenth of their income in support of their elders, and that one third of these family caregivers devote 20 percent of their income to financial assistance for the elder.[65] Some caregivers who are preretirees find that the financial needs associated with caregiving necessitates the postponement of their retirement plans.[66]

When the needs of the elder intensify, some employed caregivers decide to make a substantial financial sacrifice, quitting work to provide the necessary level of caregiving. A 1986 study in California conducted by the Family Survival Project concluded that the caregivers included in their study who had quit to respond to the needs of their dependent relatives had each lost an average of $20,400 of annual income.[67]

Research indicates that overall levels of care given to elderly parents by their daughters did not differ among working and nonworking daughters. Although the working daughters were more likely to purchase some services to help with some of the personal care or housekeeping needs, they continued to participate directly in activities such as transportation, companionship, and household management.[68] These working women have made many sacrifices.

The struggles typically addressed and felt most poignantly at home are apt to affect three groups most intensively: women, caregivers who concurrently have responsibilities to their own children, and single parents.

Women as Caregivers

There is a clear consensus among most experts in the field of gerontology that women assume the bulk of elder-care responsibilities. Most current estimates suggest that women comprise approximately three quarters of the dependent elder caregivers. For example, the Family Survival Project found that 70 percent of the caregivers participating in their survey were women.[69] Similarly, only 25 percent of the employed caregivers identified by the Retirees Advisors, Inc., were men.[70]

Attitudes are changing, but the behavior patterns for elder care suggest that women continue to shoulder most of the caregiving responsibilities despite the fact that one half of these women caregivers are employed.[71]

The changing values in our society have produced some dissonance for women who are faced with the prospect of providing care to a dependent elder. Although they seem to feel that these responsibilities should be equally divided among the male and female family members, they end up attending to most of the elder's needs, especially if paid caregivers are not readily available.

In a survey of attitudes of three generations of women about women's role and filial care, majorities of all three generations agreed that it is better for a working woman to pay someone to care for her elderly parent than to leave her job to do so (Brody et al., 1983). Most respondents stated that adult children should not adjust work schedules for parent care, but all three generations were more likely to expect working married daughters rather than working married sons to do so (Brody, 1984). Although the women were strongly in favor of sons and daughters providing equal amounts of parent care, in practice the daughters were doing virtually all of it (Lang & Brody, 1983).[72]

In comparison to men, women are not only more likely to be caregivers, but also more involved with their elderly relatives. According to the results of the 1985 Travelers survey, women typically devoted more than three times as many hours (16.1 hours weekly for women and 5.3 hours for men) to caregiving tasks.[73] As one might expect from this difference in the number of hours, the men were more likely to hire outside help or get assistance from their spouses to supplement the care they provided directly.[74] The types of care provided by men and women also tend to be different. Whereas women usually are involved in direct care (such as the administration of medicines and personal care), men are more likely to respond to other needs, such as making appointments and managing finances.[75]

It is perhaps the combination of the long hours and the demands (and rewards) of the close, interpersonal relationship with the dependent elder that contributes to the different reactions that men and women have to the caregiving situation. Women have a greater tendency to develop symptoms of stress.[76] As Abel suggests, "women may be more likely to experience caregiving as a boundless, all-encompassing activity. Some studies have found that women are less likely to set limits and more likely to assume responsibility for improving the overall quality of the lives of the elderly."[77]

At least one study has generated some statistics suggesting that employed men may be beginning to be involved in elder care. The 1989 survey conducted by the Health Action Forum found that among the working caregivers, the ratios of men and women caregivers reflected their proportions in the employee populations.[78] The women caregivers in this study, however, were devoting more hours to their caregiving responsibilities. Whereas nearly one quarter of these women indicated that they spent eleven or more hours each week on caregiving, only 6 percent of the men devoted this amount of time.[79] Future studies need to examine whether men will continue to assume increasing levels of caregiving roles.

Parents with Dual Dependent Roles as Caregivers

Statistics abound documenting the changes that have occurred in America's childbearing patterns. The baby boom generation has had fewer children, later in life, than their parents. Previous generations have enjoyed the advantage of having grandparents available to enjoy their grandchildren, and in some cases these elders made significant contributions to child care. The 1980s has witnessed such a dramatic change that not only are grandparents less available to help with child care at a time when more parents might need it, but also the family "care deficits" are exacerbated by the fact that the elders themselves may need care in addition to the children. These middle-aged adults are, figuratively speaking, surrounded by the care needs of the young and the old, and sometimes are referred to as the "sandwich generation."

Employed caregivers are more likely than their nonemployed counterparts to have dependent children and dependent parents simultaneously. They typically are younger by almost six years; one third of working caregivers are between ages 40 and 45.[80] Demographic information about working caregivers indicates that approximately two fifths of them have at least one child under age 19.[81] Some estimates of the sandwich generation are as high as 50 percent.

Although the day-to-day demands exerted by children on parent caregivers decrease as the children age, the financial strains on the family may become augmented when payments for elder-care services and college expenses are required simultaneously.

Single Parents as Caregivers

Like married caregivers, single parents who have dependent elders face demands on physical and emotional energy, financial burdens, the lack of affordable and quality services, and conflicts with the fulfillment of work responsibilities. For single-parent families the conflicts are intensified because work, parenting, and caregiving roles are all assigned to a single person. For many the resultant stresses are severer, and their impact on the family unit is, therefore, heightened.

There is some evidences that adult children who are divorced may not be able to devote as many hours to the care of dependent elders as those who are married.[82] Undoubtedly, employed single parents who also have elder-care responsibilities are facing the potential of overwhelming role strain.

CONFLICTS AT THE WORKPLACE

Despite the valiant efforts made by employed caregivers to protect their world of work from the demands of elder dependent care, the realms of work and family do not function independently or autonomously; there is inevitable spill-over—both positive and negative—from one sphere to the other. As a group, caregivers may find that these family responsibilities affect the selection of particular jobs, the ability to fulfill day-to-day job expectations, attempts to manage work and family schedules, and overall job performance.

Research suggests that both the employees and their supervisors are aware of the impact that elder dependent care can have on workers' performance. Health Action Forum data suggest that approximately two fifths of working caregivers believe that their caregiving responsibilities interfere with their jobs at least occasionally.[83] Surveys of managers and supervisors indicate that they, too, are aware of work/family conflicts among their workers who are elder caregivers. A study of senior executives conducted by the University of Connecticut found that six out of ten executives were aware of work-related problems associated with some of their employees who were caregivers.[84] Two thirds of the corporate members who participated in the research sponsored by the New York Business Group on Health reported that caregiving conflicted with employees' work responsibilities, as evidenced by absenteeism, tardiness, and unscheduled days off.[85]

Although elder-care responsibilities can develop at almost any time during the employment life of an adult, a significant number of caregivers factor in caregiving responsibilities when they are looking for a job. One national study found that nearly 25 percent of the working caregivers had already assumed caregiving responsibilities when they began the jobs they held at the time of the interview, and 8.1 percent indicated that their caregiving activities affected the selection of that particular job.[86] It is interesting to speculate how the caregiving role might impact career decisions and job selections. Do these caregivers (typically women) seek out part-time employment, and thus curtail their ability both to contribute to their places of employment and to earn an income? Do these caregivers look for jobs that will be less demanding than they might be capable of handling in hopes that they can "leave their jobs at work" because they must focus their energies after work on caregiving? This possibility of underemployment may have negative impacts both on the individual caregivers and ultimately on the companies that are unable to fully utilize the talents and contributions of its labor force.

The loss of labor potential becomes even more staggering when one considers that large numbers of caregivers would be interested in employment if their caregiving responsibilities were not as extensive and time-consuming. Statistics derived from the Long-term Care Survey (1982) suggest that many caregivers might seek employment if they did not have to fulfill their caregiving responsibilities. Among the survey participants who were unemployed at the time of the survey but who had worked within the previous year, 28 percent found that caregiving had interfered with their being able to look for work, and 21 percent had declined job offers because they anticipated that their caregiving and work responsibilities would conflict.[87] Similarly, more than one quarter of the nonemployed caregivers participating in the 1987 Family Survival Project survey stated that they would be working if they did not have their caregiving responsibilities.[88]

Caregivers who are able to maintain employment may quickly find that they need to rely more heavily on standard employee benefits to respond to some of the needs of their dependent elder. Vacation time, sick days (often extended by company policy to include the care of immediate family members for short-term, acute illnesses), personal days, and even lunch hours may be devoted to caregiving. When these benefits are exhausted the employee may be forced to make requests to take off days without pay.

Some documentation is available that provides insights into the patterns of caregivers related to their being either present or absent from work. From the corporate perspective, time lost is money wasted, and this represents a priority concern for businesses. Several studies have documented patterns of caregivers who miss work time. One exploratory study revealed that elder caregivers had missed an average of thirty-five hours a year—a sum of a full work week— because of elder-care responsibilities.[89] More than half the respondents to the 1989 Health Action Forum survey indicated that they had been late or had left work early because of caregiving; a third had missed work during the past year.[90] Other surveys conducted at different types of workplaces in different regions all indicate that working caregivers typically miss time at work—sometimes without any notice—because of conflicts with the caregiving responsibilities. Wang Laboratories, Inc., in Lowell, Massachusetts, reported that their employees who have elder-care responsibilities miss an average of six days a year as a result of caregiving activities. Research conducted by Enright and Friss indicates that more than half of those caregivers who work at least twenty hours a week report that they miss work because of caregiving.[91] Data generated from the Long-term Care Survey revealed that about one fifth of the employed caregivers took time off because of caregiving needs.[92]

Statistics from the 1986 Retirement Advisors, Inc., survey suggest that large numbers of companies are experiencing the effects of increased instances of absenteeism because employees must respond to caregiving responsibilities[93]:

Late arrivals/early departure	45.3%
Absenteeism	42.6%
Unscheduled time off	40.8%

Other studies confirm that many companies are becoming aware that signs of the conflicts associated with elder caregiving are being manifested at the workplace. One national survey of employers found that more than half (57%) have received requests for time off and an additional 39 percent had had employee requests for leaves of absences because of elder dependent care.[94] The University of Connecticut reports a similar profile of employers experiencing performance problems because of caregiving: 38 percent of the companies surveyed had caregivers who had taken unscheduled days off, 30 percent had problems with absenteeism, and 37 percent had employees who were either arriving at work late or leaving work early.[95]

Disruptions at work can become especially complicated for those caregivers whose elderly relatives live at a distance. For these workers any emergencies with the elder can necessitate the employee's having to make a sudden request for some type of leave of absence. According to a large survey sponsored by the AARP (1987), approximately one third of all caregivers are involved in this type of long-distance care.[96]

Full-time workers usually have less flexibility in providing care during the typical work day; therefore, it might be more difficult for them to arrange to help with tasks such as medical and service appointments, which tend to occur during daytime hours. The results of the 1987 Family Survival Project survey indicate that a greater percentage of full-time working caregivers (55%) experience more absenteeism than their part-time counterparts (33%).[97] However, the work/family conflicts confronting part-time workers should not be overlooked. Research conducted by Petty and Friss revealed that caregivers employed part-time who are responsible for highly impaired elders also must take time off from work. "Over half of those who work twenty hours or less said they would work more hours if they were not giving care."[98]

Another impact of caregiving involves requests for more permanent schedule changes. Some employees may indicate a need for flex time, whereas others seek a reduction in work hours. Gibeau and Anastas reported that among the eighty-five employers involved in their survey, one quarter (26%) had received requests for changes in the work schedules of their employee caregivers.[99] Their survey of employed caregivers found that nearly one third of them had considered "some change" in their work schedule.[100] Similarly, the results of the Long-term Care Survey (1982) indicate that 21 percent of the participating caregivers had reduced their hours and 29.4 percent had rearranged their work schedules in the hope that this might better accommodate their caregiving responsibilities.[101]

A reduction in work hours may become necessary for caregivers when the elder's needs increase beyond the capabilities of the worker during nonwork hours. The Family Survival Project (1987), focusing on caregivers of highly impaired elders, found that more than half (55%) had to reduce their working schedules in response to the high level of dependent care activities in which they were involved.[102] Among the employed adult daughters involved in a study conducted by Brody, one quarter had to either cut back on their working hours or were in the process of assessing the need to quit.[103]

A major issue affecting the human resources management of businesses is the anticipation of employee retirement plans. Caregiving responsibilities can cause some workers to dramatically alter these plans. In some situations the needs of the elderly parent (or other relative) may become so great and time-consuming that early retirement seems to be a reasonable solution, so that the worker will have more time to devote to caregiving. One survey of eighty-five employers found that 17 percent had had requests for early retirement so that the workers might better respond to their caregiving responsibilities.[104] Conversely, other workers might find that the increased financial strain associated with dependent care forces a postponement of retirement so that the family can access some additional years of greater income. It is significant to note that among those companies surveyed by Retirement Advisors, Inc. in 1986, 29.7 percent thought that caregiving responsibilities of employees had resulted in retirement delay.[105]

Although variables such as absenteeism are relatively easy to obtain, it is more difficult to develop measurable criteria that provide information about the effects that caregiving can have on overall work performance or productivity. Despite this fact there are some indicators that suggest some of the potential negative effects of dependent caregiving on productivity.

In a preliminary survey of working caregivers, Gibeau and colleagues found that 77 percent had experienced conflicts between the responsibilities of work and caregiving, and that 35 percent indicated that these conflicts had interfered with their work.[106] It is easy to understand how worry and concern about a disabled loved one could distract workers. The study conducted by the Family Survival Project (1987) found that more than half of those caregivers who were assisting elders with serious impairments stated that they worked at a slower pace, and more than 50 percent felt that their productivity was deleteriously affected because of distraction, worry, and distress over their elderly relative.[107] Managers and supervisors also have observed changes in the work performance of caregivers. Nearly half (46%) of the managers surveyed by the New York Business Group on Health in 1986 indicated that they had noticed declines in the work performance (quality and productivity) among workers who were responsible for elder dependent care. Furthermore, 64 percent of these managers thought that excessive use of the telephone for personal needs during work hours was exhibited by working caregivers.[108]

The 1986 survey of employers by the Retirement Advisors, Inc., summarized some of the concern about caregivers' productivity[109]:

Work Problems Associated with Caregiving	Percentage of Companies Participating in Survey
Decreased productivity	32.1%
Low morale	28.3%
Stress/emotional distres	56.5%
Personal phone calls	57.2%

More attention needs to be paid to some of the other ways in which caregivers may not be able to explore career potential because of time constraints imposed by caregiving. In one study sponsored by the National Association of the Area Agencies on Aging nearly one fifth of the workers surveyed decided to forego training opportunities and 13 percent were not able to work overtime.[110] It also would benefit corporate decision makers to gather information about the number of talented workers providing care to elderly relatives who are unable to consider promotions or more challenging jobs because they think that they cannot handle additional demands.

It would seem that one of the most significant indicators of work/family conflicts is the incidence of resignations. Although the loss of salary results in great family sacrifices, even among dual-career families (for whom the second income is seldom a luxury), turnover rates also affect businesses which must calculate the costs incurred by job searches, the time and money devoted to training new employees, and the differences in proficiency between experienced and new employees. Research indicates that the percentage of voluntary job terminations by caregivers is probably in the low teens, although there is a large variance in this rate among different populations of caregivers.[111]

There are a number of salient characteristics about the individual caregiving situation that affect whether the employed caregiver decides to leave the workforce, including severity and nature of the illness of the elder; medical prognosis; scope of the caregiving needs (according to one study conducted by Brody, 45% of those caregivers who quit their jobs were devoting more than forty hours per week to caregiving[112]); availability and expense of supplementary services; ages of the caregiver (older caregivers, who are probably closer to retirement, tend to quit their jobs more readily than younger caregivers[113]); the complexity of the caregiver's other family responsibilities; income of the caregivers; (caregivers earning lower incomes typically quit more readily than those who are in higher-income brackets [114]); and the attitudes of the caregiver toward the job.

A 1987 study by Brody found that women with strong commitment to their careers, filling high-level positions, and earning high incomes experienced the greatest work/family conflicts associated with their caregiving responsibilities.[115] These women are at risk of quitting, which would be a serious loss to their companies. Clearly, it is a priority for most corporations to retain their valued employees, and it would, therefore, be in their own best interests to try to identify ways for retaining workers who have elder-care responsibilities rather than do nothing and risk the possibility of having these workers leave the workforce.

The total impact of caregiving on the workplace has not been completely assessed. Some pieces of information, however, contribute to a better understanding of the potential effects. A recent survey of Transamerica Life Companies in Los Angeles revealed that this company loses $250,000 each year just in wages and benefits (approximately 1,600 working days) as a result of caregivers' absenteeism.[116] Current estimates are conservative because the hidden costs of decreased productivity, decreased quality in performance, and increased turnover are not included. Even without statistically sophisticated analyses, it is apparent that work/family conflicts that result from elder dependent care can be costly to business.

SOCIETAL CONFLICTS

Elder care issues are, in one sense, unique among work/family conflict issues because sooner or later virtually every person is directly affected. Nearly all of us will experience the aging of a parent or other relative, and as our life spans lengthen, almost all of today's adults will spend some of their years as an elder person who is likely to develop some dependency needs.

Like steady tributaries that branch out into new territories, the stresses and strains of caregiving begin to impact many institutions. No major sphere of our society remains unaffected by elder-care needs. Despite the fact that our society has responded to some of the identified elder-care needs, large numbers of families are bereft of services. Compounding the absence of services, the service delivery systems of some agencies actually create additional barriers for the families to confront.

The most glaring conflict our society faces in relation to elder care is part of the larger issue of the lack of a cohesive, consistent, and cogent family policy. Although our culture emphasized the value of the preservation of the family, it is ironic that many U.S. leaders refer to this value as a rationale for not "interfering" with the functions of individual families, even when the families are begging for some sort of assistance.

America's policy vacuum negatively effects elder care in the following ways:

1. There is a *shortage* of subsidized services.

2. Subsidized services target the very poor, leaving the majority of *working families to fend for themselves,* even though the cost of even minimal services exceeds the financial means of many of these families.

3. It is difficult to ensure the *quality* of many direct-care services, especially in-home services.

4. Typically, the complete range of a *continuum of care model is not available* either because of an absence of particular types of services or because a variety of programmatic eligibility restrictions prevent some elders from participating. Consequently the family needs to fill in the gaps.

5. The *coordination* of multiple service needs often is left to the family.

Several problems with the delivery of elder-care services can be identified. Although some of these seem to be discreet problems, in reality many families experience them as related aspects of an overwhelming crisis.

LOCATING RESOURCES

The need for elder care often has a rather sudden onset and frequently is precipitated by events such as accidents or hospitalizations.[117] Most families have probably not planned much for care contingencies. Unfortunately, when elder-care needs arise, the assistance usually is required immediately, and families seldom have the luxury of becoming familiar with even the basic aspects of the service delivery system.

The first hurdles for families are numerous. Families may not be able to identify the range of specific services needed and cannot anticipate how needs might change in the near future. Many families do not know where to begin to look for help and are not sure what services are provided by which agencies. Furthermore, it is difficult for most family members to independently assess the appropriateness (and/or quality) of those services with which the family might be familiar.

Adult children faced with elder-care responsibilities for the first time may not even be cognizant of the existence of the nation's network of area agencies on aging and, in all likelihood, do not have even an elementary understanding of the organization of the delivery of elder services. Among the caregivers participating in a survey sponsored by the Travelers Insurance Company, 36 percent of the respondents had not found any source of information particularly helpful, and only 8 percent had found that workplace systems (such as employee assistance programs) provided the kinds of information they needed.[118] A significant finding in a 1986 Harris poll was that only 40 percent of the elders surveyed were able to name an organization to which they could turn if they needed assistance.[119] The community-based orientation of most elder-care services offers many advantages to the elders in the community, but it can be extremely frustrating for those caregivers who live some distance from their elders. In most cases it is up to the family (who might live in a different state) to identify and help with the coordination of services provided in the elder's community. This is a do-it-yourself project for most families. From the perspective of the family caregiver who must contact a number of agencies that operate independently of one another, the system seems fragmented.

AVAILABILITY

For those families who are able to establish contact with an appropriate elder-care agency, the next problem often encountered is that the services they seek may not be available. The shortage of in-home support services, which help elders to maintain as much functional independence in their own homes as long as they can, is particularly acute. Many working families whose elders need this type of assistance think that they have only three options: to directly fulfill the role as the primary caregiver, to assume the financial burden of privately paying for some supportive care, or to assess the feasibility of a nursing home placement.[120]

In some cases, although some of the needed services may technically be available, the elder must be put on a waiting list to receive them. Demand exceeds supply, creating a significant strain on an already tenuous home situation and potentially putting an already frail elderly person at risk. In many cases the dependent elder cannot wait for assistance.

The inadequate volume of services affects both in-home and institutional care. Despite the increases in the absolute number of nursing home beds in the past twenty years, the need for this level of care has increased with the burgeoning elderly population and nearly 75 percent of nursing homes have long waiting lists.[121] There are similar indicators that the levels of in-home care are insufficient.

Some estimates suggest that nearly three quarters of the disabled elders in America live in states where home health and homemaker services are inadequate.[122] A recent survey of home care corporations (which provide direct care) in Massachusetts discovered that 1,700 elders who met the various program eligibility requirements (i.e., income restrictions, lack of family availability to provide assistance, and functional impairments) had been authorized to receive services, and yet they had not been assigned to a staff person because none were available.[123] The catch–22 for the families of the dependent elder is almost unbelievable: their willingness to make extreme sacrifices so that they can assume some of the caregiving responsibilities may make that elderly relative ineligible for some services.

The shortage of services primarily results from inadequate public funding. Small percentages of the Medicare and Medicaid budgets are devoted to much needed in-home care services.[124] Insufficient money makes it necessary for service-providing agencies to limit their programs. In addition, funding limitations dictate the low salaries of the staff hired to provide the caregiving. Like many human services organizations, elder-service agencies have a difficult time recruiting and keeping in-home workers, especially in regions that have low unemployment rates. Consider the following situation experienced by one community agency in Massachusetts: "Ten years age, Home-Health Visiting Nurse Services of Northern Middlesex . . . would receive 50 responses to a newspaper ad for a homemaker—someone to do light housekeeping, shopping, or cooking. Now, if the non-profit outfit runs an ad for a week in three newspapers, it's lucky to get 10 responses."[125]

The attrition rates also are high among paid caregivers; more than 60 percent of home health aides stay with their jobs for less than one year.[126] Many elders who start to receive services thus experience interruptions in the provision of those services because of rapid and repeated staff turnover.

COST

Quality, labor-intensive services are expensive. The lack of a national family policy means that most families bear the cost for in-home elder care either by providing the labor themselves or by paying for someone else's services. In most cases the total number of caregiving hours of purchased care combined with the family caregiving increases with the infirmity of the elder. A noteworthy finding of the 1987 Family Survival Project survey of caregivers to highly impaired elders is that those families who paid for supplementary services purchased an average of thirty-six hours of care each week *in addition* to the thirty-five hours they provided themselves.[127]

At a time when America is beginning to acknowledge the ramifications of almost unfathomable government deficits, cost containment is a pressing and very real issue. The reality of national budget constraints, however, should not supercede the validity and urgency of the needs of our elders and their caregiving families. Family caregiving is "saving" the taxpayers significant amounts of money. One estimate for substituting free family caregiving for fee-for-service is as high as $9.6 billion annually.[128] Based on 1982 figures, this amounts to approximately $4,500 worth of services per caregiving family.[129]

The shortage of quality and affordable services for dependent elders brings to the forefront another major social conflict that gets played out in the work/family conflict arena. People with more financial resources tend to have more access to better-quality services. Whereas workers with higher incomes have the option of trying to purchase the services of another person, this usually is not possible for families with limited incomes. According to one analysis of the National Long-term Care Survey (1982), utilization rates of community-and home-based services varied in direct relation to the income of the elder needing the services. Research suggests that at least two thirds of the elders who receive formal (as opposed to family) services pay for at least some of the cost of these services; almost one half of these dependent elders pay the total cost.[130] The purchasing of supplementary services makes it possible for higher-income workers to continue to work and maintain their economic status. As might be expected, full-time workers (especially men) purchase more outside help and more frequently seek residential placements for their elders than do other caregivers.[131]

The scenario for workers whose incomes are low is quite different. For each working caregiver, there is some boundary of time and energy that the person can devote to the combination of work and family responsibilities. Some caregivers are able to work full-time and devote perhaps thirty-five hours (or more) to elder care. But for most people this level of commitment quickly becomes too much, and the toll of physical and emotional strain is apparent. At some point, when the hours needed for elder care began to increase—from perhaps eight to twenty hours a week—families with limited incomes find themselves confronted with harsh decisions made more difficult by the limited availability of public assistance. One study at the University of Connecticut confirmed that lower-income employees who provide elder care are more likely to report stress and anxiety than are upper-income caregiving workers.[132] The Family Survival Project (1987) also found levels of stress among full-time workers who were not able to pay for supplementary caregiving help.[133]

The stress that results from the inability to purchase supplementary care services often is compounded by the stress experienced at the workplace. One issue most lower-income workers must face is that their jobs may have more rigid time schedules than those of professional and management positions held by higher-income earners. Office politics can mean that people in lower-income positions may not receive the same special considerations as top-management caregivers.

When the basic physical needs of the elder cannot be met unless there is a caregiver present for signficicant periods of time each day, the caregiver may be forced to put the entire family system at risk financially and quit work so that the vulnerable elder receives the necessary care. A 1987 study found that women caregivers forced to leave the labor force as a result of their conflicting caregiving responsibilities had much lower family incomes than those who were able to maintain their employment.[134] The inadequacy of our society's response to the elder-care needs creates a situation in which the entire family system is put at risk because of the reverberating impact of the growing needs of elderly family members and the lack of available quality services.

Budget constraints that limit the availability of in-home services may come back to haunt our society. Families that do not obtain the support they need to continue to offer in-home help to the dependent elder may have to explore the options of institutionalization, which is more expensive for the government to subsidize. Unfortunately many low-income families find that there also may be barriers to utilizing institutionalized care. Although Medicaid funds can be used for nursing home services, the subsidized reimbursement rate typically is lower than the cost charged to patients who pay privately. Sadly, many nursing homes (especially those with long waiting lists) prefer to accept patients who can pay the full cost. Elders who rely on Medicaid can find it close to impossible to secure a placement in a reliable nursing home on a timely basis.[135]

CONCLUSION

Working families who are responsible for elder care can assume tremendous responsibilities that exert incredible strains on the family system as a whole. Almost inevitably, these stresses begin to affect workers' performance. As Belson and colleagues conclude, "although much of the current media attention continues to focus on child care as the major new issue for employers, care of elderly dependents represents a greater potential problem for employees."[136]

Employed caregivers make significant sacrifices to ensure that their family members receive the care they need, and they seem to be asking for relatively little. First and foremost, employed caregivers are interested in receiving information that could help them in both their decisions and their caregiving activities.[137] This information needs to be concise, targeted to the caregiving audience, and available on a timely basis.

Most working caregivers neither want nor expect society to assume all the care assistance for their elderly relatives. Although the majority are requesting "just a little help," it is uncontestable that many working caregivers would significantly benefit from the increased availability of direct-care services from community resources. Increasing the availability of respite care has the potential of buttressing and stablizing both the home and the working lives of families while minimizing elder care and work conflicts.

Employed caregivers eventually find themselves confronted with the ultimate question. They must ask themselves whether it is feasible—physically, financially, and emotionally—to continue in their current caregiving roles, given the limited amount of support they may be receiving. If help is not forthcoming to working caregivers, employers will continue to lose their workers and society as a whole will find itself paying for the institutional care of elders who might otherwise remain in their own homes, fortified by the presence of their families.

NOTES

1. Gibeau et al., p. 6; Hertz, p. 134.
2. Abel, p. 4; Employee Benefits Research Institute (EBRI), p. 13.
3. Hertz, p. 134.
4. Abel, p. 4.
5. Lee, p. 110.
6. Brody, p. 20.
7. Brody, p. 20.
8. Ibid.
9. Petty and Friss, p. 26.
10. Hertz, p. 134.
11. Lee, p. 110; Robert Friedland in EBRI, p. 13.
12. Keppel, p. 12ff.
13. Weinstein, pp. 75–79.
14. Comptroller General of the United States, 1977, in Brody, p. 21.
15. Abel, p. 3.
16. Place and Wise, p. 4.
17. Abel, p. 3.
18. Weinstein, pp. 75–79.
19. Summary of research by Ethel Shannan in Abel, p. 3.
20. Brody et al., p. 201.
21. Creedon, p. 17; Petty and Friss, p. 26; *Working Age—An AARP Newsletter,* p. 4; Abel, p. 3.
22. Gibeau et al., p. 6.
23. Brody, p. 21.
24. Abel, p. 3; Creedon, p. 26; Petty and Friss, p. 26.
25. Gibeau et al., p. 6.
26. Results of *National Long-Term Care Demonstration Survey* summarized in Abel, p. 9.
27. Dietz, p. 58, summarizing of University of Connecticut study.
28. Abel, p. 24.
29. Ibid., p. 9.
30. Creedon, p. 25; *Working Age,* p. 3; *Travelers,* p. 21; EBRI, p. 14.
31. Beinecke and Marchetta, p. 2.
32. Ibid.
33. Creedon, p. 3.
34. Ibid., p. 27.
35. *Travelers,* p. 6.
36. Brody et al., p. 202; Gibeau et al., p. 6; Creedon, p. 18; *Working Age,* p. 6.
37. Petty and Friss, p. 23; *Working Age,* p. 2.
38. Gibeau et al., p. 6.
39. Creedon, pp. 2, 21; Geibeau et al., pp. 3, 6; Brody et al., p. 202; Friedman, p. 46; Beinecke and Marchetta, p. 3.

40. Petty and Friss, p. 23; Creedon, p. 19.
41. Gibeau et al., p. 6.
42. Friedman, p. 46; ibid., p. 3.
43. *Travellers*, p. 3.
44. Ibid., p. 7.
45. Beinecke and Marchetta, p. 3.
46. Creedon, p. 19.
47. *Travelers*, p. 6.
48. *Working Age*, p. 7.
49. *Travelers*, p. 5.
50. Beinecke and Marchetta, p. 3.
51. Ibid.
52. Creedon, p. 28.
53. Abel, pp. 12–13.
54. Ibid., p. 24.
55. *Working Age*, p. 8.
56. Brody et al., p. 201.
57. Friedman, p. 46.
58. Petty and Friss, p. 23.
59. Weinstein, p. 75.
60. *Working Age,* p. 70.
61. *Travelers*, p. 9; Friedman, p. 46.
62. Able, p. 10; Petty and Friss, p. 23; *Working Age,* p. 7.
63. Brody et al., p. 201.
64. Friedman, p. 46.
65. Abel, p. 31.
66. Creedon, p. 3.
67. Petty and Friss, p. 23.
68. Brody et al., p. 201.
69. Petty and Friss, p. 23.
70. Creedon, p. 2.
71. Hertz, p. 134; ibid., p. 20.
72. Brody et al., p. 202.
73. *Travelers*, p. 7; Brody et al., p. 207.
74. *Travelers*, p. 7.
75. Dietz, p. 56.
76. Ibid., p. 58.
77. Abel, p. 15.
78. Beinecke and Marchetta, p. 2.
79. Ibid., p. 4.
80. Creedon, p. 26.
81. Beinecke and Marchetta, p. 2; EBRI p. 13; Brody et al., p. 202.
82. Abel, p. 6.
83. Beinecke and Marchetta, p. 3.
84. Dietz, p. 58.
85. *AARP Newsletter*, p. 110.

86. Gibeau et al., p. 7.
87. Abel, p. 10.
88. Creedon, p. 20.
89. Gibeau et al., p. 4.
90. Beinecke and Marchetta, p. 3.
91. Creedon, p. 2.
92. Abel, p. 10.
93. Creedon, p. 22.
94. Gibeau et al., p. 5.
95. Dietz, p. 58.
96. *Working Age*, p. 4.
97. Creedon, p. 20.
98. Petty and Friss, p. 26.
99. Gibeau et al., p. 5.
100. Ibid., p. 4.
101. Abel, p. 10.
102. Petty and Friss, p. 22.
103. Brody, p. 25.
104. Gibeau et al., p. 5.
105. Creedon, p. 22.
106. Gibeau et al., p. 4.
107. Petty and Friss, pp. 22, 26.
108. Creedon, p. 26.
109. Ibid.
110. Creedon, p. 21.
111. *Working Age,* p. 11; Brody et al., p. 207; Creedon, pp. 2, 20.
112. See Brody et al., p. 207.
113. Ibid.
114. Ibid.
115. Brody et al., p. 207.
116. Keppel, p. 2ff.
117. Beinecke and Marchetta, p. 1.
118. *Travelers*, p. 8.
119. Abel, p. 42.
120. Ibid., pp. 2, 25, 26, 34.
121. Ibid., p. 25.
122. Ibid., p. 41.
123. Hertz, p. 178.
124. Abel, p. 34.
125. Hertz, p. 178.
126. Abel, p. 39.
127. Petty and Friss, p. 23.
128. Abel, p. 25.
129. Lee, p. 110.
130. Abel, p. 19.
131. Petty and Friss, p. 26.

132. Dietz, p. 58.
133. Creedon, p. 20.
134. Brody et al., p. 203.
135. Abel, p. 19.
136. Belson et al., pp. 117–121.
137. Creedon, p. 2; *Travelers*, p. 9.

Chapter 8

SOCIAL CONFLICTS

As the family struggles with balancing its work and family roles, it has become increasingly apparent that the family's ability to resolve its conflicts is directly tied to its larger environment. Private lives rely on social responses on a variety of basic issues from survival to social order. The very role of social policy is to create the social context and environment in which individuals and families can realize many shared values and carry out their daily lives supported by these values as they become operationalized through social policy and legislation.

Over the past several decades the prevailing social order has been rocked by countless episodes of turmoil and upheaval, reflecting the lack of fit between existing social policy and operating values, and the emergence of new values and behaviors. Nowhere is this more evident than in the work family arena. The changes in family structure, values, and functions have been caught in the social order of a previous generation, an order that is largely dysfunctional for the family of today. The many conflicts within the family over work/family issues have found little response in current social policy.

This unresponsiveness is not accidental, nor is it the byproduct of a cruel and heartless centralized government. Rather, it reflects the conflicts at the societal level over public/private roles, government's role in the family, and the tension surrounding basic cultural themes. Fundamental responses to issues such as child care are tied to critical social and cultural contexts that shape how we as a society should or can respond to work/family issues.

At this juncture in our society, although there does appear to be heightened conflicts within both the family and the workplace, it may well be premature to foreclose on the vibrancy and vitality of social processes to respond to these problems. What is clear from available evidence is that the family and the workplace are changing. Furthermore, the demographic changes are real, the conflicts are significant, and the shifts in social and cultural values have intensified. Indeed, some of these trends spell danger, but others open up some wonderful opportunities for our society. Whether society can respond to these challenges and overcome its current paralysis and turmoil, or whether it will continue to act as a bystander is yet to be seen.

This chapter looks at the work/family conflicts from the perspective of society, the overarching concept within which families and the workplace are joined. Although it is difficult to disaggregate family and work conflicts from the larger social conflicts, it is apparent that the social fabric that surrounds these issues is an important influence on them. Because society constitutes the "glue" that holds the institutions of work and family together, it becomes essential to understand work/family conflicts within their larger societal context.

Public policy usually reflects the existing values of the dominant culture. The pulls and tugs at established policies and the attempts to promulgate new policies are indicators of the undercurrents of social conflicts around work/family issues.

The purpose of this chapter is to promote a better understanding of the social tensions; the role of government and social policy in supporting both the family and the objectives of private enterprise; and the multiple conflicts that exist within society over ideological, political, and economic goals. This analysis begins with an examination of social values, policy, and institutions.

VALUES

At the most basic level, much of the conflict in society around work/family issues can best be understood through an examination of the social values and beliefs that surround work and family affairs. These values reflect the deeply held beliefs that our society holds important in maintaining social order. Not surprisingly, many of the values and cultural beliefs traditionally cherished are undergoing a transformation reflecting the movement of society towards a new order. To adapt to this new order through transformed institutions, roles, and social processes, a prolonged and often painful process of value change is necessary.

As is characteristic of this type of value change, there is a lack of consensus about the advisability of these shifts. Some of this is disagreement between generations because the work/family arrangements of the past are inadequate for the present and the future. Additionally, major dissensus between different population groups exists. For example, data from the *Boston University Balancing Work and Homelife Study* indicated highly significant differences between men and women on such basic attitudinal issues as the place of women and gender role expectations.

To better understand some of the current societal conflicts around work and family, it is important to briefly examine some of the central themes that are still present in American life. A Yankelovich study on basic American life values showed that a majority of the adult population associated four cultural themes with work.[1] Despite the radical changes in personal values, these themes—and their variants—are still powerful forces in American society.

Good Provider Theme

A man's identity is subsumed by his role as breadwinner. A "real man" provides for his family.

Central to this theme is the link between a traditional perspective of masculinity and one's livelihood. Until recently masculinity was primarily associated with a man's ability to make a living that would provide financially for his family. For young men the move toward adulthood entailed assuming the responsibility of getting a job.

This theme has led to considerable societal conflicts on at least two levels. In the 1970s and 1980s women began to jointly occupy the provider role. This change resulted, in part, from societal economic changes (including spiraling inflation) that made it difficult for many families to retain their economic viability on just one paycheck. Additionally, many women sought work as one important aspect of their personal development. The entry of women into the workforce was a shift that was perceived by many men as a direct assault on their masculinity. Some of the conflicts associated with women's labor force participation were expressed by gender conflict issues, such as struggles over affirmative action, comparable worth debates, and the women's rights movement.

On another level, the changes over the seventies and eighties have put the good provider theme within a broader framework: How does the income obtained by the family providers interact with the finances and services from the public sector? At what point should the public sector contribute to the provider responsibilities to relieve the family of unreasonable burdens? Is the presence of government in the role of economic provider too intrusive in family life? Has the good provider role become unrealistically tied to the family, and should some aspects of this role be shifted to the social domain?

The strongly held traditional values associated with the good provider theme has made it difficult for men with families facing poverty to give up their traditional role as the good provider and allow the public sector to move in to fill the void. Similarly, the public sector is reluctant to assume too great a role, given the strong cultural prohibitions and the active voices of those who oppose such a government role in family life.

Independence Theme

To make a living by working is to "stand on one's own two feet," and thus avoid dependence on others. Work equals autonomy. To work and be paid for one's labor means that the individual has earned freedom and independence.

The shifting work/family environment has, by necessity, forced a greater interdependence between individuals and corporations and between institutions (both family and the workplace) and government. However strong the cultural value of independence, it is virtually impossible to stand completely on one's own two feet in today's world. With no adult at home full-time many families are finding it difficult to stand alone—to raise young children and provide for all their child-care needs, to own a home, and to provide for the care of dependent family members (e.g., disabled elderly parents). To what extent can society pick up responsibilities that have previously been relegated to the family as the traditional family caregivers (women) move from the home to the workplace? Because both the corporate and the public sectors depend on these adult family members to perform other functions outside the family domain, a shared interdependence among the three spheres has emerged. Replacing independence with interdependence, however, has created a series of conflicts that have made the combination of such roles as parenting and working more difficult than in eras past. Families' dependence on either the workplace or the government for benefits or services may represent a turn from past values and the loss of independence.

One significant source of conflict is the lack of norms associated with this new movement toward interdependence. Important questions are raised about how the finances and services provided by the family interconnect with those from the public and corporate sectors. Which sector should take the lead? Who retains decision-making responsibilities? What choices are left for the family? Can services provided by the public sector preserve some of the family's autonomy? If society assumes more and more responsibility for services and financing of family needs, are families inadvertently being discouraged from caregiving?

The provision of various types of dependent care is a graphic example of the conflicts associated with the theme of the independent family. It has been a struggle in our society to determine the point at which certain caretaking responsibilities have become too burdensome, and it is necessary for the public sector to offer some relief. At this time all three sectors have a stake in dependent care, and it has become important to identify the appropriate roles and responsibilities for our society. Furthermore, it is necessary to establish reasonable boundaries for society in relation to both the family and the corporate sector.

Some women have had a particularly difficult time relinquishing their models of family independence in terms of caregiving. Because they have traditionally filled this caregiving role, handing this over to others outside the family has proved to be a conflict-laden task. The first phases of women moving into the workplace were rendered somewhat easier because of the presence of family members who had retired or who had never worked and were willing to provide child care. As this pool disappeared (partly resulting from greater labor force participation rates among women and increased mobility of the U.S. population), more families had to turn to either the public sector or the corporate sector (especially to private enterprise) for assistance. For many women this conflict manifests itself in guilt or feelings of inadequacy as their children or elderly parents have to be handed over to "strangers" for care because of the constraints of employment.

Success Theme

Hard work always pays off. The rewards of hard work usually are reflected in a steadily increasing standard of living and a solid position in the community. Hard work can lead to increased purchasing power, most notably home ownership.

Material success has become more elusive than it was for the parents of the baby boomers. Because the rising standard of living has not been accompanied by a parallel increase in real wages, the concept of hard work has been redefined. On a societal level the economic forces that have driven most women into the workplace have made it necessary to develop new expectations about what it takes to achieve success. The struggle for economic survival, or at least the ability to keep even and maintain a standard of living congruent with that of their parents, has contributed to the emergence of dual-income families and the necessity for most adults, men and women, to play an economic role in the family. For most people hard work now means that both adults have to work (possibly at the expense of family-oriented dependent care) to meet the goals of home ownership and a consistently adequate standard of living.

Both families and society face conflicts because the cultural themes of success—defined in such terms as material goods, status, power, and accomplishments—are perceived as more difficult to attain. Within the context of work/family conflicts, many families believe that success is more amorphous in light of their multiple home and work roles and the resulting role strain. Although the concept of hard work paying off continues to be a strong cultural theme, success seems less attainable and has become somewhat of a dangling carrot that is never close enough to capture.

Self-Respect Theme

Hard work of any type be—it menial or exaulted—has dignity. A person's inherent worth is reflected in the act of working. To work hard at something and to do it well is highly valued.

Because work has been tied socially and psychologically to self-respect, self-esteem, and personal identity, it constitutes a critical dimension of human existence. As Freud declared, work and love are the two cornerstones of all human behavior. And as Camus commented, life without work "goes rotten." In the past, men often have struggled with the self-respect theme during periods of unemployment or tight financial times.

Within the arena of work/family conflicts a new dimension to the self-respect theme has been added for women. Where previously societal values tended to enshrine the hardworking mother who nurtured the family (even though she did not receive pay for this labor), the new values that hold tight to the self-respect and work theme devalue housework and dependent care because the concept of meaningful work is primarily positioned outside the home. As women have begun to build careers (and as the workplace has started to open up to their talents and contributions), their investment in their occupational status has become highly valued, often to the detriment of the importance of family responsibilities. A curious situation has developed for many working women who continue to do most of the housework and family caregiving, but who often do not derive a lot of "sense of self" from these activities.

The overreliance on the workplace for deriving self-respect has created a second aspect of conflict, one that has not received a great deal of attention. In the age of working families work has taken on a more prominent position in home life. What previously was the primary domain of men has been expanded to include men and women. What was at one point the sole domain of one parent, is now the domain of both. The dominance of the workplace has succeeded in capturing not just the organizational man of the fifties, but all adults, husbands and wives.

As more and more working women associate the concept of the self-respect theme with paid employment, a type of dissonance has developed among women who are full-time homemakers, especially those who do not have preschool-age children in the household. These women may feel a need to explain "what they do all day long," "why they can't work," or "how they are 'self-actualized.'" Given the cultural shift in attitudes about women's role in society, these women (who are becoming a vanishing breed) are confronting issues about their self-respect and self-esteem.

Whereas in the past the home was an alternative source of self-respect and the other domain for hard work, the devaluing of the home as a result of the dominance of the workplace has some potentially dire consequences for family life, community life, and the balance that any society hopes to achieve among its institutions. It is possible that today's standards of self-respect may be overly concentrated in the sphere of work.

In addition to the four values discussed above, there are certainly a number of others that have shifted significantly during the past several decades. All these changes in work/family values currently are under scrutiny as the social forces attempt to support new work and family arrangements. Our society must pay attention to whether the shifting and rearranging that is currently under way leads to a new balance (however delicate) that allows individuals, families, and major institutions to function in a healthy manner. Because the values that surround work and family have been in constant motion during the seventies and eighties, it has been difficult to determine what accommodations (by whom) are acceptable. The more significant the change in values, the more gradual is the evolution of value transformations. It will be some time before the value conflicts become less intense and the social forces become more in line with the emerging new social order.

POLICY PHILOSOPHIES

Before the evolution of city-states, families were virtually self-enclosed and self-sufficient. As government began to evolve within Western civilization, the public sector began to support (and in some cases fully assumed) some of the family roles, such as education, care of dependent children, care of disabled citizens, and assistance to the elderly. The model of families as the sole providers of care to dependents gradually began to give way to a reconceptualization of society accepting some of the direct-care responsibilities. The involvement of government in the well-being of its people paved the way for the partial development of today's so-called welfare state. This evolution has not proceeded without ambiguity, confusion, and conflicts, as the boundaries between societal roles and the responsibilities of the family often were blurred. The presence of the corporate sector in social roles (e.g., industrial capitalism during the late nineteenth and early twentieth centuries, and the occupational welfare system associated with the provision of benefits) further complicated the relations among these three spheres.

Many of the cultural values that are so embedded in American society have become stumbling blocks as the public sector attempts to carve out some policy initiatives that might alleviate some of the work/family conflicts that have developed during the seventies and eighties. Key leaders continue to measure the "strength" of America's families by the proportion of two-parent families because they perceive single-parent families (and other family/household types) to be a sign of the deterioration of the family system rather than a different family structure. Public sector leaders who respect the desire for families to retain their independence are reluctant to support policies that increase the presence of the government in the family. To date, the United States has been able to develop family policy only for those who are determined to be at risk. The rest of America's families are left within a policy vacuum, and usually receive no direct government support for family responsibilities.

To appreciate the importance of the societal dimension in work/family conflicts, it is helpful to move outside the limited context of the United States and briefly examine the work/family policies in other industrialized countries. In these countries the cultural values, social structure, and, most important, the economic and public policy systems are expressed in very different configurations. Being the only industrialized country other than South Africa without a specified family policy, the United States has the distinction of lacking the public support designed to mitigate against some of the more salient work/family conflicts.

Virtually all Eastern and Western European countries provide a child allowance program, which are benefits paid to families with children regardless of income or the employment status of the parents.[2] The pregnancy and parental leave policies, for example, adopted in many European countries offer liberal benefits that can include paid time off for four to twelve months with a job guarantee on return to work. Most of these nations have developed systems in which the employee, the employer, and the government contribute to the fund that provides the financial benefits during these leave periods. Additional periods of unpaid leave often are an option for parents.[3] Most European governments believe that it is educationally beneficial for preschool-age children (starting at ages 2 ½ to 3) to participate in some type of school, and have established voluntary preschool programs. In some countries, such as Belgium, France, West Germany, and Italy, high percentages of 3- to 5-year-olds attend public preschools.[4] Afterschool child care also is typically conceived as one aspect of the total educational system rather than as a totally separate function. Some of the particularly progressive countries, such as Sweden, also have adopted such measures as leave provisions for sick child care, limited work schedules, and limited leaves (up to two weeks) for times of special transition during the life of the child, such as entry into school.[5]

Unencumbered by the American conception of the appropriate role of government, most European countries offer a range of family programs that are "free, voluntary and are available to anyone—whether they work or not."[6] Many European countries have developed family policies that respond to some of the more salient work/family conflicts across the family's developmental life cycle. For example, in some countries adults who are unable to seek paid employment because of their elder-care responsibilities are at least given social security credits that, in some way, acknowledge the importance their caregiving has for society.[7]

There are some significant differences between the approaches that individual countries may adopt to the resolution of specific work/family conflicts. For example, although the overarching principle of Hungarian policies are designed to support mothers being able to fulfill their family responsibilities at home, France emphasizes offering parents choices in their response to work/family conflicts.[8] The United States has to date failed to articulate any major policy direction from which specific programs are launched.

The change in America's cultural themes and values present some real dilemmas for public sector leaders. Policymakers who are functioning according to the work themes described by Yankelovich might decide that the best course of action is to continue a virtual hands-off policy with regard to most family issues.

According to this line of thinking, it would be in the best interests of family functioning (except for the minority of families who display clearly dysfunctional behaviors such as child abuse) for the government to support strategies that enhance the family's capabilities to take care of its own problems. In the case of dependent care traditional values might suggest that the government offer benefits or services that can help (or at least do not penalize) families with a full-time homemaker in addition to dual-earner families with dependent-care responsibilities. A proposal such as a child allowance or an increase in tax credits for the number of dependents living in the household could accomplish this objective in comparison to the range of child-care service programs or benefits, which are less likely to support the traditional family arrangement.

The consideration of social values impacts on many aspects of policy development. Should the government identify family stress as a societal problem? Which problems merit the attention of the public sector? To what degree should the government become involved? Which strategies are most consistent with which values? Of course, the central issue is whether our country should have a family policy.

INSTITUTIONS

In addition to the conflicts that exist in society's values and the philosophical context for government policies, work/family conflicts also have affected major institutions in the United States. Society establishes institutions as mechanisms that enable it to provide services to citizens. Because the institutions usually mirror prevailing values (and the conflicts that accompany them), they can provide important insights to the conflicts at the societal level.

Without a doubt, the very structure of institutional life and resulting institutional arrangements have been affected by the new era of working families and, in turn, affect the lives of these families. Before the entry of women into the workplace most institutions depended on societal arrangements that would allow them to operate and get their business done during the day. Because somebody (usually a married woman) was at home to deal with the needs of the family, it was possible for institutions to operate fairly efficiently (and profitably) on a regular nine-to-five schedule. Once the majority of nonelderly adults became affiliated with the workplace during daytime hours, social and business institutions slowly began to recognize that this shift was not transitory. It became apparent that if the institution was going to be able to respond to the needs of its customers/consumers, it would have to restructure some aspects of its operations.

Private Market Adaptations

Some institutions were able to respond to the new work/family relations more quickly than others. Commercial institutions were probably the first to recognize the shift in demographics and in American lifestyles, and they often adjusted accordingly. For example, most banks, which traditionally adopted a nine-to-three working schedule, extended the hours of their services into the early evening and offered Saturday schedules. In addition, the introduction of automated teller machine enabled basic services to be instantly available to harried and rushed working families. The availability of new technologies (such as modems and fax machines) as well as the exploitation of more traditional solutions (such as twenty-four-hour 800 numbers and mail order catalogues) have made it possible for many businesses to continue to sell their services and merchandise to families even when there is no homemaker available during the day to execute the household purchases.

These adaptations to the needs of working families occurred because they were the only way many commercial businesses could continue to achieve their profit goals in the new environment of working families. It was a matter of economic survival. By understanding the needs of the customer (including factors associated with access), these businesses instituted a series of changes that were straightforward, good business practices. Clearly, supermarkets did not decide to stay open at nights and on weekends because they felt sorry for working families and single parents.

It is interesting that other businesses have been less accommodating to workers who find it difficult to also be consumers during typical daytime work hours. Some medical clinics and appliance repair businesses are still firmly entrenched in their traditional, rigid schedules, which contributes to the stress of working adults who also must respond to the needs of every-day living. Workers must decide to either forego the services of these businesses (and put off getting the rugs cleaned) or locate a different vendor who is willing to accommodate the schedule of a working family.

Social Institutions

Social service, public, and nonprofit organizations constitute a second set of institutions that often are equally important in the daily lives of workers. Many of these institutions are at the center of the lives of working families and, at least in theory, should be sensitive to the needs of the public they serve. In comparison to most businesses, however, these institutions have been slower to acknowledge and respond to work/family conflicts. The schools, social services, and voluntary organizations provide three examples of the roles that institutions play in work/family conflicts and how these institutions are themselves affected by these unresolved conflicts.

Schools. The U.S. educational system is, in many ways, the most central institution to work/family issues. The very existence of public education was a response to a work/family conflict that emerged during earlier times when the family's involvement in work away from the home made it increasingly difficult to directly provide for all a child's educational needs. Although education had once been the exclusive domain of the family (with some assistance from the church), it was finally relegated to the public sector during the years of industrialization.

Schools were originally structured around the needs of the workplace. In rural America the workplace was the farm; school began at 9 A.M., so that there was time for the children to complete their morning chores before they hustled off to school. The peak demands of farm life clustered around harvesting (during July and August); therefore, school vacation schedules were set that enabled families to balance the family's need for their children's education with their work needs, which necessitated the children's participation in the farm work. The needs of the workplace also affected the curriculum. The changes in technology and in the world economy that occurred during the late nineteenth and twentieth centuries have impacted the emphasis on particular skills so that the future labor force would be adequately prepared to maintain the economic viability of U.S. businesses.

The rapidly expanding school systems of the 1950s reflected the values that insulated the home (especially children) from any work/family conflicts or stresses. The full-time presence of so many mothers at home made it possible for educational institutions to limit their focus just on what they perceived to be the educational (often seen as distinct from social and emotional) needs of the children. By and large, families were able to accommodate to school schedules that did not directly impact on the schedules of the families' breadwinners.

As women began to move into the workforce in large numbers, there was a lot of pressure for schools to accept a greater set of expectations associated with the needs of the children within (not separate from) the context of their working families. Many school systems began to receive requests for earlier arrival times and later departure hours so that parents could get to work on time and coordinate work schedules with the schedules of their children. Among some educational policymakers, concern was expressed about the schools becoming surrogate mothers. Many educators vociferously opposed the school's assuming caretaking roles in addition to its primary educational objectives. Resistance was evident among members of teachers' unions, professional associations, and elected school boards. Educators and administrators wanted to ensure that professional roles and standards were maintained. Community leaders wanted to be sure that their cities and towns would not have to bear the burden of additional costs to pay for additional services. In almost every community there was evidence of the institutional resistance to change. Schools had operated on relatively regular schedules and within firm boundaries for many decades. Attempts to introduce change in both function and scheduling represented dramatic change for both the staff and the larger institution.

Although some communities were able to respond to work/family conflicts with the establishment of afterschool programs, it is significant that most of these programs have been organized as independent services rather than as part of the educational system. Even though the schools may provide space for the afterschool programs, they often do not receive any local community funding (expenses typically are covered by fees to the parents), and the staff are not considered to be employees of the school system. This "separate system" approach conveys the reluctance of most public schools to acknowledge the importance of their role in responding to work/family conflicts.

Although change and adaptation seem inevitable, most schools are slowly adjusting to the new realities of American families and the workforce. Even though the schools hold great promise in their capacity to relieve some of the more stressful work/family conflicts, they have been barriers to change in many cases. If their past history can provide us clues about their future, U.S. school systems will continue to be sensitive to the needs of the nation's economic system. And it is clear that in the face of a shrinking labor force, the corporate world will need to retain as many competent workers as it can. It would, therefore, seem that as work/family conflicts become more pronounced, it is almost inevitable that schools will begin to assume a more active role in reducing the stress of these conflicts. In the long run this will be in the best interest of the children, who will be better able to meet the educational objectives that society has established for them.

Social Service Agencies. The operations of social service agencies offer a second look at the response of U.S. social institutions to work/family conflicts. Before the movement of mothers and wives into the workforce, social service agencies were rooted in the community and operated around the daily time schedules of families with adults at home during the workday. As women entered the workforce, they were less able to avail themselves of services that were accessible only during the nine-to-five schedule. Although some agencies began to offer some flexible schedules, many of them lagged behind commercial enterprises in their response to consumer need. Whereas many retail stores were quick to respond, many social service agencies displayed less sensitivity to the scheduling conflicts that existed among their working clients, and many continued to operate with traditional hours. There is a sad paradox in this situation because the explicit raison d'être of these agencies is to provide services to their clients.

One adaptation that was made by social service institutions to the newly evident work/family conflicts was the change in the location of some services to the workplace itself. This change in the delivery of services started with a response to the problems of alcoholism, which began to be seen as a problem both for business and for the worker and his or her family. The introduction of occupational alcoholism programs (later transformed into employee assistance programs) began in earnest in the late 1970s.[9] These programs made the case that there was a direct connection between the alcoholism of an employee (or in the worker's family) and corporate productivity or profits. Corporate leaders began to understand how alcoholism spilled over into the workplace, as evidenced by increased absenteeism, tardiness, and other measures of impaired performance. By establishing occupational alcoholism programs, corporations communicated their belief that the rehabilitation of the alcoholic worker would not only help to restore the health of this employee, but also be in the self-interest of the business because such programs were a more cost-effective response to the problem than suffering from lowered productivity.

Many business institutions found it difficult to even consider the development of any social services within the corporate structure because this seemed to contradict the myths about the separate worlds of work and personal/family problems. Many business leaders still clung to the notion that what was a personal or family problem was "not the business" of the corporation. Even imagining the corporation playing a distant role in helping individuals or families seemed to constitute an intolerable intrusiveness to some business leaders and labor groups.

Despite resistance to the concept of access to social services at the workplace, occupational alcoholism programs began to proliferate. The development of employee assistance programs was the precursor of many other services and benefits targeted to the personal and family needs of workers. Employees started to be able to address some of their social service needs (ranging from needed information of such diverse issues as retirement planning and acquired immunodeficiency syndrome to the provision of some direct benefits such as childcare services) through the workplace. Social services are no longer seen as irrelevant to the functioning of business. Rather, they have been brought into the mainstream of the workplace where most adults spend their days and where most adult socialization occurs.

The entry of social services into the world of work not only changed the workplace, but also affected a reshaping of many U.S. social service institutions. At the same time the linkages between social services and work began to strengthen, the role of the federal government in the provision (and funding) of services began to be reduced. The advent of this new federalism brought with it increased expectations about the role of the private sector in becoming involved in and supporting a greater share of social services and community programs. The concept of public and private partnerships inaugurated a new day for both social services and the workplace.

Voluntary Organizations. A third perspective on the institutional impacts of work/family conflicts can be detected within voluntary agencies. The United States is somewhat unique in the community of nations in that it has developed an extraordinary sense of volunteerism. The rise of the private not-for-profit sector occurred, in part, because of the strong currents of free enterprise that believed in the axiom of "the least governed, the best governed." Thus, our society has looked less to the government for a response to the social problems of individuals and families and more to the private sector. The spirit and tradition of philanthropy and a generous volunteerism have come from many sectors, including organized religions, and has benefited a range of social service, educational, recreational, and health needs. In fact, most hospitals and social service programs are quite dependent on volunteers. Medical institutions, for example, heavily utilize volunteers in a wide range of personnel capacities from board members to assistance with fund raising to direct service assistants like members of the women's guilds and even Candy Stripers who supplement staff as a strategy for minimizing expenses. This pattern of depending on volunteers can be observed in agencies from the large-scale efforts of the United Way to small community-based programs such as drop-in centers and hot lines. In the absense of a more comprehensive welfare state, which is common in most other industrialized countries, volunteerism is indispensable to the functioning of American health and welfare institutions.

A major threat to volunteers came as women began to enter the workforce in large numbers. Although the upper levels of volunteerism had been dominated by men on boards of directors, the vast majority of volunteers had been women, particularly housewives who were able to devote some time during the day to assist with the delivery of health, educational, and social services. The transfer of women from geographical communities, where they lived, to work communities put an increased squeeze on most agencies, which were simultaneously beset with government cutbacks resulting from the federal revenue–sharing policies of the 1970s. The next decade brought an even more stringent environment as the trickle of women going to work turned into a torrent. At the same time, President Reagan was swept into office, promising to get government off the backs of people, and he looked to volunteerism to "take up the slack" as the federal government backed away from a presence in the delivery of many services. All of this was not good news for those institutions that were dependent on volunteers. Although the possibilities of volunteerism continue to be highly touted, the realities have become increasingly problematic for many agencies. Organizations from boy scouts to town boards to groups that visits elderly shut-ins are all becoming endangered by the new structure of America's working family.

There is an irony in this crisis of volunteerism. Although most of today's working adults have less time and energy available to devote to volunteer activities, the stress that has developed in their families often results in their needing the services provided by these agencies even more. At a time when many agencies are being forced to reduce some of their services (or increase their fees), working families may be looking to community programs such as their local YMCA or the public library for expanded services.

As is evident from a cursory glance at some of the prominent U.S. institutions, their structure and functions have been affected by the changing nature of work and family systems. Social conflicts will continue to be manifested in institutions such as these as the dynamics of work/family conflicts continue to evolve in the public and private sectors. These institutions both reflect the conflicts and offer some of the mechanisms by which the conflicts will ultimately be reduced.

THE INADEQUACIES OF WORK/FAMILY SUPPORTS

Even under the best of circumstances, existing social policies and programs fall far short of providing the type of support to assure working families that their needs are recognized, that basic standards of living will be protected, and that basic social supports will be provided. Although some attention has been paid to the more visible needs of working families (e.g., child care and parental leave), large gaps remain in the fulfillment of basic needs for many working families.

At the end of the 1980s a great deal of national attention was focused on the problems of the working poor and moderate-income families, which must undertake extraordinary measures against slipping into poverty. Many of these families face critical work/family conflicts associated with the fact that their employment does not provide them with sufficient money for even the basic necessities of daily living. To date, much of the debate about work/family conflicts has centered on those families in the upper reaches of the socioeconomic ladder. It is the Yuppies and representatives of dual-career families who have seemed to be at the forefront of this issue. Interestingly, these are also the families who usually have the most resources at their disposal to address their conflicts. As a society, we also must confront the conflicts experienced by families with more limited incomes.

Tentatively, some public leaders are attempting to define society's role for those families that cannot independently provide for the basics (including shelter and medical care) and whose employers have not taken the initiative to respond to their needs. The functioning of individuals and families ultimately affects the social fabric of the society at large. Furthermore, it is often these same individuals and families that participate in the workforce that contributes to the nation's performance in the global arena of economic competition. The prosperity—and perhaps even the survival—of our society may depend on its ability to ensure that families receive adequate levels of food, shelter, clothing, and medical care.

Work/family issues are not just dilemmas of the middle and upper middle class, but must be seen within a broader social framework. Unlike the European countries, which have established strong social support systems of health and welfare benefits and programs, the United States has left such benefits largely to the discretion of individual corporations and to the bargaining power of labor. Consequently balancing work and home life is more a matter of corporate benevolences than a system of supports guaranteed by the public sector.

Not surprisingly, there are many casualties as a result of this philosophical orientation. Poor families with children and elders feel the impact most immediately.

FAMILIES IN POVERTY

One of the most obvious gaps in the nation's social policies is the virtual absence of programs that extend their services to the working poor. The United States has developed policies and programs for some of those who are identified as "truly poor," and although participation in these programs often stigmatizes the recipients, the services do provide a baseline of assistance with some needs such as food, shelter, and medical care. Working poor families, which are struggling to provide as much as they can, often are resentful of the fact that they are worse off in terms of both income and benefits because their income makes them ineligible for even limited assistance. The perils of poverty thus become an important dimension of work/family conflicts because many working poor families may have more in common with families that are formally recognized as living at the poverty level than they do with other members of the labor force.

The increase in poverty that has accompanied the economic resurgence of the past decade brings with it the ultimate irony and contradiction within the current social and economic policies that drive the country. According to Robert Greenstein, director of the Center on Budget and Priorities, "we're now in the sixth year of the longest recovery in several decades, yet the poverty rate is higher than in any year in the 1970s even in the deepest depression." Additionally, the seventies and eighties witnessed a widening gap between the rich and the poor.[10]

There are some glaring discrepancies between society's public values about cherishing and nurturing the potentials of children and the lack of policy assurances that even minimal physical needs will be met. Despite the fact that the United States must rely on its children to ensure its future, it is often the youngest who are most vulnerable to inadequacies in social policy. The growing number of poor children in America is spread even more widely than in previous generations across racial, social, and geographical lines; poverty is no longer confined to ghettos of the unemployable and the chronically ill.

Although research has for many years attested to the financial savings that can be realized if adequate health care is provided to pregnant mothers and to children, great numbers of children do not have access to such care. According to the Children's Defense Fund, 40 percent of children in working poor families have no health insurance.[11] Furthermore, more than one third of those people who do not have health insurance coverage are employed. Among full-time wage earners who are not covered, a third are heads of families.[12]

One of the most significant challenges of working single parents is keeping their families out of poverty. Half the children born in 1989 will live with one parent for a significant period of time before they reach age 18. Among these, three quarters of the children who spend part of their first ten years in a single-parent home will experience poverty.[13] One factor that influences the plunge of single-parent families into poverty is associated with the scandalously low levels of support provided by fathers to their children once they have left the family through separation or divorce. The large number of families living in poverty because of the failure of fathers to provide financial support is a testimony to a failed social policy. The inadequacy of most enforcement mechanisms permits mothers and their children to fall further into poverty. The remarriage of the father may further reduce the amount of child support that the father pays, particularly if the man's new family includes children either from his new wife's previous marriage or from their current marriage.[14] Although some policy initiatives are beginning to surface concerning the father's responsibility for child support, additional focus on these issues is critical.

Children who belong to a racial minority group also are at risk financially. Nearly one out of every two African American children and one out of three Hispanic children are poor in comparison to one out of every six white children. These statistics have led Isabell Sawhill of the Urban Institute to label childhood poverty the "unfinished business of the civil rights movement."[15]

It is necessary, however, to combat stereotypical images of poor children. The "new" poor reach far beyond the inner-city images. "Fewer than 10 percent of America's poor and fewer than 20 percent of poor blacks live in urban ghettos. Almost 40 percent of the nation's 12 million poor children live with two parents, many in homes where at least one parent works. Two-fifths of poor children are non-Hispanic whites. More than 40 percent do not receive welfare, up from 29 percent in 1979."[16]

Perhaps even more germane to the series of work/family conflicts is the transitory nature of poverty. Although there is a small population whose entire life is spent within poverty and who are supported by public assistance, the majority move in and out of the poverty status because of downturns in the economy, plant shutdowns, and health problems not covered by insurance. It is not uncommon to find families that are able to put a number of jobs together that enable them to achieve a semblance of economic security, only to have that thrown out of kilter because of changes in their work lives that were essentially out of their control.

Poverty among the children of working poor families affects the corporate world in both immediate and long-term ways. For today the challenge to our nation's businesses is to provide some of the leadership to address the dilemma of helping workers to access a "breadwinner's wage" that can take care of the very basic family needs of food, shelter, and medical care. Looking ahead, corporations must begin to understand that the children of today, who may not be receiving the minimum requirements to promote their physical, social, and cognitive growth, are the labor force of tomorrow. Their continuing existence within the culture of poverty will directly impact the nation's ability to remain competitive within the world market. The declining birthrate translates into fewer workers for the economy in the twenty-first century. Increasingly, corporations will have to turn to this population of poor children to fuel the economy and maintain productivity. There is a strong connection between the health of families and the health of our economy. A workforce that remains uneducated and medically vulnerable will not be an asset in this regard.

Poverty among families with children is clearly an issue with which society must grapple. A vital society depends on utilizing the maximum contributions of all its members. As the 1987 report by the corporate-backed Committee for Economic Development states, "this nation cannot continue to compete and prosper in the global arena when more than one-fifth of our children live in poverty and a third grow up in ignorance."[17] The tragedies that result from what we do not give to these children are at our doorsteps. Although the current social policy reflects the laissez-faire philosophy of the economic principles driving it, the nation as a whole will wind up paying for the inadequate education, the unemployment of large numbers of people, and the absence of policies and programs such as child care that can act as a catalyst in moving people out of the ranks of the working poor.

Finally, it is these children to whom most of us will have to turn for any financial support that we may need in our elder years.

THE INSECURE FUTURE OF FINANCIAL SUPPORT FOR TOMORROW'S ELDERS

Some of the changes that have occurred in the United States during the 1970s and 1980s have cast significant doom on the social policies that the nation has adopted to ensure that senior citizens can anticipate a certain level of financial security.

When the Social Security Act was passed in 1935 one objective was to provide a minimum floor of income for the retired elderly. About 95 percent of the labor force today is covered by Social Security (89 percent) or some other public retirement program (6 percent). . . . Dependence on Social Security alone, without coverage by an employer-provided pension, is increasingly likely to mean poverty or a very low income for retirees. Indeed, according to a report from the President's Commission on Pension Policy . . . "one of the results of the near universal coverage of social security and the lack of coverage of employer pensions is the creation of a two-class retirement income system." Employees themselves view entitlement to a pension as the second most important benefit they receive at work, after health and medical insurance.[18]

Two factors have affected the conflicts associated with the financial support that the nation offers to senior citizens. The demographics of an aging society translates into proportionately fewer working adults who contribute to the Social Security system that will need to make payments to the burgeoning number of citizens in the baby boom generation who will become elders starting in the year 2010. The budget context for the policies of the Social Security system creates some additional financial limitations. Many people are asking whether society can expect to finance and care for a growing elder population when it is unable to meet the fiscal realities of current social policies that depend heavily on family care.

The care of the young and the old used to be private family concerns, but the emergence of new work/family conflicts has thrust these issues into the public agenda.

ROLES AND RESPONSIBILITIES

Within the arena of work/family conflicts, perhaps the single greatest challenge for society is the determination of which spheres accept which roles in responding to the resultant stresses. Although there is general agreement that the vehicles of the past are inadequate to address the increasing complexities of the conflicts, there is a wide-ranging debate over what roles different levels of government and the corporate sector should assume. Public debate about the relations between the family and the government will increase as the work/family dilemmas become more apparent. Similarly, the legislative agenda during the next decade will increasingly identify work/family issues as social issues rather than relegate them to the privacy of individual families, which are left to respond to their problems independently. As these discussions proceed, several important questions will begin to surface. To what extent should society encourage government to move in and fill the vacuum left by the family that has moved into the workplace? Can legislation serve to reduce the social conflicts without upsetting the delicate cultural beliefs surrounding the relative independence of the family? To what extent will the United States move more toward the family policies of most of the industrialized countries to remain competitive? In sum, is it time to reshape both family and industrial policy so that the corporation can remain viable within the global economy and so that the family can thrive within the context of rapidly changing social and economic conditions?

Although a great deal of attention has been focused on such issues as maternal leave policies and child-care programs, the social conflicts run considerably deeper and constitute a much more complex reality than the piecemeal approach to legislation on work/family issues that continues to evolve. The failure of public leaders to approach these issues as an interconnected web that outlines the components of a national family policy is an indicator of the social turmoil associated with the development of a coherent policy. To date, partisan politics has dictated both the definitions and the interpretations of some of the more salient work/family conflicts. Further, most of the debates about the appropriateness and potential levels of intervention into these work/family conflicts are grounded in partisan philosophies. Most of the discussions about the potential roles for the government in addressing some of the more salient work/family conflicts begin to echo party platform jargon. The reality is that most of these issues supercede political ideologies.

Inherent in the discussion about responsibilities for the resolution of work/ family conflicts is the determination about who must assume the costs of needed services and programs. There are some glaring inequities in our society that need the immediate attention of public sector leaders. Some of the existing policies, such as child-care tax credits, offer some assistance to higher-income groups but do not provide any relief to the working poor. According to Census Bureau statistics, women in poverty who pay for their child care devote nearly a quarter of their income (22%) to child-care expenses in comparison to average working mothers who devote 6 percent of their monthly income to child care.[19] The U.S. government must address gaps in policies that further jeopardize the status of poor families.

The reluctance of the government to confront these conflicts may cause some of them to go full circle, returning to haunt the government as complicated public responsibilities. It is quite possible that many working families that have critical family needs, such as the care of an elderly parent, and that do not have sufficient resources (e.g., time, money, energy, stamina, and space) to adequately address these needs might decide to quit work to attend to family concerns and apply for some type of public assistance. Inadequate family policy, which does not address the range of family needs, such as child care to health care, may force people to give up the role of productive employee and become dependent on the government to meet basic survival needs. In one recent survey two out of three welfare recipients indicated that "trouble with finding and keeping child care" is the number one problem they face in joining the workforce. The lack of sufficient quality child care at an affordable cost contributes to the expenditure that the United States makes to Aid to Families with Dependent Children.[20] The lack of a national family policy is counterproductive to a sound fiscal policy because it becomes costlier to provide total financial assistance to a family rather than offer some assistance that enables the adults to supply as much support as they can. With regards to family policy, the U.S. government be "penny wise" but "pound foolish."

Despite the public debates about work/family conflicts, there is still a prevailing sentiment in the nation that the problems of families are primarily theirs and should, therefore, be solved through strategies largely developed by themselves. Given the projected labor shortage, combined with the perceptions about the fragility of the family system, the wisdom of this perspective is questionable. "Perhaps the most glaring in all the recent discussion of work-family conflicts is any mention of collective, rather than individual, solutions involving societal changes that draw on this country's long progressive tradition."[21]

Our society cannot afford to adopt an ostrich-like posture that ignores the changing environmental and demographic realities. It is no longer reasonable to assume that families will be able to resolve all the conflicts associated with these changes, either on their own or with some voluntary help from an enlightened employer. The continued lack of a national family policy is highly questionable in light of the urgent needs of children and the growing stresses of families.

The seemingly haphazard confluence of changing values, new demographic profiles, the shrinking labor pool, the movement of women into the workplace, and the growing globalization of the economy serve to refocus existing family policy. The glaring deficiencies of current policies in light of these developments become more acute as the conflicts become more apparent through public perception and the attention of the popular media. What was once a problem largely among the poor and working-class citizens has become a problem that affects the economic and social stability of the vast majority of American families.

As the perception of the family's inadequacy to cope with all its work and family roles and responsibilities grows, increased pressure mounts to resolve the conflicts. The more transparent, universal, and problematic these conflicts become, the more demands will be placed on the public arena to determine appropriate responses. Given the many political, religious, and cultural values that underlie the most basic of social institutions, forging any acceptable legislation will be difficult. Nevertheless, the social conflicts will not abate in the coming years, nor can society afford to ignore the conflicts that abound. One thing is certain: resolving the conflicts will constitute a critical public policy challenge requiring increased dialogue among America's families, the corporations, and the public leaders.

NOTES

1. Yankelovich, pp. 22–23.
2. Kamerman, "Child Care and Family Benefits," pp. 23–28.
3. Stautberg, p. 284.
4. Gordon, "Nation Confronted by Day Care Crisis," p. 91.
5. Sharon Johnson, p. A20.
6. Kamerman quoted by Gordon, "Nation Confronted," p. 91.
7. Brody et al., p. 208.
8. See Kamerman, "Child Care," pp. 23–28.
9. For an excellent discussion of this, see H. Trice and M. Schonburn, "A History of Job-Based Alcoholism Programs 1900–1955," *Journal of Drug Issues,* 11, no. 2 (1981):171–198.
10. Sege, "Growing Gap Shown Between Rich, Poor," p. 17.
11. Sege, "Poverty's Grip on Children Widens," p. 21.
12. Kamerman and Kingston, p. 164.
13. Sege, "Poverty's Grip," p. 20.
14. Cherlin and Furstenburg, p. 13.
15. Sege, "Poverty's Grip," p. 20.
16. Sege, "Poverty's Grip," p. 1.
17. Ibid.
18. Kamerman and Kingston, p. 154.
19. "Report Says Poor Spend Proportionately More for Child Care," p. 68.
20. Place and Wise, p. 42.
21. Gordon, "Work, Work, Work," p. 60.

Chapter 9

SOCIETAL RESPONSE

As debates swirl around child care, latchkey children, and other work/family concerns, one overarching observation appears evident: policy responses remain few and reflect the diversity and debate around the political and social attitudes to work/family issues. Those that do emerge from the process are muted, relatively impotent, and usually far from the mark. The increased debate of the seventies and eighties has resulted more in a stalemate than in resolution. No consensus has yet begun to develop in terms of policy direction or formulation. What has emerged is a patchwork of programs that have managed to find a piece of the response that can be accepted in the context of this standoff. Public policy responses are faced with a number of serious barriers that impede its ability to respond to the work/family issues described in this book. For example, the sharp separation of government and family dictated by the strongly held cultural and social beliefs around the sanctity of the family continue to perceive government as an intruder into family space. This is even more manifest within political realms, where responses to work/family issues become mired in political, religious, and ideological debate. Even the most basic child-care proposal becomes caught in these whirlwinds of dispute, largely resulting in inertia, status quo, and nonexistent policy and programs.

The primary purpose of this chapter is to explore existing and proposed social responses, in an effort to understand what the potential roles and responsibilities of the public sector either are or could be within the larger framework of work/family issues. Are we—or should we be—moving toward a society in which work/family issues are social issues for which government has a major responsibility? All this must be put in the context of existing cultural and political realities and the continuing social policy debate surrounding national family policy.

BACKGROUND OF SOCIAL RESPONSES

In examining work/family conflict it is important not to lose sight of the forces that have brought this issue onto the public agenda over the past few decades, as well as the role of government and society in trying to maintain a healthy social order (including that of the family). Although there appears to be minimal evidence that children who receive adequate child care are negatively impacted by working parents, we do know that many children do not in fact have child care. The breakup of families through divorce has brought with it a number of consequences, including a lowered standard of living and a movement into poverty by large numbers of citizens. Many children experience at least short-term trauma. Even those so-called intact families experience the absence of socially sponsored child care, leaving their desired family health at risk and in some degree of stress. The issue of child care, however, is but the tip of family policy; the question currently facing society is whether we can continue to ignore the costs of a society without an explicit family policy and can be satisfied with allowing the family to drift within the current public policy of minimal intervention. Are there ways in which the public sector can reshape existing public policy to better assist the family in coping with its new reality? And, most important, to what extent can the strong sociocultural themes of leaving the family alone be tempered by the detrimental impacts of families that are feeling increasingly unable to go it alone? Can we collectively afford a society that is fast becoming socially and economically dysfunctional and uncompetitive in a global environment in which virtually all other societies have found it necessary and desirable to support their families?

Although families have known for some time that dramatic changes have occurred in the lifestyles of most American households over the past several decades, it is only now that the issue has come so forcefully onto the public agenda. This "public" discussion, however, in no way implies that a social response to work/family issues is close, or that government is about to redefine its traditional hands-off policy toward the family. The heat of the debate reflecting conflicting societal values currently precludes any immediate adoption of formal and informal work/family policies.

The 1988 presidential campaign provides an interesting insight into the basic dynamics leading to the current policy stalemate. For the first time in campaign history all the major candidates commented on the need to address work/family issues. Some of them tied it to family values, whereas others related it to the need for greater competitiveness within the world economy. In either case, the perception of the need for family-responsive policy had moved the issue from the periphery to the center of the national agenda. Not unexpectedly, the candidates expressed wide differences on the appropriate role of the government in work/family issues, reflecting the competing ideologies surrounding public participation and policy in family issues.

"We must have a president who understands that no family should be forced to choose between the jobs they need and the children they love," stated Michael Dukakis in July 1988.

"Child care has become the sleeper issue of 1988," wrote William Safire of the *New York Times* in July 1988.

"If I had to make a list of 10 issues that are going to sway people's votes, this [child care] wouldn't be in the top five but it might be in the second five," commented Republican Campaign official Kevin Phillips in July 1988.

While these quotes danced around the positions and ideologies relative to social supports for the family, at the very least there seemed to be a common recognition that these issues need some exploration and attention.

As stated in earlier chapters, a primary reason for the apparent "inertia" of the government is that there are no historical precedents of government involvement in American society in supporting the functioning of typical middle-class families. Previous government involvement has been restricted either to the small percentage of families that experience some type of distress (e.g., poverty and disability) or to unusual historical circumstances that are limited in time, such as World War II and the Depression.

For most government officials there is a genuine conflict of values between what they think needs to be done and ought to be done in promoting a legitimate set of family supports with the prevailing values of keeping government off the backs and out of the living rooms of the family.

Many people have bemoaned the fact that among the advanced countries, the United States is the only nation that does not have a family policy to ensure that the children of working parents are well cared for. . . . The contradictory viewpoints that exist regarding government responsibility for child care are that (1) quality child care is expensive and it is government's responsibility to help parents pay the cost of this kind of care, and (2) the ultimate responsibility for child care falls on the parents and thus a federally funded structure for a child care facility is therefore unnecessary.[1]

This clash of values was probably best put by a ranking Republican conservative, Senator Orin Hatch of Utah, who, in introducing a child-care bill, commented that "it's better for parents to be at home but that isn't the reality. Maybe there is a role the federal government can play without being too intrusive."

In many ways the challenge to current public policy parallels that of the economic crisis facing the United States. Can the traditional laissez-faire economics carry us into the era of a world economy in which our major competitors have policies that put them at an unfair advantage over the United States? Take, for example, a case seemingly unrelated to work/family policies, the case of high resolution television. The United States currently trails badly in the high-stakes race for world wide supremacy in the technology of the future of high-resolution television. In large part because of the close working partnership between the government and the business community, the Japanese have been able to invest millions in research and development funds, with the understanding that the payoff of hundreds of billions of dollars will have a positive impact on the Japanese economy.

In the United States, despite having a superior technological base in research and development, the game has yet to be played, and the country is far behind in what may prove to be a costly error for this next state technology. Government and industry, always uneasy with each other, have not been able to work out an acceptable partnership, largely because of the traditional taboos against such joint partnerships. A recent study by the American Electronics Association concluded that with the proper mix of industry coordination and government incentives, including relaxation of tax breaks and antitrust laws, the United States could overtake the leaders and regain its prominence. The struggle continues, however, at the highest levels of government as to whether the government should get involved at all, and to what extent.

The issue is not dissimilar to that of social responses to work/family conflicts: To what extent should the government get involved, if at all? Responses to this question range up and down the continuum, but there seems to be a growing consensus that some reponse will be necessary if we hope to keep our nation's families intact and at the same time have a labor force that can compete with the labor force in countries where the work/family issue is addressed through corporate and social policies.

SOCIAL RESPONSES

Conceptualization of society can be subject to exhaustive theoretical and political debate. For the purpose of this chapter society refers to the institutionalized responses made by local, state, and federal governments. Because there is general agreement that no family policy currently exists in the United States, any discussion of social response must be qualified by what does exist and what is proposed. For example, Social Security, workman's compensation, and other federal legislation could be considered part of an overall family support system. So, too, could the tax codes that allow corporations to deduct certain benefits and services that benefit the family. Although these undoubtedly do impact positively those families that are part of the labor market, they do not address many of the programs and policies that working families need and that other industrialized countries have routinely included in their social response to work/family conflicts.

Four distinct areas of social response to working families can be examined: child care, parental/family leave, disability policies and benefits, and health care.

Child Care

Because the care of young children is the lightning rod for work/family issues, it is not surprising that much of the attempt to create national family policy has centered around this topic. A rationale for this focus can be viewed from several perspectives.

1. For the most part American society views itself, or likes to think of itself, as a child-responsive society, and values providing nurturing care to its children.
2. Children constitute the nation's most valuable resource. Its future depends on them developing into productive and caring adults. It is not accidental that the push for child care, and a changing environment more hospitable to the idea, is coming in the midst of a threat to the country's leadership in the world economy.
3. The entry of the baby boom generation into the mainstream of parenting and the workroles has resulted in its experience of work/family conflicts. The demand for child care can be traced to this cohort of the population coming on line in large numbers.

All these factors have led to an increased level of support for a national child-care program. A number of recent polls show strong support for government involvement in child care. A 1988 poll of 901 registered voters found that 86 percent saw child care as an important national issue. Of those favoring a federal child-care program, 57 percent were voters with no children under age 12.[2]

Sixty-three percent of those surveyed by the Children's Defense Fund and the American Federation of State, County, and Municipal Employees supported policies to make child care more affordable and available for working parents. Even among Republicans, who tend to favor less government spending and involvement, 45 percent supported such policies.[3] A recent Yankelovich survey of the American Association of Retired Persons found that children were seen as the most in need of government help.[4]

The founder of the interest group KidsPac was "knocked out" by the results of a poll they sponsored that indicated that 51 percent of voters strongly favored spending several billion dollars over the next five years to help working families afford child care and to increase the availability of child-care services.[5]

This ambivalence toward socially sponsored child care reflects the absence of a consensus in the United States that our government should assume responsibility for making it possible for parents to have some assistance and flexibility for staying home with their children during the first year to eighteen months, and that all children receive safe and high-quality child care outside the home when needed and desired. What currently exists is a patchwork approach to child care that offers one type of program for one population and a little assistance through another type of program. And even though there is no federal program for child care, federal expenses for 1986 totaled more than $6 billion[6]:

Expense	Billions of Dollars
Tax credits and deductions	4.0
Head Start	1.2
Food programs	0.8
Block grants	0.6

On a state level these programs are even more scattered throughout the budget. In Massachusetts, for example, $151 million was spent from budgeted items in the Department of Social Services, employment training programs, early childhood education, Head Start supplements, licensing, capital planning and renovation, resource and referral agencies, child care in public housing, worker training, affordability scholarship assistance programs, and corporate child care outreach.[7]

It is interesting to note that in the absence of policy, a system often begins acting on an informal or back door strategy when the demand and the need have not reached political consensus. Clearly on both federal and state levels child care is being addressed in this manner. Even on the local level there are numerous examples of the government responding to perceived needs. In Seattle voters approved a levy to spend $5 million to place mobile units for child care in fourteen elementary schools. San Francisco zoning laws require developers of all new office buildings in excess of 50,000 feet to provide on-site child care or contribute $1 per square foot to an Affordable Child Care Fund.[8] Similar legislation has been enacted in other cities.

Perhaps the most widely touted provision for child-care programs (at least by the Republican party) is the dependent care assistance program, better known as Section 129 (referring to the Internal Revenue Code). This program is the primary strategy of the federal government for child care (and potentially elder care). The law, passed as part of the 1981 Economic Recovery Act, provides that employees of participating employers can set aside up to $5,000 of pretax dollars to be used for dependent-care expenses. The benefit can represent a real decrease in the family's taxable earnings. (This legislation also offers some incentives to employers who offer on- or near-site day-care centers with the provision of new advantageous depreciation systems.) Unfortunately this program is not widely used as a result of the following regulatory requirements:

- If the worker earns less than $20,000, it is economically more beneficial for the family to take the tax credit for child care.

- The family must have a formal agreement with the caretaker to participate in this payment plan. Many families are using informal arrangements (typically with babysitters or relatives or in unlicenced homes) in which the caretaker does not report earnings to the Internal Revenue Service. For obvious reasons, these child-care providers do not want to have formal arrangements with the families.

- The amount being set aside must be determined at the beginning of the tax year. Any money that is set aside but not used is forfeited. This poses a major stumbling block to many families that do not have that amount of disposable income to front-end this program. It also is difficult for many families to accurately project their child-care expenses for the coming year (e.g., hours fluctuate, rates are subject to increase, child-care placements change, and parents' work hours change. This program penalizes those who estimate too much. On the other hand, parents don't want to underestimate or else they won't take full advantage of the benefit.

- Some companies have found it difficult to communicate the procedural complications of this program to employees. Hewett Associates, an acknowledged leader in benefits options, has estimated that only 4 percent of employees at any given time are making use of dependent care assistance programs when they exist.[9]

PROPOSED CHILD-CARE RESPONSES

Although what exists is scattered and relatively sparse, several options have recently been introduced that provide a glimpse into the social response of the future and that illustrate some of the issues that surround societal and governmental responses to work/family issues.

In 1971 President Nixon vetoed a bill introduced by Senator Walter Mondale (D.–Minn.) to establish a comprehensive national day-care system because the authority of the national government would become aligned with communal approaches to child rearing which he felt was un-American and anti-family.[10] Quite a bit of water has gone over the dam since that early initiative, and now public policy on the government's role in child care is back on the agenda. More than seventy day-care bills were introduced in Congress in 1988, reflecting both the pressing need to get this on the public agenda and the complex political, programmatic, and ideological disputes that surround any publicly sponsored child-care legislation. The rush for child care has begun in earnest. The real spark for this came from the ABC bill, the Act for Better Child Care Services, which was drafted by a 107-member coalition of child-care providers and advocates. Introduced by Senator Christopher Dodd (D.–Conn.) and Representative Dale Kildee (D.–Mich.), this bill proposed giving grants to states for expanded child-care services for families earning up to 115 percent of the median income. Two and a half billion dollars are allocated for the first year and after that such sums as are necessary.

Conservatives, understanding the political suicide of coming out against child care in an election year, acted quickly to introduce their own bill, Child Care Services Improvement Act, sponsored by Senator Orrin Hatch (R.–Utah) and Senator Johnston (D.–Louisiana). The provisions of this bill provided for $300 million a year to expand day-care programs, give tax breaks to firms providing child-care services for employees, and set up insurance pools to lower liability costs.

The two approaches couldn't be much further apart in terms of a social response to this growing problem. Political analyst William Schneider of the American

Enterprise Institute called child-care legislation "a practical program to serve a visible social need." Republicans see it ideologically, he added; "they see it as a subsidy for the disintegration of the family, and as a program that will produce social change."[11] In contrast, the Democratic-sponsored bill sees the change as already having happened. The lines are clearly drawn: tax credits versus subsidized services, a debate not uncharacteristic of Democrat–Republican skirmishes.

The defeat of this bill and all child-care (and parental leave) bills through early 1990 illustrates the political and ideological currents that run wide and deep. Many business interests had prevailed on the Senate to reflect their views that the bill would be too costly for business at a time when it is trying to be more competitive, and any mandated benefits were decidedly not in the spirit of America. These interests were joined by conservative profamily groups who fought both bills, but particularly the child-care legislation, since it represented federal interference with child-rearing. Even among the proponents, however, other issues arose again, reflecting the constraints of the democratic processes in promoting family policy. The American Civil Liberties Union, the National Organization for Women, and the National Education Association all had problems with ABC provisions that allowed church participation in delivering child-care services. A number of black women leaders, including Coretta Scott King and Marion Wright Edelman, challenged the ABC supporters to work harder because political leaders have buckled to the pressure of a few organizations, primarily the National Education Association.[12]

Politics within and without are critical factors in limiting child-care legislation (and other family issues) from becoming part of the social agenda and public policy. Any attempt to create a government initiative on child care will be met with predictable and forceful opposition by those who see such legislation as antithetical to the public good and to the role of the government. When Senator Hatch introduced a $375 million bill that would provide block grants to the states (setting up insurance risk pools and establishing revolving loans for day-care homes) to supplement—not replace—the ABC legislation, George Gilder, writing in the *National Review,* lashed out on "Hatch's surrender on day care, the single most shocking event in a recent bout of conservatism."[13] Gilder went on to defend his position by postulating that women prefer to leave their children with family friends, not at a day-care center. In addition, some critics thought that the bill would be unfair to men and women who chose to forego work to stay at home with their children. On a separate front, a study for the Cato Institute (a public policy think tank in Washington, D.C.) contended that the government's poor track record in providing public education is precisely the argument against any public programs for child care.

The ABC bill and the legislation by Hatch are far from the final word on child-care legislation. In fact, they are more likely the beginning. A brief examination of other bills introduced provides a flavor of the thinking and direction of child-care legislation for the 1990s:

- The Family Day Care Provider Act would allocate funds to provide for training and technical assistance and to establish a national resource center for day care.
- The New School Child-Care Demonstration Projects Act would allocate funds to support the provision of day care to children between the ages of 3 and 12 years by public school systems; establish a family support system for the parents of newborns; and provide support for family day-care providers and information and referral services.
- The Smart-Start program for day care for 4-year-olds would fund all-day prekindergarten programs.
- Tax credits would be given to employers who provided on-site day care.
- The Long-Term Home Care Bill would establish a benefit under the Medicare program for children and certain chronically ill elderly for home-care services.
- Kids, a $2.5 billion program, would help to create child-care programs for businesses, technical assistance for employers, and afterschool services for children. The bill also would authorize $100 million for an insurance pool for day-care providers.

All these point to the future as the debate over public involvement in child care continues. There will be little progress until the more fundamental disagreements are resolved over the public role and responsibility to the family.

PARENTAL/FAMILY LEAVE

Although child care is the focal point for much of the public policy debate over work/family issues, the parental and family leave debate touches on an issue that is even more central to the public response to working families: policies, benefits, and programs that mediate the relation between work and family and that support working adults in their family care roles and responsibilities, particularly during the early childhood years. The absence of clearly formulated and universally agreed on policy reflects the same set of political and cultural value conflicts that frustrate a national family policy. As with most family policy issues, the United States lags far behind the rest of the industrialized world in recognizing and providing for parental leave after the birth (or adoption) of a child.

Unlike 75 countries including all other advanced industrialized societies, the United States has no statutory provision that guarantees a woman the right to leave from employment for a specified period, protects her job while she is on leave, and provides a cash benefit equal to all or a significant portion of her wage while she is not working because of pregnancy and childbirth.[14]

Even Japan, against whom the United States is most pitted economically, and where the rights of women are practically non-existent, provides twelve weeks of leave with 60 percent pay to its working women. Not surprisingly, the absence of parental leave in the United States is tied to the same set of values and ideological beliefs that limit the adoption of family policy.

In fact, no coherent policy has emerged in either the private or the public arena to support working families in coping with the transitions after the birth of a child, which has to be one of the more difficult times for parents balancing job and home responsibilities. The adaptation of the family to this new event consumes time and energy and, in the case of dual-earner or single-parent families, is a potentially high-stress situation.

Many mothers are expected to return to work even before they are physically, no less emotionally, able to; this return may take place within a matter of days or weeks. Fathers are typically granted no more than a few days, if any time at all. The father's need to be at home during the first months after birth as the entire family adjusts to the new member is little recognized by the general public. The nation's response to the influx of working mothers has been for individuals and employers to create a hodgepodge of policies surrounding the circumstances of childbirth and the parent's return to work. These policies range from extremely supportive to extremely limited, depending on an employer's needs and concerns.[15]

Current federal legislation for leaves is restricted to disability leaves. At a minimum, those employers (usually the larger employers) who offer disability insurance must extend the coverage to pregnant women (typically starting one to two weeks before birth and ending eight to twelve weeks after birth, depending on birth complications). Employers who do not offer any disability benefits don't have to offer anything to pregnant workers.

Existing federal law prohibits discrimination in employment on the basis of pregnancy. The Pregnancy Discrimination Act of 1978 requires that pregnant employees be treated the same as employees with any temporary disability, and that women who are unable to work because of pregnancy can be granted leaves. Federal policy, however, does not mandate that employers set up new disability benefits or provide leave to parents to care for newborn infants. Thus the law is not so much a benefit as it is a safeguard or protection for pregnant women who cannot work because of their pregnancy and childbirth experience.

Kamerman's 1981 study of the impact of the Pregnancy Discrimination Act found much less extensive coverage than was assumed.[16] The study revealed that only about half the private sector workers in large companies (even less in small companies—thus nationally considerably less than half the employees) were covered by some form of disability or sickness benefits providing income replacement for about six to eight weeks at the time of childbirth. Even in those few states that have greater coverage or in the most progressive firms there was no instance of paid maternity leave that went beyond twelve weeks. In Europe no country provides less than twelve weeks. Even unpaid leave after birth is relatively unusual, although no current data provide reliable detailed statistical information.

The policies adopted by Sweden are noteworthy. Paid parental leave is available for twelve months, and is covered by government social insurance paid at 90 percent of gross earnings. The leave is quite flexible and can be shared by husbands or wives as they see fit. It extends up until the child is 8. This has served to encourage men as well as women to use this benefit, and the latest statistics indicate that about 25 percent of men are now doing so.[17]

Proposed Initiatives

Because family leave is a fundamental building block of family policy for working adults, there has been increased interest in trying to get the policies of the United States more in line with those of other industrialized countries. One federal response to families' need to respond to temporary medically related situations was the introduction of the 1987 Parental and Temporary Medical Leave Act. The House form of this bill proposed to provide employees with up to twenty-six weeks in response to a serious health condition (i.e., the worker's health, including pregnancy) and to have up to eighteen weeks to care for the health needs of a family member. One form of the proposed legislation stipulates that these leaves would be unpaid, but the employees' benefits (e.g., health insurance) would be continued. This bill was written so that leaves would be available for a wide range of family needs, including the care of a newborn, care of children after adoption, care of dependent elders, care of special needs family members, and care of family members during acute health crises.[18]

In 1987 twenty-eight states introduced some form of parental leave legislation. Five states have established a mandatory revolving fund to pay for maternity leaves under worker disability statutes. But no state has made such a fund available to fathers or to employees who need to care for ageing parents.

A two-year study by the Bush Center for Child Development and Social Policy at Yale University crafted a carefully designed infant leave proposal that merits consideration. The advisory committee recommended that the United States provide all employees with the option of a six-month leave. The leave would be paid at 75 percent of salary up to three months, with an option for an additional three months of unpaid leave.

Because a leave provides the time for parents to respond to the infant, grow in their identities as parents, and establish routines and patterns of interaction, they are also strengthened in their ability to attend to work tasks when they do return. Early research shows that when parents are given support for substantial leave time (three months or longer) they are willing to make a greater commitment to the employer in return, are less likely to need to take sick days out of concern and anxiety over the new infant and are often energized and strengthened by the sense that they have taken care of family matters to their satisfaction (Catalyst 1981; Kammerman 1980; Kammerman and Kahn 1981).[19]

Although movement toward a parental or family leave policy seems inevitable, given the changing demographics, it also should be noted that little discussion has been held to date about dependents other than children. Because infant care is so emotionally charged and so immediate to the cadre of working mothers entering the workforce, it tends to overshadow other, equally compelling needs in the area of dependent care that also constitute family need. Any public response to working parents will soon have to be aware of how to shape leave to accommodate employees with elderly parents, whose care can be as perplexing as that of children. A crippling disease or a chronic situation that involves a parent who lives alone can mean trying times for working families. Some modification of parental leave would enable employees to respond to these short-term episodes.

The plight of disabled or chronically ill dependents also falls under this heading. Workers with such dependents can make an equally poignant plea for the need for leave provisions. How national social policy responds to these situations and how public and private sectors can accommodate the need of dependent care poses a formidable challenge over the next decade.

DISABILITY

Disability represents one of the most traumatic and disruptive events for working families. Through accidents or sickness the family can experience severe hardships that are exacerbated when medical costs and loss of income are uncovered. This is particularly true for the hourly employee, whose benefits and income usually are not able to absorb absences, even on a short-term basis. Because of the lack of a national policy or a health insurance that would cover such events, most employees are left to fend for themselves, and their families feel the impact economically and socially.

Whereas most other countries in the industrialized world have provisions within their national health insurance that cover short-term disability, there are no such provisions in the United States. The Social Security Act includes a federal disability insurance, but that is intended to meet long-term disability and does not apply until a person has been disabled for six months. Because most disability is short term, the absence of social legislation in the United States to cover the first six months is left to the individual family or the corporation. Six months can cause unreasonable hardships for most families who are a paycheck or two away from financial crisis.

A number of states have begun to step into this vacuum. Five states (California, Hawaii, New Jersey, New York and Rhode Island) as well as Puerto Rico and the railroad industry, have temporary disability insurance laws requiring employers to cover their workers under a plan that pays a benefit replacing part of the worker's wage, usually for a period not to exceed 26 weeks (39 in California). The 1985 benefit maximum in the five states ranged between $145 and $224 weekly, usually replacing about half the wage.[20]

For many families a safety net for short-term disability lies with the coverage of the company. For large companies an estimated 60 percent of employees are covered.[21] For the vast majority who work in small firms, however, the likelihood of coverage is minimal. Furthermore, most disability plans last for a minimal amount of time, usually a few weeks' pay. The absence of mandatory coverage does not bring much assurance to families who face such disability.

In examining disability provisions from the perspective of social response, the characteristics of a comprehensive and effective policy would resemble provisions of a national health insurance. The reluctance to provide disability insurance on a short-term basis to U.S. employees has its roots in the same two principal objections often raised to national health insurance proposals: the less government, the better, and the family should be there to provide for its care within a free-market capitalism.

HEALTH CARE

Although most employees are covered by some type of health insurance, the absence of a national health insurance policy leaves many families, both working and nonworking, uncovered or grossly undercovered. As discussed in Chapter 8, one of the most basic work/family conflicts occurs when a worker's wages plus benefits do not cover the cost of even the most basic family needs, such as shelter and medical care. Health insurance (including short-and long-term disability as well as sickness and medical coverage) is primarily a corporate responsibility, and part of the web of occupational benefits that accrue to those in the workplace. Unlike other industrialized countries, the United States has but a minimal and selective health coverage, usually for those who are destitute or aged. Meanwhile approximately 23 million workers of the population have no protection at all, and another sizable segment exists with only the barest coverage.[22] "The number of uninsured Americans currently estimated at 37 million is increasing at a rate of about 900,000 annually and [Senator] Kennedy said most of the 5.2 million jobs projected between now and 1992 will not offer health care benefits."[23]

Families that are devastated by inadequate or no health coverage represent one of the major drawbacks of a system that relies primarily on corporate responsibility and absents the public arena from playing a major role. For many people who are marginally above or below the poverty line, employment without health benefits is commonplace. It is this large and growing population that is falling through the safety net put in place by the private sector and whose families often are transitioning in and out of the labor market because of health problems. Ironically, the very families that are most in need of health coverage and least able to cope financially with medical expenses are those for whom coverage is least likely.

Any policy or set of policies aimed at responding to family needs would have health insurance as a cornerstone. With the projected labor shortage and the push to become competitive with the world economy, it also is in the interest of society as a whole to keep as many people as possible in the labor pool and at the worksite as healthy and productive employees. Thus the absence of a health insurance for a significant number of current and potential employees poses a distinct threat to the social goals and the economic imperatives for the next decade.

Much of the debate over health insurance, not unlike other social benefits, can be reduced to two basic questions: Whose responsibility is it to provide coverage? And who should pay for such health insurance? At the current time the occupational welfare system has been picking up a sizable portion for working adults and their families, and has been desperately trying to curtail health benefit costs, which have been spiraling upward far in excess of the rate of inflation. In fact, the most recent labor struggles are focused on corporate "take-backs" in terms of insurance coverage and the attempt to increase the employee's share or copayment. For many corporations these health care costs have moved from an insignificant benefit during the sixties to a major expenditure. General Motors, for example, spends more on health care than it does on steel. Other companies get hit because of downsizing to the point where the number of retirees and their dependents outnumber current employees and their families. Many employers are instituting control measures such as second opinions, managed health care, and a movement toward alternative health plans, such as health maintenance organizations and preferred provider plans, to rein in these costs. Other businesses are cutting back the benefits in subtle and not so subtle ways by increasing the copayments and the deductibles and eliminating some areas that were previously covered.

Although the corporate response is one of containment and strategic cutback, it is becoming clear that the scandal of having significant segments of the population without health insurance is not only an issue of justice and social obligation for a country at the upper end of the distribution of wealth, but also a serious barrier for promoting family life. To this end there have been some proposed health initiatives within the federal government, all of which begin moving the system toward a national health plan of some type.

Perhaps the most far-reaching of the current proposals is that introduced by Senator Edward Kennedy (D.–Mass.) and Representative Henry Waxman (D.–Calif.) to cover the basic health-care costs of all Americans by the year 2000. This proposal would expand private health insurance to 23 million workers who currently lack coverage. The unemployed would be covered under a federal–state plan. Although this is a far-reaching plan, its specifics would allow a gradual phase in and modest copayments and deductibles. The mandatory plan would create minimum benefits designed to cover basic medical and hospital costs with cost-sharing by beneficiaries. Policyholders would pay no more than 20 percent of the premium along with annual deductibles limited to $250 for individuals and $500 for families, along with copayments of 20 percent for each covered service. No employee or family would pay more than $3,000 in any calendar year.[24] There also are a number of provisions for small businesses, many of which are unable to absorb mandated plans such as this.

Although health insurance does not, at first blush, appear to be an essential component of social response to work/family conflicts, it is clear that the absence of such basic coverage can not only aggravate existing family conflicts, but also threaten the ability of the family to maintain its employment status, and thus it assaults the economic viability of the family. Because there has been so strong a corporate role in this area, crafting an adequate response to reduce work/family conflict will require careful maneuvering between private and public interests. Similar to other family policies, the role of the government will, in all likelihood, become more prominent, thus enabling the workforce to become more productive and competitive, while providing families some basic supports in managing their multiple roles and responsibilities.

PUBLIC RESPONSES TO PRIVATE ISSUES

Societal response to work/family issues is itself a novel and controversial proposition. What was unthinkable a few decades ago in terms of government's role in addressing family issues has only recently been elevated to the public agenda. This has happened primarily as a response to a broader set of events within society that has focused on the harried and stressed working parent, along with the broader issues of dependent care and the need for a more competitive workforce as we approach the year 2000. Social responses to the conflicts between work and family discussed in earlier chapters have experienced a political paralysis, and thus continue to avoid the difficult decisions that are needed to readjust social behavior to existing policy. The deeply held values in both the private and the public sectors, along with the absence of clear strategies and solutions to work/family conflicts, continue the stalemate. Any movement toward a new policy is met with a barrage of opposition from those who consider state intrusion into this area inappropriate. Some take this position on ideological grounds relative to a laissez-faire economics that argues for a hands-off role for government, whereas others take this position on the grounds that such issues are left to the discretion of individuals and/or their employers. All these objections reflect longstanding debates around the role of government in assisting families to cope with their environments. The legislation of the New Deal, particularly social security, marked a decided break with a longstanding American tradition, and came about only because of the extraordinary circumstances of the Depression. The case can certainly be made today that a new set of social responses and policies is warranted in light of the dramatic movement of mothers into the labor force, the inability of the family to provide basic care to dependents, and the increasing lack of fit between current policies, structures, and institutions and the ability of families to meet basic social needs.

By all accounts the debate over family policy will be intensive and energetic during the 1990s. Although there has always been a strong, albeit small, group of advocates for instituting a national family policy, the social and demographic changes of the past several decades have brought forth a new set of voices, which argue for such policies as child care, parental leave, and health care on the national and state level. Their concerns are linked with those whose focus has been on the state of the family, but who now are linking the family to the workplace. The movement of the primary caregiver into the workplace has served to upend the comfortable accommodations and arrangements that allowed for both family functioning and a familial caregiving, along with undisturbed work environments. This rather abrupt change has brought concern, some of which is coalescing into organized advocacy. For example, the Older Women's League of Massachusetts whose members consider themselves part of a sandwich generation that bears responsibility for both school-aged children and aging parents, began endorsing legislation for paid family leave and other profamily bills. An examination of those who are supporting this type of legislation reveals the increased active participation of such groups as parent-teacher associations, the league of Women Voters and the Federation of Business and Professional Women, all of whom are testifying to the strain on today's working families and the need for an expanded public policy.

The range of public policy issues touched on by work/family concerns continues to expand as this issue unfolds. What began as a concern over children and the need to find high-quality, affordable child care is quickly moving to embrace an agenda that wraps itself around the quality of life and the very role of government in our times. Public policy concerns reach out to address serious gender inequalities, neglect of children, the fragility of families, and the scandal of abandoning citizens who are unable to take care of themselves. What, on one hand, appear to be broad philosophical issues, such as those related to quality of life and the role of society in supporting family life, become concretized as the challenge of working and living becomes more and more difficult for the average American.

The major benefit of the growing debate around work and family is the opening up of the public–private relationship for reexamination. Minimal social responses to families will be an increasingly difficult position for any society to embrace. What has remained deeply entrenched in the American tradition and fabric is gradually being freed from its ideological mire, so that the most basic societal functions can be considered.

- What kind of society do we want, and what can we do to protect and promote family life?
- How can caregiving be valued and equitably shared between society, workplaces, and families?
- How can the burden of providing care be lifted from families—and especially from women—so that all can share equally in the most basic act of humankind?
- How can we make our institutions and social structures more responsive to work/family issues, so that both families and workplaces can realize their goals?

Reconciling work and family poses more problems than solutions. If such a reconciliation is to come about, however, then the role of the public sector is essential. No society can expect individual families or the private sector to respond without primary public sector participation. In addition, it is the very role of society to address these issues and provide the leadership and resources necessary to overcome what are admittedly difficult conflicts.

As the United States faces a thorough reexamination of its public policy in responding to work/family issues, it will clearly require both a new direction and leadership to achieve a more responsive society. The new direction will reshape the current dysfunctional configurations through heightening awareness of the need to change, along with specific shifts in policies and the development of family-sensitive programs. Through creative partnerships with the private sector, public policy makers can establish a new standard for family protection, family supports, family leave, and whatever other policies and programs will enable the family to thrive and grow.

There also can be a tendency to overrely on the government, a sort of rush to legislate, which can have equally deleterious consequences. Expanding social response to work/family issues is not the nostrum by which work/family conflicts will be resolved. The role of government in the social economic system of the United States was not created and is not intended to provide the final answers, but to work with its citizens and institutions in finding solutions for the commonwealth of the larger society. In this light the response of society to work/family conflicts is not to completely own or resolve such issues, but to serve as a catalyst and active agent in relieving the stresses of working parents and overwhelmed families and corporations.

The public sector also can serve to build a dependency infrastructure of institutions to address the difficult areas of elder care, child care, latchkey children, AIDS victims, and the like. In this respect it carries out the true purpose of government to support family life not by intrusion, but by support on both the policy and institutional levels.

In the final analysis no set of carefully crafted policies or programs can advance too far without forceful and articulate leadership on the national, state, and local levels. Clearly, work/family conflict is an issue for which there are few quick fixes. Despite the attempts to focus on child-care centers, the issues, as we have explored them in this book, run much deeper. The fact that these conflicts do not lend themselves to facile solutions speaks to the complexity of the social, economic, and political forces that surround work/family issues. Perhaps the most valuable contribution of the public sector is to provide leadership as a symbol to the family, the private and the public sectors. A great deal of discussion, deliberation, fact-finding, and trade-offs needs to take place if there is to be meaningful reduction of work/family stress and reconciliation between the demands of work and those of the home.

Furthermore, a deeper set of changes will lead society toward a higher level of living and working, one that impacts the very quality of life. Through such transformation, children begin to be seen not as problems squeezed between workplace and home demands, but as a national and social resource. Likewise, parenthood will be seen as a social function whose products and processes are as much of a concern to public policies as are the state of our environment or infrastructure. Real and symbolic leadership is essential on all levels of government to bring together and create imaginative solutions to these difficult conflicts.

NOTES

1. Sekaran, p. 200–201.
2. Wyman, p. 26.
3. Sege, "Child Care Debate Shifts from Personal to Political," p. 20.
4. Hanafin, p. 1.
5. Sege, "Child-Care Debate," p. 1.
6. Hanafin, p. 8.
7. Ibid.
8. Hernandez, p. 20.
9. Place and Wise, p. 51.
10. Sege, "Poverty's Grip on Children Widens," p. 1.
11. Sege, "Child-Care Debate," p. 20.
12. Levine, p. 82.
13. Gilder quoted in Sege, "Child-Care Debate," p. 20.
14. See Kammerman et al.
15. Zigler and Frank, pp. xvi-xvii.
16. See Kammerman et al.
17. Rapoport and Moss, p. 4.
18. Place and Wise, pp. 7,16.
19. Zigler and Frank, p. xvi.
20. Kammerman and Kahn, p. 53.
21. Ibid.
22. Knox, p. 11.
23. Ibid.
24. Ibid.

Chapter 10

MEETING THE CHALLENGE OF WORK/FAMILY ISSUES IN THE TWENTY-FIRST CENTURY

Work and family problems, although not new, have come to a dramatic crossroads in the United States as the twenty-first century draws near. Perhaps like Gorbachev in the East, struggling with an archaic economy and a bureaucratic maze that are threatening the superpower status of his country, the American system finds itself straining under the weight of an ideology and social structure that are unable to cope with or meet the needs of its populace. Ideology—whether capitalist or communist—can work at cross purposes with the economic and social development of a society. There have always been work/family conflicts for large segments of the population. The work/family conflicts of today, however, are not simply another adjustment to changing technology or shifting social values. In fact, the work/family issues of today bump up against profound cultural and social changes, changes that have not been well reconciled or integrated into the delicate balance of working and living. The repeated difficulty of acknowledging these conflicts, and, more important, finding a political response to them, only speaks to the deep roots and core values that are being touched and in a real sense threatened.

What differentiates this work/family crisis from past episodes is the extent to which the issue has impacted the population. What previously was felt most immediately by the lower working class now reaches into all households, irrespective of class and income. Finding adequate and satisfying solutions to child care, elder care, and womens' career tracks is no longer a side bar issue, but a front-page phenomenon. Conversations about work/family conflicts abound in the home and office. Added to the universality of the issue are the other social changes, including the increased number of single parents and divorced couples, the mobility of the population as a whole, women's participation in such large numbers in the labor force, elders living longer, the shrinking size of households, and the postponment of child-rearing—all speak to the revolution in mores and living arrangements. Much of this can be tied into the economic changes of the past few decades. The plain economic reality of the necessity of all adults in a household to work has forever changed the fabric of life as we know it in the United States.

And although the demographics and social characteristics of society and its families have undergone this radical transformation, the institution of the workplace has reluctantly begun to shake off the sleepy complacency of past decades to realize that its cultural and organizational environments are considerably different then those of even a decade ago. Its employees' bring a new set of values and energy into the workplace that needs to be understood, integrated, and managed if the workplace is to remain relevant and competitive in a global environment.

Throughout this book significant indications of unrest, conflict, and social dissonance around what has loosely been termed work/family issues signal the beginning of a society that is coming to grips with major social and cultural change. When Freud cited work and love as the foundations of human behavior, he might well have substituted work and family. These are the two major institutions on which any society is based. It is not surprising that institutional responses to the changes of such magnitude that have occurred in our society do not happen overnight, but rather evolve through incremental stages to give sufficient time to break down the cultural and organizational resistances to change and to provide adequate lead time for people to adapt. Institutional change is never quick or easy; change of this order in two institutions as complex and central as work and family takes place only with the patience of time and the process of adaptation.

In the final analysis the period within which we currently find ourselves can best be characterized as confusing, harried, and, above all, rushed. The rapidity of changes, the absence of role models that tie the past to the present, and the general lack of discretionary time create an environment and a generation of tired and frayed members. In the interviewing for the *Balancing Work and Homelife Study* the one characteristic that was repeated throughout the interviews was the prevailing sense of tiredness, a generation of fatigued, exhausted people who accepted their dependent-care responsibilities gladly, but who had either run out of strategies for successfully integrating work and living or given up out of desperation.

What, then, are the sources of the conflicts that are behind the inability of most Americans to find a satisfying balance between their work and family lives? Sons and daughters have experienced severe value conflicts far beyond the usual generational tensions that mark the coming of age. Husbands and wives wind up in daily skirmishes around roles and division of labor, symbolic of the larger social forces that are rumbling on all sides. Families themselves feel less and less secure, protected, and coherent, and the frenetic pace and demands of work, coupled with decreased leisure time, radically alter most family structures and interactions. Social institutions such as schools and retail operations struggle to adapt to a society whose adults are primarily at work, leaving the traditional hours of daytime operation somewhat irrelevant to working families. Corporations are at a loss as to how to filter these changes through their traditional dominance of the family and maintain their ability to keep it separate from the corporate sphere. The very hegemony of the corporation is threatened by the new work/family agenda. And government, through its public policy bodies, whose purpose is to define and serve the common good, is faced with a new order that in many cases turns traditional values and institutions on their head and forces a thorough reexamination of the role of government and its relation to families and to the corporation.

It would be difficult to find a more fundamental set of cultural shifts than those surrounding work and family issues. As a society, we have come to the point of acute denial, a situation many alcoholic and other dysfunctional families find themselves in. On the outside, everything seems to be functioning well. On the inside, however, a radically different story unfolds. In place of a smoothly functioning system, conflicts are breaking out all over, creating a high level of stress and anxiety, all of which is covered over by masking the problem, denying its existence to maintain a semblace of stability. The price of such denial inevitably gets too high. Although individuals, families, and society have an incredible ability to deny the realities of the present to preserve some dogma or image of the past, the level of stress eventually becomes too great a price, and the system begins to unravel. It is at this crossroads that we find ourselves as we contemplate what to do about the work/family equation. What is in place is clearly inadequate to support families, but visions of a more satisfying set of social arrangements have not been forcefully conceptualized or advocated by social, political, or economic leaders.

At the heart of this crisis (at least so proclaimed by the media) is the fundamental threat to family life. Parents, whether single or married, have moved from a rather prescribed and predictable society to one in which the basic cocoon of the family is threated by high divorce rates and widespread economic and social stress unknown a generation or two before. Even in the midst of the economic disaster of the Great Depression there was a sense that this was an economic cycle, and despite its severe pain, it, too, would pass. Not so for this generation. The economic and social crunch that has turned one-earner households into dual-earner households is most likely the beginning of a long and protracted period in which declining standards of living will be experienced for some time, and higher productivity (usually in the form of increased work by family units) is the most immediate antidote.

Directly or indirectly, almost all Americans confront repercussions of work/ family conflicts. This is not simply an issue of changing womens' roles, or a case of too few resources devoted to caring for children and elderly parents.

Whether dual-income, single-parent, or single-nonparent, the work/family issue hits home on both the individual and the personal level as well as the more complex social level.

Although all this should be seen within a broad framework, such is not always the case. In fact, a major piece of the problem is that it is often seen as a woman's problem, or the wife's problem, or the family's problem. Much like the proverbial hot potato, responsibility for ownership gets tossed at the most vulnerable or the most convenient. For years the family bore this burden. Because of the ideology that had built up around the industrial workplace, the family was seen as subordinate to the needs and goals of the corporation. The most widely held perception was that work/family conflicts belonged to and stayed within the home. For the most part issues such as child care and role overload stresses were seen as family matters that properly belonged within the domain of the home. Government and corporate roles dictated that they were to keep out of the "business" of the family and let the natural forces work so that the family would ultimately find workable strategies and solutions to these conflicts. The direct or indirect message from the corporation was "we will tolerate mothers who make the choice to work but don't tell us about your child-care problems, aging parents, and impossible scheduling conflicts. And above all, don't let arrangements for your children interfere with your work." The myth about separate spheres of work and family was alive and well. In effect women entering the labor force were to conform to the same mandates as their husbands did, except that they had no wife at home to fulfill all the dependent-care responsibilities.

Corporations worked diligently to maintain this arrangement, through services, benefits, and, later, subtler means, as exemplified in Whyte's *Organizational Man*. Later, as women became more prominent in the workplace, they bore even more of the burnt of work/family issues. Becoming freed from such a strongly inculcated cultural value as "a woman's place is in the home" was no small matter. Even now, despite the widespread presence of women in the workplace, there is broad support for this cultural theme among both men and, surprisingly, although to a lesser extent, women. Despite the economic necessity for women to work, the cultural messages present obstacles that only ferment the conflict even further.

Although much of the attention in the nineties has begun to focus on corporations and corporate responses to work/family issues, the role of government is coming under increased scrutiny. At the most basic level, there is no national family policy. Standing alone among the developed countries of the world, the United States has adopted a curious brand of capitalism that leaves no room, ideologically speaking, for a family policy. The overwhelming ideology of laissez-faire capitalism and the preeminent rights of the individual overshadow a common good to the extent that adopting a family policy cuts against the grain and represents a form of ideological heresy. This has led to an almost total silence and abnegation by society for any social supports that would alleviate the stress now carried by the family. Without a family policy and a government that sees as part of its responsibility developing strategies, policies, and programs to support working families, it is unlikely that families will find any significant relief.

Although there is no apparent conspiracy or even concerted strategy to scapegoat women or families to independently accept the work/family issues, the end result is that there is no broad ownership to this issue by our society. Consequently the movement toward resolving or lessening work/family conflict has been slow in developing. Unless society at large begins to feel some ownership for an issue, it is unlikely that it will be highly motivated to find a solution. The perceptions of the problem, however have recently begun to shift. The demographic trends that indicate a labor shortage toward the turn of the century is but a few years away. The mechanisms and responses from both the private and the public sectors are inadequate and insufficent to significantly reduce the conflicts. Families are being stretched to a point of crisis, with the vulnerable (children, elderly, single parents, and the economically disadvantaged) assuming a large share of the burden. Most corporations have been more or less immobilized because the "traditional" values policies and practices are not synchronized with the needs of their current labor pool. Although the government is beginning to proceed with some public discussions about work/family conflicts, pressing budget limitations and conflicting ideologies have many legislators trying to find quick and simplistic solutions.

ACCEPTING AND MOVING INTO A NEW ERA

It is not accidental that work/family issues are increasingly bubbling to the surface toward the end of the century. The forces that have driven this issue from the beginning (demographics, changing values, and economics) are intensifying, and the options of denying the problem and doing nothing are rapidly decreasing. Not only are the times changing, but the institutional and social structures and behaviors are beginning to feel the dissonance between the old and the new. The family as we have known it for much of the twentieth century is not there. As much as we try to hold on to outmoded and antiquated remnants of a past era, the demands and realities of the present will force the changes and require new responses. The nation is quickly learning that it cannot continue to live under past myths. America the producer, the leader of the free world, the economic miracle of the twentieth century, is quickly realizing that its supremacy and dominance on the world stage are being challenged from several quarters. To maintain its edge and compete effectively, society will have to adapt, to move out of the complacency that previous circumstances have luxuriously allowed it, and to move into a new era in which competition, particularly on the economic stage, will be considerably more difficult.

It is within this context that the changing American family, in unison with the changing American corporation, will have to confront the multiple conflicts of work and family discussed throughout this book. No longer is there an option of whether these conflicts can continue to exist without resolution. The price for inaction is becoming too high. A dauntingly close parallel is that of Daniel Moynihan's call for national action on the black family in America. Although his predictions have proved to be all too prophetic, the failure to act resulted in incalculable costs. It does not take too much foresight to make a similar case for the American working family. Without a dramatic reversal of the current policies of inaction and nonintervention, the ability of the American family to cope and ensure healthy and productive members is minimal.

FUTURE DIRECTIONS AND RECOMMENDATIONS

An awareness of the conflicts related to work and family issues is far more evident than prescribed solutions. Frustrations with the problems have not yet been translated into resolutions. In fact, the road toward resolving and reducing work/family conflicts is long and tortuous, a minefield of political and cultural obstacles. Nevertheless, it is becoming clearer by the day that the need to move toward solution is pressing. The costs of inaction are mounting, and the necessity for an agenda to act is growing. Although such a mandate for change has not reached the policymaking bodies, it is festering in homes and offices throughout the nation. The clouds of change are on the horizon, and the signs of dysfunctional and overstressed families and workplaces are all too apparent. Postponing any longer the identification and implementation of solutions can only perpetuate existing dysfunctional and highly stressful individuals, families, and organizations. The conflicts of today will constitute the crises of tomorrow. Ignoring or not responding to the problems connected with work and family issues carries with it equal, if not more serious, consequences.

Many of the resolutions to these conflicts have seeds in already existing programs and initiatives. Much of what has been discussed in this book constitutes the early development and germination of viable solutions. Most of these initiatives are grounded in the political, social, economic, and cultural realities of America toward the end of the twentieth century. Neverthless, there has not been a strong leadership to carry this issue in either the public or the private sector. Not surprisingly, the electorate is far ahead of elected or appointed leaders on these issues. Most certainly the forces building around the work and family agenda will translate over the coming decade into legislative initiatives, policy changes, and program initiatives in both the public and the private domain.

Effective resolutions to these issues will not be found in a prepackaged program or even a series of legislative packages. The threads the intertwine work and family are intricate and require action along a broad front. To this end a number of recommendations can be made that can begin to spark some concerted action. Before delving into the recommendations, however, it might be well to lay down a number of fundamental principles or building blocks on which these recommendations can flow.

Fundamental Principles

New and creative approaches are needed that cut across traditional lines.
Traditional methods of resolving these issues are doomed to failure primarily
because of the limited ownership of them. As long as these problems are seen
as women's problems, or even the family's problems, the solutions will be geared
toward helping them cope better. This misses the point. Work and family issues
are a social problem whose roots are deeply embedded in our culture, our
economic system, and the arrangements between private and public
responsibilities.

If effective resolutions of these problems are going to emerge, they will do
so from a considerably broadened ownership and constituency. Corporations and
unions will see such resolutions as essential to their mission and well-being.
Their response is every bit as important as the family that bears its appropriate
share. Government will have to move away from its non-interventionist position
to assume responsibility in supporting American families. Using schools and
public facilities for child care, restructuring long-term care and community care
for elder parents, and revisiting leisure time as an essential component for healthy
and productive employees and families will all require a marked departure from
the old solutions of the present day.

*Clear roles and responsibilities must be identified and agreed on by the public
and private sectors.* The current status of work/family as a no-man's-land must
be changed if appropriate and effective participation is going to occur. Building
on the principle above, new dialogue is necessary between public and private
sectors to determine appropriate responses and responsibility. The current system,
in which everybody does a little, leaves a confusing vacuum in which in effect
no one takes charge. Some states have child-care initiatives, and some corporations have built day-care centers. Some have not. If we fought a war or built
highways in this manner, pandemonium would break out in all quarters. Yet the
current absence of policy and program boundaries has resulted in an unhealthy
state in which concerted action is next to impossible, since there are no formal
or informal agreements or contracts that address the problem of whom should
be doing what. This is not to argue for some centrally planned approach, but
for a better understanding between local, state, federal, and corporate sectors
on what might be appropriate roles and how coordination can begin to build
systematic responses to the complex issues of work/family conflicts.

There is no single or correct solution. One of the most effective means of
disarming and diminishing any issue is to oversimplify. Thus the rush to set up
a child-care center often is shrouded with the assumption that this solves the
work/family problems for this family, company, or community. Although this
goes a long way toward helping one aspect of a family's work/family dilemma
and assists the corporation or community in being more responsive to an aspect
of the problem, it is a far cry from solving work/family conflicts. The diversity
of the workforce, families, corporations, and communities defies any one ap-

proach or solution. Instead, a multifaceted approach will be necessary that can both identify and appreciate the diversity and begin to work within this diversity to create multiple pathways and opportunities as we prepare for the new social and economic environments that await us.[1]

Solutions must move beyond accommodations. If the goal of resolving work/family conflicts is to find meaningful solutions, then building a child-care center here and installing an elder-care information and referral service there will not suffice. To date most of the responses to work/family issues have been family-centered. For example, setting up a child-care information and referral service for employees, although assuredly most helpful, is basically accommodating the current status of a family and its employer, who need to have the adult in a position of a productive employee. These responses place the responsibility for child care on the family, and the corporation or governmental unit agrees to help them carry this out. By adopting this accommodating strategy the responsibility is kept off the corporation or government and on the family, thus denying ownership of the problem. The family winds up getting help, but it still has exclusive ownership. If the fabric of work/family issues were to be examined in its entirety, there would be a recognition that genuine cultural, organizational, and social change is necessary if the conflicts are going to be handled at the root. Attacking a problem above ground only ignores and postpones the more genuine and lasting response. Accommodating stressed parents through programs and services denies the more fundamental roots that need to be examined and modified. Not surprisingly, this is a more difficult and higher degree of change, one that will impact the dominance of the workplace and the current socioeconomic ideologies that prop up current approaches to working families.

Leadership must emerge to champion work and family issues. Work/family conflicts have become more publicly acknowledged, and creative solutions have begun to emerge, albeit for the most part on an anecdotal basis. Such a process could continue to limp along for some time, but the underlying conflicts would not be addressed or resolved to any great extent. Given the mounting concern over these conflicts, and the potential harm of allowing current conditions to prevail, it would appear that the call for leadership will be essential to the realization of effective responses. This leadership will have to emerge from both the private and the public sectors, leaders who can add voice to vision in articulating the direction for work/family policy and programs. If indeed such essential issues as the competitiveness of America, the preservation and growth of the family, and the future of our children are tied to new structures, policies, and programs, then leadership will be necessary to provide the political might to gain consensus and obtain "buy-in" from the many stakeholders in work/family affairs. No movement can emerge from the fray of competing social issues without strong leadership and advocacy, and work/family issues are no exception.

Recommendations

All the principles above lay the ground work for fundamental change in the work/family arena. To this end a number of far-reaching recommendations are made to better inform the reordering of society to respond to work/family conflicts.

The work/family debate will have to move to the next step. The current agenda for work and family is much too narrowly focused. If an outside observer were to define the work/family issues by the current efforts within the public and private sectors, the issue would probably be defined as an absence of child care and a growing concern for providing information on aging parents. Although this is acceptable as a first stage, any genuine response to work and family issues must go far deeper than information and referral. Just as the women's movement has matured, learning from its interactions with the social environment and culture, so, too, does the work and family movement need to mature. In fact, probably the essence of the next step is that work/family issues have to take on the shape of a movement. The isolated pilot programs of a few progressive corporations and governmental units have to be broadened into the mainstream. Advocacy groups will have to arise in some number and become strengthened if the work/family agenda is to compete with the multiplicity of other public policy issues.

Many of those who are on the front lines of work and family issues are quickly coming to the conclusion that if meaningful societal and corporate response is going to take hold, the current initiatives fall far short. Simply providing services changes little except to give some concrete relief to a select few individuals who are the most acutely affected individuals. But triaging work/family issues so that only the neediest get services misses the larger, underlying issues. Deeply held stereotypes and attitudes need to be changed both at work and in the community. As long as gender discrimination and attitudes about women belonging at home prevail (as was evident in our study), then the real issue is not the absence of child care, but attitudinal change throughout society. Until corporations and communities begin to understand their stake in work/family issues the problem and the burden continue to be on the backs of families. This is the next-stage agenda—structural, organizational, and social change that supplements the current responses of services and benefits. Work/family issues are not simply family problems, but corporate, community, and social problems.

Corporations and government should work toward breaching the wide chasm that exists between men and women. As long as work/family issues are defined and perceived as women's issues, little substantive change can occur. The long simmering battle of the sexes has taken on a new life as women have entered the workforce and the work/household role distinctions between genders have all but disappeared in many households. But as stark testimony to the tenacity of fundamental beliefs, the shift in these roles has not significantly altered either behavior or attitudes. Both the household and the workplace still exhibit relatively rigid gender role expectations and behaviors, reflecting the deeply held values that support these practices. Some have observed the absence of family pictures on the desks of women executives, a fear that the wrong message may be portrayed on their way to the top. On the other side, an informal survey of men at a soccer game during work hours revealed that all of them reported that they were going to a meeting rather that openly admit that they wanted to attend their children's soccer game. Current cultural norms tend to trap men into existing stereotypes, particularly from within the male-dominant workforce.

Although the gender issue has tended to become synonomous with women, the evolving work/family dynamics have increasingly refocused male roles away from the traditional rigid parameters of wage earner. This more open role is still not widely embraced by the prevailing norms of the culture, and this makes it even more difficult for men to break out of the traditional stereotypes. After all, there is no equivalent to *Working Women* magazine for men, (unless it is something like *Esquire*), and men have tended to be either the villians in the work/family drama or crowded out of the picture because of the long neglect of women, for whom the workplace is relatively new.

Men and fathers are, for the most part, on the sidelines, excluded from the work/family picture except as objects to be changed. Partly because of the culture, men have been rather passive and seemingly disinterested in the issue. A reversal of this situation will be required if meaningful change is to take place on both attitudinal and behavioral levels. Solutions such as that proposed by Felice Schwartz in setting up what has become known as the Mommy track will only reinforce work/family as primarily a women's issue. New mechanisms have to be found both in the community and in the workplace to bring men off the sidelines and into the equal partnership of family members trying to balance their family roles with their work roles. As difficult as it may be to admit, the integration and cooptation of men into the heart of work and family debate are two of the essential keys to lasting change. As long as work/family issues are defined or perceived as women's issues there is little hope for resolving even the most superficial conflicts.

How this gets accomplished will require a great deal of creative problem solving and focused attention on those barriers that currently prohibit such balance. Advertising, which forms such a powerful socialization process, can become much more sensitive to stereotypes in the media. Some men will have to take more leadership in discussing this issue and the cultural barriers that keep men on the sidelines. Mechanisms at the worksite and in the community, such as focus groups, will be needed to break down the cultural impediments and allow the necessary interactions between men and women. The educational sphere also will need to assume some leadership so that these issues get addressed at an early age. Moving men into the mainstream and away from the sidelines is no small task, but one that has tremendous potential for making substantial progress toward better work and family balance.

Corporations will have to examine their benefits and policies in light of family needs and supports. For the corporate sector, change has been the most difficult. Given the historical and cultural myths of the separate worlds of work and family that have predominated this century, corporations, more than families or government, have had to come the most distance in understanding and becoming sensitive, adapting, and responding to work and family issues. And yet they still have the farthest to go. On one hand, the expediencies of a changing economic climate and a shrinking labor pool have forced them to make dramatic changes in their operations so that they can survive and compete. In addition, the rising expectations of employees, weaned from the traditional government supports, are demanding increased corporate participation and responsibility. The workplace of the twenty-first century in the United States will take on a radically different configuration than that of a generation ago. This workplace community is the location of most adults during the greater proportion of the day. As such it represents a new reality of how citizens and family members exercise their nonwork roles and responsibilities, in that most of their time is captured by the workplace. This fact alone catapults the workplace into a major player in reconfiguring society in issues as disparate as child care and leisure time. Despite any actions and responses by courts, legislatures, or community institutions, corporations will increasingly be cast within a leadership role in resolving work/family conflicts. Because the corporation has captured most of the time available to adults and because the social benefits have increasingly been shifted from the public to the private sector, the corporation has been made the de facto environment from which many of the mechanisms for reducing this conflict will emanate.

This does not imply that the corporate sector will embrace this role or these responsibilities willingly. There are still significant cultural and economic obstacles that not only mitigate against corporate involvement, but also strive to keep the status quo in place. Nevertheless, the corporation will need to move from benefits and policies that have largely been devised along an individualistic line to those that are focused on the needs of the working family. Workplaces now employ families or households, not simply individuals. The recent proliferation of benefits and policies pertaining to dependent care and flexible workplace environments speaks to the momentum of this movement. The strategic corporation will become proactive in seizing the work/family issue as a means of recruiting and retaining employees within a shrinking labor pool. Whereas some corporations may offer programs or policies as part of being a good employer, the more forward-thinking and -acting companies will be actively promoting their family policies and programs.

To be more family-sensitive, corporations will have to have mechanisms for better understanding the work/family conflicts of their workforces and for responding. This will require them to establish some type of functional unit, probably within human resources, that will monitor such data, bringing critical issues to the fore, weighing alternative policies and programs, and remaining responsive to the shifting dynamics of working families. Some corporations have found great value in such mechanisms to sort out the information and to weigh the difficult policy and program decisions. By adopting benefits and policies that are family-sensitive, corporations will ultimately be acting in their own interests. Understanding the full dimensions of their vested interests, however, is neither self-evident nor politically easy.

Corporations are going to be increasingly faced with greater involvement with what were once purely social issues. Take child care as an example. Although the public sector will play a large role in shaping policy and programs around this issue, there is ample room for corporations to join into an alliance with the government to respond to dependent-care issues. The opportunity to assume a leadership role is not tied to some new sense of corporate social responsibility, but a much more pragmatic reality—vested interests. Reshaping benefits and policies and joining public ventures around work/family concerns represent a strategic move by which the corporation positions itself for the future. Ensuring that benefits and policies are reflective of corporate needs as well as family needs ties business goals to good employee and community relations. To allow benefits and policies to become separate from the changing environment and employee needs loses a unique opportunity to marry business objectives to employee needs.

Government will have to play a larger role in shaping family policy. The United States can no longer become the anomaly within the industrialized community of the world, continuing to ignore family policy. The social contract of the past is dysfunctional for families and increasingly so for society as a whole. The current political paralysis that has characterized deliberations around family policy is becoming more unacceptable from both an economic and a social perspective. If the current stance of containing family policy within a minimalist position continues, the costs will exceed the benefits of upholding an anachronistic and dysfunctional ideology. Political leadership, although seemingly in short supply, is desperately needed to break through the log jam of competing values and morals to create some form of family supports.

The family agenda spills across a wide spectrum of government legislation, from long-term disability insurance to provisions for child care. But it must be clear that the government role is not simply focusing on the most immediate (such as child care), but also on the total array of family issues, which range from family stability to latchkey children. Even if the federal government can legislate some form of child care—which appears to be simply a matter of time— the role and responsibility of the government to ensure healthy and productive families go far beyond simple child care.

One of the primary reasons government has been reluctant to embrace a family agenda and create a family policy is linked to the strong cultural taboos against interfering with the sacred independence of families. In fact, a significant segment of the population would argue that government and corporations should not become involved in the "caring business" because it weakens the family. From this perspective, children should be taken care of by parents, elders by their children. There are, however, a few fallacies in that position. First of all, there is a significant number of elders for whom care by relatives is virtually impossible by reason of distance from children or absence of other family members.

Indeed, most families that are not seriously dysfunctional do not want the government to take over family responsibilities, but rather to support them so that they can succeed in meeting their needs. Elder care provides a good example of the need for a new role for government that breaks out of the noninterventionist ideology of the present, but avoids the feared role of a government bureaucracy swallowing the family. Studies have shown that few families want to place their parents in nursing or retirement homes. But the fact is that the drain of women from the household into the workplace makes home care a limited option. Without some type of supplemental assistance few families of today are in a position to assist their aging parents. By creating a partnership between families and government not only can the desired goal of home care be realized, but there also is some evidence that the level of services delivered by family members remains constant when formal help is provided. Thus the two types of care—home-based and community care—complement each other.[2]

What is the proper role of government, and to what degree should family supports be provided by the government? Few would argue that the United States should adopt the social policies of Sweden, for example, in relation to family policy. Forcing a solution from one economic system on another seldom works well. On the other hand, few can argue persuasively today that the United States can continue without an expanded and more explicit family policy. The time has arrived for honest reexamination of the consequences of the current system. Families cannot continue to maneuver their way through the current times in the way they were able to in the 1940s and 1950s. This does not require an overthrow of the system, but a major reshifting to accommodate the new order.

The social contract entered into by the state and its citizens is seriously flawed under current conditions. Pretending that families will be able to meet their responsibilities for children, elders, and the disabled and find a quality of life that is fulfilling within a context in which work allows little space for such responsibilities simply uses denial as a primary defense mechanism for survival. This is a system that barely recognizes that the family structure has been radically changed, that women are in the workplace and not at home, and that meeting the needs of children, elder parents, and the family as a whole is practically impossible, given the absence of policy and supports. All the formal and informal movement toward responses to work/family conflicts, such as child-care programs, parental leave policy, and comparable worth, have been mostly met with resistance, which is an indicator of the inability of the existing system to create a society that can balance its work/family systems.

The federal government, in both the executive and the legislative branches, will have to reduce its rhetoric around work/family issues and redouble its efforts to enact legislation that will create the supports and programs necessary for families (and corporations) to achieve a healthy work/family life. Because this is a political decision, movement in this direction will have to be mobilized on many fronts. Although there are numerous political, social, and economic issues that tend to either immobilize or foreclose any action, advocacy groups, coalitions, and strong leadership will have to guide this process.

Whatever the final disposition of a family policy and system of supports adopted in the United States, it should result in a society in which the needs of the family unit as the nurturing affective haven can be preserved while families pursue economic goals. "The social fabric relies on our ability to nurture the weak and to respond to the needs of intimates. Although we should respect the determination of some women not to engage in caring for aged parents and spouses and seek to alleviate the burdens of those who do, we should not automatically subordinate this work to the pursuit of individual achievement."[3]

In the early 1980s many mothers who worked felt guilty or inadequate, and became apologetic about their employment. Today, many mothers who stay at home full-time think that they have to explain themselves. Their choice to provide care to their families is perceived to be devalued or unnecessary. The absence of strong family policy exacerbates this situation, leaving the responsibility and the increasing conflicts solely on the backs of women and men. If society is to play any role in mediating work/family conflicts, it might opt to create environments in which families can realize a less frenetic existence, and in which many of the conflicts can be reduced by means of programs, policies, and benefits weighted to encourage family life and reduce individual, organizational, and social stress associated with the current disjointedness around balancing work and home life. The role of government in all this is not to solve the problem, but to find a better balance. Unquestionably this is no minor adjustment, but a major cultural shift that will require government to play a more active role without becoming too paternalistic and intrusive. However difficult a balance to realize, the end product is a society in which its members appreciate the need for individual and family systems to work out arrangements so that they can be both economically productive and nurturing.

The key to reducing work/family conflicts is the creation of new partnerships. From all perspectives the issues swirling around work/family conflicts become more complicated the more we understand them. If the conflicts were simply a question of more government expenditures, then an effective lobbying and advocacy movement would quickly remedy the situation. If the issue was one of getting corporations to be more responsible in setting up day-care centers, then the conflicts could be resolved almost immediately. The conflicts, however, are reflective of a much more complex web of strong cultural values, social and institutional transition, economic restructuring, and a set of interlocking issues that require movement across multiple systems.

Much of what we have seen throughout this book is the failure of past and present efforts to successfully integrate work and family into one system. One of the three spheres of work, family, or government has been expected to resolve these issues, or in some instances has tried to proactively move on work/family issues largely on its own. In fact, what is interesting about the current gridlock over work/family conflicts is that no one sector wants ownership of the issue and, consequently, is looking to others. Families have just about had it with the impossible set of expectations heaped on them by cultural expectations and institutional neglect. Corporations are feeling similar in that having to deal with employees' family and personal problems not only is new, but goes against a longstanding tradition that has kept them out of these affairs. Now that employee expectations for corporate involvement in these issues have risen and government cutbacks have increased, many sets of eyes are turning to the private sector for relief. This creates much discomfort and annoyance in corporate boardrooms as corporations are trying to fight international competition and the challenges of a new workforce. And the public sector, overwhelmed by budget deficits and trying to get government off the backs of people, is in no mood to initiate a major new spending program around families.

Because the problem of work/family conflict is so enormous, and the solutions not self-evident, it is understandable why none of the three institutions is eager to carry the primary responsibility. Indeed, any effective solutions transcend the ability of any of them individually to adequately resolve the conflicts. As with past attempts, the response by one sector is doomed to failure. Thus it will be necessary for partnerships to be formed on all levels to bring together the different spheres, each of whom have vested interests in resolving work/family conflicts. These partnerships will be born out of a growing recognition that the problem and the conflicts, as well as the resolutions, reside in all three spheres. The essence of partnership is a joining of forces in the recognition that together a more comprehensive and integral response can be developed and implemented. Many of these partnerships have already begun and others are in the developmental stages.

Partnerships often evoke the images of complicated systems, lengthy negotiations, and endless political posturing, all of which can be true. The work/family partnerships, however, will require not so much complicated negotiations between strange or estranged parties as explorations based on common interests and action based on expediency of the common good. A number of these partnerships can be examined on the micro and macro levels.

1. Family Partnerships. On the most basic level, new partnerships need to be developed within families both for the sake of survival and for a return to a healthy level of family functioning. Husbands and wives, parents and children will need to develop new mechanisms and new contracts by which family roles and responsibilities get apportioned. This partnership arrangement recognizes the longstanding cultural differences and role expectations between men and women, and how dysfunctional these are in today's society. The family compact will entail more open communication about attitudes, stereotypes, and behaviors that currently add to family conflict. Much of this is trivial and even petty. Nevertheless, it is at the most basic level of conflict: Who cleans the house, who is able to get to school functions, and who feels saddled with the care of an aging parent can be fought over, argued about, and the subject of much tension without leading to any productive resolution. Simple methods such as regular family meetings, writing out a contract, or spending time with an outside arbitrater in an informal session can be productive in taking the focus away from

the problem and onto the solutions. Families, like corporations and government, find it hard to change and adapt. They, too, need to recognize the trade-offs necessary to reduce tension and enter into a healthy and productive family life.

2. Workplace Partnerships. The need for partnerships between management and labor is becoming increasingly clear as economic competition, a shrinking workforce, and the changing nature of human resources and employee relations compel workplaces to enter into a new compact. The entrenched hierarchical, bureaucratic corporation will not survive in today's environment. Similarly, the old labor and management relationship, often cast in adversarial terms, will not be particularly useful in solving the problems of the 1990s. The partnership with the workplace will probably have the most difficult time, since it has to overcome what has been a one-sided and often competitive relationship, qualities that do not make for effective partnerships.

The multiple factions of labor and management, men and women, employee relations and benefits will have to examine the work/family issues from a different perspective, one that begins with a recognition of a common set of problems. Everyone within the corporation is affected by work/family conflicts, and the beginning of any genuine partnership is to recognize that everyone shares the problem. The time for finger-pointing and blame is over, and the time for jointly trying to find effective solutions is now. Job-sharing may appear to present more problems for the corporation than it solves, but it needs to be explored within an open system, trying to understand the dilemmas any solution poses for some sectors. Today's corporation may anxiously fear the costs in setting up child-care centers at every location, when in fact what is called for is something quite different and considerably less expensive than imagined by management. Through a partnership of open communication and problem solving some new and innovative work/family programs and policies may emerge. It is necessary to acknowledge, however, that the partnership will revert to preordained battle lines if the basic ground rules do not change. Work/family conflicts are set down in the midst of existing employee relations. If a climate of suspicion and mistrust characterizes the environment, then the partnership cannot be fruitful, and old attitudes will be left to deal with new challenges—a proscription for failure.

Leadership within the corporation and the unions or labor groups will have to offer bold new directions if the current situation is to become unstuck and useful dialogue and action planning undertaken. The list of worksite conflicts are long and emotionally charged. This form of partnership is essential, however, if the necessary breakthroughs are going to be realized in areas such as child care, flex time, parental leave, and job-sharing.

3. Corporate/Community Partnerships. As corporations have become more imbedded with work/family issues, they also have come to appreciate that the solutions for many of the problems are to be found within the communities in which the corporation is located. Work/family issues are not simply corporate problems, but community and social problems that require active community participation. Trying to provide child care to employees within the confines of

corporate partitions is unrealistic as well as misdirected. The community is more ideally suited for such family supports as child care, and to attempt to define and resolve the child-care issue primarily within a corporate context is to miss the opportunities of linking community needs and resources with corporate needs and resources.

Corporate/community relations define the corporation in terms of its inter-dependence with the community. In the case of work and family issues, the American corporation is beginning to move beyond the benevolent good citizen of previous decades that provided corporate philanthropy to worthy community causes in order to protect and enhance its corporate image. Today the relation of the corporation to the community is considerably more dynamic and essential—it is tied to survival. This is most evident in the area of education that is at the top of just about every corporate agenda. Because the shrinking labor pool is coupled with the deteriorating educational institutions in our society, the corporation has begun to realize that it will have to actively participate in the community educational ventures if it hopes to stay competitive over the next generation. Through this assessment of self-interest the corporation breaks the previous rules and boundaries between corporate and community involvement to act in its own interests.

A similar agenda is growing within the American corporation around the work/family and dependent-care issues. The issues of elder care, sick care, latchkey children, and adolescent drug and alcohol problems, along with child care, are now the problems of both community and corporation. Just as the problems of schools have led to joint partnerships such as the business–school compacts that have sprung up in many larger cities, so, too, will the work/family issues call for new and innovative partnerships at the community level with corporate buy-in. Already corporations such as the Bank of America have acted as a catalyst for a statewide coalition of child care in California. Other corporations have joined with hospitals to sponsor programs for sick children. The more progressive, such as Stride Rite, have even broached child care and elder care through their imaginative intergenerational care project. In all these the interests of the corporation and those of the community have found a common ground in which joint participation reduces conflict and more systematically approaches the solution of the problem.

4. Corporate/Government/Family Partnerships. The last and most comprehensive of the partnerships links all three spheres in a new partnership that redefines the traditional social contract as the essential relationship between citizens and the state. Under this partnership a new dimension—that of the corporate sphere—is added to truly reflect the total system of policymakers and service providers. American capitalism toward the end of the twentieth century has evolved into a complex of public and private benefits that, in large part, define the social contract. The corporate sphere has become much more dominant over the past several decades primarily because of its large investment, as reflected in its benefit plans. Thus the partnership is no longer simply between a

citizen and his or her government; it has become enlarged to include an equally important segment—the corporation.

This partnership is perhaps least understood, since there are few formal links between the three. In recent times, however, a growing number of advocacy and special interest groups have arisen, on the state level as well as in Washington, that have focused on many of the aspects of work/family issues, such as child care and elder care. An equal number have focused on the perceived results of unbalanced work/family roles and responsibilities, such as adolescent drugs, suicide, and latchkey children. All of these, although independent and loosely connected, are beginning to discover the power of coalition building among themselves.

Likewise, corporate interests, from both management and labor, are quite active in representing their interests, particularly in reacting to proposed legislation. Unions, such as the AFL-CIO, and management groups, such as the U.S. Chamber of Commerce, have become quite forceful lobbies on a variety of fronts.

What has yet to emerge in any significant manner, is the mutual planning and deliberations that mark a partnership. There will have to be increased realization of common interests as well as the price that will have to be paid for adversarial stances. Because this is the most macro of all partnerships, there are many obstacles to realizing it even at the most minimal of levels. This is the most important partnership, since it is in the arena of policy—setting national priorities and policy on the whole range of work/family issues. Unless and until increased interdependence and joint programming emerge from these three spheres, the problems of work and family will continue to be dealt with in a fractured manner. The many critical issues necessary to make the country productive and the family healthy, issues such as parental care, child care and elder care, all require new problem-solving mechanisms and new relationships between these established institutions. The central planning mechanisms of the Japanese and their close working relationship between government and corporate sectors (more typical of all countries with the exception of the United States) suggest that this partnership is essential for American survival and the quality of life for American families. Clearly our system will not and should not emulate the partnerships found in Japan and in many European socialist systems. Creative entrepreneurship, the spirit of inquiry, and the freedom to strike out on one's own cannot be lost or stifled in the quest for increased interaction between public, private, and family spheres. Nevertheless, the barriers to what will become American-type partnerships must be broken down to avoid the continued slippage that is taking place in the country owing in part to the separateness of the three spheres, their adversarial stances, and their inability to find common ground. Partnerships at this level not only promote dialogue and interaction, but also serve to reduce those characteristics that keep the work and family problems from being put into a more systematic problem-solving cauldron.

All these partnerships will be necessary if the work/family conflicts that characterize much of today's environments are going to be reduced. Solutions cannot come from any one of the spheres, but from the working together of all parties that have an equal interest in reducing and resolving the conflict. A number of the work/family conflicts could have relatively simple responses, such as educational support for caregivers, counseling, information and referral, and support groups. In many ways these responses are good starting places for cooperative ventures. For example, the government might fund a project that develops necessary training material and information for purposes of dissemination. Community agencies might be able to provide the technical expertise, and to pretest these. Corporations and families might then be willing to bear the cost of the actual services.

One such example is the formation of the Child Care Resource and Referral Centers in Massachusetts. These organizations offer services to both the child-care providers and consumers (training information and referral, consultation) on a fee-for-service basis (subsidized by government funds). Special package programs often are sold to businesses, which offer these as benefits to employees.

Despite all the talk about recent private/public partnerships, particularly in the area of education, there are few meaningful links between government efforts and corporate activities. The two spheres remain more separated by reason of cultural differences, mistrust, and an inequitable distribution of power. The rhetoric behind partnerships has not caught up with the tough political realities of joining together for a common purpose. This breakdown is further complicated by the fact that consumer participation in most policymaking groups tends to remain at a level of tokenism. Clearly one hand does not know what the other is doing or needs. This does not bode well for work/family partnerships. Nevertheless, it does present the challenge. If partnerships are overlooked or avoided, then the chasm will only grow between those sectors who need each other if accommodation and realistic and effective responses to work/family conflicts are to be developed. There is much to learn from the failures of past partnerships, and a great deal of leadership needed to break down the barriers to such partnership. Staff in organizations such as state area offices of aging and child-care coalitions will have to give greater priority and develop better skills at interacting and communicating with corporate human resources personnel. They are both struggling with the same issues.

In the long run we need to break down the walls of isolationism. In our own self-interests, the ancient question of "Who is my neighbor?" gets paired with "Am I my brother's keeper?" Corporations can no longer afford to think that work/family issues should be resolved at home; neither should they assume that these issues are now the primary responsibility of the corporation. Government at both the state and national levels cannot postpone its responses until the budget crisis passes. That may never happen. In addition, the very nature of government in protecting the commonwealth of its citizens must be answered in the context of the new century. Partnerships will be necessary to both share the burden and creatively find solutions by which all of society is effected and around which the future of families, corporations, and society as a whole is shaped.

Work/family issues must be linked to the broader quality of life issue. Lurking immediately below the work/family issue is a more elusive issue, yet ultimately one of equal importance—the quality of life. Unless work/family issues become linked to quality of life issues, a major opportunity is lost in addressing the fundamentals of working families. At the heart of all the work/family conflicts discussed throughout this book is a desire to reverse a quickening of life, a diminuation of quality time with spouses, children, relatives, and friends. The economic forces that have sent women into the workplace have also served to create a more frenzied lifestyle for most American households. Leisure time has diminished, children are seen on the run, and what nonwork time is available is spent trying to catch up on household chores, and obligations to friends and neighbors. In the interviews conducted for the research in this book there was an almost universal exhaustion reported by working couples and single parents. Everyone seems to be working and running twice as fast as they were a decade ago, only to keep pace. The noticeable reduction in time for friends and family was sadly recorded. The presumed rise in the standard of material goods made possible by dual-income families appears to have had little impact on improving the overall quality of life.

The movement for addressing work/family issues in reality is a call to improve the quality of living and working. Finding child care or taking care of parents is not simply looking for the government or the corporation to take over family responsibilities; it is a plea from those who have found their lives too full to respond and too captured by economic necessity to abandon the workplace.

On the corporate front the rush to productivity and to maintain competitiveness has taken the spotlight off quality of life issues and placed it on more immediate and pragmatic economic goals. And indeed, the rush to compete cannot be treated lightly. The Japanese and, probably even more important, the Europeans have created two strong markets that are more than able to compete with the United States. There comes a point, however—and the work/family issues may be the spearhead of such a point—at which individuals and families ask, "Productivity? For what and at what expense?" Interestingly, this question is impacting the other markets as well. In Japan the newer generation is seriously questioning the current order in which there is a relatively materially deprived generation of their parents, whose long work days, oppression of women who subsidize the family enterprise, and high cost of consumer goods have exacted a heavy price on the quality of Japanese life. In Europe, now the largest market, the traditional set of family supports are under attack on the grounds of competition. The traditional month off in August and five weeks' mandatory vacation cannot hold up against their major competitors, Japan, where vacation time is widely downplayed and subordinated to work, and the United States, where two weeks' vacation is the norm.

Thus the work/family issue may present an unusual opportunity to reexamine the quality of life within the American context. Its very essence is a call to reorder the existing system, to restructure the overly dominant workplace for a more balanced approach to living and working. This may be a side door approach to addressing the many ills of society that have, by most accounts, grown worse. Indeed, much of the appeal of this work/family movement is its universality and widespread recognition that things as they are not very satisfying to anybody.

At the workplace the quality of working life has its own history and development. What had begun during the 1970s with a great flourish now appears to have been sidestepped by the rush toward productivity. One of the great tragedies of the current scene is that women are emulating men's work, rather than questioning the basic arrangements and assumptions that are largely nonresponsive to family needs and the growth of individuals and families. Yet there is great opportunity for reviving the quality of life programs, to try and humanize the workplace, and this time make it more responsive to parents and those with dependent-care responsibilities. The workplace has ample room to make itself more responsive without sacrificing quality or productivity; in fact, the very process of being responsive may constitute the best strategy for improving productivity.

Meanwhile the quality of living, although far-reaching and multi-itemed, remains at the core of our society, and represents one of the more critical mandates for our elected officials. By heightening the quality issue and placing it toward the top of the social agenda, it will get the type of attention that most working citizens hope for. Communities struggle daily with a range of issues from pollution to decaying infrastructures, but none can be any more important than the status of families and the overall quality of life. It is to these issues that policymakers on all levels of government should be turning increased attention, not in any quest for a utopian existence, but in an attempt to recognize this as a legitimate and important set of issues and as a society to commit ourselves to finding better solutions and strategies than the current environment offers.

SUMMARY

The growing conflicts discussed throughout this book have described the widening gulf between the changing characteristics of the American population, and the policies, institutions, and social supports necessary to ensure a healthy and productive society. Work/family conflicts, at their most basic level, can be seen as historical maladaptations between economic and family functioning. A great number of conflicts arise because major institutions of society (e.g., government agencies, private business, and schools) are primarily oriented to and have organized their structures, schedules, and resources around a society and family structure that no longer exist. Although the private marketplace of banks, with automated tellers, have pioneered alternatives designed to offer services that better coincide with the working families of the 1990s, many mainstream institutions remain irrelevantly rooted in a past era.

The problems of balancing work and home life have become homogenized throughout American society. A generation ago dual-earner families were typically confined to lower-income families, or if the wife worked, it was considered nonessential. Currently the majority of all classes are characterized by dual-earner or dual-career families. Like so many other social problems, once the problems of balancing work and home life move from the minority of the lower class into the majority of working and upper class, they become mainstream and, consequently, defined as problems or conflicts. Once professionals, blue-collar workers, and the poor share concerns about child care and problems of limited family/personal time, the likelihood for finding a solution increases dramatically. The problem of the few has become a problem of the many.

In the midst of this attempt to resolve and reduce work/family conflict it is important to recognize that other problems press up against work/family issues, and inadvertently there is a danger that some of the proposed solutions may conflict with other issues, such as classism, racism, and sexism. For example, if it is left to the private market to respond to the increasing unmet personal and family needs, the wealthiest members of society will typically get the best services. The benefits afforded by the *Fortune* 100 companies will not be available to the small businesses and concerns that employ the vast majority of American workers. Even many nonprofit community agencies are looking for clients who can pay on a fee-for-service basis so that the agency can respond to funding cutbacks.

All this returns the work/family issue to the context within which much of the social policy issues, particularly the social welfare benefits, must be viewed: Who pays, what are the entitlements, and what is the basis on which services such as those around child care and elder care are received by the population? If the response assists the minority within the *Fortune* 100 companies, the gap between the haves and have-nots will increase, and the economic problems related to work/family, as well as the family stress associated with these issues, will only grow larger.

Although the debate may focus on tax versus subsidy and program money, the real debate within the government is whether the traditional laissez-faire policies that have guided our economics and our government are adequate in responding to the work/family conflicts of today. As these conflicts have become more pronounced at the macro levels, and as their shortcomings become more evident, it may be that the absence of government through these policies will lead to economics that cannot effectively compete globally because of a labor force shackled by dependent care for which it does not have adequate supports and that keeps it from working during a period of acute labor shortage. The continuation of this same laissez-faire philosophy may ironically serve to continue the deterioration of the American family which is finding it more and more difficult to manage within the current policy of nonsupport. Although the philosophy of keeping government out of the family may have been functional for the past, it appears that the continuation of such a policy will only serve to continue the fragmentation and stress currently experienced by the family.

Whereas some groups are focusing on governmental intervention, others are reexamining the role of women as central to the resolution of the work/family conflict. Although there is no doubt that women have borne the brunt of the conflicts, and continue to be perceived as both the primary caretaker and the factor in the equation that has undergone the most change, focusing on women as the center of the work/family conflict can have political and policy ramifications far beyond the particulars of their role.

As the uproar over Felice Schwartz's piece in the *Harvard Business Review* on creating special lower-paid, low-pressure career tracks demonstrated, a solution may create more problems than it solves. Leaves of absence for caretaking may in fact reinforce women's subordinate position in the labor market. As mentioned before, the relegation of this issue to women continues to pose serious problems. If issues such as parental leave are taken only by women, then the work/family issue will remain primarily a women's issue. If those speaking out and writing about these issues are predominantly women, then the likelihood of this moving into the mainstream of policy deliberations will be minimal. Leadership is needed from women and men on all facets of the work/family conflicts, leaders from the corporate and the government sectors who can articulate the conflicts and argue passionately for the solutions. Until work/family issues are seen within a gender-free light, the issues will be pigeonholed and pushed to the periphery by the majority.

Work/family issues are increasingly being understood within a more global context, particularly within the framework of competition. From this perspective, it touches on a basic social and economic challenge to the country: Can we mobilize our resources to assume economic competitiveness and can we maintain a healthy functioning family unit as the core of our society and civilization? The responses to both these issues will require large-scale and dramatic change. Trying to tinker with existing structures and policies will not achieve the desired outcomes necessary to attain these goals. The growing realization that the goals of economic productivity and family health and functioning are inextricably intertwined will force a new approach, one that recognizes the interrelations of work and family.

In the midst of the reexamination of work/family arrangements is the need to question the basic premise on which these fundamental roles operate. From some perspectives the dominance of economic productivity has hampered a healthy interchange between the two domains. If work overly dominates the family, the imbalance of power will create disincentives for the family to work cooperatively with the workplace toward mutual gains. This approaches the quality of working life issues that have been difficult to integrate into the mainstream of corporate and family life.

In too many discussions on work/family conflicts the emphasis is placed on the problems of family responsibilities impinging on work responsibilities. It is as if people are saying, "If we could only get good child care, I could pay more attention to the priority, which is work." Adults should not feel as if they have to make a choice between work and family, nor should they need to prioritize these important components of their lives. For example, managers should not feel any more guilty or apologetic when they have to cancel a meeting because their children are sick than they do when they have to cancel a meeting because of competing work responsibilities. We have to grow beyond a mommy track, a daddy track, or even a daughter track (referring to working women whose careers are threatened by the amount of time they must devote to elder care). As difficult as the trade-offs are in balancing work and family responsibilities, we need to find a better balance, rather than continue the inequitable and dys-functioning systems now in place. This may in effect be one of the goals of reshaping work/family relationships, of achieving of a new level of maturity that can be defined as meeting the challenges of productivity (paid or unpaid labor) and the forms of intimacy (family relations).

This book has discussed a number of the changes that have contributed to some of the work/family conflicts. It is possible that some unforeseen oppor-tunities lurk in the midst of these conflicts. Opportunities are always on the opposite side of the coin to crisis. The glue that has served to hold together the current arrangements around work and family over the better part of the century has begun to feel the ravages of time. The clear and pressing needs and demands for new work/family structures, policies, and programs at the societal, corporate, and family levels, constitute a distinct challenge for society and all its citizens. The somewhat radical overthrow of institutional and social values and behaviors necessary to achieve this new state has not been fully appreciated, and certainly not accepted by the majority. As the negative consequences of trying to stick with the old structures increase, the momentum toward the new will increase. Judging by recent events and the increasing awareness of workforce 2000 de-mographics, the momentum is quickly building. The opportunities to rebuild America and its families rely on the very qualities of entrepreneurial spirit and creative problem solving that have brought the United States to where it is in the late twentieth-century. Finding solutions and reducing the conflicts around work and family constitute a national agenda of great importance. Given the universality of such an issue and the will to find effective solutions, this period may well be one of those timely periods that every institution and society must go through as a means of transforming the old into the new. The challenges await us.

NOTES

1. See, for example, *The Governor's Task Force on Work and Family.*
2. Abel, p. 36.
3. Ibid., p. 26.

BIBLIOGRAPHY

Abel, Emily. *Love Is Not Enough*. Washington, D.C.: American Public Health Association, 1987.

Allen, Donna. *Fringe Benefits: Wages or Social Obligation?* Ithaca, N.Y.: The New York State School of Industrial and Labor Relations of Cornell University, 1969.

American Council of Life Insurance. *Baby Boom Generation Settling Down*. Washington, D.C.: Health Insurance Association of America, December 1983.

Amott, Teresa. "Working for Less: Single Mothers in the Workplace." In *Women as Single Parents: Confronting Institutional Barriers in the Courts, the Workplace, and the Housing Market*, edited by Elizabeth A. Mulroy. Dover, Mass.: Auburn House, 1988, pp. 99–122.

Axinn, June, and Herman Levin. *Social Welfare: A History of the American Response to Need*. New York: Longman, 1982.

Barnett, R., and Grace K. Baruch. *Multiple Roles and Well-being of Preschool Children*. Wellesley, Mass.: Center for Research on Women, 1979.

Barton, Paul E. *Worklife Transitions: The Adult Learning Connection*. New York: McGraw-Hill, 1982.

Baruch, Grace K., Lois Biener, and Rosalind Barnett. "Women and Gender in Research on Work and Family Stress." *American Psychologist* 42, no.2 (February 1987): 131–133.

Bass, Alison. "Researchers Debate Day Care's Effects on Kids." *Boston Globe*, July 7, 1988, pp. 29–30.

Beinecke, Richard H., and Anne Marchetta. *Employee Eldercaregiving Survey: Summary Results*. Boston, Mass.: The Workplace Caregivers Project Health Action Forum of Greater Boston, Inc., May 1989.

Bell, Carolyn Shaw. "Small Employers, Work and Community." In *Families that Work: Children in a Changing World*, edited by Sheila Kamerman and Cheryl Hayes. Washington, D.C.: National Academy Press, 1982, pp. 144–208.

Belson, P., J. Dopkeen, and W. Getchell. "Meeting Employees' Needs for Elder Care." *Compensation and Benefits Management.* 4, no.2 (Winter 1988): 117–121.

Berenson, Harold. "Women's Occupational and Family Achievements in the U.S. Class System: A Critique of the Dual Career Family Analysis." *The British Journal of Sociology* 35, no.1 (March, 1984): 19–44.

Berg, Barbara. *The Crisis of the Working Mother: Resolving the Conflict Between Family and Work.* New York: Summit Books, 1986.

Bettelheim, Bruno. "Uniting the Family." *The Center Magazine,* September-October 1976, pp. 5–10.

Blumenstein, Philip, and Pepper Schwartz. *American Couples.* New York: Pocket Books, 1983.

Bohen, H., and A. Viveros-Long. *Balancing Jobs and Family Life: Do Flexible Work Schedules Help?.* Philadelphia: Temple University Press, 1981.

Bolles, Richard Nelson. *The 1987 What Color Is Your Parachute?.* Berkeley, Calif.: Ten Speed Press, 1987.

Brandes, Stuart D. *American Welfare Capitalism: 1880–1940.* Chicago: University of Chicago Press, 1976.

Brody, Elaine, "Parent Care as a Normative Family Stress." *Gerontologist* 25, no.1 (1985): 19–29.

Brody, Elaine, Morton H. Klehan, Pauline T. Johnsen, Christine Hoffman, and Claire B. Schoonover. "Work Status and Parent Care: A Comparison of Four Groups of Women." *Gerontologist* 27, no.2 (1987) 201–208.

Bronfenbrenner, Urie. "The Roots of Alienation." In *Influences on Human Development,* edited by Urie Bronfenbrenner and Maureen A. Mahoney. Hinsdale, Ill.: Dreyden Press, 1975, pp. 658–677.

Bronfenbrenner, Urie, and Ann Crouter. "Work and Family Through Time and Space" In *Families That Work Children in a Changing World* edited by Sheila B. Kamerman and Cheryl D. Hayes. Washington, D.C.: National Academy Press, 1982, pp. 39–83.

Burden, Dianne S. "Single Parents and the Work Setting: The Impact of Multiple Job and Homelife Roles." *Family Relations* 35 (January 1986): pp. 37–41.

Burden, Dianne S., and Bradley Googins. *Balancing Job and Homelife Study.* Boston: Boston University School of Social Work, 1987.

Calhoun, Arthur W. *A Social History of the American Family from Colonial Times to Present.* New York: Barnes and Noble, 1945.

Caple, Frances Smalls. "Restructuring Family Life." In *Women as Single Parents: Confronting Institutional Barriers in the Courts, the Workplace, and the Housing Market,* edited by Elizabeth A. Mulroy. Dover, Mass.: Auburn House, 1988, pp. 73–98.

Castro, J. "More and More, She's the Boss." *Time,* December 2, 1985, p. 64.

Chapman, Fern Schumer. "Executive Guilt: Who's Taking Care of the Children?" *Fortune* February 16, 1987, pp. 30.

Cherlin, Andrew. *The Changing American Family and Public Policy.* Washington, D.C.: The Urban Institute, 1988.

Cherlin, Andrew, and Frank F. Furstenberg, Jr. "The American Family in the Year 2000." *The Futurist* June 1983, pp. 7–9. Adapted from *The Shape of the American Family in the Year 2000,* a report for the Trend Analysis Program of the American Council of Life Insurance.

"Child Care Economics." *Boston Globe,* March 20, 1989, p. 16.

Combe, J. "Management and Marriage—Push and Shove." *SAM Advanced Management Journal,* Summer 1978, pp. 32–39.

Cooper, Cary. *The Stress Check: Coping with Stresses of Life and Work.* Englewood Cliffs, N.J.: Prentice-Hall, 1981.

Cowan, Ruth Schwartz. "Women's Work, Housework, and History: The Historical Roots of Inequality in Work-Force Participation." In *Families and Work,* edited by Naomi Gerstel and Harriet Engel Gross. Philadelphia: Temple University Press, 1987, pp. 164–177.

Creedon, Michael, ed. *Issues from Aging America: Employees and Eldercare—A Briefing Book.* Southport, Conn.: Creative Services, Inc., June 1987.

Deetz, James. *In Small Things Forgotten: The Archaeology of Early American Life.* Garden City, N.J.: Anchor Press, 1977.

Demos, John. *Little Commonwealth: Family Life In Plymouth Colony.* New York: Oxford University Press, 1970.

Dietz, Jean. "Care of Aging Parents Could Produce Daughter Track." *Boston Globe.* May 24, 1989, p. 58.

"Dual Careers—A Family Killer?" *Human Behavior* 7 (March 1978): 49–50.

Editorial Research Reports on the Changing American Family. Washington, D.C.: Congressional Quarterly, June 3, 1977, p. 8.

"Education Really Does Matter in the Job Market." *The Wall Street Journal* October 20, 1988, p. B1:1.

Elkind, David. *The Hurried Child: Growing Up Too Fast Too Soon.* Reading, Mass.: Addison-Wesley, 1988.

Emlen, Arthur C. "Panel on Child Care, Work and Family." American Psychological Association Annual Meeting, New York City, August 28, 1987.

Emlen, Arthur C., and Paul E. Koren. *Hard to Find and Difficult to Manage: The Effects of Childcare on the Workplace.* Portland, Ore.: The Workplace Partnership, 1984.

Employee Benefits Research Institute. *EBRI Issue Brief.* Vol. 85. Washington, D.C., December 1988.

"Employment Trends-Women." *Women and Work Research and Resource Letter* 1, no.1 (Summer 1986): p. 2. Publication of the Women and Work Research Center at the University of Texas Graduate School of Social Work.

Epstein, C. F. "Law Partners and Marital Partners: Strains and Solutions in the Dual-Career Family Enterprise," *Human Relations* 24 (1974): 68–85.

Eurich, Nell. *Corporate Classrooms: The Learning Business.* Princeton, N.J.: The Carnegie Foundation for the Advancement of Teaching, 1985.

"Family Members Care for over Half of Workers' Pre-School Children." *The Numbers News* 4, no.1 (January, 1984):4.

Fernandez, John P. "Child Care and Corporate Productivity." Report for AT&T, March 1984.

———. *Child Care and Corporate Productivity: Resolving Family/Work Conflicts.* Lexington, Mass.: Lexington Books, D.C. Health, 1986.

Ferree, Myra Marx. "Family and Job for Working-Class Women: Gender and Class System Seen From Below." In *Families and Work,* edited by Naomi Gerstel and Harriet Engel Gross. Philadelphia: Temple University Press, 1987, pp. 289–301.

Fowlkes, Martha R. "The Myth of Merit and Male Professional Careers: The Role of

Wives.'' In *Families and Work*, edited by Naomi Gerstel and Harriet Engel Gross. Philadelphia: Temple University Press, 1987. pp. 347–360.

French, Desiree. "Second Marriages." *Boston Globe*, September 9, 1989, pp. 61, 66.

Friedman, Dana. "ElderCare: The Employee Benefit of the 1990's." *Across the Board* 23, no.6 (June 1986): 45–51.

Furstenberg, Frank F., Jr. "The Family Since '80: Rhetoric vs. Reality." *The Wall Street Journal*, September 1, 1988, p. 20:3.

Gardener, Marilyn. "Better Child-Care Options Top Working Parents' Wish List." *Christian Science Monitor*, January 23, 1986, pp. 25–27.

Garland, T. Neal. "The Better Half? The Male in the Dual Profession Family." In *Toward a Sociology of Women*, edited by C. Safilios-Rothschild. Lexington, Mass.: Xerox College Publishing, 1972, pp. 199–215.

Gibbs, Nancy. "How America Has Run Out of Time." *Time* 133, no.17 (April 24, 1989): 58–67.

Gibeau, Janice L., Jeanne Anastas, and Pamela Larson. "Breadwinners, Caregivers and Employers—New Alliances in an Aging America." *Employee Benefits Journal*, September 1987, pp. 6–10.

Gilbert, Neil. "The Welfare State Adrift." *Social Work* 31, no.4 (July/August, 1986): 251–254.

Gladding, Samuel T., and Charles H. Huber. "The Position of Single-Parent Father." *Journal of Employment Counseling* 21, no.1 (March 1984): p. 13–17.

Googins, Bradley, and Judith C. Casey. "Dynamics of Alcoholism in Working Families." *Alcoholism Treatment Quarterly* 4, no.3 (Fall 1987): pp. 47–66.

Googins, Bradley, Margaret L. Griffin, and Judith C. Casey. "The Role of Work for Wives of Alcoholics." Submitted for publication to the *Journal of Studies on Alcohol*, November 1989.

Gordon, Suzanne. "Nation Confronted by Day Care Crisis." *Boston Sunday Globe*, January 12, 1986, p. 91.

———. "Work, Work, Work." *Boston Globe Magazine*, August 20, 1989, pp. 16, 60.

The Governor's Task Force on Work and Family. New York, March 1989. Project Director: Ann E. Forsythe.

Grief, Geoffrey. "Mothers Without Custody and Child Support." *Family Relations* 34 (January 1985): 353–357.

Groves, Ernest R., and Gladys Hoagland Groves. *The Contemporary American Family*. Philadelphia: J. B. Lippincott, 1947.

Haavio-Mannila, Elina. "Cross-Gender Relationships at Work and Home Through the Family Life Cycle." In *Family and Support Systems Across the Life Span*, edited by Suzanne K. Steinmetz. New York: Plenum Press, 1988, pp. 197–212.

Hanafin, Teresa. "A Debate Centering on Money." *Boston Globe*, July 12, 1988, pp. 1, 8.

Hanson, Shirley, and Michael Sporakowski. "Single Parent Families." *Family Relations* 35, no.1 (January 1986): p. 3–17.

Hareven, Tamara K. *Family Time and Industrial Time*. New York, N.Y.: Cambridge University Press, 1982.

———. "The Dynamics of Kin in an Industrial Community." In *Families and Work*, edited by Naomi Gerstel and Harriet Engel Gross. Philadelphia: Temple University Press, 1987, pp. 55–83.

Harris, Louis. *Inside America*. New York: Vintage Books, 1987.

Hecksher, Charles C. *The New Unionism*. New York: Basic Books, 1988.

Hernandez, Peggy. "Flynn's Approach to Child-Care." *Boston Globe*, July 10, 1988, p. 20.

Hertz, Sue. "Taking Care of Mom and Dad." *Boston Magazine*, April 1988, pp. 132, 182.

Hill, Reuben. "Life Cycle Stages for Types of Single Parent Families: A Family Development Theory." *Family Relations* 35 (January 1986): 19–29.

Hirst, Michael. "Young Adults with Disabilities: Health, Employment and Financial Costs For Family Careers." *Child Care Health and Development* 11 (1985): 291–307.

Hochschild, Arlie Russell with Anne Machung. *The Second Shift: Working Parents and the Revolution at Home*. New York: Viking Press, 1989.

Hodgkinson, Harold L. "Guess Who's Coming to College?" *Academe*, March-April 1983, p. 16.

Hoffman, Lois. "The Effects on Children of Maternal and Paternal Employment." In *Families and Work*, edited by Naomi Gerstel and Harriet Engel Gross. Philadelphia: Temple University Press, 1987. pp. 362–395.

Holahan, Carole K., and Lucia A. Gilbert. "Conflict Between Major Life Roles: Women and Men in Dual Career Couples." *Human Relations* 32, no.6 (1979): 451–467.

Holmstrom, Lynda Lytle. *The Two Career Family*. Cambridge, Mass.: Schenkman, 1972.

Hughes, Diane. *Child Care and Working Parents*. New York: Bank Street College of Education Report, 1987.

Hughes, Diane, and Ellen Galinsky. *The Fortune Magazine Child Care Study*. New York: Bank Street College of Education Report, 1986.

Hunt, Janet G., and Larry L. Hunt. "Male Resistance to Role Symmetry in Dual-Earner Households: Three Alternative Explanations." In *Families and Work*, edited by Naomi Gerstel and Harriet Engel Gross. Philadelphia: Temple University Press, 1987, pp. 192–203.

Immerwahr, John. "Building a Consensus on the Childcare Problem." *Personnel Administrator*, February 1984, pp. 31–37.

Johnson, Colleen Leahy, and Frank Johnson. "Parenthood, Marriage and Careers: Situational Constraints and Role Strain." In *Dual Career Couples*, edited by F. Pepitone-Rockwell. Beverly Hills, Calif.: Sage, 1980, pp. 143–161.

Johnson, Representative Nancy. "Recognizing Child Care Realities." *Institute for American Values* (newsletter), New York: 1988, p. 5.

Johnson, Sharon. "Working Families in Sweden and U.S." *The New York Times*, May 25, 1984, p. A20.

Johnston, William B. *Workforce 2000: Work and Workers for the 21st Century*. Indianapolis: Hudson Institute, 1987.

Jones, Sherrill C. "Going to Work: A Challenging Time for Single Mothers." *Journal of Employment Counseling* 21, no.1 (March 1984): 7–12.

Kamerman, Sheila B. "Child Care and Family Benefits: Policies of Six Industrialized Countries." *Monthly Labor Review*, November 1980, pp. 23–28.

———. *Parenting in an Unresponsive Society: Managing Work and Family Life*. New York: The Free Press, 1980.

———. "Meeting Family Needs: The Corporate Response." *Work in America Institute Studies in Productivity: 33*. New York: Pergamon Press, 1983.

Kamerman, Sheila B., and Cheryl D. Hayes, eds. *Families That Work: Children in a Changing World*. Washington, D.C.: National Academy Press, 1982.

Kamerman, Sheila B., and Alfred J. Kahn. *The Responsive Workplace: Employers and a Changing Labor Force*. New York: Columbia University Press, 1987.

Kamerman, Sheila B., Alfred Kahn, and Paul Kingston. *Maternity Policies and Working Women*. New York: Columbia University Press, 1983.

Kamerman, Sheila B., and Paul W. Kingston. "Employer Responses to the Family Responsibilities of Employees." In *Families That Work: Children in a Changing World*, edited by Sheila B. Kamerman and Cheryl D. Hayes. Washington, D.C.: National Academy Press, 1982, pp. 144–208.

Kanter, Rosabeth Moss. *Work and Family in the United States: A Critical Review and Agenda for Research and Policy*. New York: Russell Sage Foundation, 1977.

Kantrowitz, Barbara. "Love in the Office." *Newsweek*, February 15, 1988, pp. 48, 52.

Keith, Pat M., and Robert B. Schafer. "Correlates of Depression Among Single Parent, Employed Women." *Journal of Divorce* 5, no.3 (Spring 1982): 49–59.

Keppel, Bruce. "The Sandwiched—New Challenge for Employers: Workers Responsible for Care of Their Elderly Parents as Well as Children." *Los Angeles Times,* May 15, 1988, p. 12.

Kett, Joseph F. "The Stages of Life, 1790–1840." In *The American Family in Social Historical Perspective* (3rd ed.), edited by Michael Gordon. New York: St. Martin's Press, 1983, pp. 229–254.

Kidder, Tracey. *The Soul of a New Machine*. Boston: Little, Brown, 1981.

Knox, Richard A. "Kennedy Cosponsors Proposal for Universal Health Care." *Boston Globe*, April 13, 1989, p. 11.

Krauskopf, Marian S., and Sheila H. Akabas. "Children with Disabilities: A Family/Workplace Partnership in Problem Resolution." *Social Work Papers* 21 (1988): 28–35.

Leavitt, Judith. *Dual Career Families: A Bibliography*. Chicago: Council of Planning Bibliographies, 1982.

Lee, Eliot D. "Firms Begin Support for Workers Who Look After Elderly Relations." *The Wall Street Journal*, July 6, 1987, p. 13.

Levine, Suzanne Braun "Caring about Child-Care." *Ms. Magazine* 28 (March 1987): 31.

Long, L., and T. Long. "The Unspoken Fears of Latchkey Kids." *Working Mothers,* May 1982, pp. 88–90.

Marks, S. "Multiple Roles and Role Strain: Some Notes on Human Energy, Time, and Commitment." *American Sociological Review* 42 (1977): 921–936.

Masnick, George, and Mary Jo Bane. *The Nation's Families: 1960–1990*. Boston: Auburn House, 1980.

May, Leslie Steven, and Cynthia Ingols. "A Place to Work is a Place to Learn: The Corporate Training Exercise." *Alumni Bulletin: Harvard Graduate School of Education Association Bulletin* 32, no.1 (Fall/Winter 1987): 15–17.

McCubbin, Marilyn A. "Family Stress and Family Strengths: A Comparison of Single and Two-Parent Families with Handicapped Children." *Research in Nursing and Health,* August 1988, pp. 101–109.

Melli, Marygold S. "The Changing Legal Status of the Single Parent." *Family Relations* 35 (January 1986): 31–35.

Miller, Joanne, and Howard Garrison. "Sex Roles: The Division of Labor at Home and in the Workplace." *American Review of Sociology* 8 (1982): 237–262.

Mintz, Steven, and Susan Kellogg. *Domestic Revolutions: A Social History of American Family Life*. New York: The Free Press, 1988.

Moore, K. A., and I. V. Sawhill. "Implications of Women's Employment for Home and Family Life." In *Women Working: Theories and Facts in Perspective*, edited by A. H. Stanley and S. Harkness. Palo Alto, Calif.: Mayfield, 1978, pp. 201–225

"More Working Wives Expose Their Hubbies to the Joy of Cooking." *The Wall Street Journal*, October 16, 1980, p. 1.

Naisbitt, John. *Megatrends 2000: Ten New Directions for the 1990's*. New York: William Morrow, 1989.

Norton, Arthur J. "Keeping Up With Households." *American Demographics*, February 1983, pp. 17–21.

Owen, John D. *Working Lives: The American Work Force Since 1920*. Lexington, Mass.: Lexington Books, D.C. Health, 1986.

Parsons, Talcott and Robert F. Bales. *Family, Socialization and Interaction Process*. Glencoe, Ill.: The Free Press, 1955.

Pett, Margorie A., and Beth Vaughan-Cole. "The Impact of Income Issues and Social Status on Post-Divorce Adjustment of Custodial Parents." *Family Relations* 35 (January 1986): 103–111.

Petty, Diana, and Lynn Friss. "A Balancing Act of Working and Caregiving." *Business and Health*, October 1987, pp. 22–26.

Piotrowski, Chaya, and Mitchell H. Katz. "Women's Work and Personal Relations in the Family." In *Women: A Developmental Perspective*, edited by Phyllis W. Berman and Estelle Ramey. Bethesda, Md.: National Institutes of Health, 1982.

Place, John, and Nicole Wise. *Work and the Family: Does Employer Involvement Pay Off?* Human Resources Advisory: Strategies and Practical Solutions, vol.#1:1. Greenvale, N.Y.: Panel Publishing, 1988.

Pleck, Joseph H. "The Work-Family Role System." *Social Problems* 24 (1977): 417–427.

———. *Changing Patterns of Work and Family Roles*. Working Paper no.81. Wellesley, Mass.: Wellesley College, Center for Research on Women, 1981.

———. *Husbands' and Wives' Family Work, Paid Work, and Adjustment*. Working Paper no.95. Wellesley, Mass.: Wellesley College, Center for Research on Women, 1981.

———. *Married Men: Work and Family*. Working Paper no.96. Wellesley, Mass: Wellesley College, Center for Research on Women, 1981.

———. *Working Wives/Working Husbands*. Beverly Hills, Calif.: Sage, 1985.

Pleck, Joseph H., Graham L. Staines, and Linda Lang. "Conflicts Between Work and Family Life." *Monthly Labor Review*, March 1980, pp. 29–31.

Pond, Constance S. *And Along Comes Baby: What Happens When the Working Woman Becomes Pregnant*. Lanham, Md.: University Press of America, 1986.

Prince, Sylvia. "A Self-support System for Single Parents." *Journal of Employment Counseling*, March 1984, pp. 38–45.

Quinn, R., and G. Staines. *The 1977 Quality of Employment Survey*. Ann Arbor, Mich.: Survey Research Center, Institute for Social Research, 1979.

Radloff, L. "The CES-D Scale: A Self-report Depression Scale for Research in the General Population." *Applied Psychological Measurement* 1 (1977): 385–401.

Rapoport, R., and P. Moss. *Exploring Ways of Integrating Men and Women as Equals at Work*. Report to the Ford Foundation, November 1989.

"Report Says That Poor Spend Proportionately More for Child-Care." *The Washington Post*. Reprinted in *Boston Globe*, July 27, 1989, p. 68.

Reynolds, Pamela. "Moonlighting: More and More Women Find They Need Two Jobs." *Boston Globe*, March 14, 1989, pp. 25, 27.

———. "Time for a 'Daddy Track'?" *Boston Globe*, March 17, 1989, p. 43.

Reynolds, Pamela, and Desiree French. "Who's Minding the House?" *Boston Globe*, September 7, 1989, p. 81, 86.

Richter, Judith, and Douglas T. Hall. "Psychological Availability and Daily Transitions: A New Way to Examine the Relationship Between Work Life and Personal Life." Boston, Mass.: Boston University School of Management, February 1987. (Paper available through the School of Management at Boston University, 621 Commonwealth Ave., Boston, MA 02215.)

Robinson, B., B. Rowland, and M. Coleman. *Latchkey Kids: Unlocking Doors for Children and Their Families*. Lexington, Mass.: Lexington Books, D.C. Health, 1986.

Robinson, J. P. *How Americans Use Time: A Socio-Psychological Analysis*. New York: Praeger, 1977.

Rodman, Hyman. "From Latchkey Stereotypes Toward Self-Care Realities." In *Family and Support Systems Across the Life Span*, edited by Suzanne K. Steinmetz. New York: Plenum Press, 1988, pp. 99–104.

"Room for Diversity in Household Definition." *The Wall Street Journal*, October 20, 1988, p. B1:1.

Ross, Catherine E., John Mirowski, and Joan Huber. "Dividing Work, Sharing Work, and In-Between: Marriage Patterns and Depression." *American Sociological Review* 48 (December 1983): 809–823.

Saltzberg, Marjorie, and Carl Bryant. "Family Systems Theory and Practice at the Workplace." *Social Work Papers* 21 (1988): 16–27.

Sanik, Margaret Mietus, and Teresa Mauldin. "Single Versus Two Parent Families: A Comparison of Mother's Time." *Family Relations* 35, no.1 (January 1986): 53–56.

Schilling, Robert F., Maura A. Kirkham, William A. Snow, and Steven Paul Schinke. "Single Mothers with Handicapped Children: Different from Their Married Counterparts." *Family Relations* 35, no.1 (January 1986): 69–77.

Schwartz, Felice N. "Management Women and the New Facts of Life." *Harvard Business Review*, January-February 1989, pp. 65–76.

Sege, Irene. "Child Care Debate Shifts from Personal to Political." *Boston Sunday Globe*, July 10, 1988, pp. 1,20.

———. "Poverty's Grip on Children Widens." *Boston Globe*, March 12, 1989, pp. 1, 20–21.

———. "Growing Gap Shown Between Rich, Poor." *Boston Globe*, May 15, 1989, pp. 1,31.

———. "Couples Working, Parenting in Shifts." *Boston Globe*, September 26, 1989, pp. 1,8.

Sekaran, Uma. *Dual Career Families*. San Francisco: Jossey-Bass, 1986.

Sekaran, Uma, and Douglas T. Hall. "Asynchronism in Dual Career and Family Linkages." In *Handbook of Career Theory,* edited by Michael B. Arthur, Douglas T. Hall, and Barbara S. Lawrence. New York: Cambridge University Press, 1988, pp. 159–180.

Seward, Rudy Ray. *The American Family.* Beverly Hills, Calif.: Sage, 1978.

Sharf, Lois. *To Work and to Wed: Female Experience and the Great Depression.* Westport, Conn.: Greenwood Press, 1980.

Sidel, Ruth. *Women and Children Last: The Plight of Poor Women in Affluent America.* New York: Penguin Books, 1986.

Simpson, Peggy. "Child Care: All Talk, No Action." *Ms.,* December 1988, pp. 81–82.

Stautberg, Susan S. "Status Report: The Corporation and Trends in Family Issues." *Human Resource Management* 26, no.2 (Summer 1987): 277–290.

Steinmetz, Suzanne K. "Parental and Filial Relationships: Obligation, Support and Abuse." In *Family and Support Systems Across the Life Span,* edited by Suzanne K. Steinmetz. New York: Plenum Press, 1988, pp. 165–182.

Stocker, Carol. "Make Room for Baby: Equality Plus Parenthood Equal Stress for Couples." *Boston Globe,* November 16, 1989, pp. 93,101.

Thomas, Sandra, Kay Albeicht, and Priscilla White. "Determinants of Marital Quality in Dual Career Couples." *Family Relations* 33 (October 9, 1984): 513–521.

The Travelers Employee Caregivers Survey. Hartford, Conn.: Travelers Insurance Company, June 1985.

Trost, Cathy. "Men, Too, Wrestle with Career-Family Stress: Few Firms Offer Working Father Much Support." *The Wall Street Journal,* November 11, 1988, B–1.

United States Bureau of the Census. *Current Population Reports.* "Household and Family Characteristics: March 1986." Series P–20, No. 419. Washington, D.C.: Government Printing Office, 1987.

———. *Current Population Reports.* "Households, Families, Marital Status, and Living Arrangements: March 1987 (Advance Report)." Series P–20, No. 417. Washington, D.C.: Government Printing Office, August 1987.

———. *Current Population Reports.* "Marital Status and Living Arrangements: March 1987." Series P–20, No. 423. Washington, D.C.: Government Printing Office, 1988.

———. *Current Population Reports.* "Changes in American Family Life." Series P–23, No. 163. Washington, D.C.: Government Printing Office, 1989, p. 8.

———. *Historical Statistics of the United States: Colonial Times to 1970.* "Annual Estimates of the Population, by Age: 1900 to 1970." Series A 29–42. Washington, D.C.: Government Printing Office, 1975.

———. *Historical Statistics of the United States: Colonial Times to 1970.* "Birth Rate-Total and for Women 15–44 Years Old, by Race: 1800–1970." Series B 5–10. Washington, D.C.: Government Printing Office, 1975.

———. *Historical Statistics of the United States: Colonial Times to 1970.* "Households, by Number of Persons: 1790–1970." Series A 335–349. Washington, D.C.: Government Printing Office, 1975.

———. *Historical Statistics of the United States: Colonial Times to 1970.* "Labor Force, Gainful Workers, by Age, Sex, and Farm-Nonfarm Occupations: 1820–1930." Series D 75–84. Washington, D.C.: Government Printing Office, 1975.

———. *Historical Statistics of the United States: Colonial Times to 1970.* "Labor Force,

Marital Status of Women in the Civilian Labor Force: 1890–1970.'' Series D 49–
62. Washington, D.C.: Government Printing Office, 1975.

————. *Historical Statistics of the United States: Colonial Times to 1970.* "Marital
Status of the Population, by Age and Sex: 1890–1970.'' Series A 160–171.
Washington, D.C.: Government Printing Office, 1975.

————. *Historical Statistics of the United States: Colonial Times to 1970.* "Marital
Status of Women in the Civilian Labor Force: 1890 to 1970.'' Series D 49–62.
Washington, D.C.: Government Printing Office, 1975.

————. *Historical Statistics of the United States: Colonial Times to 1970.* "Married
Women (Husband Present) in the Labor Force, by Age and Presence of Children:
1948–1970.'' Series N. 63–74, Washington, D.C.: Government Printing Office,
1975.

————. *Historical Statistics of the United States: Colonial Times to 1970.* "Median Age
at First Marriage, by Sex: 1890–1970.'' Series A 158–159. Washington, D.C.:
Government Printing Office, 1975.

————. *Historical Statistics of the United States: Colonial Times to 1970.* "Median Age
of Population, by Race, Sex, and Nativity: 1790–1970.'' Series A 143–157.
Washington, D.C.: Government Printing Office, 1987.

————. *Statistical Abstracts of the United States: 1988.* 108th edition. "Children Under
18 Years Old, by Presence of Parents: 1970 to 1986.'' No. 69. Washington, D.C.:
Government Printing Office, 1988.

————. *Statistical Abstracts of the United States: 1989.* 109th edition. "Labor Force
Participation Rates of Wives (Husband Present), by Age of Own Youngest Child:
1975–1988.'' No. 640. Washington, D.C.: Government Printing Office, 1989,
p. 386.

United States Congressional Committee on Foreign Affairs. *UN Decade for Women:
Hearing Before the Subcommittee on Human Rights and International Organi-
zations of the Committee on Foreign Affairs.* Washington, D.C.: Government
Printing Office, 1985.

United States Department of Health and Human Services. "Advance Report of Final
Divorce Statistics, 1984.'' Final data from National Center for Health Statistics,
Monthly Vital Statistics Report, 35, no.6 (1986). Supplement (September 25,
1986) Table 3, p. 7.

Voydanoff, Patricia. "Work Role Characteristics, Family Structure Demands, and Work/
Family Conflict.'' *Journal of Marriage and the Family* 50 (August 1988): 749–
761.

Waldrop, Judith. "Inside America's Households.'' *American Demographics* 11, no.3
(March 1989): 20–27.

Wallerstien, Judith, and Sandra Blakeslee. *Second Chances: Men, Women, and Children
a Decade After Divorce.* New York: Ticknor and Fields, 1989.

Walker, K., and M. Woods. *Time Use: A Measure of Household Production of Goods
and Services.* Washington, D.C.: American Home Economics Association, 1976.

Weinstein, G. "Help Wanted: The Crisis of Child Care.'' *Ms.* 18, no.4 (October 1989):
75–79

W. E. Upjohn Institute for Employment Research. *Work in America.* Cambridge, Mass.:
MIT Press, 1973.

White, Lynn K., and David B. Brinkerhoff. "Children's Work in the Family: Its Significance and Meaning." In *Families and Work*, edited by Naomi Gerstel and Harriet Engel Gross. Philadelphia: Temple University Press, 1987, pp. 204–218.

Whitehead, Ralph, Jr. "Courting the Baby-Boom Vote." *Boston Globe*, January 4, 1987, p. A:17.

Whyte, William Hollingsworth. *The Organization Man*. New York: Simon & Schuster, 1956.

Wilensky, Harold L., and Charles N. Lebeaux. *Industrial Society and Social Welfare*. New York: The Free Press, 1965.

Women and Work Research and Resource Newsletter, Summer 1986, vol.1, no.2, p. 3.

"Women Gain Ground in Wages, Study Shows." *The New York Times*, February 9, 1989, p. C:11.

Work and Family: A Changing Dynamic: A Bureau of National Affairs Special Report. Rockville, Md.: Bureau of National Affairs, 1986.

Work in America: Report of a Special Task Force to the Secretary of Health, Education, and Welfare. Cambridge, Mass.: MIT Press, 1973.

Working Age—An AARP Newsletter About the Changes in the Workforce 3, no.5 (March/ April 1988).

Wyman, Anne. "Area Child-Care Activists Say Dodd Proposal Has the Answers." *Boston Sunday Globe*, February 26, 1989, pp. 12, 26.

Yankelovich, Daniel. "The Meaning of Work." In *The Worker and the Job*, edited by Jerome Rosow. Englewood Cliffs, N.J.: Prentice-Hall, 1974, pp. 22–23.

———. *New Rules: Searching for Self-Fulfillment in a World Turned Upside Down*. Toronto: Bantam Books, 1981.

Zahavi, Gerald. *Workers, Managers and Welfare Capitalism: The Shoeworkers and Tanners of Endicott Johnson, 1890–1950*. Urbana: University of Illinois Press, 1988.

Zigler, Edward F., and Meryl Frank, eds. *The Parental Leave Crisis: Toward a National Policy*. New Haven, Conn.: Yale University Press, 1988.

Zill, Nicholas, and Carolyn C. Rogers. "Recent Trends in the Well-being of Children in the United States and Their Implications for Public Policy." In *The Changing American Family*. Washington, D.C.: The Urban Institute Press, 1988, pp. 31–116.

Zussman, Robert. "Work and Family in the New Middle Class." In *Families and Work*, edited by Naomi Gerstel and Harriet Engel Gross. Philadelphia: Temple University Press, 1987, pp. 338–346.

INDEX

ABOUT THE AUTHOR

BRADLEY K. GOOGINS is an associate professor at the Graduate School of Social Work at Boston University. He is author of a monograph entitled *Boston University Balancing Job and Homelife Study* and an article, "Vulnerability of Working Parents," which appeared in *Social Work* in 1987. He is now working on a companion volume on work/family conflicts from the corporate perspective.